Praise for *Welcome to the Urban Revolution*

"Jeb Brugmann is a strategist of great analytical power. His book with great acuity captures important moments in cities around the globe. It is a fundamental reference for all those who wish to understand how cities can change the world."

—Jaime Lerner, architect and urban planner; former mayor of Curitiba and governor of Paraná State, Brazil; president of International Union of Architects, 2002–2005

"Writing from his long on-the-ground global experience, Jeb Brugmann has provided a rich and accessible menu of deep insights, engaging stories, and surprising facts about a world of cities. His *Welcome to the Urban Revolution* is a prophecy of hope and a political challenge to us all."

—Michael Cohen, director of the International Affairs Program at The New School and former senior advisor for environmentally sustainable development at the World Bank

"Absorbing." **—*Next American City***

"For a deep dive into creative city-watching and prognosis it would be tough to top [Brugmann's] insightful *Welcome to the Urban Revolution*." **—Neal Peirce, Citiwire.net**

"Brugmann is arguing for the collective power of a dense city as the ultimate form of grassroots living." **—*New York Review of Ideas***

"Important and immensely engaging." **—*Winnipeg Free Press***

"Urbanization may be a global-scale phenomenon, but Brugmann finds that the movement's magnitude is best observed with a highly localized viewpoint." **—*Zócalo***

Welcome to the Urban Revolution

Welcome to the
Urban Revolution

How Cities Are Changing the World

JEB BRUGMANN

BLOOMSBURY PRESS
New York · Berlin · London

Published by Bloomsbury Press, New York

All papers used by Bloomsbury Press are natural, recyclable products made from
wood grown in well-managed forests. The manufacturing processes conform to the
environmental regulations of the country of origin.

Library of Congress Cataloging-in-Publication Data

Brugmann, Jeb, 1957–
Welcome to the urban revolution: how cities are changing the world /
Jeb Brugmann.—1st U.S. ed.
p.   cm.
Includes bibliographical references and index.
ISBN 978-1-59691-566-4 (alk. paper hardcover)
1. Urbanization. 2. Cities and towns—Growth. 3. City planning. 4. Urban policy.
I. Title.

HT361.B78 2009
307. 1'16—dc222
2008046952

First published by Bloomsbury Press in 2009
This paperback edition published in 2010

Paperback ISBN: 978-1-60819-092-8

1 3 5 7 9 10 8 6 4 2

Typeset by Westchester Book Group
Printed in the United States of America by Worldcolor Fairfield

In memory of my brother, Bob Brugmann, and colleague Judy Walker, mentors in life and in the cause of sustainable development.

Contents

Preface to the U.S. Paperback Edition

When Rebuilding an Urban Nation . . .

When Hurricane Katrina struck New Orleans in August 2005, I was in Mumbai, exploring the workings of that city's low-income districts. Mumbai is famous for its floods. The monsoon that strikes each year—carrying with it winds of 150 miles per hour—is one of most powerful natural phenomena in the world, pouring some five feet of rain each season on a mega-city whose drainage infrastructure lags its growth by decades, and where six million people live in seeping shacks. In July 2005, the monsoon dumped thirty-nine inches of rain on the city in one day. Within hours, flash floods hit the heart of the metropolis and shut down its airports, telephone networks, trains, and roads.

The reaction of my Indian colleagues to the unfolding Katrina crisis was telling. It was one thing to see Mumbai's conditions mirrored in a U.S. city—the disrepair of essential infrastructure and the disregard of warnings, the lack of cooperation between jurisdictions, the human toll. It was something else for them to witness the tattered social fabric, the National Guard patrols behaving like an invading force in the lower-income inner city, the silence and inaction of the White House. They had never imagined, it seemed, that that kind of societal fragility could be revealed in the fabric of America's cities. As the political damage to the Bush administration became irreversible and the New Orleans port suffered a multibillion-dollar toll on international trade, we saw just how easily the fate of a great nation can turn on the events of a single city.

Yet we rarely—if ever—anticipate those events, nor do we even try.

Take the major civil uprisings in Urümqi, China, and Tehran, Iran, in June 2009. Both events were anticipated in this book's analysis of the urban origins of contemporary political revolution. As the media focused hyperbolically on student "Twitter revolutionaries," they overlooked the more basic economic and social geographies of conflicts: ethnically and economically fragmented urban districts, harassed urban migrant communities, and competing strategies of urban commerce. In the urban tectonics of these still-simmering uprisings, the extended social networks of each city's traditional bazaar economies were confronting the political patrons of each city's distinct forms of new state capitalism as each laid its claims over precious urban land, location, and the rules of local commerce. Such deep-seated tensions are what make urban uprisings far more than ideological mobilizations or the ventings of harassed minorities. Urban revolutions, like the 1960s civil uprising in our own country, are rooted in competing urbanisms: in the unique ways that different city-building communities design, build, govern, and colocate their activities to support specialized economies and lifestyles.

Urümqi marked a new stage of China's simmering Urban Revolution, which finds expression in tens of thousands of street demonstrations each year, generally sparked by the police-backed claims of firms and developers upon locations where demonstrators have long plied more traditional forms of commerce. The initial demonstration around Urümqi's international bazaar and the subsequent ethnic clashes were enough to bring President Hu Jintao home from a G8 meeting to an emergency politburo meeting, which led to new national laws on police deployment and public demonstrations. Tehran's events shifted the global political calculus even more dramatically.

How can something as parochial as a local commercial tradition or as mundane as an urban development pattern or infrastructure problem be so nationally and globally influential? The answer is only clear when we begin to understand that the urbanization of the world—from 29 percent of the world's population in 1950 to half the world's population today to nearly 70 percent in 2050—is more than a matter of shifting head counts. Urbanization is the substratum of globalization itself, a restructuring of the basic geography of human opportunity. Already today, for instance, 82 percent of the U.S. gross domestic product is produced in its metro regions. Wealth creation, in other words, has steadily shifted from rural and resource-rich territories, over which nations struggled in the past, to the designed, manufactured, and ever-malleable urban locations over which nations, corporations, local merchants, migrant communities, criminals, corrupt officials, and political-guerrilla movements compete today. This shift is driven by a far more open source than Twitter and the Internet. We are witnessing the opportunistic, self-organizing pursuit of the most basic economies of urban settlement, a phenomenon explored at length in these pages. Every person and organization of every size in every place can leverage and shape the raw efficiencies of urban proximity, density, scale, and association to build their route to wealth and power. Through urban infrastructure they can then connect the footholds they create in one city to scores of footholds in cities globally to pursue a worldwide economic and political strategy. The result is the emergence of a global system of cities, a nervous system of myriad chaotic, competing networks, through which the events in one city can rapidly register across the planet.

Everything is affected by this worldwide pursuit of urban location and the advantage it gives: the use and spread of new technologies, the way we mate, the economic health of nations, the world's ecosystem. Today, 80 percent of Americans live in urban areas. The populations and economies of our urban areas account for 80 percent of national energy consumption and 65 percent of vehicle miles traveled. Most children are born, churches are built, food is eaten, and ball games are played in metropolitan areas. By 2050, 90 percent of Americans will live in cities and metro areas. Most will be located in a handful of mega-urban regions that cross state and even national borders.

The world itself is being transformed into a City—the mega-geography of what has heretofore been abstractly described as "globalization." As this vast new landscape of processing, planning, trading, and migrating evolves within the borders of urbanizing nations, the work of those states will change. The path through this tectonic shift in global economics and politics will be paved via the design, development, and governance of cities and metro areas—for better or for worse. Those nations that innovate and build the most robust city regions will win the first urban century.

But today we still seek to build America's future in denial of our urban dependencies.

Over the last decade, in small patches of our metropolitan regions, we have been renewing and updating the urbanisms that once made us a great industrial nation. Still, in denial of those traditions, most construction and infrastructure investments in the United States are being used to expand a semi-urban landscape that offers neither the benefits of rural life nor those of urban form. The American suburban project—a cultural, political, and fiscal denial of demographic and economic reality—even continues in the wake of the global economic crisis it has touched off.

As in the examples of New Orleans, Tehran, and Urümqi, the epicenter of the 2007–2008 global financial crisis—which spread from metropolis to metropolis worldwide—is itself traceable to a handful of American metropolitan areas. The crisis might never have happened if not for the unique fragilities and proclivities of these regions.

According to a comprehensive assessment of real estate foreclosures by urban planner William Lucy of the University of Virginia, the housing crisis was not truly a national affair. Foreclosures in thirty-eight states were well below the national average. The bulk of foreclosures struck the suburban sprawl of recently expanded metros lacking traditional urban cores. An astounding 62 percent of the country's foreclosures were in the fast-growing metros of Arizona, California, Florida, and Nevada. Of these, metropolitan Las Vegas accounted for 88 percent of Nevada's foreclosures. Metropolitan Phoenix accounted for 91 percent of Arizona's foreclosures. The Miami, Orlando, and Tampa–St. Petersburg foreclosures accounted for 62 percent of the Florida total; metro Los Angeles, Sacramento, San Diego, and San Francisco about the same for California.[i] Tracing the crisis fault line even closer to its source, the foreclosures were ten, fifteen, even thirty times greater in the suburban counties than they were in their central cities. This was a crisis of a suburban construction boom, significantly concentrated in a few suburban counties of a few of America's fastest growing urban regions.

The ongoing global economic crisis, in other words, is the logical conclusion of one model of city building. Aggressive and lax mortgage lending was the catalyst, but not the full cause.

For sure, the hocus-pocus of property finance *was* a nationwide phenomenon. Starting in the 1980s, the business of property finance was transformed from a business of asset management (in which the investor knows and tracks real local property value and local borrower credit-worthiness) into a business of risk management (in which the investor effectively places a wager on a unit share of a very large portfolio of properties and lessens attention to local conditions). The investment decision was entirely severed from knowledge of the underlying economic conditions being designed in fast-growing metros, which ultimately determine the borrowers' solvency and real property values.[ii]

One of those underlying conditions, well-known but little highlighted, is the evolution of homes, offices, and condominiums into tradable products, distinct from their function and economic performance in a place. In a true urbanism, buildings are designed and combined in creative ways to bring production, commerce, culture, and residential life together to create specific economic, social, and political advantages for their user community. The value of a building, like a downtown office space, is tied to the economic synergy it and its users create together through the colocation of different kinds of buildings and activities in, say, a central business district. But since the 1950s, the American mass-produced suburban model, with its reliable profitability, has hampered the creation of robust economic places through unique arrangements of buildings and activities into productive neighborhoods and districts—a far more expensive proposition.

In suburbanism, the essential synergies of a true urbanism—the unique mixing of production, commerce, culture, and residential living achieved through numerous innovations in design, business models, and technology together in a specific place—are abandoned through both physical design and zoning law. The building product, such as a residence or retail outlet, becomes an end in itself. It is "value-engineered" and produced as a standardized, single-purpose product. The product is then batch produced to gain economies of scale—in the forms of a residential subdivision, an office park, or a retail mall. The building and the place in which it is located—appropriately described as a "development"—has been reduced to offering a very basic, predictable utility, such as a nine-to-five workspace for employees. Then for sentimental marketing purposes it is proclaimed as a place with a dynamic life: It is evocatively called a "village," a "neighborhood," an "entertainment district," or a "town center." Given the lack of a true economic dynamism that creates value above and beyond the stand-alone market price of the building, the business of the "developers" is only possible with considerable public subsidy of infrastructure and services required for the building's basic utility—sewerage, roads, water supply. These subsidies generally exceed what the developers and user-residents will pay in fees and taxes, creating a structural fiscal deficit.

In the 1990s, this separation of a building's value from the real economics of a place was taken to an even greater extreme. This time the value of the building was separated not only from the value of the economic opportunities made possible in a place, but even from the basic utility of the building itself as a place of residence. In this ultimate form of suburbanism, vast new tracts and condo districts in metro Las Vegas, Phoenix, Miami, and Los Angeles were built to be traded as speculative investments as much as they were built to be used. The popular emergence of speculative buy-hold-flip demand for new developments started driving the market and the shape of America's urbanizing landscape. By 2005, reports MIT economist William Wheaton, the development industry, with its municipal and funny-finance collaborators, produced 60 percent more new residential homes to serve this demand than the actual growth in the number of American households.[iii] The result was a flash flood of oversupply, often held by overextended small investors. The modus operandi of suburbanism—the publicly subsidized denial of basic urban economics—had come to its logical conclusion.

But if funny money and speculation were the only problem, then the foreclosures would be less concentrated in certain metro areas, and more evenly distributed across the suburbanizing country. Another factor behind the crisis is even less discussed and understood: the diseconomic nature of the new cityscapes in these particular high-growth areas. It's not enough to say that banking became a form of sophisticated gambling or that property became valued as much for its speculative purposes as its actual uses. Something had to trigger the collapse of the whole investment scheme. The accepted explanation is that sudden, built-in increases in subprime and other high-risk mortgage rates pushed millions of homeowners into insolvency. But increased housing payments only break a household budget if other costs are also high and inflexible—if there is no margin for either savings or spending error. This was the case in the most crisis-ridden areas. The fixed cost of living and working in the regions' supersized properties and their sprawling, fractured landscapes—for vehicles, energy and gasoline, services, and communication—left no margin for error. People and businesses might tighten their belts, but the costs of just occupying and maintaining their property and living and working in this kind of landscape were too high to absorb. Living costs were going up (notably including a rise in gasoline prices) while real incomes and public subsidies started going down. It would seem that these metro areas did not generate enough local wealth to cover the burgeoning, underlying cost structure that was designed into those cityscapes.

The remedy that has been offered, in the form of the American Recovery and Reinvestment Act (ARRA), represents the largest single bundle of federal subsidy to the American suburban enterprise since the federal highway program of the 1950s. While substantial recovery funds have been allocated to stabilize older urban neighborhoods and even to introduce new urbanist approaches into metropolitan planning, reports on the use of ARRA infrastructure funds indicate that they have been predominantly allocated to suburban and rural infrastructure investments and highway expansion. The policies, subsidies, and business models of American urban development have been geared to the suburban model. When it comes to creating new metropolitan landscapes at scale, that's about all we know how to do.

The fate of the U.S. economy thereby continues to be driven by a model that was only viable in an era of cheaper resources and greater fiscal largesse. To come out of this cycle of boom-bust urbanization and declining competitiveness, the United States needs a new and truly urban American Dream, built by a development industry that specializes in more robust urban places.

Reversing our fifty-year abandonment of real urbanism is neither rocket science nor mystery. People have been creating and renewing robust urbanisms for millennia. Bazaar districts, port districts, university districts, central business districts, and the distinctive manufacturing-commercial-residential neighborhoods of American industrial cities have long been centers of wealth creation, culture, and political power.

New and renewed American urbanisms have succeeded across the country. We just have to get back into the game of producing them at scale.

On a morning walk in central Houston before business meetings, I am trying to discern the place for such a turning point. Contrary to reputation, Houston was one of the last large U.S. metro areas to succumb to the suburban model; its growth was concentrated in the central city until the most recent building cycle. But on this walk I find no hint of urbanism, only a landscape of supersized building products hosting supersized business models. This is America's inner-city counterpart to suburbia's narrowly conceived designs.

The mile stretch of central city corridor combines retail, services, and office spaces, in principle a key aspect of real urbanism. But rather than being arranged into a district of firms and services of various sizes and specialties that work closely together as an economic community, almost every building is purpose-designed for a stand-alone large firm or scaled-up franchise that depends on a global supply chain and logistics operation. Only one property offers an entry point for local entrepreneurship: a rundown sex video shop next to a big highway overpass, clearly a holdover from an earlier time. The corridor-district is an oddly affluent yet sterile landscape, divided by large parking lots, lawns, and physical barriers that almost require navigation by car. There is no place for chance encounters or a morning greeting. Even the cafe, a sidewalk business traditionally designed for such a social purpose, is a drive-through Starbucks with a half dozen cars queued up.

This place does not support the notably convivial character of Houstonians nor invite their collaboration and invention. It is a place for a commute or to drive through, not really a destination or the center of anything. It is purpose-built for the same franchises, offices, and gas stations that one finds on arterial corridors everywhere. It expresses the one-dimensional economics of American city building. Everything is about economies of scale—and only economies of scale—which requires highly capital-intensive building and infrastructure. All the other basic economic principles of robust urbanism are entirely missing.

The first missing principle is proximity: By positioning the things that people need close to each other, the time and expense required to obtain those resources is reduced. Such self-evident economics are what led to the creation of cities in the first place. Traders would meet at a crossroads or river bend to create a market. But proximity has been lost as a first principle in American city building. The more we deny the logic of proximity, the more we add to the burden of getting things done, and the more we must compensate with expensive technology, e.g., the car, and the valuable urban land and resources that it consumes. It's only possible to violate proximity if surpluses exist to compensate.

The second missing principle is density. Density builds on the economics of proximity, but is poorly understood. We tend to think of density as concentration: lots of people and buildings per square mile. For Americans, that's not a very appealing idea. But the true economic meaning of density is more nuanced than this—and much more fundamental to the economic success of urban nations. Density is design that optimizes the economic use of land, buildings, and infrastructure.

There are three main kinds of density. *Spatial density* optimizes the use of land, and is particularly important in prime locations: it builds in more economic activity per acre of square mile. *Colocation density* optimizes the use of buildings by clustering them in ways that efficiently support the specialized production, trade, and living of specific user communities. For instance, the colocation of all the daily activities of a diverse research community together in a single district—laboratories, classrooms, libraries, residences, restaurants, cultural facilities—is historically associated with increased research productivity and patent applications. It increases the number and variety of collaborators conveniently located near each other in one place, and supports both planned and spontaneous interaction. Finally, *network* or *system density* optimizes the use of infrastructure. Urban design is used to increase the frequency and variety of uses of an established network, like a road or transit system, making it both more efficient and more productive.

Smart metros and organizations develop scale and density economies together, not unlike large companies whose operations extend over large geographic areas. But we compensate for missing economies of density in our metros with a mix of fiscal subsidies for underutilized infrastructure and service systems, and with ever-larger economies of scale, as in this Houston corridor.

Consider the successful growth of Wal-Mart in the United States.

Wal-Mart is popularly understood as a story of brute economies of scale and the market clout it affords. But a 2005 study of the growth of Wal-Mart's national network of 4,300 stores by Federal Reserve Bank economist Thomas Holmes shows that Wal-Mart grew by using both economies of scale *and* density to dominate local retail markets.[iv] The retailer would establish a foothold in a market catchment area and then create a network of stores three to four miles apart to achieve penetration in that area, optimizing the use of its local logistics and distribution systems. Holmes concludes that Wal-Mart grew by developing economies of density in selected locations rather than by using its scale economies alone to access prime locations across the United States as quickly as possible. Just as companies like Wal-Mart use economies of density to create efficiencies, metro regions need to develop economies of density to create more affordable, sustainable infrastructure systems and competitive local enterprise.

The third missing principle of robust urbanism, largely missing in the American metropolis, is economy of association: the way that urban design can increase opportunities for efficient meeting and collaboration. Back on my morning walk in Houston, I am looking for an opportunity just to say good morning to someone. I try to share such basic friendliness with two strangers who are waiting for a city bus— the only two people outside—as the ruckus of commuting cars rolls by. I get no response. Perhaps my suit and pale skin color, contrasted to their worker's clothing and darker skin, has already put us a world apart. If so, then there is no place built in this landscape that might bring us together. Even for people of my own social group and status, there is no built-in place that entices others like me to meet and discuss the better potential of this city or to venture a new idea together. This landscape is built for strictly instrumental interactions, not for the renewal or forging of a community.

Division has always been a part of the American suburban project— suburbia was nearly conceived as a racial, economic, and political separation from the inner city. The machinery of politics in this country often seems more interested in exploiting the urban-suburban divide than eliminating it. The fate of New Orleans and Mumbai, and the revolutionary stories of Detroit, Gdańsk, Nairobi, Tehran, Johannesburg, and others probed in this book, highlight how the development of such divided landscapes can destabilize whole nations and seed revolutions.

But this book also offers cause for a practical, even mundane hope. The stories of Barcelona, Chicago, Curitiba, and other cities show how the nuts-and-bolts work of urban regeneration can reshape economic and social life into new urbanisms where citizenship, collaboration, and unity of purpose can thrive. By applying the basic principles of robust urbanism, the same dynamics of urban revolution that left us a blighted Detroit and the destroyed Ninth Ward of New Orleans can be harnessed differently in order to rebuild a strained urban nation.

PART I

The Urban Revolution

CHAPTER 1

Look Again

A View from the Expanding Edge of the Global City

In 1994, during a visit to Machala, Ecuador, I was taken to a scattered collection of shacks, suspended on stilts eight feet above an open marshy field at the southern edge of the coastal city. There were no paved roads to the place, none of the elements that we associate with our idea of a city—no permanent buildings, walkways, drains, water pipes, or lights. The dozen or so shacks were made of scrap boards, sticks, and thatched grasses. They had appeared over the course of a single night a few months before.

The only adults around were women. My host, the city's vice mayor, explained that the men had left in customary fashion to take up work on banana plantations, on construction jobs, or in the new shrimp farms. The women had organized their new community into a barrio association to fight for their claim to the land. As we entered the settlement, the women watched but avoided us, remaining focused on their chores. In contrast to the crowded sidewalks, blaring music, and broadcast political appeals in Machala's busy little commercial center a mile or so away, this place seemed deadly quiet. But it was a deceptive stillness.

When I think of this place today, after looking at recent satellite photos of the region, I feel like an astronomer might, peering through a high-powered telescope, watching and measuring the clustering gases of a birthing star. For this new settlement in Machala—which itself was a town of only seven thousand in 1950—has proven to be far more than the isolated encampment it appeared to be in 1994. It was the expanding edge of a sort of organism, remaking that remote part of the world and connecting its people, commerce, and politics with cities everywhere.

Today, Machala is still a small city with its population of two hundred thousand. That makes it a tiny place on a planet with a population approaching seven billion. Even on the urbanized part of the planet, which counts 3.5 billion residents and nearly two hundred metropolitan areas with more than two million people, Machala is but a half-made town. It's the kind of place you might pass through without even noting its name. But look again. Something truly revolutionary is happening in these small and isolated places.

A group of landless rural people—locally they are called *invasores,* or "invaders"—came down from the forested Andean foothills in the middle of the night to claim a ten-acre piece of waterlogged land on the lip of the Pacific's mangroves. Like those before them who had built the other barrios of Machala, this group arrived with tools and materials and a clearly planned division of labor. While some constructed the stilt houses, others stood guard with machetes. By the dawn of their first Machala day the construction work was done and they had started their new city life: creating animal pens, securing new jobs, and organizing politically to secure land titles, rights, roads, and water systems. Together, they were joining the largest grassroots movement ever known to this world: a movement of hundreds of millions of people that has transformed marshlands, estuaries, forests, fields, and hillsides everywhere to build and secure their claim to the emerging global City.[1]

These so-called invaders were part of a fantastic phenomenon, for Machala, despite its remoteness and anonymity, has become a big player in the world. For instance, as much as a quarter of the world's annual commercial supply of bananas is now shipped from its port. Over the course of the 1990s, the city leveraged its port along with its local culture of land seizure, plantation development, and labor-seeking migration and literally reengineered Ecuador's southern coastal zone. It transformed the region's natural fish-breeding mangroves into aquaculture plantations, which since 1994 have spread pond by pond over hundreds of square miles, making Machala a major point on the global industrial supply chain for shrimp. At the same time, the city has also reengineered the urban landscape, covering its drainage canals and streams to address the city's persistent cholera and typhoid problems, and channeling the city's untreated sewage into the remaining mangroves, further degrading the remaining natural coastal fishery.

Meanwhile, the city was also fomenting regional political change. A citywide strike against the Ecuadorian national government in 1994 fueled the election of a populist national government in 1996. Machala's director of community participation, a grayed Che Guevara look-alike who had organized and worked with the local barrio associations, was appointed Ecuador's first minister of environment. In hindsight, we know that Machala was at the front line of a wider populist revolution brewing in the region's cities, which has since transformed the politics of South America, electing governments in Venezuela, Ecuador, and Bolivia.

Machala is one of thousands of little-known, small cities that have been shaping and connecting our world in ways far beyond their size or stature. The impacts of these cities reveal a fundamentally new characteristic of our world today: that local affairs are no longer just local. Our incessant city building, in particular over the last half century, has created a connected, worldwide system of cities through which we have been reengineering global economics, politics, and ecology in ways still barely understood. The evolution of individual cities into a city system, which I just call *the City,* has radically changed the relationship between local and global affairs. Through the City, local conditions and events, even at the margins of a provincial town, are amplified into global events and accelerated into global trends, often overwhelming the systems and strategies that nations, corporations, and international institutions use to manage their affairs.

Take, for instance, the city of Tiruppur, India. With a population of fifty-two thousand in 1950 and still only three hundred thousand in 1991, Tiruppur made itself into one of the world's top manufacturing centers for cotton knitwear, successfully competing against India's wealthier textile mega-cities, Calcutta and Mumbai. Its industrial rise is substantially based on local traditions. Members of an ancient community of rural peasants, called the Gounder caste, migrated to industrial jobs in Tiruppur where they learned the occupations and operations of small garment mills. They then applied their traditional approaches to sourcing and organizing village agricultural labor to build a region-wide system of just-in-time labor recruitment and contracting for the city's knitwear industry.[2] From their small production units, this urban migrant community developed a tight network of five thousand local firms and thousands of other small supporting units, which together produce and export goods worth more than a billion dollars each year for companies such as Wal-Mart, Tommy Hilfiger, and Reebok. Tiruppur's knitwear industry may supply global brands, but look again. The industry can't really be understood as a "global" corporate phenomenon in the traditional sense. It is based on deep and, until recently, undocumented local traditions of seasonal agricultural production and labor management. Through the Gounder community's urban migration and its members' grassroots investments in their adopted city, they have been giving real shape, as in Machala, to a more diverse and unpredictable kind of globalization than the popular notion suggests. In a world that is fast becoming a City, the local realities of places like Machala and Tiruppur are gaining increasing global significance.

Take another example from an entirely different area of human endeavor. In 1950 the small university city of Irvine, California, did not even exist. It was built out of ranch land in the 1960s and 1970s. Then, in 1989, Irvine played a catalytic role in starting global action to address the destruction of Earth's stratospheric ozone layer and global climate change. With a city population of only 105,000 at the time, the Irvine municipal government estimated that 1/800th of the worldwide emissions of CFC-113, a major ozone-depleting compound, were being emitted by the aerospace and high-tech industries and other institutions located in its jurisdiction. The big-picture orientation of Irvine's university population supported passage of the first North American law requiring a phaseout of ozone-depleting chlorofluorocarbon (CFC) compounds. Irvine's mayor Larry Agran and the famous atmospheric chemist Sherwood Rowland (later awarded the Nobel Prize) then hosted a meeting in Irvine of city leaders from across the United States and Canada to urge them to pass similar laws. The political pressure mobilized in Irvine, as cities like Denver, Los Angeles, Miami-Dade, Minneapolis, and Newark began passing their own local laws, was made evident by a legislative deal struck soon after in Washington, D.C. Sitting in the White House one day, a group of senior Senate, industry, and environmental professionals agreed on terms for supporting ratification of the United Nations' Montreal Protocol (to phase out CFC production globally)—on the condition that the federal government would ban the growing number of Irvine-inspired local laws.[3] The movement of cities that began in Irvine then went on to convince and assist more than eight hundred cities in fifty countries to dramatically reduce their greenhouse-gas emissions.[4]

While Irvine was seeking solutions to global environmental problems, a deteriorating Los Angeles district called Pico-Union, only forty miles away, was hosting the development of a different kind of movement. During the late 1980s, some of the millions of El Salvadorian war migrants settled in Pico-Union as so-called illegal aliens. Here they were introduced to the traditions and practiced methods of Los Angeles street gangs. Unable to get jobs, social services, or rights as citizens, and rejected by the established gangs, the Salvadorian youth of Pico-Union created the notorious Mara Salvatrucha, or MS-13, gang. What followed is similar to the stories of other criminal organizations—the establishment of a parallel, illegal economy in one urban slum area, which the gang scales across a network of cities and eventually merges with other urban criminal networks into today's trillion-dollar transnational criminal economy.

MS-13 started as one local gang among many. At first it was preoccupied with controlling its particular city turf area. But when the war in El Salvador ended in 1992, a new wave of migrants arrived, including members of the former guerrilla force, who brought new military skills to the gang. During these years, crime and intergang violence was on the rise in the notorious L.A. police district called the Rampart Division, of which Pico-Union is a part. The police cracked down and arrested MS-13 gang members, who were incarcerated together. In prison, the gang's development was severed from its dependencies on a single local geography. As Los Angeles police chief William Bratton put it, "To them prison is like going to finishing school." The model that they had mastered was based on expertise in controlling and exploiting marginalized urban territories. So when the U.S. government began deporting MS-13, or "mara," members back to El Salvador in 1996, they set up cells in the low-income districts of El Salvador's cities, recruiting other former guerrillas and unemployed youth. By 2005, wrote Ana Arana in *Foreign Affairs*, the maras "effectively ruled" fifteen municipalities in El Salvador.[5]

MS-13 expanded operations to Honduras. Then, fleeing crackdowns in both countries, it evolved into a transnational criminal organization with operations extending across a network of cities in Canada, the United States, Mexico, Guatemala, El Salvador, and Honduras. The maras have forged alliances with the Mexican mafia. The extensive infrastructure they built to connect this city network—advanced communications equipment, airplanes, and arsenals—and their professional management structure have allowed them to extend their activities from criminal commerce into political and paramilitary territorial control. Their rapid evolution in the course of a decade from a small-scale neighborhood gang in Los Angeles into an integrated drugs, stolen goods, and smuggling operation in Central America, and then further into a transnational political, military, and commercial operation demonstrates how the mismanagement of local urban affairs gets amplified through the extending reach of the global City.

Most telling about these examples—and many others like them—is how even the small districts, the remote provincial towns, and entirely new cities play a major role in world affairs today. Not long ago, developments in places like Machala, Tiruppur, Irvine, and Pico-Union went largely unnoted and had little consequence. Today, they are directly changing the greater world in measurable ways. These places have been the expanding margins of something much bigger: a global City of more than three billion people, soon to be five billion, that is changing the nature of human affairs and of nature itself.

Ideas like globalization, the "flattening" of the world, or the growth of a "network society" are abstract attempts to try to explain this change. But the world is a material place. Its economic and information flows, technologies, business processes, and social relations are not ethereal. They occur within geographies, infrastructures, buildings, and organized communities with very local histories and cultures that are all organized into distinct, tangible, three-dimensional city places that create the economies and social dynamics for particular kinds of activities and living. They are anything but virtual or flat. Those local conditions

8

and histories both constrain and enable the markets for wealth creation, the application of technologies, and the development of new politics.

Consider the Internet, a technology that Thomas Friedman argued had flattened the world, because it allows us to collaborate together 24/7 across the planet without the restrictions of place. The Internet is an urban infrastructure, wedded to the markets and social realities of individual cities. Like the shipping port, electrification, the telegraph, telephone networks, airports, and fiber-optic networks, the viability of Internet-based activities depends on the economics created through our organization into cities. The Internet started as a quintessentially urban network of university scholars in the United States.[6] Public Internet services were then made available in cities, because only cities provided the economics of density and scale to support them. The companies and social networks that have scaled their operations through the Internet have built their operations city by city.[7] Whether in the United States, China, or Afghanistan, it was only after dense networks of urban Internet users were formed that rural Internet services became economical. But these rural networks are not really *rural* in any traditional sense; they are extensions of the urban markets, networks, and services back into rural settlements and society, linking their populations into the global City system and accelerating its growth.[8]

In this book we will explore the tangible form of globalization, which exists in longitude and latitude and three-dimensional space. It rests on the bedrock structure of the world's growing cities and gains definition through their particular designs, values, and routines as they interact in a billion undocumented ways in the emerging global City system. In the early 1990s, Machala's vice mayor established a health clinic that offered (of all things) Indian ayurvedic treatments to the residents of that new stilt-shack barrio; a community of peasant-workers built a global industry; a group of Los Angeles migrants built a transnational criminal organization that is monitored by the U.S. Southern Command[9]; and a group of cities led the global effort to reduce greenhouse-gas emissions—all initially *without* the Internet, multinational companies, or breakthrough business processes. Something more fundamental and more concrete than just "globalization" was happening.

If we think about it, that fundamental force has been obvious. It has been so much a part of our own family stories of migration from rural to urban life and of our everyday lives in cities today that we have failed to recognize it for the revolutionary event it is. This is hardly the first time we've underestimated the significance of events that we only later understood to be of revolutionary importance. The mechanization of production that started in England in the 1760s, for instance, was only understood to be an "Industrial Revolution" in the 1840s. Not until the 1880s did people widely study and debate the process of and word for "industrialization." In the one hundred or so years between the start of the Industrial Revolution and the emergence of conscious efforts for industrial development and "modernization," the great debates of that era focused on the revolution's secondary manifestations: for instance, on land clearance and the rise of pauperism, on the decline of monarchies and the rise of the nation-state, or on machines and technologies themselves and their adverse affect on artisan guilds—much as we, for instance, focus on the phenomena of urban pollution and traffic congestion, mega-cities, and illegal immigration when trying to understand the Urban Revolution today. European society had already been fundamentally reorganized by industrialization before the new phenomenon was given a name. Today our world has been fundamentally reorganized by the Urban Revolution but we discuss it almost cryptically, through demographic trivia. The media have been keen to report that "half the world's population now lives in cities," but we are overlooking the main event: half the world *has become* a City.

For a few decades, a network of visionary thinkers and scholars has been drawing attention to the emergence of what they call "the world city system," but their work has been overshadowed by the twentieth century's dominant paradigm of global order as an international system of nation-states (with their states, provinces, and municipalities), international organizations like the United Nations and the International Monetary Fund, large military organizations, and large corporations. These institutions still dominate the way we study, debate, and try to manage world affairs. But the concrete order of the world has been changing radically. For example, even though the severe acute respiratory syndrome (SARS) crisis in 2003 was a distinctly *urban* epidemic, spread from one city-region in China's Pearl River Delta to other city-regions throughout the world, the World Health Organization only reports SARS cases and deaths by *countries*, even though the mutation of the SARS virus, its transmission from animals to people, and its initial spread within the delta's cities were fundamentally determined by local urban form, traditions, markets, climate, and building designs. Like this example, the management of global affairs has been viewed as a matter of alignment and cooperation between nations, military alliances, and corporations, as with the "coalition of the willing" in Iraq, the negotiation of the United Nations (UN) Kyoto Protocol, or the response to the December 2004 tsunami crisis. With alignment, the collaborative ability of modern institutions to reengineer societies and achieve shared global objectives was assumed, as in the 1960s Green Revolution. Local ethnic, cultural, and political conditions (as in Iraq's insurgent cities); the local, urban origins of global pollutants (as in the case of most climate-changing greenhouse gases); and the emergence of new industries and market crises in the unique contexts of cities (such as the 2007–2008 subprime mortgage crisis in the United States) were secondary concerns in the strategies of modern institutions—until now. Now the inescapable development of the City regularly inserts local details into global affairs in the form of epidemics and disasters, political revolutions and disruptive new business models, global social and consumer movements, transnational criminal organizations and urban insurgencies. The City constantly catches the old order of modern institutions by surprise.

Between 1950 and 1980, in countries everywhere, more than a billion people migrated from rural areas to cities.[10] This movement was counted as little more than a demographic shift, imposing housing, infrastructure, and congestion problems. But a new City system was evolving parallel to the old order. Now we can't understand world events without understanding the City's workings. We can't shape world developments without designing, governing, and managing the cities that are rapidly evolving as a City system.

Studying the rising economic centrality of cities in the world, scholars like John Friedmann, Peter Hall, and Robert Cohen documented how cities were having direct relationships with each other independent of relations between nations, even during the era of Cold War controls. As the Cold War came to an end in the late 1980s and national governments relaxed market controls, there was a dramatic increase in global migration, travel, investment, and information flows—between cities. Urban scholars like Peter Taylor, Manuel Castells, Saskia Sassen, and Fu-Chen Lo started analyzing how these flows were organized, and they discovered that global activities were patterned according to networks of cities. They combed what data were available at the city level to document these patterns. They looked at the origins and destinations of telephone calls, Telexes, faxes, and new Internet connections, and at airplane travel, immigration, commodity flows, container shipments, corporate office locations, product sales, and professional group concentrations. Their conclusion has been that the growing commerce between cities has created hierarchies between cities that define the new global economic order. Cities and their networked systems, not countries or individual corporations, are the new command and control centers of a world City system.[11]

But their analysis has painted only part of the picture. While establishing the economic reality of the global City system, we still hardly understand the ecological dimension of global change that has been caused by urbanization. Ecologists have long focused their studies of urban ecology on the adaptations of natural species, like birds and plants, to harsh urban environments. We are only beginning to explore how the growth of cities and their networks have been creating a quasi-ecological order parallel to the natural world, much as world urbanization has created a new social order parallel to the twentieth-century international system.

The scale of the Urban Revolution's ecological impact is hard to grasp. Consider a simple example—the primary material of the City itself: concrete. Data from the cement and concrete industry suggest that the provision of this one building material to cities involves an annual movement of material weighing eight times more than the total global automobile fleet. That's equivalent to 5.5 billion Toyota Corollas. By volume, this conservative estimate of concrete consumption in cities each year is equivalent to 730 Great Pyramids of Giza.[12]

World concrete production depends on local supply chains and production facilities to extract the limestone, shale, sand, and gravel required to build and renew the extant centers and growing margins of the City each year. The trucks that transport these materials cover millions of miles annually. The energy used in production and the carbon dioxide (CO_2) emissions released during the mixing of the concrete account for an estimated 5 percent of global CO_2 emissions—equivalent to the national emissions of Russia or India.

But this is just the start. The concrete buildings, roads, and infrastructure in cities are also constantly being renewed. It is estimated that more than one billion tons of construction and demolition waste are generated each year.[13] This waste has to go somewhere. Most of the material used to build the world's constantly transforming cities is reused to extend waterfronts, to fill marshes, or to create new airports. The global cycle of material accumulation in cities is reshaping the world's coastline. Similar dynamics and impacts apply to the cumulative energy, water, plastics, chemicals, and organic materials used in cities and to the wastes they generate. The scale of the global City's mundane forces is so great that it has revolutionized Earth's ecology. To sustain our economies and social order, we must learn how to steer those forces in revolutionary ways.

The second force not yet fully understood about the City system is its revolutionary social and political effects. Once again, our modern intellectual bias has been to view global changes as top-down processes, driven largely by central government investments and global corporate interests. When cities are described as economic command and control centers, the world-cities scholars are particularly referring to the corporate power concentrated within them, particularly in central business districts, in certain industries like finance and business services, and among certain population groups, like white-collar professionals or what Richard Florida calls "the creative class." But this describes only one part of the City. A much larger "creative class" has also been building the City—hundreds of millions of urban migrants like those in Machala, Tiruppur, and Pico-Union, who have created urban land from marshes, built settlements that cover much of the global City's landscape, created new industries and massive global investment flows with their remittances, and formed the political movements or criminal and paramilitary organizations that now perplex the old international order.

Consider the annual global financial flows of these grassroots city builders. In 2006, some 150 million global migrants sent an estimated

$300 billion, predominantly earned in foreign cities, back to their countries of origin. These funds are reaching an estimated 10 percent of the world's population. The annual sum of migrant "remittances"— another generic term, like "globalization," that hides the underlying urban nature of the phenomenon—equals nearly 40 percent of the total investment of foreign corporations and private investors in all developing countries.[14] These financial transfers serve as a sort of global urban development fund, transferred household to household, small business to small business. It is from this fund that new family members are brought to the city, that their houses are built, that their new livelihoods are capitalized, and that their televisions and mobile phones are purchased, allowing them to build their own networks across the City. This fund dwarfs worldwide government and international development assistance to developing countries. It accounts for one tenth of the gross domestic product (GDP) of forty-three countries, including Morocco, Bangladesh, the Philippines, Vietnam, Bosnia, Serbia, and most of Central America. Fourteen countries receive more than one quarter of their GDP from these grassroots transfers. Remittances involve, on average, an estimated 4.1 million transfers *each day* (a total of 1.5 billion each year), thanks to the integration of urban markets and telecommunications infrastructure across the City system.

Global migrant financial flows, through both the legal system and parallel informal financial systems, reveal the extent to which the Urban Revolution is a bottom-up process. Cities can't be effectively understood as the products of national infrastructure building or as nodes in a new global corporate order. Many and diverse interests converge and struggle in each city and create parallel systems of finance, governance, planning, enterprise, and regulation to steer the city's development to their advantage. They create parallel cities of informal slums, security-guarded planned communities, and ethnic, sectarian, and criminal territories within each metropolis, each networked to others across the City. The competition in and between our cities is certainly economic but in more trenchant ways than the celebrity-styled competitions for best business location or the next Olympics venue. The competition for cities is a struggle over the most basic stuff of economic opportunity— over the raw, malleable economics of cities that we design and build in hundredfold ways to create some unique economic advantage. The efforts of *invasores* and transnational corporations are actually very similar. They are both urban migrants trying to shape cities to their advantage. One group leverages its vast human numbers, the other its vast financial accounts. Both develop tenacious, specialized ways to secure their rights and opportunities in the global City.

From the time Homo sapiens first began migrating from Africa to Eurasia about fifty thousand years ago until the first known cities circa six thousand years ago, our species lived as nomadic hunter-gatherers or in small agricultural villages. It was no more than about four thousand years ago that a city's population first surpassed one hundred thousand people, in the cities of Ur and Avaris (in today's Iraq and Egypt, respectively). Even then we remained a predominantly rural, agricultural species until the twentieth century. By 2040, nearly two thirds of the world's people will live in cities.

In the most recent phase of the Urban Revolution (for our purposes, between 1950 and 2000), cities grew largely beyond our control, inefficiently and problematically. In this book we'll explore how their underestimated and mismanaged growth seeded many of the problems that we wrestle with today: climate change, transnational crime, political instability, terrorism, epidemic disease, supply chain breakdowns, congestion, and riots. As the world urban population grew, we failed to understand what drove its growth. We failed to hone basic practices of urbanism—how to govern urban markets, develop shared urban culture, and design urban form and systems—to viably create a City with less poverty, less inequality, and less environmental degradation. Now the scale of those problems, and the City's continued growth, demands a new strategy.

In the nineteenth- and early-twentieth-century era of nation-building, the practices of military strategy were mastered to control territories and manage trade. In the late twentieth century, global business strategy was developed as a distinct practice to secure market share in the City's integrating markets. We have refined strategic practices for global agricultural development, industrial economics, intelligence gathering, and global disease control, but the world's best practices in urbanism are barely known and are rarely supported by our institutions.

We cannot anticipate or shape global change today without a strategy for the remaining decades of the Urban Revolution. Governments and corporations alike have been consistently caught off guard by local urban revolutions in Iran in 1979, the Philippines in 1986, Central and Eastern Europe in 1989, and South Africa in the 1980s and early 1990s; urban disasters (New Orleans in 2005), epidemics (SARS in Guangdong in 2003), uprisings (Paris in 2005, Gaza City in 2007, Beirut and Nairobi in 2008), and business practices (subprime mortgage lending in 2007). These events document the vulnerabilities created when societies rapidly urbanize without effective practices of urbanism. Our lack of preparedness for them reflects the degree to which the City's fundamental forces remain out of focus.

Lewis Mumford, the famed historian of science and technology, once wrote: "The blind forces of urbanization, flowing along the lines of least resistance, show no aptitude for creating an urban and industrial pattern that will be stable, self-sustaining, and self-renewing."[15] But we *do* have an opportunity to develop that aptitude. As the next two billion people join the ranks of "Homo urbanis," today's cities will be redesigned and rebuilt to absorb that growth. Over the next thirty years, cities will replace much of their stock of housing and infrastructure. Their demographics will radically change as well. Along the way, we have a chance to replace much of the thinking, politics, design, and technology that dominates (and burdens) our cities today. If we can just learn how to better grow our cities, we can also design solutions to many of the global problems that confront us. We can create cities that increase social cohesion rather than accentuate our social divisions. We can create cities that dramatically reduce their encroachments and demands on natural ecosystems. We can create cities and a global economy in which spatial form and design are used to boost productivity and innovation rather than sapping them through congestion and instability. But if we fail to advance sound practices of urbanism, continuing on the blind urbanization path we have been taking, we will be designing the global crises of tomorrow.

CHAPTER 2

The Improbable Life of an Urban Patch

Deciphering the Hidden Logic of Global Urban Growth

To make this all more concrete, we can begin by exploring a typical city neighborhood to understand how it works as a microcosm of the global system of cities. To begin, imagine the classic image of Earth seen from space. You will surely see the familiar pattern of great seas and continents; deserts, polar regions, and forests; the blues, tans, whites, and greens that we have come to know through astronauts' eyes. These vast natural systems and territories are what ecologists call our planet's *biomes*. Each has its distinct currents and cycles; each has its unique, complex communities of plants and animals.

But there is something truly odd about this image. You'll note that in this view your city neighborhood does not appear. In fact, in this prevalent image of Earth—ironically photographed during Earth's most rapid period of urbanization—we see a world without a single city. This deceptive view of our planet, and its widespread embrace, epitomizes the extent to which we have left our cities, and thus our future, out of view.

To find your city neighborhood, we have to put this image aside and look at Earth from a different perspective. Imagine that same view from space, but this time at night.[1] In this view, all the natural biomes are hidden in solar shadow and a totally different reality is exposed. Dense concentrations of light dominate continents and cluster on coastlines, revealing their own patterns. The United States and Europe are completely alight. A thick band of light extends all the way from Europe and the Middle East, across Russia and Siberia, to northern Asia. The lights then spread down the brightly profiled landmasses of Japan and South Korea, spill along the eastern half of China to Indonesia, and collect into a pool that illuminates the entire Indian subcontinent. The southern and northern coasts of Africa are ringed with light, and the glow in the eastern regions of South America extends around the southern and western coastlines. Light trickles out into the Amazon basin and up the western rise of the Andes.

These vast areas of light are evidence of a new ecological order—of the urban biome we are creating.[2] We have only partial measures of urban populations, economics, health, financial flows, and resource consumption. But we know this much: we cannot see the few lights of a village from space. The dots, dense clusters, or long bands of light that extend across our continents are the growing City. The flow of energy represented by the continental constellations of light is indicative of many other Earth-changing flows that connect cities into metropolitan clusters and regional systems that, in turn, connect into the City, a phenomenon now as vast and commanding in Earth's order as the great oceans.

One point in this system of light is your city neighborhood. Zoom in from space, and the blues, tans, and greens give way to urban grays and browns. At first, the city structure looks like some kind of industrial hive or a piece of modern art, but because you have become habituated to it, you will recognize its patterns. You will discern the arrangement of streets and city blocks, of residential and industrial areas, and of canalized rivers and ports. Zoom in further and you will find the unique arrangement of streets, buildings, and green spaces that distinguish your urban patch—the urban equivalent of a tiny mountain crag or a ripple in a river. Now we can begin to understand the familiar yet ever-surprising character of the City.

To take in my own urban patch I leave my computer and go to the rooftop of my home. This is a quiet, mixed-income neighborhood in Toronto, Canada. From here I can see about five hundred feet in all directions. The two- and three-story homes of my neighbors face me to the east, across the street. Behind them lies the small neighborhood park. Beyond the park, I can see the rooftops of a small social housing project and a large high school. To the west, behind a row of trees, I see the back of another row of houses like mine. These houses face one of the bigger, mixed retail-residential avenues that border our neighborhood in each direction. There is another school across this avenue and to the southwest I can see a high-rise housing complex. Directly to the south of my house, the single-family homes extend as far as I can see, and to the north, through the full canopy of mature maple trees and above the tops of other homes, I can glimpse the taller buildings on the district's main avenue. It seems a typical, uneventful place.

An average day unfolds. A few weeks ago, the neighborhood held its annual fireworks display and organized a cleanup in the park. Neighbors have been commiserating about the noisy, swearing teenagers on the basketball court and sharing a consoling word about the passing of an elderly neighbor who had lived here since the neighborhood was built. A century ago this man's parents saw a pasture on this place, where it met a small, wooded ravine whose stream flowed down past the old brickyard and under the train tracks, and then passed through a colony of factories and workers' houses before it reached the shore of Lake Ontario two kilometers to the south. Our urban patch sits over the filled and leveled top of that ravine.

Among the accomplished writers, actors, musicians, and artists and the established professors, journalists, advertising professionals, lawyers, and civil servants who own property here, a stunning variety of recent immigrants have also laid claim in this small area. Some came from distant villages and are building their first footholds in the City. They have brought trades, extended families, and customs with them. They have not abandoned their places of origin but use our patch to extend their opportunities across those chains of light on the darkened Earth.

Twenty years ago this area was dominated by Greek and Italian immigrants. Most came in the 1950s, leaving behind countries unsettled by war. Now the annual Greek Independence Day parade on the main avenue seems like a relic of another time. An Ethiopian family owns and runs the corner store across from the school. A Korean family owns the discount store, and a Turkish family owns the shoe repair shop. These shops are across the street from a new Starbucks. Down the sidewalk from Starbucks, a Mexican immigrant has set up a burrito shop. Across the street, a Japanese man purchased a building for his sushi restaurant, and nearby two Jamaicans run a barbershop for the local Caribbean population. Another barbershop was located near the subway station for the Greeks and other Europeans, but when the two Greek barbers retired, they leased their shop to a barber from Bangladesh. The Greek men who ambled by the shop every day to their cafés and political clubs have been replaced by the daily flow of hundreds of predominantly South Asian men on their way to prayers at the neighborhood mosque. When we take our sons into the barber's now, we are invited to sit not with a copy of *Sports Illustrated* but with a copy of the Qur'an.

In the fifteen years I have lived in this place that calls itself "the Pocket," it has developed a whole new community of Muslim immigrants from India, Pakistan, Bangladesh, Afghanistan, and East Africa. Fifty percent of the children at our neighborhood elementary school do not speak English as their primary language. Cricket has become a regular sight in the park where our sons play baseball and hockey. Single-family homes and simple retail storefronts are used in new ways. Some have been divided into rooming houses, where new arrivals first take up residence as they look for work and wait for family members to arrive. Other homes are used during the workday as informal day care centers. On the avenue immediately west, next to an old Estonian church, an extended family from a small town in Gujarat owns four homes. Here the multiple couples, parents, in-laws, aunts and uncles, siblings, and cousins have re-created a life typical of the traditional "joint homes" in their native western India. On the main avenue five hundred feet to the north, near the old Italian grocery shop and the Baptist church (that still attracts worshippers of Caribbean origin each Sunday), another successful Gujarati family has established a clothing manufacturing and retail business. When I buy my business clothes there, I am treated with a courtesy and level of service that is extremely rare in the franchised retail landscape of North America.

The public stolidity and discipline of our new Muslim village contrasts sharply with other developments in this urban patch. One of the rooming houses became the residence of a drug dealer, and then of a prostitute who openly did fast favors for her roadside recruits behind an apartment building on a nearby street. To track the drug trade, the police placed undercover agents at the local doughnut and coffee shop. One January night a dead man was dumped in the alleyway behind our neighbors' homes immediately across the street. More recently, three men threatened a couple in the park with razors when they would not surrender their wallets. Life in our patch of settled affluence and aspiring immigrants continues, although it also hosts an underworld of crime and illicit commerce that does not fit the image of a good neighborhood, even if this is a normal reality in most parts of the urban world today.

I increasingly notice similarities between life in my Toronto neighborhood and life in cities like Mumbai, Bangalore, Manila, and Johannesburg, where I have been conducting business. In those cities, low-income garbage scavengers who sell their materials to recyclers have long been an unofficial part of their city's system of solid waste management. Here in Toronto, subsistence scrap collectors do regular late-night rounds to scoop up metal appliances and furnishings that have been left for the municipal collectors. Other scavengers pick the valuable aluminum cans from our recycling bins, a practice that became so widespread that it cost the municipal recycling program an estimated million dollars each year, forcing the city to pass a law to stop it. A new deposit fee on wine bottles has spawned another specialization, whose "proprietors" have staked out territorial routes, which they "service" with repurposed shopping carts to collect the spoils from stoops and verandas of the area's wine-drinking homes.

Just a few hundred feet beyond the abstract border of our urban patch, people from other distant lands have created a microcosm of world affairs in a low-income housing complex. Women from different parts of the Caribbean run their traditional micro-banking activities, in which members make monthly contributions to savings pools and disburse the proceeds to a different woman each month. A group associated with the Dinka rebel movement of southern Sudan—refugees from their country's twenty-two-year civil war—plan their return. Afghani exiles from Taliban rule have been returning home to rebuild their businesses. Senior officials of Somalia's new national government have recently resided here, and the current prime minister of Somalia lived in a low-income housing project a few miles away.

Beyond the housing project to the southwest is a predominantly Chinese commercial district where we often shop. Here, rival extortion and drug gangs profit from the many restaurants and grocers. They occasionally have shoot-outs on the streets and have recently felled an innocent bystander. Stolen and contraband goods can be purchased from backrooms and basements. People wonder why the police cannot contain the gangs that operate so openly.

Students in our neighborhood high school, to the east, commute from an area where Sri Lanka's Tamil Tiger insurgents have long operated an extortion scheme, which generates as much as $12 million a year for their insurgency. Human Rights Watch reports that extortion fees in this neighborhood are set at $1 for each day that each Tamil family has lived in Toronto. Tamil small business owners are "asked" to pay as much as $25,000 to $100,000 per annum.[3]

These are some of the increasingly common signs of the changing life within any urban patch in the world today. I cannot begin to document or even imagine the connected worlds that are invented and taking root in this little place, which little more than a century ago was a stream, some field, and trees.

Even the natural order of things in our neighborhood defies expectations and stereotypes. People think of urban environments as depleted and spoiled, but they are not. They are enriched by hundreds of species, native and exotic. Toronto's urban neighborhoods host substantially greater numbers of species than the temperate rural landscapes that surround the city. In addition to domestic pets, some from continents far away, our patch hosts populations of woodland raccoons and skunks that live in denser populations than those found in their natural habitats beyond the city limits.[4] These animals have fully adapted to urban living, digging nests into our rooftops and feeding surreptitiously on our leftover food. Foxes have been seen visiting the neighborhood, following the remnants of the old ravine through the train yard to the neighborhood park. The varieties of plants are even more exotic. We have avid gardeners in this patch. My twenty-foot-by-twenty-foot front yard hosts nearly one hundred perennial plant species. As a result of the exceptional ecological richness of our urban patches, greater Toronto has more plant and animal species than many whole countries.

The biology of a metropolitan area like Toronto may be unstable in comparison to natural ecosystems. Our patch depends on vast quantities of materials, commodities, and energy that are extracted from distant other ecosystems, processed in far-flung patches of the City, and shipped to us here. But managed properly, our cities are full of untapped efficiencies and potentials. For example, one of the primary efficiencies of Earth's green and blue ecosystems is the way energy is recycled along an entire food chain, passing itself in ever new nutrient forms from one species to the next. Mimicking this pattern, energy recycling is becoming an important aspect of Toronto's evolving brown and gray ecosystem. The city government established a company that uses the waste steam from four downtown energy plants to provide an efficient heating solution for 140 high-rise office buildings, running the steam through a twenty-five-mile system of pipes. Then, in 2004, the same company opened a district cooling system that draws cold water from deep in Lake Ontario to serve one hundred major office buildings. The deep lake water, which is extremely clean, then flows into the Toronto water system. From there the used water is treated and returned to the lake (albeit with many different new trace chemicals). This clever infrastructure creates an urban ecology that is more symbiotic with the natural one. It reduces the electricity used in standard air-conditioning systems by 90 percent, it reduces air pollution and massive discharges of hot water into the lake from electrical plants, and it eliminates the use of ozone-depleting CFCs.

Our five-hundred-foot patch has also hosted odd ecological conflicts. For some years, a network of Greek and Eastern European immigrants made a living by collecting large earthworms at night from, among other places, the high school playing field, to be sold along a value chain to distant recreational fishermen. One resident of Greek heritage was a veritable kingpin in the so-called dew worm trade, a supplier to a regional industry that exported more than five-hundred million worms to the United States each year. Nightly worm-gathering sorties in our high school playing field so depleted the worm population that the field became barren. Even weeds struggled to survive. The municipality eventually challenged the local worm industry, which one study described as including a daily informal auction in a restaurant where freelance pickers met with refrigeration truck operators to transport the worms to the U.S. border.[5] The city's crackdown on the trade was part of a whole new regime for managing the urban environment, in which neighborhood trees, fields, wildlife, pets, waste, household chemicals, and parking spaces became, at least in theory, centrally regulated.

In spite of all this exotic detail, when guests visit our neighborhood, they remark that our area is comfortable, interesting, and charming. Our quaint neighborhood resembles many urban neighborhoods that we take for granted throughout the world. The faces and players might be different, but the dynamics of this Toronto urban patch are probably little different from the dynamics of the neighborhood that you can see from the roof of your city home or office. These are the dynamics of the fast-evolving world order that I have proposed we simply call—much as we refer to the ice caps, the steppes, the rain forests, or the seas—the City.

It is important to understand what drives the enterprising convergence of so many different undertakings in a single city block—a Starbucks located two hundred feet from a drug house in the midst of a new outpost of the Gujarati diaspora close by where distant insurgencies are financed and foreign governments planned. Further, we need to understand the imperatives that drive the merging of cities throughout the world into a single, converging system that is re-ordering the most basic dynamics of global ecology, politics, markets, and social life.

At its root, we can only comprehend and ultimately steer the City's growth and the new pressures, competitions, and struggles it creates by understanding what makes cities places of so much opportunity. People and organizations don't go to cities for their problems. If cities were primarily the problem centers of the world, as they are so often portrayed, then it would seem logical that people and money would flee them. Their populations would not be increasing. Multinational companies would not be competing for new building sites. Dubai would not be host to thirty thousand (or 24 percent) of the world's construction cranes, just as Shanghai had a quarter of the world's cranes in the 1990s. People and organizations build and flock to cities and will continue doing so because they are massive generators of opportunity. Cities offer *advantage* in the world—*unique* chances to secure greater income, to organize for political rights, to benefit from education and social services, to meet other entrepreneurs or gain competitive position in a market. Cities, relative to other forms of settlement, offer what we can simply call *urban advantage*. The further concentration of hundreds of millions in cities, whether through risk-taking squatter communities, multinational companies, ethnic groups, social movements, guerrilla movements, or transnational gangs, reflects the multitude of strategies to claim some bit of control over a city's urban advantage so they can leverage it *for their own advantage.* If we don't understand what makes up urban advantage, then we can't understand the City.

Most cities, unless they are entirely new, have accumulated a unique legacy of urban advantage, bequeathed by the strategies of earlier urban pioneers who designed and built their cities in specific ways to secure their own advantage. If your city is lucky, those pioneers had insight about the basic elements of urban advantage that could be developed from the city's location and historic circumstances. Often this took the form of a strategic location itself, like Toronto's location by a protected harbor during a time of colonial warfare, or Chicago's location at the meeting point of two great shipping basins, or Bangalore's location on a high plain between the strategic centers of Mysore and Madras. Then, if your city's fortune holds, its pioneers learned how to arrange a mix of activities—production, commerce, culture, and residential life—into a fixed spatial relationship with each other to create an efficient social and economic dynamism, which economists have explored as "agglomeration economies," but which I call a local *citysystem* to also embrace its social and ecological elements.

Take Bangalore, for instance. In the 1990s, it became a world-changing city, seemingly from nowhere. But its growth into a leading center of high-tech industry was built on a centuries-old foundation of developed urban advantage. Consider the city's historic practice of developing through distinct, specialized districts. First there was the old city where textile production, commerce, and residential activities were clustered efficiently together. Then came the nineteenth-century military cantonment, which joined barracks, housing for officers, military grounds, and later military research and production in another distinct citysystem. In the twentieth century, the city developed specialized industrial townships, where large primary manufacturers and supporting small workshops were built adjacent to workers' housing and the retail establishments and vendors that served them. Then successive national and state governments endowed the city with every imaginable kind of scientific and research institute, again using a clustered campus model of urban development. This process started with the establishment of the Indian Institute of Science in 1909 and with its numerous spin-off research institutes over the decades. The process of scientific endowment within a clustered area of the city never really stopped. It extended to the National Aeronautics Laboratories (1960), the Indian Space Research Organisation (1969), and the Indian Institute of Management (1973) and to more recent institutes on information technology (IT), telematics, electronics, physics, and every other imaginable field of scientific inquiry.

By 1980 the city had scores of colleges—and hundreds of thousands of students—producing a fresh labor supply for its technical industries. Further hands-on training was offered through an explosion of private sector training companies. By 2000, Bangalore had 760 firms offering IT training alone. As its industries and technical institutes developed, the city created and attracted young talent. And while other major Indian cities became congested and unmanageable, Bangalore had physical room to grow and intellectual room to experiment.

Repeating the industrial township approach used decades earlier, in the late 1970s Bangalore's state government created the setting for the future IT sector in the form of an industrial park called Electronics City. In the 1980s, new software start-ups like Infosys joined the city's first generation of electronics companies in Electronics City. Here their proximity, shared needs, and shared frustration with the poor infrastructure engendered both the politics and economics for the country's first scaled broadband communications system in 1992. So great was Bangalore's legacy of urban advantage that with the simple addition of a new fiber-optic infrastructure in Electronics City, the city's software companies stood ready to profitably meet the huge new challenge faced by expanding transnational companies—the integration of their separate national business operations and acquisitions into more seamless global operations through new software systems. Bangalore's rise did not appear from nowhere. It was built on a foundation of urban advantage that could support unprecedented growth.

When people are asked to describe the basic stuff of cities, they tend to mention streets, sewers, drains, housing, factories, and skyscrapers. Or they get even more basic and list concrete, steel, brick, glass—and lots of busy people. These are the *things* that visibly make what was once a marsh or village or small town a budding city. But clearly, a place like Bangalore—just one of countless specks of light on that extended global City—derives its energy from more potent forces, from some other raw stuff of a city. That stuff is the four basic elements of urban advantage, which make cities everywhere magnets for every kind of ambition: what I call their economies of *density*, *scale*, *association*, and *extension*.

The first thing that anyone notices on entering a city is the concentration of people and their activities. Simple as it is, this density has been little understood, and its benefits are too often squandered through the low-density development of cities today. The density of cities is their most basic advantage over any other kind of settlement. Without density of settlement, most of what we learn, produce, construct, organize, consume, and provide as a service in the world would simply be too expensive. Density increases the sheer *efficiency* by which we can pursue an economic opportunity.

The scale of cities is the second building block of urban advantage. It increases the sheer *volume* of any particular opportunity, producing what we call economies of scale. Scale permits the splitting of fixed costs and known risks over a large enough group of users to make an activity attractive or service profitable *in a big way*. In this way, the scale of cities increases the range of opportunities and level of ambition that can be viably pursued in them and thereby the scale of the impacts that urban pursuits can have on the world.

The scale and density of interactions among people with different interests, expertise, and objectives then combine to create the third basic economy of cities. Together density and scale exponentially increase the variety of ways and the efficiency with which people can organize, work together, invent solutions, and launch joint strategies for urban advantage. I call this collaborative efficiency economies of association. Like-minded people have only so much time and opportunity to happen upon the people and organizations with whom they can invent, plan, and launch their strategies for advantage in the world.

Finally, economies of density, scale, and association together provide the cost efficiencies and user communities to extend their organized strategies to other cities through infrastructure investments and technology applications. Shipping ports, airports, telephone, cable television, and fiber-optic networks depend on the combined economies of density, scale, and association in cities. We accurately call these systems *urban infrastructure* because their economic viability is uncertain without the supply efficiencies created by density and scale and the demand efficiencies created by association. The net result is a new kind of advantage: economies of *extension*. Extension is the ability to economically use technologies to link the unique advantages of different cities to create whole new strategies for advantage in the world.

These elements of urban advantage are what allowed an unknown Los Angeles neighborhood gang to develop into a transnational criminal organization in less than fifteen years, just as it allowed Bangalore software entrepreneurs to leverage their relationships with companies in Europe and North America into a new business process outsourcing industry. Cities, and specific groups within cities, design and use urban infrastructure to extend their strategies and forms of association (e.g., commerce, politics, and crime) across a network of cities. They combine the unique advantage of one city with others to create whole new strategies for advantage in the City. Globalization is this process of developing new advantage from the unique economics of an extended group of cities—from their spatial designs, infrastructures, cultures, and local markets. Local urban affairs, therefore, are more (not less) important in the global era. They define the potential and the burdens of the expanding City.

There are two aspects to density in the growth of cities. *Proximity* reduces the time and energy and therefore the cost required to move people and materials around to achieve any objective. It is easy to do the math. Take an urban water system. If we are building a water system for a suburban neighborhood where homes are 120 feet apart versus a downtown neighborhood where homes are twenty feet apart, we have to use one hundred feet of extra pipe for each home in the lower-density neighborhood. If each neighborhood has one hundred houses, then a higher-density neighborhood saves an impressive two miles of pipe— not to mention the costs for installation and maintenance and for pumping the water through it. But in my city, a person living in a low-density neighborhood pays the same rate for water as the people in my high-density neighborhood. The water department loses money on the low-density neighborhood, and our neighborhood must help make up the difference through our water rates and tax payments. The same basic math applies to every other service. If the city's average density goes down, then the underlying economics of the city deteriorate. Someone has to make up the difference. If people in low-density suburbs had to pay the full cost for their infrastructure, a great many of them would likely reconsider where they live.

When mutually supportive activities are located in proximity to each other, their *concentration* has a further synergistic effect. The economics of collaboration generally improve. Expensive infrastructure and service systems are used more fully and in multiple ways, making them more cost efficient. Cities can exponentially increase these economies by clustering complementary activities together. One of the most basic and least practiced arts of city building today is the creative use of density—proximity and concentration—in the city's built form.

The economics of concentration were further driven home to me in Mumbai, where low-income vendors of bananas or tomatoes set their tables right next to each other on the street. There might be fifteen tomato vendors on one sidewalk together. On the surface this seems unwise—they are placing themselves right next to their competition. But the economic dynamics of density are such that by concentrating, they gain the benefits of a more scaled grocery operation. They create a unique go-to destination for tomatoes.

One can see this use of clustering to create the proxy advantages of scale on city streets all over the world. If you walk along the main avenue of our Toronto neighborhood you will find a group of individual stores that specialize in home décor and furnishings. They have organically concentrated together without any coordination or plan. On the surface, like the Mumbai fruit vendors, they are in competition with each other. But by concentrating together, they are using density to create what amounts to a specialized home furnishings market that attracts and serves customers from across a much larger area of the city, increasing the total pool of patrons for each individual store.

Like proximity, concentration can also provide physical economic benefits. Take high-rise apartment buildings as an example. In a world struggling to increase its energy efficiency, the high-density high-rise is an obvious solution. A free-standing home that is thirty feet long and twenty feet high has four walls of six hundred square feet each and a nine-hundred-square-foot roof—a total of thirty-three hundred square feet exposed to Toronto's winter cold or Miami's summer heat. However, a condominium of the same size that is located in the middle of an eight-story building has just one wall—six hundred square feet—exposed to the elements, through which winter cold or summer heat seeps in. Everything else being equal, the energy efficiency of a high-rise district adds in a very basic way to a city's urban advantage.

Density is the first thing that distinguishes a city from other forms of settlement because it is the city's first and most basic source of advantage. The second thing that you'll notice on entering any city is its scale. Ten years ago the restaurant and shop owners along a mile stretch of our main avenue decided to organize an annual festival in which they all sell their foods and goods on the sidewalks—to the entire city. Now the festival attracts one million visitors in a two-day period alone. Festivals in cities around the world are the most traditional and accessible form of scaled market operation. The same economic dynamic that made this work in our little urban patch also transformed a collection of competing, individual commodity traders in Chicago into the world-renowned Chicago Board of Trade or supported the investments required for dozens of clustered software start-ups in Bangalore to grow into a global high-tech hub with hundreds of thousands of employees.

The combination of density and scale economies underpins the third basic advantage of cities: association. The concentration, proximate convenience, and number of interactions between the people in a city—with their different ideas, talents, desires, and intentions—allow societies to efficiently organize into myriad groups with shared pursuits and strategies. The economics of association starts as a simple self-organizing process among small groups of like-minded people. For instance, the Muslim families in my neighborhood, from very disparate places and backgrounds, can join together into a common religious community and pool their resources to expand and upgrade their austere mosque. Like-minded neighbors can easily raise funds to upgrade and manage the activities in our neighborhood park. The businesspeople on the main avenue, from so many different countries and cultural backgrounds, can associate to create a common festival and commercial identity.

On a larger scale, city dwellers from many places and backgrounds meet, mix, plan, and engineer electorates, companies, NGOs, shadow governments, systems of criminality, and insurgencies. The economics of association in cities permits the efficient organization of talent into labor markets (like the huge new market for software technicians in Bangalore), research collaborations (like the development of e-mail and the Internet in Cambridge), and industries (like the organization of the Gounder migrants in Tiruppur). The efficiency of urban association underlies the basic process of human invention and innovation. People of all backgrounds are drawn to cities to break from the restrictions and injustices of traditional rural societies and to reorganize themselves into new communities. By facilitating new forms of association, our cities increase the pace and variety of human invention and social change.

Finally, when people and organizations associate to leverage advantages from their city, they also raise resources to build the infrastructure to tap into the opportunities of other cities. Extension from city to city is the story of my neighborhood's globally collaborating artists, activists, businesspeople, and diaspora communities, and of its criminal organizations, war extortionists, and multinational franchises alike. What starts as a local criminal gang in Hanoi or Los Angeles can extend its influence here to Toronto and thereby find new opportunities in the global City. For instance, not long ago Toronto-area police uncovered an alliance between Asian and Hungarian criminal organizations, reportedly involving one family in our urban patch, which had jointly stolen $7 million in postal checks from regional post offices. Similarly, what starts as an insurgency in Sri Lanka can develop into an international financing system that uses personal identification numbers (PINs) to track the annual payments of tens of thousands of households and small businesses in Toronto's Tamil diaspora population.

Once associates extend their reach across a group of cities—for instance, connecting New York retailers and marketers, and their unique advantages, with the design industry that emerged from the unique advantages of Milan and Barcelona, with the manufacturers that emerged from the unique advantages of Tiruppur—the shared urban advantage of these places can be leveraged to support a new value chain in the global City. These alliances have developed what I call an urban strategy. Others call it something less precise: globalization.

Today, extended urban networks drive the political developments of entire countries, as in the case of my urban patch's influence on Somalia, or the earlier worldwide urban networks of South Africa's émigré anti-apartheid leadership, which sourced the finance, know-how, weaponry, and political support to overthrow the Afrikaaner apartheid regime. Likewise, local commercial communities demand and enable investments in new extension infrastructure, like the early demands of Bangalore's budding high-tech companies for a fiber-optic network. The shipping ports and airports, telephones, and Internet services that these extended networks demand provide the nervous system for the City.

Density, scale, association, and extension drive development in every urban patch, whether in a Toronto neighborhood, a Machala squatter camp, a little inner-city immigrant district like Pico-Union, or a high-tech incubator district in Bangalore. People and organizations of every sort have joined the rough-and-tumble clamor to shape the raw economics of urban patches everywhere into spatial arrangements and building forms that offer them unique advantage. This makes the development and spatial designs of each city a constant around-the-clock competition. The most basic challenge of every city is to transform that competition into a governed negotiation to create shared urban advantages for all whose ambitions bring them to the city. The distinct ways in which cities and their different urban patches succeed or fail in creating these shared advantages determines their contributions, for better or worse, to the world City system.

CHAPTER 3

The Great Migration

The Rise of Homo Urbanis

When Arum wakes to another morning, he plans his revolution anew. His eyes open in a makeshift, one-room shack in Madurai, a city of one million located deep in the agricultural regions of southern India. The dirt floor that is his bed emits an earthy smell evocative of his village home. But this shack of scrap wood, metal, and fabric is clustered with others against the high, thick wall of a brick-making compound. A few feet away, through the compound wall, a city is coming to life.

Arum listens to the sounds of the brick makers across the dusty, hard-packed compound yard. He listens to their movements to judge the time of day. They work in small family groups, a father and mother and one or two teenaged sons, beginning at one o'clock in the morning. For three hours, while the city sleeps, they dig, wet, and knead the soil. From four to ten o'clock, as the sun rises and heats their backs, and as morning birdsongs give way to the traffic noise outside the compound, each team hand-molds a daily output of two thousand to three thousand bricks. Later in the afternoon, with the city's heat and dust bearing down on them, they work three more hours to clean and stack their day's production for the kiln. This twelve-hour process earns them a shared daily wage of less than $10 for a three- to four-person crew, or an average of 17 cents an hour for each worker.

For the brick makers, this is an impressive sum. It is three times the earnings that they could make for off-season agricultural labor back in their villages. Each year during the dry months from March to September, when the region's rural harvest season gives way to its urban construction season, these families migrate back to Madurai. Here each family unit reclaims its residence in a shack or simple canvas tent, producing another four hundred thousand bricks over the course of six months to build the offices, temples, walls, and homes of this growing city.

Madurai and the region that surrounds it have been defined for centuries by seasonal migrations between rural and urban areas, binding village and city into a single economy and culture. The city is known for its elaborate temples and has long been a center of religious festivals and of the markets and occupations that accompany each festival. Every year, hundreds of thousands of villagers, pilgrims, and traders travel hundreds of miles to Madurai with their savings and thirst for camaraderie, renewal, and profit. Each festival draws its own traders and migrants, specializing in the scaled markets it creates for gifts, traditional foods, and religious accessories.

For twenty-two years, Arum's father has migrated back and forth between his village and this brickyard. While he and his wife have raised their family by the seasonal cycle of brick making and agricultural labor, they have invested their savings not into home improvements or better appliances but into Arum's schooling in Madurai. Today the aging father makes fewer bricks and less money. He has also had to save dowries for Arum's two sisters, so there is not enough to continue Arum's schooling. But the parents are using what savings remain to rent the crude brickyard shack for Arum so that he can surmount the annual rhythm of seasonal labor that has defined their family's life for generations. When the dry season is over and Arum's parents return to work in the fields, Arum will not go to the village. He will stay in the city to search for permanent work.

"He should not lead a life like us," his father says in an austere, loving manner. This decision does not require elaboration. It reflects a new regional logic that his family has come to accept as self-evident. Arum is not permitted to make bricks or to join his buddies as laborers in construction jobs. He must discover a new path for himself, and for his family's future, in the world of cities.

So Arum does not rise with his father and mother and the other brick makers in the adjacent tents and huts. Neither does he venture to meet his buddies as they warm their bones with milky tea before their construction work begins. When Arum awakens, he hears the brick makers slapping, patting, and scraping the mud within the molds. Meanwhile, the city rattles awake to the surges of auto rickshaws, buses, and trucks and their growing chorus of horns. If Arum searches the familiar din outside the compound, he can hear small groups of boys and girls passing just beyond the wall, jesting as they navigate the traffic en route to school. Whereas the villagelike sounds of the brick makers and the morning birds within the sheltered compound might lull him back to sleep, the sounds of the school youth trigger his planning anew.

When he emerges from the shack, he is wearing Western trousers and a tucked-in shirt. The morning sun is getting high. I can see him approaching us from the shaded area of the workers' encampment. I'm speaking with the brick makers who are resting in the middle of the compound yard. Arum has an easy, alert gait that is different from the deliberate, sparing walk of his father. It is the walk of a different culture.

"All my friends are doing construction work," Arum tells me as we move to a shaded place. The steamy air slows our movements and conversation. "But I don't want this work," he says in front of the listening workers. I search their body language for a sign of offense but notice none. "I want to use my schooling," Arum says, "to get a job in the shops."

Arum's strategy is to become a shopkeeper. After our talk he will spend his day approaching the proprietors of Madurai's ubiquitous little shops, offering his labor for free to create relationships and collect scraps of advice or gossiped opportunity that might open a pathway for his ambition. "I don't even want to earn money from them, but to learn the skill of running a shop, so I can set up my own," he confides, not quite aware of the many other impediments he will face in securing the space and capital required for this new livelihood. He will return late from his investigations, maybe catching a waking moment to report to his parents. Soon, Arum's parents will depart to find work in the fields, having invested their dwindling savings in Arum's search for a lasting entry point into the expanding City.

Humans are an extremely migratory species. Archaeology chronicles the migrations of our prehistoric ancestors across all the world's landmasses and seas. History chronicles the invasions, global trading, and labor migrations of millenniums of globalization before us. Most cultures, even the most seemingly sedentary and agricultural ones, had seasonal migrations through which families patched together livelihoods from combinations of farm labor and skilled trade activities in separate, often distant locations. In many parts of the world, these migratory traditions defined the prominent caste, class, occupational, and cultural communities of their societies. In Arum's region in southern India, for instance, distinct communities still follow ancient migratory livelihoods, such as the livestock herders who each year cross great distances with their goats to inhabit and graze fallow fields in exchange for providing welcoming landowners with their traditional mowing and fertilizing service.

Though human migration has been extensively studied, most of the thousands of patterned human migrations across history remain undocumented. It might seem foolish therefore to make general observations about them, except for the simple fact that, with the exception of slavery, they have a shared characteristic. Even when people flee hard times—disaster, famine, and conflict—they engage that quintessential human survival instinct to secure a livelihood through some niche economic advantage.

So-called primitive hunter-gatherer cultures aligned their movements with animal migrations as a strategy for livelihood. Nomadic societies shepherded their domesticated herds between distant seasonal grasslands. In more recent times, distinct groups developed skills and nurtured relationships to access specialized urban labor or commercial markets. Once established in a city, they then extended their tested local strategies to secure new opportunities from migrations across larger urban territories. The Chettiar, Marwari, Sindhi, and Parsi caste communities in India and Pakistan, for instance, established specialized roles in business and finance in their traditional home regions and then extended these specializations into dominant positions in commerce and banking in towns across the whole country, then across South and East Asia, and then across the globe.[1]

Similarly, specialist European groups, like the skilled stonemasons and statue makers from the Chiavari region near Genoa, used the migratory strategies that they had honed over centuries in Europe to establish niche roles in the young North American economy, in this case establishing a beachhead in the welcoming market of fast-growing Philadelphia.[2] Another Indian caste community, the Nadars from districts south of Madurai, first learned how to gain dominance in the local retail sector in Tamil Nadu state and then adapted their local strategy to establish a prominent presence in the retail sector of towns throughout India—not unlike the evolving strategies of immigrant South Korean families who have established a ubiquitous presence in the convenience store business of North American cities today. As summarized by scholar Adam Mckeown, "Entire villages [in Asia, Europe, and Africa] specialized in skills such as banking, stonemasonry, letter writing, or trade in particular products, and sent migrants to ply their trade across the region."[3]

Much like Arum in India today, millions of European peasants, in the time before industrialization, combined their local farming activities with seasonal migrations to urban markets to secure a viable annual livelihood. These migratory livelihoods, as in Asia and Africa today, varied for different communities from different regions. As documented by Jan Lucassen and further elaborated by Saskia Sassen, after Europe's peasant families annually harvested the crops that their weak soils could grow and exhausted local opportunities as farm laborers for large landholders, many would migrate hundreds of miles to other harvests, construction and sailoring jobs, bog draining projects, peat-cutting, and peddling activities across all parts of Europe.[4] German peasants migrated annually to grain and peat harvests, brick making and dock work, and canal and dike construction jobs in the Netherlands. Sassen reports that German and Norwegian migrants from very specific regions accounted for a major part of the growth of Amsterdam's population and skilled labor force, including nearly 60 percent of its sailors. The permanent migrations that built Europe's major cities evolved, she writes, "from temporary rural migrations that began to take place at the end of the Middle Ages."[5]

Then, some three hundred years ago, the predominantly seasonal migrations in Europe started taking on a different character, beginning a whole new era of human migration. Although migratory livelihoods were common, particularly among artisans and merchants, residency in most of medieval Europe was restricted by systems of serfdom that tied people to landowners and subsistence agriculture. The decline of those systems in the seventeenth century enabled the beginnings of the global urban migration process that can still be observed today in regions like Madurai, where traditional agricultural systems are more recently being supplanted by urban industrial economics.

The steady emancipation of European peasants from their indentures to landowners in the seventeenth and eighteenth centuries coincided with major crop failures and with the efforts of cities to rebuild their populations and labor forces after plagues and epidemics. Seasonal migrants increasingly took permanent residence in cities to secure their urban livelihoods and political rights. Those with skills were often invited to become citizens. "German records for the eighteenth century," writes Sassen, "show, for instance, that about half of the burghers in trading towns were migrants."[6] These migrants created what Sassen calls "chain migrations" in which one family member establishes a foothold in the city and masters the livelihood strategies and contacts there, to be used in the later migrations of family or community members.

With the rise of global mercantile trade and early industrial technology in the eighteenth century, urban advantage grew. Migration to gain from that advantage accelerated, starting the massive European urban migration in the nineteenth century that grew into the great global urban migration of the twentieth century. Europe's early development as the world's first predominantly urbanized continent, with its city-states before the creation of modern nations, explains the advanced nature of its urban practices, the efficiency and vibrancy of many European cities, and the richness and resilience of its urban culture. The revolutions that created Europe's modern nations in the nineteenth century arose from its cities and their aspiring migrant populations.

The end of ancient seasonal migrations, which connected the economics and social life of towns and their agricultural hinterlands, was often provoked by large-scale events like revolutions, wars, colonization, plagues, and famines. But the patterns of migration and settlement of those who fled the countryside to rebuild their broken livelihoods in cities show that theirs was not a passive, impulsive, or victimized response. Throughout the centuries and even today, urban migrants have generally responded to the pushes and pulls of major events as active agents, not as passive victims. The urban migrant can often be distinguished from his village peers by his attitudes, entrepreneurial ambitions, and tolerance for change and risk. He crafts a strategy for a new livelihood that builds a chain of opportunity for his family, clan, or ethnic community. These pioneering acts—creative and opportunistic responses to large-scale pressures—define the first phase of the great, global migration from humankind's agricultural past to its current urban reality.

Nothing matches the sheer numbers, momentum, and universality of the Great Migration to cities that began in eighteenth-century Europe and accelerated exponentially into a global phenomenon in the twentieth century. As migrations reinforced the growth of towns and their diversifying markets, the variety and effectiveness of migrant strategies also increased. A cycle of migration, urban market growth, more migration, and more market growth created a self-reinforcing momentum. It provided the scale and density of labor supply and consumer demand, and the mercantile association required for industrialization.

But the continuing story of the Great Migration has rarely been told, and its enormity, involving hundreds of millions of people, is hardly understood. Compared with the Great Migration, the most chronicled and widely recognized migrations of history were linked to systems of agricultural labor supply and involved tens of millions. For instance, slave trading over a millennium relocated some twenty-eight million to forty million Africans to the Near East, Europe, and the Americas. The transatlantic slave trade documents eleven million forced relocations between the landing of the first documented African in the Western Hemisphere in 1519 and the constitutional abolition of slavery in the United States in 1865.[7] The plantations of the British Empire replaced African slavery with the Indian indentured labor system, which sent 1.5 million migrant laborers forth between 1834 and 1917. From 1850 to

1940, another six million lower-caste Indians "freely" emigrated to plantations in Sri Lanka, Burma, and Malaysia through a new labor contracting arrangement called *kangani* that bound migrants to foreign employers through debt contracts. Similarly, the nineteenth-century migration of Chinese laborers amounted to some ten to fifteen million people, predominantly to plantations and towns in the European colonies of Southeast Asia and the Caribbean but also to railroad projects and gold rushes in North America and Siberia.[8] But the sum of all these rural labor migrations together does not begin to match the scale of the more voluntary Great Migration that exponentially built the world's cities.

The immigrant settlement of North America was one of the largest, longest migratory flows of people in modern times. The transatlantic migration of an estimated fifty-five million between 1846 and 1940 is associated with the American and Canadian legends of pioneer nation-building, but its bigger, more tangible meaning has been hidden in the demographic data: the waves of migration were dominated not by plans to homestead and build new rural communities but to build livelihoods in the growing markets of North America's cities.[9] Migration to the United States built America's urban population from less than 10 percent of the total population in 1840 to 23 percent in 1880 at the peak of European immigration. During this time the number of city dwellers increased from 1.4 million to 11.3 million. By 1900 an estimated 73 percent of all immigrants were settling in the nation's cities. At the end of the great European immigration, around 1940, America's urban population had increased to 57 percent of the total, with seventy-five million living in cities. By 1990, after yet another phase of immigration from all parts of the world, America's urban population grew to 75 percent. By this time 187 million people were living in American cities.[10]

Today, almost all immigration to North America is to its cities. The United States received around 5.5 million immigrants between 2000 and 2005; nearly all settled in the fifty largest metropolitan areas. Although Canada's vast landscape is full of affordable arable land, clean air and water, and security so scarce in much of the world, 75 percent of Canadian immigrants decline these rural possibilities for a place in the more risky, expensive, and congested urban markets of Toronto, Montreal, and Vancouver. The national governments of Canada and the United States, and the visas and citizenship that they offer, have become an administrative mechanism to facilitate international access to a bigger prize: the markets and opportunities of their cities. Their social support programs, like welfare and employment training, serve as a kind of personal insurance policy on the trial-and-error economic strategies of their urban migrants, whose families are fast becoming the majority of their countries' urban populations.

No migration in history has thus matched the scale or global reach of the Great Migration and the transformational changes, like industrialization, the Information Revolution, and globalization, that are made possible by the remarkable increase in urban advantage that this has created. Although urban growth has taken place in different ways and time spans across the world's economic regions, the underlying process of the Great Migration exhibits similar patterns almost everywhere. It happens in three general stages.

In the first stage of urban migration, pioneers like Arum break traditions of seasonal migration and establish their families' first permanent residences in a regional town. An accelerating cycle of migration, commerce, and investment, followed by further chain migration, transforms the town into a full-fledged city. The chain migrations that feed this cycle change the city's politics, economics, culture, and institutions and ultimately breach its traditional symbiotic relationship with its rural hinterland. This first stage of the Great Migration continues in smaller cities all over the world today, which together will account for the largest part of world urban growth in coming decades. In Africa and Asia alone, the United Nations estimates that cities with a population of fewer than 500,000 will grow by 273 million people between 2005 and 2015, a number equal to the combined populations of Germany, France, Italy, and the United Kingdom.[11]

Having established their strategies for urban living in the more familiar regional towns, migrant families often begin a second stage of migration to the larger cities of their home country. To succeed in these larger cities, they create family and ethnic networks, which support their specializations in new occupations, their dominance in particular industries, and the creation of new political movements in those emerging metropolitan areas. While these migrant networks are uncounted, the projected growth of cities with populations from five hundred thousand to ten million gives an indication of the trend. Between 2005 and 2015, 162 additional cities will grow to this size, increasing their combined population by three hundred million people, a number equivalent to the population of the United States.

Finally, a third stage of the Great Migration can be observed: how second- and third-generation urban migrant families emigrate from the urban centers of their country and extend their economic reach across a network of cities around the world, at once building and laying claim to the global City.

At this late, accelerated period of the Urban Revolution, these stages of migration take place simultaneously. First-generation migrants join established city dwellers whose families left the countryside generations before and immediately begin to extend their strategies to cities worldwide. But we can still observe all three of the Great Migration's stages in individual cities. By understanding them, we can comprehend the forces through which urban growth will continue to transform our world.

Madurai, a typical mid-sized Indian city, is a fascinating place in which to observe the Great Migration's first stage. Some 780 million Indians, or 71 percent of the country's population, still live in rural villages and agricultural areas. This makes India the most rural of the world's large countries. By comparison, only half of the populations of Indonesia and Nigeria, and one quarter of Russians, still live in rural areas. At the far extreme, only 10 percent of the populations of Australia, the United Kingdom, Argentina, and Chile remain rural. Even China, historically the world's largest rural peasant society, has faced a more rapid decline than India in its rural population due to urban migration, with 60 percent of China's people living in rural areas today. An urban majority in India will not be reached until the latter half of this century.

Because of this late migration, it is still possible to directly observe the kinds of seasonal and chain migrations in India's smaller cities that finished long ago in more urbanized regions. One can directly observe the personal logic of urban migration and how the character of the migrant city builder contrasts with that of people who stay in the village. We can also observe how specific social communities evolve their rural traditions into urban economic and political strategies by leveraging the raw potential of association.

I was first invited to Madurai to advise an organization that was seeking to stem the steady migration of villagers to their city. The Covenant Centre for Development (CCD) was founded by a group of social workers who responded to the rise of addiction, crime, and exploitation of migrant youth in their city's growing slums.[12] My hosts at CCD had studied how traditional rural livelihoods, maintained over centuries by different rural caste communities, were in decline. This left young villagers like Arum to forge new livelihood strategies, unsupported, in the city. One result was a growth in Madurai's population from 239,000 people in 1940, when Arum's father was born, to more than one million people today.

The strategy proposed by CCD for slowing urban migration and rebuilding village economies was to adapt and reorganize traditional livelihoods into scalable market-based companies, owned by the villagers. They had organized a company that specialized in traditional herbal medicines, for instance, that was owned by hundreds of traditional growers and gatherers. Its products were being sold in markets throughout India and Europe. With such ventures, CCD hopes to reestablish the economic synergy between the region's rural and urban ways of life.

The CCD team tended to view the city, and urban migration itself, as a problem. By their account, a family's decision to migrate to the city was pushed on them by colonial history, drought, soil erosion, and the division of land into smaller parcels through the generations. Madurai, by this kind of logic, was a city that grew because of the pressures of crises and not because of the imperatives of human ambition and entrepreneurship.

To understand the changing relationship between the village and the city, we agreed to set aside our contradictory views about cities and take a shared reality check. Together, we spent weeks surveying and interviewing scores of low-income migrant households, listening to their firsthand accounts of migration and new city life.[13]

On a relatively cool November morning, toward the end of Arum's first monsoon sojourn in the city, we visited a small settlement at one edge of Madurai's sprawling, unplanned fringe. The loose cluster of new homes, made of concrete blocks, illustrated why Madurai is sometimes called "a city of villages." The place was distant from the cacophony of horns, weaving traffic, and workshops in the old city. Cows, goats, and chickens roamed about. We had to walk on wooden planks through swampy land to reach the houses; the land, we learned, had recently been a rice field. Some of the homes were carefully tiled; others were simple, unfinished structures. They had been spatially arranged like those in a typical regional village.

One two-story house stood out from the others. It sported a special stone memorial at its doorway, commemorating the family's village and its guardian diety, Murugan, the god of health and youth. The woman of the house, Iswari, greeted us at this doorstep, a broad smile permeating every feature of her round face. Receiving a foreign guest is an honor in Tamil Nadu, and she was clearly happy to be the first to welcome us today to her village-in-the-city. We had hardly finished introducing ourselves when ten of her female neighbors and some of their children gathered around us to listen and talk.

In south and central India, people of modest backgrounds, particularly those with village roots, are extremely open and frank. They will tell you their incomes—and then ask you to reveal yours. They will openly contradict each other, share their personal thoughts, and discuss their medical problems and financial details. It is with this kind of frankness that these women told us their stories.

Iswari's father-in-law and her future husband migrated to Madurai in 1985 during a drought. The family were agricultural laborers in a village forty miles south of Madurai. The father-in-law began selling dried fish from a bicycle in the streets. "He brought his son along to help," Iswari explains, teaching her future husband this livelihood as well. Her young husband developed a friendship with another boy whose family was from the caste community that specialized in carpentry. Already the dynamics of urban association were working on him. Different rural castes were mixing and helping each other. "This friend introduced him to a job as a construction worker. After five years he was trained to do masonry work. He saved his money to purchase the equipment of the mason's trade," she explains, as if she was telling a legend that she had recited many times before. He eventually established himself as an independent contractor doing small jobs and now has an operation with a few laborers of his own. He not only moved to the city, but like many other migrants, he is now physically building it.

In the meantime, Iswari's entire family moved to Madurai. Some were introduced to the mason's trade by her husband; another brother started a grocery shop. In 1990 she and her husband bought their piece of land on the old rice paddy from a speculator. By 2000 they had saved enough money to build their house.

They have also saved and invested in their children's education. Iswari was proud to report that her eldest son, born the year of her migration to Madurai, now studies computers at a polytechnic institution. "My husband wants his children to go for other kinds of jobs, not for masonry," Iswari explains. "He's suffered a lot in life, because he is not educated. He has to work with cement. My children should be educated and go for a better job. My son will go to an office and come home well dressed. This generation wants to be neat—civilized," she emphasizes. "If they are educated they will be civilized." She indicates the women who have gathered around us and she adds, "We are villagers."

A younger, quiet woman named Muneeshwari elaborates on their attitude about the city. She and her husband migrated from a small village in 1990, following her elder sister who had already moved to the city. Her brother-in-law then introduced her husband to construction work, which now takes him to jobs in regions beyond Madurai.

"It's like a dream come true, coming to Madurai," says Muneeshwari. "I was born in a village and married to a villager and I always dreamed of being in the city, and now I'm here. We say it is because of no rain that we leave the village," she elaborates, "but to move to the city is big, and we want to move here. If there was plenty of rain," she says, almost appreciating the drought that triggered their move, "we might not have come. My family thinks I'm more civilized because I live in the city."

It is the second time that I've heard them describe the city as "civilized" and I check with my interpreter to make sure that she has given me a literal translation of the women's words. Muneeshwari elaborates. "In the village everybody has to toil in the sun. Here only our husbands toil in the sun. Also in my village there is a school only to the fifth grade. Education is very bad. Teachers don't come regularly, and in the town it is not like that." Muneeshwari's argument is reflected in global statistics: literacy rates are far higher in cities worldwide, particularly for women. Another neighbor explains that in the village people would get into fights and hurt one another, and that in the city they tend to talk things through more. Another interjects that she has a niece who has recently married a young Madurai software engineer. They are now living in London.

In the course of only twenty years these families came from marginal backgrounds and used the city to revolutionize their lives. They have created entirely new livelihoods and started small businesses. They were able to buy expensive urban land and have built homes far larger and more elaborate than they had ever dreamed of owning. Their children are training for professional careers and beginning to move to larger, more affluent cities abroad. Their achievements are a testimony to their ambition and fortitude as well as to the raw possibility that the City has provided them.

But Iswari interrupts Muneeshwari. She takes exception to her wholesale preference for the city. "When youngsters like her come to the city, they forget village life," she says, suggesting that she has witnessed an evolving urban preference in the younger generation. "We [older women] still cherish village life. It was peaceful in the village. In the village we [women] were independent. We had work to do, and we could earn. But we don't know how to use our time here." I ask her whether she has ever thought to start some kind of small enterprise to fill her time, at which point the other women glance at each other. Our CCD colleague then shares that the more elaborately housed Iswari has already built a business as a moneylender. Many of the women gathered with us are her indebted clients.

Of the forty-two people we are to interview, only nine echo Iswari's fondness for the village. And even these nine people plan to stay in the city because of the benefits that it offers their children. None of the women in Iswari's group has had relatives move back to the village. Over the course of a week of discussions with migrant families, from early morning till sundown, only a few people say that they will try to move back to the village once their children are grown, educated, and settled into an urban occupation.

Many more extol the opportunities of the city, even if their lives have been extremely difficult. We visited one group in a soggy, fly-infested slum along the riverbank. This settlement of some five hundred fami-lies came from ten villages not far from Madurai. They live the most marginal life that a city has to offer.

The approach to the slum from a hectic main road in the heart of Madurai passes through a run-down residential neighborhood. This neighborhood's paved road dissolves into a dirt track, which narrows into a puddled footpath lined by dozens of thatched-roof huts and shacks made of scrap materials. These villagers-in-the-city have lived here without even basic water pumps and sanitation for decades, work-ing as construction laborers and housekeepers. Goats and chickens roam alongside the path, supplementing the residents' meager diets and earnings. We stop at a small grocery shop to ask directions, and a crowd of young men and elderly women gather to learn who we are. The di-rector of CCD explains our purpose and then the people vie to talk with us.

Some of the adults say they have had neighbors who returned to the village. "In a good year"—a year with good rains, says one man—"we can make as much money doing work in the fields as in the city, and it is cheaper to live there." But the sons of these elders take a different stand.

Karthick, a gentle-mannered fifteen-year-old, reports, "My father wants to keep me in school to become an engineer." Twenty-eight-year-old Tanalakshmi will let his three daughters stay in school "as long as they want" so that they can "take a step up" in the city, in contrast to the village tradition of marrying off one's daughters with just a basic edu-cation. Another, nineteen-year-old Arumugam, reports in his polished, assertive manner, "I want to become a [construction] contractor." Five years ago he started working as an unskilled construction laborer. He reports that he is now a skilled mason. Then he elaborates his plan to be-come a contractor. "For this I'll need fifty thousand rupees [$1,200]. I want to save this by the time I am twenty-six. For this I want to get sea-sonal work in other cities like Madras and Coimbatore to make more money." He represents the patient, long-term ambition of the migrant.

At the edge of the slum we introduce ourselves to Krishnaswamy, the proprietor of the kind of grocery kiosk that can be found by the thou-sands in any Indian city. Krishnaswamy started his urban life as a lone child living on a Madurai street at eleven years of age. His move to the city was triggered by a different event from that experienced by most families we will meet. He left his village to escape family problems, not drought. Krishnaswamy was too young to have a strategy or contacts in the city, and his family did not help him. Yet he took the same first steps toward urban life as all the others.

Living on the street, he met another, more established migrant, a young man whose family lived not far from Krishnaswamy's village. This man took Krishnaswamy into his home and helped him get a job as a table cleaner at a hotel. After someone moves to the city, we find, the second step on the urban migrant's path is gaining a slim opening into the city's markets through a relationship with an earlier migrant. Krishnaswamy then worked his way up to the position of tea maker and then bread maker at the hotel. From these early years, Krishnaswamy was taking the third step on the typical migrant's path: developing a skill in an urban trade. By the age of thirty-two he had saved enough money to fulfill his real ambition: to start a little grocery and snack shop. He thereby took the fourth step on the urban migrant's path: saving a small pool of capital with which to attempt a further claim on the city's opportunities. Finally, with savings in hand, he took the fifth step: with a loan from a moneylender, he started his own small business, a little eight-by-ten-foot shop attached to the front of his equally small one-room family home at the slum's fringe. Here he sells the bulk grains, tea, sugar, snacks, and milk that net him an income of $5 per week.

Krishnaswamy failed in two earlier attempts to achieve his goal of becoming a shop owner. During his first try, he took a $100 loan from a moneylender, paying a weekly interest rate of 1.5 percent, or 80 percent per year. He says he lost $4,500 in that attempt before he closed his shop and went back to work at a tea shop to start saving again. The second time he avoided the moneylender and instead borrowed money from forty-eight different local people. But the shop did not succeed this time either. "It got very rough," he says, "and I had to run away and stay in another area until I had fully repaid all the money." He did this with the help of his elder son, who developed an occupation as a skilled marble mason. But through all of this, Krishnaswamy never considered going back to his village.

In contrast to the accepted notion that people migrate to cities to find work in a factory, we found, and many other studies confirm, that first-generation urban migrants are a self-selected entrepreneurial breed, building their own livelihoods along the paths of chain migrations. Along their pathways, a single city's migrants experiment with hundreds of strategies to secure their own stake in an expanding market. The "job market" that the migrant enters does not have advertised openings and defined positions, or regulated hours, wages, tax deductions, and training programs like the official or formal labor markets of most countries. Instead, the migrant enters an informal, experimental economy of petty trade, micro-enterprise, and labor contracting that is governed only by the unique rules of the unofficial city and the raw opportunity to leverage and shape urban advantage. The lands upon which hundreds of millions live are not legally deeded to them. Businesses are not registered. Employment laws are not followed. Whole new professions arise to serve the workings of this ballooning informal economy. Large slums have lawyers who specialize in real estate transactions over properties that have never been deeded in the legal system. Indian cities have self-proclaimed "consultants" who advertise services for illegal connections to the electrical grid. Entirely different rules of governance prevail, involving unwritten codes of loyalty between family clans and ethnic groups. Even as the informal economy does the work of constructing the city and servicing its growing formal economy, migrant families and communities are working to build their own urban advantage. They would join the formal city if its rules were designed to include them and offer them benefit. This not being the case, they will build a million parallel cities to create their own forms of advantage across the divided City.

Of the forty-two migrants we interviewed, only five had ever secured a job in a registered company or a regulated occupation. Two had worked in a textile mill, another in a rice mill; one was a unionized folksinger and another was in the actors' guild. Most were introduced into their livelihoods by relatives or friends who had pioneered their occupations before them: in petty hawking and trading; in construction, housework, or small-scale production; in grocery or clothing retail shops; in auto rickshaw driving or jobs with small trucking companies operating in a gray zone between the formal and informal economy.

This discovery is consistent with findings around the world. A 2003 study of urban migration in the cities of Colombia found that

52 percent of new urban migrants worked in informal, underground economic activities, with the rest either gaining formal jobs or remaining unemployed.[14] A survey of migrants conducted in 2000 in Guangzhou, China, revealed that they primarily secured employment in the market-based "new economy" sector and in self-employment. The more that migrants gained experience through work in the city, the more they shifted to self-employed commercial activities. In fact, this study indicated that a substantial group of migrants to Guangzhou had higher education levels, greater commercial success, and higher income levels than established, nonmigrant residents.[15] Similarly, a 2004 study in South Africa found that urban migrants are more likely to end up in informal sector work, but they are also more likely to be successful in avoiding unemployment than settled, nonmigrant neighbors of the same economic status. In Morocco another study showed that unemployment of urban migrants was less than half the average urban rate. "There is something about the motivation or quality of the migrant," conclude the authors of the South Africa study, "which affords them greater success in avoiding unemployment."[16]

"If you move to town you can start a business," says thirty-seven-year-old Anand, as if to confirm the conclusion that can be drawn from these studies: that the typical migrant is a special, entrepreneurial breed. Anand left his village in 1983. Through the connections of a relative who had migrated before him he obtained his first job in a small informal workshop where he polished eating utensils. Then he learned how to lathe the utensils. "But I was not making enough, so I switched to driving," he explains. A CCD colleague told me that Anand was one of the first auto rickshaw drivers (a position at the bottom of the city's transportation services sector) who got a mobile phone. The phone made it possible for CCD to rely on him to serve colleagues on demand as they attended meetings around the city. Through Anand's entrepreneurial investment in the mobile phone, he soon had a clientele. "I got a loan and bought an auto rickshaw," he reports proudly. "I was just a worker; now I give work to someone."

"Madurai is a big town where you can do anything to make a living," says twenty-three-year-old Kumar, who like Krishnaswamy has started his own little six-by-eight-foot grocery shop. His father earned his migrant's living as a peddler of firewood. "It was my father's idea to start a shop," he admits. The organization and orderliness of Kumar's shop belies the unfinished, ungathered nature of his surroundings at a street corner. Sweets are decoratively stacked inside large, wide-mouthed jars. Branded groceries are perfectly arranged on crude shelves, and medicines, razors, toothbrushes, and single servings of detergents are hung like festival ribbons. In spite of his diligence, Kumar's shop sometimes earns only enough to pay his monthly interest on a $1,200 loan from a moneylender. "If I want to come up in life I have to suffer, but I am fully committed to this business," he says before providing a detailed report on the shop's operation. Having interviewed some twenty-five migrants prior to this conversation, I got the impression that their openness with a wealthy foreigner is part of a strategy. Kumar has bigger plans, and there is a chance that I could advise or even help him. "Once it [the shop] is successful I want to get into a bigger supermarket business," he says, expressing the entrepreneurial sensibility for continuous advancement that is common in this dusty, still half-made place.

More established urbanites around the world forget the enterprising mission of the migrant. They misjudge his tenacity and innovative temperament. They forget that the migrant has no intention of returning to an unequal position in life. This perspective is validated by research that colleagues and I have done for corporate clients who wanted to better understand what we call the consumer pathway: how low-income, marginal consumers who live in villages steadily connect to the world's markets through seasonal migration or daily work commutes into the city, followed by full migration.

Again and again these studies indicated that the rural poor are making very different choices based on underlying temperaments. Our first task was to characterize these different psychological profiles of rural households and to understand their impacts on household consumption. One cluster of villagers was accepting, if not seemingly content, with their pastoral, traditional lives in the countryside. Another group was restive. Families in this group struggle to upgrade their conditions, at least for their children. Yet another group was fully committed to changing their lives and that of their ethnic group. They were risk-taking agents of change.

When we mapped these different groups, a clear pattern emerged. The accepting families were most concentrated in the villages, involved in agriculture and other village-based economic activities. The wishful strugglers were reaching out to opportunities in the small regional cities, either through periodic recreational shopping trips or seasonal work in the city. You could see a bit of the city in their homes—in their decorations, small appliances, and the types of fuels they used. This group could also be found in the slums on the peripheries of these cities. Finally, the bulk of the enterprising, change-oriented group had already made some kind of committed shift toward the cities. They had city-based jobs, were sending their children to schools in the towns, and had family members who had migrated to cities before them. The change agents were the dominant profile of the urban migrants.

Urban migrants, in other words, are a self-selected breed. Many planners and political leaders fail to note the migrant's tenacity and methodical ways, and many critics of globalization conceive the migrant as a victim, constrained by the strategies of corporate capital and established institutions. But the city is by economic nature a center of empowerment, where new strategies are hatched between established pushes and pulls. Migrants, through their strategies to gain some urban advantage, are often revolutionary agents of change. The question is not whether they find a niche within the growing city but where and what that niche will be. When access to the formal city is blocked, migrants build parallel cities with new kinds of residential and commercial development, new systems of finance, trade, policing, and policy, to suit their means and ambitions.

Thirty-seven-year-old Mayandi illustrates how chains of migration give specific ethnic or caste groups control of whole sectors of the urban economy. He comes from Virudunagar district, twenty miles from Madurai, from a low-level caste community of landless agricultural laborers. He came to the city in 1997. His wife, Pechi, is bashful but eventually discusses her life. She says she prefers the village, "but the main convenience is children's education . . . It is better in the city." They both proudly introduce me to their young son, who has already decided to become a computer engineer.

"I moved to the city when I was ten, to be educated," Mayandi explains. "I didn't want to be a farmer. I wanted a job in the town. My generation was the first in my village to get educated." He laces his personal story with the story of the rise of his caste, called the Thevars.

"My community migrated to Madurai and Madras in the 1970s," he explains. "We came looking for wage jobs in factories. We were treated like *kandupatti* [a local word for whores]. But during the last fifty years we became moneylenders and then we learned the transport business. A relative on my maternal side had a job in a transport company. In this way I got a job managing the office of a transport company. Then we invested to create our own businesses. Now my [caste] community controls the transport business in southern Tamil Nadu. We learned a lot about how to start private business and we realized these big cities should be our stronghold."

Mayandi also volunteers that the city has had a "civilizing" influence on the people of his community. "When my community was civilizing," he says, "we wanted to leave the village and come to the town."

I ask him to define what he means by "civilizing."

"I can't define 'civilizing' but I can give an example. We never allowed our children to study but now we encourage them to do so." Indeed, he has sent his children to English school and says, "I wouldn't mind if my children choose any field, but I want them to shine in that field and come up in life." Today the Thevar community, just a step up the ladder from the better-known and long-oppressed Dalits, has dramatically increased its clout across Tamil Nadu, leveraging the economic power gained through urban migration into a dominant influence in a major statewide political party. They are like so many migrant communities around the world who have leveraged the power of urban association: like the Gounder caste in Tiruppur, or the Punjabis who have gained control of the taxi industry in New York City and the trucking industry in Toronto and southern Ontario—or like the Irish of Boston or the Cubans of Miami, who became their cities' power elites.

Today's anti-immigration debates lack essential perspective about the nature of migration, the character of the migrant, and the imperatives that drive the world to the City. Those who fight against the Great Migration are fighting against the momentum of history and the most fundamental kinds of economics. To the extent that they deny the migrant rights to the City—to its jobs, property markets, basic urban services, education, and security—they are encouraging the organization of millions into parallel, informal cities and underground economies. As happened with the Salvadorians of Pico-Union, the legal and economic marginalization of the migrant only increases the major social and economic conflicts that burden the world today. It does not and cannot stop the Great Migration, for one simple reason: access to the raw potential of urban advantage cannot be entirely controlled. The risk-taking, entrepreneurial migrant will always seek to capture a piece of it and use it creatively in countless unanticipated ways.

Efforts to keep our cities exclusive to an established citizenry or elite may be popular or profitable, but they are doomed to fail. Recent history offers too many examples of rebellions and insurgencies, and even the wholesale collapse of political and economic systems, arising from blind denial of the powerful rise of Homo urbanis.

CHAPTER 4

Anatomy of Urban Revolution
The Inevitable Democracy of the City

When rioting broke out between the Kikuyu and Luo people of Kenya in Nairobi, Mombasa, Kisumu, Nakuru, and other smaller cities in January 2008, it was reported as another case of African political intransigence, rigged electioneering, and ancient tribal rivalries. But beneath the surface of this familiar story line another reality stood plainly: the riots were another violent lurching in an epoch of urban rebellion. For all practical purposes, Kenya's political crisis in 2008, though manifested through a unique local history and social structure, was not unlike urban uprisings from Detroit to Manila, Beirut to Caracas, Johannesburg to Gdańsk during this last phase of the Great Migration.

Established elites can succeed for some decades to deny growing migrant populations access to economic and political rights. But short of mass relocation and murder, as in Pol Pot's dystopian anti-urban regime, there is an inevitable democracy in the Urban Revolution that continues to revolutionize world politics. Centralized, inegalitarian governments, initially empowered by their control of rural territories and populations, have steadily lost their exclusive grip over economic resources and international relations as their countries urbanize. Once settled in cities, even the most marginalized populations, under the most totalitarian regimes, can leverage urban density, scale, association, and extension to build their own economies, wealth, power, and political alliances. Their rebellions on every continent have continuously taken modern regimes and the mass media by surprise because they have not understood the nature of urban advantage. Urban advantage is a classic form of public good. The potential offered by a city's density, scale, association, and extension infrastructure is accessible to all who determine to use and shape it, regardless of the impediments put in their way.

Until 1963, colonial-era Pass Laws prevented Kenyans in the largely rural country from establishing permanent residency in Kenya's cities. As in South Africa, Zimbabwe, and other African colonies, migrants were encouraged to come to cities for temporary jobs, but they could not fully settle there. They lived in workers' barracks and colonies, and they maintained their social ties and homes in their rural tribal areas. With the end of colonial rule, things did not fully change. Kenya's urban migrants were allowed to reside in the city, but every imaginable economic impediment and social indignity were still set against them. Migrants have since become the majority in cities like Nairobi and Kisumu, and they have established much deeper urban roots than in colonial times, but most migrants still maintain a dual life between their rural tribal area and their struggle for advantage in the city.

Kenya's urban population has grown elevenfold since the end of Pass Laws. Lacking options for housing, formal employment, and basic urban services, they have taken city building into their own hands, honing strategies for informal labor and commerce, tenure, and governance, out of reach of official planning, policy, or law. Two thirds of Nairobi's slum dwellers eke out a living in the underground informal sector. The result is a parallel city within each of Kenya's cities. The dynamics of these informal cities may now govern Kenya's development more than Kenya's official government actions.

Seventy percent of Kenya's slum dwellers are less than twenty-four years old.[1] Poverty in the youthful slum-cities has increased as the wealth of its governing elite in the formal cities has grown. The poverty rate in Nairobi doubled between 1992 and 1997. These conditions breed an inevitable new politics. In rural areas, the lack of density, scale, and extension leave poor communities with little opportunity to build an economic and political base that can stand up to the concentrated power of a national elite. But even with the smallest toehold in the city, whether in a colonial labor barracks or in a postcolonial slum, the migrants can access the city's more robust economic potential. They refine strategies for securing a margin of the wealth that flows through each city's ports, factories, and wealthy households, incrementally building their own wealth, their support networks, and shared resentments. But lacking opportunities to invest their savings in the city, they feed them back to their rural home and community.

This basic urban-rural dynamic explains the tribal nature of Kenya's recent uprisings. As in most countries, ethnic solidarity is a powerful social force, predating the country's urbanization. In a successful period of urban migration, the cities would be places of ethnic integration. But the largest ethnic conflict in postcolonial Kenya has emerged in its cities. This is not by chance; it is effectively by design. Migrants from many different tribes live side by side in Nairobi's slums, but it is a shallow integration because they are not truly enfranchised there, economically or politically.

The dominant strategy of chain migration in Kenya is called split migration. The larger the nuclear family in rural Kenya, the more likely the family splits between a few wage earners in the city and a main family unit in its rural homeland.[2] Lacking a route to property ownership and stable work in the city, the migrants minimize investments there. Ninety percent of Nairobi's slum residents are tenants.[3] The migrant's purpose is to accumulate savings in the city for family consumption and investment in the village. One survey found that Nairobi slum dwellers send up to 20 percent of their earnings back to their extended rural families,[4] where the funds are invested in land and upgrades to their rural homes. The migrants' identities, bonds, and economic strategies therefore remain tribal.

Tribal tensions in the slums were fueled by the land speculation practices of the increasingly Kikuyu ruling elite, whose members are often slum landlords. When pressed against the wall by an intransigent urban elite dominated by one tribe, tribal identity and kinship networks become the most available channel of rebellion to gain further urban advantage.

At current rates, Nairobi alone will have three hundred thousand new slum residents by 2015 and one to two million more by 2030. This pattern is repeated in every Kenyan city. Without a revolution in urban investment and management from above, providing routes to secure tenure, home ownership, and small enterprise in the city, there will be more angry rebellion, if not a full-fledged revolution, from below.

At the height of the Urban Revolution in the United States, when cities became home to half the population in the early twentieth century, the country had its own unique Great Migration. Joining the millions who migrated from Europe to American cities, millions of rural African Americans left the economic dislocation and cruelty of the U.S. South to secure opportunities in the industrialized cities of the country's North and West.[5]

Just like migrants around the world, African American claims to U.S. cities started with seasonal labor migration to proximate regional cities in the South. Sharpening their migration strategies in these southern towns and encouraged by labor recruiters, African Americans then pursued bigger opportunities in the factories of the wartime North.[6] The migration is generally chronicled in two stages: the first between 1910 and 1940 and the second between 1940 and 1970, each time triggered by wartime factory employment. By the waning of migration in the 1960s, African Americans had forged dense economic and social networks between the country's northern, western, and southern cities and their earlier rural communities, thereby heightening their group identity, resources, and communication channels as a new *national* cultural and political community.

The history of Detroit, America's primary mid-century manufacturing city, illustrates the revolutionary political impact of efforts to disenfranchise this community in the city. From 1910 to 1930, Detroit's black population grew nearly 2,000 percent. As earnings from factory jobs and word of urban settlement strategies flowed back to African American families in the South, chain migration continued to Detroit until the 1950s. By this time, the number of African American migrants to Detroit exceeded the sum of European immigrants from more than twenty countries combined.

Even as manufacturers welcomed black migrants at the lowest wages into their booming metalworking and automobile manufacturing workforces, they were greeted by Detroit's extant populations with often violent exclusion. Both the established and new European migrant communities had developed proven strategies, through their earlier migrations, for securing their own advantage in the city. These strategies involved their own hardships, risks, and violence as they wrested economic opportunities and political control from earlier, entrenched groups. The white migrant strategy for urban dominance in Detroit and other northern industrial cities had five aspects: First, these migrants organized labor unions to gain control of the city's labor markets. Second, they sought dominance in small-scale commerce through control of neighborhood real estate and specific trades. Third, they leveraged these gains into local political control in the form of city hall machines that, in addition to policy, managed the distribution of patronage opportunities and rents (e.g., taxes, bribes) between different white European immigrant groups. Fourth, to bring the force of law to their side in support of these economic strategies, they secured control of the city's police forces, including the use of targeted recruitment drives. And last, with this leverage, white groups could also gain control of the city's underground trades, in particular the lucrative bootleg liquor markets of the Prohibition era. The African American newcomers from former slave and sharecropper backgrounds, often recruited into nonunion jobs, did not fit into this strategic equation.

The white response to black migration therefore combined deep-seated racism with a defense of white urban advantage. The mix was caustic. In the early decades of black migration, white neighborhoods throughout Detroit organized into so-called neighborhood improvement associations whose primary strategy for "improvement" was keeping black families out. When black families with established trades and professional occupations managed to purchase homes in predominantly white areas, they were greeted with mob violence.

Industrial unions excluded black members. Companies sent recruiters south to sign up new black workers particularly during union labor actions. In these times the local response to blacks was particularly violent.

In 1917, the Detroit police actively recruited white southern officers with racial prejudices. By the mid-1920s, Detroit hosted the largest membership of the Ku Klux Klan (KKK) in the northern United States. With an estimated thirty-five thousand members, the Detroit KKK had two members for each black household in the city.[7]

Living on meager incomes, most black migrants initially resided along-side recent European newcomers in the St. Antoine Street District, abutting downtown's east side. As Europeans freely made claims to the city's employment, real estate, and business opportunities in other districts, this first-stop migrant neighborhood became predominantly black. By the mid-1920s it was renamed the East Side Colored District. The district expanded southward with increasing black migration into a new dense, Dickensian slum derisively called Black Bottom. Here residents scraped the bottom in Detroit's world of opportunity.

As Europeans abandoned East Side homes, landlords divided buildings into small apartments, and the economics of tenement housing took hold. Landlords extracted rents three times the market rate in white neighborhoods. One report showed that rents in Black Bottom increased 500 percent between 1915 and 1920.[8] The market was so lucrative that owners did not bother to maintain buildings to secure new renters. Instead, they further subdivided, added new stories to buildings, converted stables, and built shacks to pack more migrants into their lots. To pay the escalating rents, more than half of East Side residents themselves took in lodgers, further exacerbating crowding.

As poor migrants pressed into this area, middle-class home-owning black families relocated to the downtown's west side. Even as these residents organized to improve their neighborhoods—in part to combat the white claim that black neighbors would drive down property values, thus rationalizing their exclusion—these skilled, professional blacks were denied fair access to most of the resources available to European migrants. They received second-class public services and political representation from the white political machines, even as they built their professions; purchased homes; established firms, stores, and newspapers; and paid their taxes. Blacks of all classes and residential districts were restricted in their movements by invisible networks organized through white neighborhood associations, business groups, unions, political organizations, and the police. These networks could organize mobs at any time, frequently backed by police, as in Detroit's large-scale anti-black riots in 1925, 1942, and 1943, and in many smaller mob attacks during this period. Scores of blacks were killed. A "hatred strike" was held at an automobile plant over hiring and shop-floor desegregation of blacks. Rioting erupted over black use of a major city park in 1943, forcing the state governor to declare martial law.

The white associations' strategies also took more subtle racist forms. Whites developed legal and business arrangements to exclude blacks from home ownership. White owners placed legal covenants on properties to restrict them from being sold to African Americans. Real estate agencies established codes preventing agents from doing business with African Americans or from showing them properties in attractive neighborhoods. Banks and insurance companies charged higher rates to black mortgage applicants. Zoning laws were passed to prevent the development of new housing for African Americans near "white areas." Black leaders fought these legal barriers all the way to the U.S. Supreme Court, but segregationists created new impediments replacing any that were struck down.

As a result, beyond unstable, low-wage factory employment, the average black migrant's access to the city's opportunities was contained to those in just a few city wards. In 1940, nearly half of Detroit's black population was concentrated in just three of the city's twenty-two political wards, where two thirds of the population was African American. By comparison, foreign-born whites represented no more than a quarter of the population in any city ward.[9]

Migrant ethnic groups around the world have used concentrated settlement to establish the density, scale, and association economies required for success in that district, from which they can extend to secure citywide opportunities. It is from these ethnic districts that migrant communities establish dominant positions in specific kinds of commerce and skilled trades like baking, jewelry, carpentry, masonry, cleaning, or leatherwork. The ability to build equity in a home, then to leverage this into a neighborhood business or educational investment through refinancing, and then to access a citywide market, allowed these migrants to draw new resources into their communities from the wider city. But the majority of black migrants gained limited leverage from their ghettoization. With limited access to property ownership and bank finance, and no access to white neighborhoods and their markets, they became a class of renters and struggling homeowners in rapidly deteriorating neighborhoods.

It might seem a stretch to compare America's historical black urban migrants with the shack-dwelling migrants in many developing country cities today. After all, the African American migrants often gained access to whole, developed city districts. They did not have to start their urban life in swamps and hillside shantytowns. But this seeming advantage created its own burdens.

In the typical slum in Asia, Africa, or Latin America—though every individual slum has its own untypical history and dynamics—the migrant generally arrives dirt poor. But like the Machala *invasores*, she is often able to steadily build wealth because costs are minimal when she is beginning her urban life. From the start she begins to create an asset. Her first strategy for urban advantage is land invasion—the de facto taking of vacant, generally low-quality land on steep hillsides, in floodplains, or in marshes. Through squatting she often gains informal ownership of the land. Even in the face of natural disasters and violent slum clearances, she can organize with her squatters' community, rebuild the shantytown in a less challenged location, and begin to make incremental investments to transform a shack and wasteland into a more secure property. In future years she adds a workshop or another floor as a rental unit. Then the organized slum community builds roads, constructs collective water and sanitation facilities, and organizes makeshift services like garbage collection or volunteer fire squads. In this way, the slum-dwelling urban migrant can manage the costs of upgrading her "property" against her meager cash flow. She converts a marginal piece of land into an asset, which can eventually secure an appreciated price on the market, whether through a legal transaction or through the parallel market of the underground economy.

But black American migrants confronted a very different set of economics. Their economic transition was more sudden and stark. Roads, sewers, multistory buildings, and electrical and plumbing systems were all factored into prices, and these systems all had to be maintained. The new migrants' collective incomes could not support these costs, and their ability to build and retain wealth within their area required the cooperation of a municipality. This cooperation was nonexistent. Resources flowed to neighborhood improvements elsewhere, including to the subsidized new suburban communities to which white and European householders and businesses fled as their market opportunities expanded and the downtown black ghetto grew. Private finance was limited and generally available only at usurious rates.

Confronted with high costs and institutionalized neglect, the black districts deteriorated over a matter of decades. Their city was never upgraded or renewed, and its asset value declined, creating a structural impoverishment that still dogs American society. A nationwide study of African American families in 2007 revealed that nearly half of the children of solidly middle-class black families in the 1960s—the success stories of America's Great Migration in neighborhoods like the west side of Detroit—had dropped into poverty or near-poverty forty years later.[10]

Battle by battle, the aspirations that black migrants brought to the city were impeded and steered into their own ghetto-cities. By the 1950s these cities had matured into worlds of their own, creating a parallel urban universe and quietly seeding one of the first urban revolutions of the twentieth century. These city-worlds were not without their own economic dynamism. They had their own black-owned businesses and social clubs and lucrative underground markets of bootleg liquor, drugs, gambling, and prostitution. They also developed areas of economic expertise and competitive advantage, particularly in entertainment and music. In spite of its growing squalor, Black Bottom in Detroit became nationally famous for its blues, big bands, and jazz music, hosting performers like Duke Ellington, Ella Fitzgerald, Count Basie, and many others.

African Americans found density and scale in their ghettos, but they could not use these advantages to leverage larger opportunities—at least in the legal economy—because of the constraints imposed on their association within and extension to metropolitan-wide markets. As a result, their ambitions could only be advanced through alternative forms of political and countercultural association, extended ghetto to ghetto, city to city, and back along the chains of migration to rural areas throughout the United States.

We have viewed the major political revolutions of the late twentieth century as separate national events, but most share the distinct character of urban rebellions, created by failed national responses to the Great Migration. New migrants, as we saw in the last chapter, are not randomly selected warm bodies, making generic additions to the city's census. They are self-selected, risk-taking people with specific ambitions and entrepreneurial aptitudes. Along their paths of migration they establish dense networks of solidarity, creating latent forms of new social organization. After decades of legal and civic appeals for equity and mutual coexistence, urban black Americans ultimately developed two broad new strategies to gain advantage in their adopted cities.

The first strategy started with the local institutions they developed in their new cities—churches, and civil rights and professional associations—and their association and extension into nationwide organizations, coalitions, and campaigns, creating the civil rights movement of the 1950s and early 1960s. "Black urbanization," writes historian Jack M. Bloom, "freed blacks from . . . tight social control prevalent in rural areas and provided the base for the development of a much more independent leadership."[11] The movement transformed the migrants' informal association networks into a disciplined political machinery that could coordinate simultaneous sit-ins and boycotts across scores of cities. Its focus was on voting rights, antidiscrimination laws, and desegregation of schools, public services, and business establishments. As they won passage of landmark national civil rights laws and Supreme Court rulings, blacks also cultivated a new generation of urban political leadership. Often the first political target was the election of blacks to city governments. Fights for local political representation produced political organizations that eventually elected black mayors to many American cities in the 1970s and 1980s, giving African Americans a nationwide political voice. Some of Detroit's first black city councillors, for instance, became some of America's most senior and influential congressmen.

But new laws and political representation did not change ground realities in poor black neighborhoods. Entrenched white political machines and association networks could easily confound implementation of laws and court rulings. Even in the late 1980s, as I traveled to small cities throughout the American South to interview local black activists, they were still struggling for effective voting rights and representation. (In most rural areas, they had no political representation and still faced the KKK and other violent hate groups.) Political bosses, business interests, and urban planners fought black progress with clearances of black slum districts and forced relocations, financed through federal programs for public housing and highway construction. These clearances destroyed the equity, local markets, and social ecology of the black community. The displaced families used their new rights to move into other ethnic neighborhoods; some were relocated to new public housing, which quickly transformed into high-rise slums. White police forces remained a constant source of harassment.

By the mid-1960s, the civil rights movement had achieved its boldest objectives, yet life in the cities was worsening. As the movement's middle-class leadership floundered, a new wave of leaders emerged in the cities. They spoke of a second strategy for "Black Power" via threats of insurgency. The focus was not on legislation and legal rights but on street-level issues: combating the police and the political machines, and gaining control in the new black neighborhoods. The young militant leaders both threatened and tried to mediate against open conflict, but as a *Life* magazine cover story expressed it at the time, the local street conflicts soon broke out into a "predictable insurrection."[12] In 1967 alone 164 riots broke loose in 128 cities, creating smoldering conflict zones that had to be secured by the National Guard.

The Detroit riot illustrates the typical evolution of conditions for such surprising rebellion. Detroit's black population enjoyed higher incomes than blacks in other U.S. cities. The Irish political machine had elected a pro–civil rights mayor. He had appointed a black police commissioner. There were black city councillors and judges. But in 1962, the city bulldozed the dilapidated but nonetheless vibrant Black Bottom as part of its so-called urban renewal scheme, wiping out four decades of black investment. One of the neighborhoods to which the displaced resettled was the Twelfth Street area on the northwest side of downtown. The district's middle-class Jewish homeowners were already moving to the suburbs. As middle-class black families moved into their homes, the old residents kept their stores and shops in the area.

Black relocation quickly created a population density in the Twelfth Street area that was twice the city average. Black Bottom survival strategies also appeared: drugs, illegal liquor, prostitution, and the subdivision of homes. When police raided an underground bar on one midsummer night they were unprepared for the response. "The Negroes in Detroit feel they are part of an occupied territory," wrote the *Detroit Free Press* in January 1965. "The Negroes have no rights which the police have to respect." Through their dense living and enforced association, the black community gained one particular advantage: network efficiency. The riot itself did not have to be organized by some new Black Power group; although the Federal Bureau of Investigation (FBI) and government commissions looked for a source of subversive leadership, there was none. White businesses and homes were particularly attacked. More than two thousand buildings were burned down. Forty-three people were killed, 467 injured, and 7,200 arrested.

Across the United States, the riots occurred in areas where black residency had historically been excluded. But within a few years of the riots, writes urban sociologist Max Herman, "small businesses changed ownership from white to black. Black residents moved into homes abandoned by whites. Blacks entered the rolls of police and firefighters in substantial numbers."[13] Violent insurgency provided a vehicle for what Herman calls ethnic territorial "succession."

The otherwise stable and developed nature of the United States clouds our appreciation of the scale of its urban revolution and the extent to which it caught the political establishment and even civil rights leaders off guard. Insurgency began in Philadelphia, New York, and Rochester in 1964; it moved to Los Angeles in 1965; then to San Francisco, Cleveland, and Omaha in 1966; to Detroit, Newark, and Baltimore in 1967; and finally on to New York, Washington, and Chicago in 1968.

American politics was never the same. The riots and subsequent flight of white residents and businesses to new suburbs created new crises that remain unresolved. For African Americans, however, a major chapter in their Great Migration was closed. In only a few years, black leaders, many from the civil rights movement, won political control in dozens of cities where their Urban Revolution had begun.

America's exclusive white "machines" were felled in relatively young cities. On the other side of the globe, the shah of Iran had nearly five hundred years of history on his side when he was toppled in 1978–1979 by an urban revolution that surprised both him and the world. The shah had control of Iran's finance system, oil production, and factories. He had power over all political institutions and policy. With the United States government as his closest ally, he had command of the military and a brutal secret police force (the SAVAK) to suppress any resistance.

But his ambitious program for transforming Iran into a modern nation had a major, critical flaw. His programs drove the country's resources and people into its cities, and his government naively believed that it could control the life and development of cities just as it could dominate life in villages, factories, oil fields, government bureaucracies, and universities. The shah and his men, like the Americans who coached them, did not understand the most basic principle of urban life: the public nature of urban advantage.

The more the shah's policies accelerated urbanization of his country, the more Iran's competing interests were forced to use urban advantage for their own, revolutionary purposes. Their most potent advantage was urban association. After marginalizing the ambitions of traditional merchants in Iran's urban bazaars; after repressing the cities' radical students, trade unionists, and conservative clergy; after controlling the opportunities of Iran's new urban classes, the middle-class professionals, and landless urban migrants, the shah was deposed by an improbable alliance of all these city groups. The alliance lasted little more than a year, long enough to drive the shah into exile before it splintered back into factions, along the way creating new forms of association and seeding conflicts and crises in Iran's postrevolutionary cities.

In other words, the popular revolution in Iran, which has cascaded into other urban revolutions throughout the Middle East, took more than a cabal of radical *mullahs*. Middle Eastern insurrection and political shifts remain less about Islam than journalists and pundits insist. They also arise from the region's failed urban migrations and from fights for control of each city's advantage.

The revolutionary alliance in Iran established its first roots in the bazaar. The bazaar is more than a market location in the city's center. It is the physical, commercial, and social product of a strategy for urban advantage that has evolved from age-old bonds between merchants, small-scale producers, shopkeepers and moneylenders, clerics, and rural landowners. It is in the bazaars that urban economies of density, scale, and association have been most refined into an efficient process; organized into distinct markets with different codes, standards, and norms; and crowded into a physical space where commerce has joint ventures with religion, where extended family relationships insinuate into business, and where urban living connects to rural roots. The bazaar, as both a culture of commerce and as a designed urban space, is a system of urban advantage, a city-system for accumulating and distributing the city's power and wealth. In the decades preceding the revolution, the shah's reform program was naively attacking the seemingly antiquated bazaar system that traditionally accounted for much of the country's trade and trading culture.

The smallest unit of the bazaar is the trader himself, known as the *bazaari*. The bazaari draws power from command over money flows at this foundation of urban society as well as from his relations with religious clerics at the local level. In Iran, notes Robert D. Kaplan in his 1996 article "A Bazaari's World," bazaars and mosques are traditionally located together.[14] Bazaari traders and clerics often come from the same families, and the profits of the traders often finance the clerics' religious activities. In his detailed study of Middle Eastern cities, *Urban Unrest in the Middle East*, Guilain Denoeux writes that "the self-contained world of the Iranian bazaar" has been a vital center of social activity for the lower classes.[15] "Through the 1970s the bazaar remained the location of a host of urban voluntary associations, religious groups and brotherhoods, gymnasiums, and traditional coffeehouses, teahouses, and restaurants. It is also in the bazaar that rumors and information are circulated and that many of the contacts that cut across kinship and residential solidarities have been established."[16] As the last shah accelerated his strategy to build a modern, centrally managed society, often in alliance with non-bazaari Christian, Baha'i, and Jewish merchants as well as with Western industrialists, he also imposed a series of reforms that taxed bazaari trade and rippled through the financial relationships connecting the bazaaris, clerics, and landowners.

But protest and resistance from bazaaris and clerics, even with the rising influence of the Ayatollah Khomeini among the grassroots clergy, was not enough to defeat the shah's regime. Since 1890, bazaars had been centers of political protest. Bazaaris had helped organize and finance numerous demonstrations, strikes, and political movements of teachers, seminarians, and workers, and they had distributed protest information in times of repression, but never to fully revolutionary effect.[17] The historical alliance of bazaaris and clerics was never enough to substantially advance their political power, particularly in the face of the SAVAK. It took new ties of association to create a viable revolutionary coalition, each made possible by the shah's partial understanding of emerging urban realities.

The shah's modernization drive rapidly built three new urban classes: industrial workers, a technical-managerial middle class, and an amassing second generation of poor urban migrants. Many of the industrial workers were unskilled migrants from the countryside seeking the rights and respect that they had long been denied in their peasant lives. When their labor unions were outlawed in the 1950s, these workers turned to underground unions and quasi-political organizations.

Meanwhile, between 1966 and 1976 the number of professional technicians and managers in Iran grew from 416,000 to 1.5 million. This second new urban class was also denied a role in politics. As the shah's regime outlawed their independent political parties, NGOs, and publications, their association strategies were driven into underground opposition. Rather than absorbing and negotiating concessions with these aspiring urban populations, the repressive regime effectively shepherded them into alliance with the bazaaris and clerics.

But a bigger transformation was required to finally upend Iranian society. That transformation came in the form of massive urban migration created by the shah's 1962 land reform program. Land reform seemed a brilliant strategy for the shah, serving multiple purposes on his agenda. It would stave off potential communist insurgencies in impoverished rural regions. It facilitated the creation of mechanized, large-scale farming. And by increasing agricultural productivity it freed laborers to become workers in his new city-based industries and construction projects. It also helped him to settle an old political score. Many traditional landowners had themselves become bazaaris or clergy in the cities, and by weakening their hold on rural society he could limit their resistance to his regime. But the land reform program distributed land and farm support to only one caste of the peasantry. The new landowners from this caste established mechanized farms and employed their own families, forcing the excluded landless castes to migrate for jobs in the cities.[18] Among the urban migrants during this period, 75 percent to 85 percent were drawn by word of jobs and high wages in the booming construction sector.[19] The result was the creation of a third dispossessed urban class, and a fourfold increase in

Iran's urban population in only fifteen years, between 1950 and 1975. The population of Tehran, the center of the impending revolution, grew from one to four million on the eve of the revolution.

The migrants came from different regions and from diverse ethnic, clan, and linguistic backgrounds. When they settled side by side in their new urban districts, they had few common bonds. Some groups even had historical antipathies. But their new association in the large, dense squatter camps and low-income housing districts on Iran's urban peripheries gave them common cause. Suddenly these diverse groups shared their poverty, their battles against forced eviction, their dependency on unpredictable temporary jobs, and their anger at the land reform program. When a credit crunch slowed the construction industry in the mid-1970s and inflation drove up the cost of living, the citizens of these marginalized districts became easy recruits into opposition. Some of the recruiters were lower-level religious leaders, allies to the bazaari world, who had regular contacts with the poor through local mosques and welfare programs.[20] More important, a network of politically motivated consumer cooperatives extended assistance to the migrant communities, providing them with goods and fuel during strikes and shortages in the revolution's final stages.[21] These cooperatives thus launched a new strategy for revolutionary change that has spread throughout the Middle East, in which Islamic political organizations provide urban settlement and development assistance to new low-income migrant populations in order to broaden their political base and alliances.

Leveraging the economics of urban association, groups with disparate backgrounds, needs, agendas, and politics built expedient citywide coalitions with the numbers and combined influence required for true revolutionary influence.[22] The isolated protests of seminarians, bazaaris, students, and unionists evolved into demonstrations involving mixed masses of hundreds of thousands. In the later stages, when striking workers and unemployed migrant laborers joined them in the streets, the demonstrations grew to the millions. Never before, and nowhere but in the efficient, connective milieu of fast-growing cities, could such an admixture of groups ally politically. This revolutionary alliance took everyone, including its own participants, by surprise.

Such alliances have become a force of political change throughout the Middle East. As ruling elites have tried to build cities into secular, modern, Westernized centers for their own urban advantage, they have competed for political and economic control against traditional groups such as clergy, bazaaris, and neighborhood strongmen (each with its own unique systems of urban advantage), while also curtailing opportunities for new migrant and middle-class groups. The rise of revolutionary organizations was often a response to the failed governance of these competing interests as urban growth accelerated between 1940 and 1970. As Denoeux writes, the efforts of modern governments to secure urban control in the face of strikes, demonstrations, and riots fostered "groups that operate in an informal manner and under the surface of the political system in 'zones of autonomy' that political opponents can use to organize against the regime" and to advance their different claims to the city.[23]

There appear to be three distinct ways that these new "zones of autonomy" and their associated revolutionary movements have evolved in low-income city neighborhoods in the Middle East, typified by the splintered militia movements in Lebanon, the decentralized Muslim Brotherhood in Cairo, and the Islamic-based political parties that swept Turkish city elections in 1994, assuming national political dominance.

In Lebanon, power was traditionally wielded by local urban "strongmen," who built district-level machines through neighborhood-based kinship, sectarian, and patron-client networks. These strongmen would negotiate services and benefits for their neighborhood communities in exchange for representing the interests of outside powers in their territories. "In societies where the state delivered few public services," writes Denoeux, "neighborhoods and neighborhood-based groups often took upon themselves functions that, in other contexts, are performed by the central government" including "distributing water, cleaning the streets, providing lighting, and maintaining order and security."[24] While the development of industry and global trade created new sources of political power in Lebanon, such as labor unions and the new middle-class political parties, these entrenched neighborhood-based organizations dominated Lebanese politics and society until the 1975 civil war. They commanded not just loyalties but also territorial citysystems, not unlike the bazaar, with their own militias and local bureaucracies for tax collection, school systems, hospitals, enterprises, radio and television stations, and even ports in their urban zones of control.[25]

But mechanization of agriculture and the conflict with Israel in southern and eastern Lebanon created a massive Shiite migration to Beirut in the 1960s and '70s. By 1974, more than 60 percent of the country's southern rural population had migrated to Lebanese cities, largely to Beirut. They settled in vast suburban slum areas in the southern and eastern city, which became known as the "misery belt." The neighborhood strongmen of the older central city were unable to extend their model and services to incorporate these new settlers into the established political system. Two kinds of social-political movement organized to fill this vacuum. On the one hand was a collection of competing left-oriented militias with their associated political leaders and parties; on the other was the clerical-based Islamic movement known today as Hezbollah, imported, financed, and receiving its militia training from the new Islamic Republic of Iran. For fifteen years, from 1975 to 1990, these militias warred for control of Beirut. But as they destroyed the city, they also entrenched their own territories in it, where they established welfare associations, schools, and radio stations. In 2000, for instance, Hezbollah operated twenty medical centers and had a commercial network of shopping malls, petrol stations, and construction companies.[26] They built new extension infrastructure, like Hezbollah's independent fiber-optic network, which the government unsuccessfully attempted to seize in May 2008.

Leveraging the advantage gained through direct territorial control over city districts, these militias extended their power into nationwide paramilitary and political coalitions. In the 1998 elections, Hezbollah's party lists won a majority of the country's municipal elections. The different militias forged alliances with Syria and Iran, and created "charitable support" networks with their respective diaspora communities in the West. From their deep-set roots in disenfranchised migrant districts, they established a tenacious advantage across the City, waging international wars, building substantial drug and smuggling operations, and influencing world affairs for more than three decades.

In Egypt, where repressive central government is consolidated, similar informal, low-income zones of autonomy serve as places where, as Middle East expert Asef Bayat explains, the migrant poor, struggling young middle-class professionals, Islamic radicals, and charitable organizations develop a "utilitarian politics" in which they exchange supportive services to each other.[27] Banned political organizations gain anonymous haven in exchange for their organizations' welfare services for the local poor. The outlawed and violently suppressed Muslim Brotherhood has built its legitimacy in underserved low-income areas, working in both utilitarian and ideological alliance with many other charities, volunteer groups, and student and professional associations, whose constituents and activities are concentrated in informal migrant areas. Their school and health clinic networks surpass the quality of government facilities. They provide legal clinics, housing, and disaster recovery assistance. They build partnerships with politically powerful professional associations by offering struggling young professionals, who often live in these areas, access to health insurance, finance, and training. The low-income districts thus provide spaces where disparate interests support each other's autonomy to pursue their different strategies for advantage. These districts have multiplied across Egypt as the country's population shifted from 32 percent to 57 percent urban between 1950 and 2000, adding twenty-two million more to its cities. With such autonomous scale, density, and association, these migrant settlements are targets of occasional, violent police raids as well as state-funded development investments to prevent their sudden emergence as a revolutionary force.[28]

Turkey's electoral landscape was transformed by its grassroots urban migrant districts in 1994 when the Islamic Welfare Party won local elections in Ankara, Istanbul, and many other cities to the shock of established political powers. Here again, the provision of health centers and schools by informal Islamic social welfare associations anchored their political rise. In the 1996 elections, the Welfare Party gained the prime ministership, only to be forced out of power by the military in 1997 and banned in 1998. Yet its leaders reorganized as the Justice and Development Party and have been entrenched as the ruling party since 2002.

Anchored in their urban strongholds, the region's Islamic movements have extended their urban strategies and political movements internationally, forging a new transnational religious identity among diasporas in Europe and North America. Founders of the Turkish Welfare Party, for instance, were directly involved in the establishment of perhaps the largest Islamic movement in western Europe. Called Millî Görüş or "the

Community View," it has established more than three hundred mosques in German cities and claims eighty-seven thousand members throughout twelve European countries. Its Web site also states that it maintains 1,833 "women's, youth, sports and educational facilities."[29] Millî Görüş is listed as a "threat" by German security agencies and has been the focus of recent anti-immigrant and financial controversies in the Netherlands.

Meanwhile, the Muslim Brotherhood is reported to have a long-standing foothold in Europe via an affiliate called the Islamic Society of Germany (IGD). The IGD is said to have centers in thirty German cities and it sponsors many youth and student organizations there. According to the *Middle East Quarterly*, it also has been associated with a number of radical Islamist undertakings.[30]

The roll call of grassroots associations, political parties, militias, and eventually governments that arose from the urban advantage developed in and by marginal districts in Middle East cities—including the revolution in Algeria in 1990 and the emergence of Hamas in Palestine—has dominated international news for decades. Like the rise of the MS-13 or the development of the business process outsourcing industry in Bangalore, their rapid ascendance to global influence reflected the powerful forces loosed by the Urban Revolution. By the time the rest of the world learned the names of these urban movements, they had already changed the politics of the region and, ultimately, of the world.

CHAPTER 5

The Tyrants' Demise

The Irrepressible Economics of Urban Association

After the urban revolutions in the United States and Iran captured the world's attention and transformed those regions; after the People Power movement in Manila deposed dictator Ferdinand Marcos in 1986; and as we watched the unfolding revolution in the cities of South Africa, we were nonetheless surprised when the communist regimes of Central Europe collapsed in a cascade of urban revolution in 1989. From the cities of Poland, a nearly defeated Solidarity trade union movement stepped out from the repressed underground and negotiated political power. Months later, the citizens of Berlin took home their souvenir pieces of the Wall. The world's collective jaw dropped ever lower as regimes in Hungary, Czechoslovakia, Bulgaria, and Romania proved oddly impotent in the face of crowds of peaceful, celebrating protesters in cities across the region.

Whole generations in both the East and West had fixated on the might and repressive power of the centralized Soviet empire. In less than a year, it was all gone. Only two events since—the attack on New York's World Trade Center in 2001 and the Indian Ocean tsunami of 2004—have matched the unexpectedness of that global moment. Yet, we again failed to notice the distinctly urban nature of the Soviet demise.

It was clear to anyone who had a chance to spend time with Communist Party apparatchiks running the cities of the Soviet bloc in the late 1980s; or to anyone who visited factories and local cultural organizations; or to anyone who played cat-and-mouse with the plainclothes KGB agents en route to visits with disgruntled musicians, artists, academics, and scientists, that people were together working up the courage to simply, peacefully abandon the system. A parallel society, made up of multiplying tiny zones of autonomy, had formed in these cities. The informal networks of disaffected citizens in and between the region's cities were linking up, extending across Central and Eastern Europe, and gaining support from their so-called solidarity cities in the West.

The final collapse of the world's most authoritarian regimes was a logical consequence of their own centralized designs. Though state police tried to track every movement, open every letter, and record every conversation, the uncontrollable life of the city and its raw economics of association just unfolded around them. Ultimately, their attempts to manage the billionfold acts of urban association—the phone calls; pamphlets; conversations with colleagues, neighbors, and spouses; association meetings; petty defiances; and protest plans of the grassroots resistance—turned their efforts into a farce. For the sake of official status within the system, most people played along, but their hearts were no longer in it. When they went home from the May Day parades they resumed the constant probing of the system's limited control over their increasingly bolder forms of independent association, weaving myriad parallel webs of unofficial social life and political thought at the system's margins.

My job in the mid-1980s put me in regular contact with people in the cities of the Soviet Union (USSR), where we did our own testing of the space for informal association: building relationships between U.S. and Soviet cities independent of Moscow and Washington designs, and meeting with the environmentalists, ostracized professionals, closet nationalists, and dissidents of these cities.

The mentality of the Cold War required that people in both the East and West subscribed daily to the myth that power resided with central governments, while the life of cities was understood narrowly as an arena of municipal affairs under central control. It was this same mentality, in many respects, that blinded the modern dictators of the Middle East, and the urban renewal planners of America's inner cities, to the shifting sociopolitical tectonics of the Urban Revolution.

When we first started developing city-to-city partnerships in the Soviet Union in 1985, local opposition to the system there was observable everywhere: in living rooms, cafés, workplaces, universities, and churches. There was a new boldness in the expression of resistance, even in small ways. On arrival in Moscow I would regularly visit a once-prominent musician who had been professionally demoted and economically marginalized for her views. She would use the occasion of these visits to flagrantly demonstrate her independence. Whereas we held our first meetings in the presumed privacy of her apartment on Moscow's periphery, she developed the confidence during these years to flout her contact with foreigners right in the lobby of the downtown, KGB-riddled Intourist hotel. Once inside she'd unveil a basket of rare meats for us to eat under their noses. This was a costly picnic for her. Meat was in short supply. But it was a way of saying, "You cannot stop me from having a good life." Then she would openly receive the scarce tennis balls that I'd brought for her as a gift. Elsewhere in another major Soviet city, refuseniks hosted us for dinner and took us on Sunday strolls. Environmentalists met with us to discuss the creation of an independent laboratory for analyzing the pollution from the regime's factories, and over the years we brought them the equipment they needed. People in the cities were emboldened by the invisible autonomous zones they were forming that gave them access to the opportunities of the emerging City.

These efforts were a small part of the re-networking of society's grass roots in the Cold War's waning years, relinking societies city to city across the Cold War's borders and restrictions. Together we openly mocked the lines of authority. We called it "citizen diplomacy." The global NGO activism that blossomed in the 1990s first achieved political status through city governments in the 1980s, which asserted their independence through activist local laws, "sister cities," "sanctuary cities," solidarity movements, nuclear-free zones, and other "municipal foreign policies." Through city governments, American opposition to the Cold War gained public sanction and reached out to communities in Central and Eastern Europe and the USSR. It was all part of what historian Padraic Kenney describes as the "carnival of revolution," a free-for-all improvisation of new kinds of resistance, amplified through the internationalization of the Urban Revolution.

Kenney resided in the heart of the drama. When he documented life in Central Europe as a student in Poland, following the military's crackdown on Solidarity in the early 1980s, he discovered not monolithic totalitarianism but societies that were parading openly and out of government's control. His account in *A Carnival of Revolution* chronicles the transition from underground dissidence to aboveground countercultural activism.[1] This new, open activism took the form less of confrontations at the barricades than of street festivals, marches, rock concerts, poetry readings, art happenings, professional exchanges, social support committees, and legal support funds, remarkably similar to the carnival-like Western peace movement.

In the mid- to late 1980s, these motley activities spread through Central European cities like a virus of association. The revolutions' protagonists, according to Kenney, were not just unionists and iconic dissidents but "radical environmentalists, hippies, performance artists, and pacifists." Their diverse movements, he writes, "paid a great deal of attention to one another. When possible, they visited one another, regardless of communist border guards and Kafka-esque passport restrictions. This interaction is a central feature of the carnival story . . . Protest became a ubiquitous part of everyday life in the major cities."[2]

This spectacle was in many ways the logical conclusion of communist planning and investment. The communist regimes of Central and Eastern Europe had come to power with a mission to remove the "backwardness" of their prewar societies. For all the inefficiency of central planning regimes, they mastered the rapid development of their countries' cities, thus creating dynamics of urban social organization that they could not control.

With ownership of all urban land, finance, and industry, the new regimes could rapidly build an urban civilization in the image of urbanized Western Europe. In thirty-five years, Poland went from a rural society with 60 percent of its population relying directly on agriculture to a country with half of the population living in cities in 1965. On the eve of revolution in 1985, Poland's economy and culture were predominantly urban, involving nearly 60 percent of the population. Similarly, Hungary was a rural society prior to World War II, dominated by an old nobility against which its majority of subsistence-level peasants rallied for land reforms and against the country's urban, Jewish elite. When communists assumed power in 1947 they began a wholesale reorganization of both rural and urban society. This created unprecedented social mobility and mixing in the cities. Collectivization of farms and forced industrialization drove urban migration, and erstwhile parochial peasants joined the ranks of trade unions and the growing technocracy. Altogether, the countries of Eastern Europe transformed the character of their civilization from a 61 percent rural society in 1950 to a 66 percent urban one in 1985.

Within the cities, further social engineering reorganized populations from disparate villages, regions, and social strata into new, city-centered groups: into layers of official political party organizations, unions, cultural and student groups, and housing and workplace committees. All of these engineered forms of association were designed as mechanisms for management, obedience, and control. In due time, they created their own elites of party faithful, with privileged access to the cities' jobs, promotions, housing, and cultural opportunities. The majority, particularly the growing ranks of industrial workers and free-thinking professionals, thereby increasingly lost access to benefits of the new urban order through official associations.

Yet by reorganizing society into dense urban clusters and networks the regime actually reduced the ability of rising *nomenklatura* elites and apparatchiks to control society's self-organizing potential. Density and scale prevented the regimes from controlling association altogether. It would only be a matter of time before the marginalized urban majority mastered strategies of association to secure their own urban advantage.

Some formed quiet alliances to work for change from within organizations of the system, in response to which many were expelled, exiled, imprisoned, or worse. Others organized at the fringes of organizations, using the contacts, meetings, and routines of the system to build independent, informal networks. As the security apparatus was extended to discipline or expel these people, the resisters formed underground unions, newspapers, and groups of dissident intellectuals like the Worker's Defense Committee (KOR) in Poland and the Charter 77 group in the former Czechoslovakia. When the machinery of repression extended to divide, demoralize, and control these groups, yet new networks of resistance formed. What the regimes didn't realize was that the only way to stop new forms of association was to remove large numbers of people from the cities.

The further the system pushed to control its urban populations, the larger the marginalized segment discovered, in trial-and-error fashion, the zones of autonomy that the regimes could not control. Even in a system where every component of urban society—economics and employment, the police and courts, phone lines, neighbors' apartments, jobs, doctors, license bureaus, passports, and prisons—was employed to try to stop free association, it could not be stopped. The communist regimes only proved that control of the city was contrary to the nature of cities.

The system's responses evolved from harsh and tragic to comic and pitiful. For all the layers of administration, not to mention brutal repression, the system remained surprisingly permeable because of the social networks and relations that emerged outside its control. I remember drafting letters in 1984 to mayors in half a dozen Soviet cities. American cities were not legally supposed to have any contacts whatsoever with Soviet cities; the United States had terminated all cultural relations between the two countries in 1979. So direct communication faced security prohibitions on both sides of the Iron Curtain. Somehow the letters made their way to disaffected cities in Estonia, Lithuania, Kazakhstan, and Armenia on the Soviet Union's periphery. (To send a message to the Soviet officials, our only letter to a Russian city was to Dubna, the nation's high-security, off-limits center for nuclear research.) Months later, we received responses, inviting formal relations without any hint of Moscow's intermediation.

Emigré groups and conservative scholars called us naive: All of these responses must have been cleared by Moscow, they said. The fast responses were an indication of the efficiency of the Soviet's system of control. Anything we would do or say would remain under tight, central control. The Soviets would manipulate us, they charged. But history revealed that the world had changed. Bilateral noncooperation in the Cold War had begun between cities on both sides of the Iron Curtain.

Negotiations, political visits, and exchanges followed. Our first test of the independence of our cooperation was a request to release a group of Jewish refusenik families, whom we had met on our first trip, as a condition of the formalization of our relationship. Within months these families were in Israel. There was nothing underground at all about our efforts. We had no independent communication infrastructure, like the Internet. Everything was monitored by the intelligence apparatus of both countries. Yet we helped environmentalists build independent cases against the system's polluting enterprises. Diaspora communities used their sister city relationships as a channel for independent relations with nationalists and marginalized church officials. These were tiny deeds in the scheme of a revolution, but each rebellious act in the mid-1980s tested the limits of autonomous association. It was in exactly this way that the *real* revolutionaries of Central and Eastern Europe tested their limits in the years to come.

For many in the Eastern bloc, it was the Chernobyl nuclear disaster in 1986 that pushed activists from novel experimentation toward open resistance. Elsewhere, pitiful responses to disasters, like the December 1988 earthquake that killed twenty-five thousand and left half a million Armenians homeless, made people realize that there was less and less to lose. A true civil society emerged in the cities and started claiming its independence.

In Central Europe's cities claims were made through diverse kinds of grassroots association, unique to each city. Polish citizens held art happenings, organized support committees for recently arrested dissidents, started church revivals and a temperance movement. They launched student clubs, a homeless shelter movement, and retiree groups. In East Germany, people organized peace seminars and prayer groups in churches. In Czechoslovakia they organized underground churches, punk music scenes, school discussion groups, and a group opposing dam construction. After Chernobyl, environmental groups sprang up in every city throughout the Soviet bloc. These groups seemed small, diffuse, and eccentric in the face of the system, but as they synchronized from their different zones of autonomy they amassed a swarm attack against it.

At first there was no aligned social movement. There was a fractious "Network of Free Initiatives," as one Czech network called itself. This was a confusing landscape for regimes designed for uniformity and bureaucratic control. To functionaries it must have seemed more like anarchy than opposition. But that was exactly the point. Underground music, for instance, "was not a form of opposition in itself," writes Kenney, that the regimes knew when or how to crush. It "was a milieu where some people would discover opposition, and a resource (of contacts, and of strategies) for that opposition . . . Any independent activity, no matter how apolitical it seemed, weakened the regime's hold on power."[3]

These tests of "what one could get away with" provided citizens with a topographic map of autonomous spaces and viable forms of association. Map in hand, by the mid-1980s many groups reorganized into more open, challenging opposition. There were the petition campaigns in Czechoslovakia and the formation of the Independent Peace Association in Prague. New opposition political parties were launched in Hungary's cities. Poland's movement of military oath resisters filled the void left by Solidarity's repression in the early 1980s.

The latter movement evolved into the peace and human rights organization called Freedom and Peace, and it started actively networking with Western and other Eastern European peace groups. From the early 1980s there was a steady trend toward the extension of resistance networks into a transcontinental movement. First, local associations networked across the controlled borders of Eastern bloc countries, bridging the historical, nationalist resentments of Central and Eastern Europeans along the way. These cross-border support networks emboldened the local opposition in cities throughout the region. The networks then linked with peace and human rights movements in the West, securing further support from western NGOs and foundations. In 1987, Poland's Freedom and Peace network organized the first pan-European peace conference held in communist Europe. Few understood just how emboldened people had become in the "carnival" of trial-and-error resistance and broad-based activist networking. Then in 1988 the seemingly impossible occurred. The sum of the region's grassroots activism became much greater than its diverse, small-scale local parts.

As with the solidarity networks created by privations of the African American Great Migration in the United States, few foresaw the power of intercity association in Central Europe. And much like the 1960s rioting in American cities, the final stage of urban revolution in Central Europe was generally triggered by blunt state repression that threatened multiple established micro-zones of autonomy and misunderstood the emboldened mood of the populace. In Poland, it was the response to a strike in Krakow. In Slovenia, it was the trial of a journalist. The disparate movements had already tested the spaces for urban autonomy. Now, in response to these events, they found themselves filling them all together for the first time.

Surely, the economic crises of these regimes, after decades of bad investments and subsidized production and consumption, was a precondition for the events of 1989. But their economic teetering began decades earlier. The actual events of 1989 required another dynamic that caught these governments unaware. The reason for the sudden collapses also cannot be pinned on the rise of Gorbachev or on some new North Atlantic Treaty Organization (NATO) military advantage or Central Intelligence Agency (CIA) plot. Glasnost had already started in Central Europe's cities before Gorbachev even came to power as Communist Party secretary, and grassroots glasnost was already forcing perestroika on unwitting regimes. Gorbachev was the bold messenger of this new reality to party elites.

Neither is it sufficient to attribute revolutionary change solely to networks of courageous unionists and peaceniks. These grassroots movements were also caught off guard by their revolutionary achievements. Revolution started, was concentrated, and persisted in the region's cities, while the countryside remained relatively passive, because of an irrepressible dynamic of cities themselves.

The possibility of revolution under dictatorship or totalitarianism, without free access to information or communications technology like the Internet, arises from the fundamental logic of urban network efficiencies—what I have called urban association. The ways that people associate are shaped by many influences. These include inherited traditions, social routines, and motivations to meet and collaborate. Culture, routine, and personality are central parts of association. But at its most basic level, the possibilities of association are shaped by the efficiency with which people of different motivations, interests, knowledge, and connections can meet and interact. This efficiency of association can be understood using simple math.

Consider five people, each needing to make a loaf of bread, but none knowing exactly how. Let's assume that a bread recipe has twenty steps, but each of the five people only knows four of the steps. So they have to meet and exchange their respective steps with each other before any of them can make a loaf of bread.

If bread making is the problem to be solved, let's consider the role of density in their ability to solve it. Assume that each baker lives one mile from the others, but because of time limitations, they can move only a half mile each day. They also have to go home every night, which is the only place they can bake their bread. Like everyone, they have constraints on their time and ability to connect with other people. Whenever they meet an aspiring bread maker they can learn a new step. Under the best of conditions, where every day they all move a half mile toward each other and meet in the middle, each person can go home with four new bread-making steps every day. So on the night of the fourth day, they can all go home and make a loaf of bread.

But life is never so easy, especially in a repressive system. Imagine what happens if the party decides that independent bread making is a threat to society and therefore posts a KGB officer at the one location where they can all meet together. If anyone goes to that spot, the officer will put him or her in jail, and none of them will ever learn how to bake bread. Now under these conditions, at best, only two meetings can happen each day. (Two people will each move half a mile toward another two people, and the fifth person will be left out until it is his turn.) Now it will take twenty days before all five can bake a loaf of bread. If it takes that long to learn, they may die of starvation! So rather than spending time trying to learn how to bake bread together, they'll each find their own independent way to scrounge for food. They'll never associate autonomously. In a figurative sense, such was the lot of the villager in Central Europe in 1950. It's just too hard to reach critical mass against a highly organized regime. Under these conditions, totalitarianism looks sustainable.

Let's take these same people and put them together in cities. (The regime itself will take care of most of the moving expenses and provide them with a new home, too.) Now each lives a quarter of a mile from the others. They still move one half mile per day and can exchange one step per day with each person they meet. Because of density, they can now each meet with at least two different people per day. So under these conditions, in spite of the police controls that keep them all from meeting together, it will take only eight days before all can make a loaf of bread. One will have all the steps in only six days and can share them with another group. Density has automatically produced extraordinary efficiency and growth in their bread-making movement. If the regime moves them even closer together—say, by locating them in a run-down housing complex at the city's fringe—then the speed at which they can bake bread increases even faster.

But the city offers more than density. It also offers scale. When they are moved into the city, they meet other people who want to bake bread. Let's say that each comes across another person who wants to make bread. So now we have ten baker-conspirators all living a quarter mile apart. By adding the element of scale, under the same conditions, we can get more loaves in even fewer days—an *exponential* increase in efficiency.

The basic economies of density and scale can create different economies of association for specific activities depending on the design of city blocks and buildings, and on the mix of land uses and types of people within concentrated areas. For instance, if work, family, school, and recreation are all located adjacent to each other, then people can multitask along their symbolic half mile of daily activity. Careful design of density multiplies the number of achievable activities and interactions. Similarly, if a regime forces people who share an inclination toward bread making into one area of the city, creating a scaled bread-making community, then efficiencies arise. The original bread makers may meet someone who can make bread in only fifteen steps, and her innovations will rapidly diffuse.

We can mathematically model the above network efficiencies provided by scale and density. But when we consider the effects of density and scale made available through different patterns of urban settlement and design, calculating network efficiencies requires extremely complex models. This explains why most people, communist rulers and dissidents alike, have a hard time understanding the revolutionary possibilities that emerge from urban design and growth.

The revolutionary potential of cities gets even more complicated. People don't move into cities as blank slates. They bring legacies of association—established networks, and cultural and occupational traditions. Whatever the nature of their existing networks—be they political cells, *bazaari* merchant networks, neighborhood gangs, or poetry clubs—they can now link up to create scaled networks of a different nature. In a scaled network, each basic network becomes a node for collaboration with a number of other networks. People from diverse starting points who nonetheless share a common challenge or interest thereby efficiently develop new innovations, identities, norms, ways of communicating, and ultimately shared strategies. Network efficiencies make cities the world's strategic centers of social innovation.

Network efficiencies can then be extended from city to city through urban infrastructure. Extension infrastructure further increases the effective scale of association, but it also contributes another dynamic to the equation: an accelerated *speed of association and change*. Shipping, transit, and air travel systems as well as telephone networks and the Internet speed the rate at which dense networks can be established and link individual cities into a functioning, extended City. They reduce the friction and costs of networking activity.

Today, because of the most recent addition to urban infrastructure, the Internet, we can find and link a thousand bread makers together in a day and scale their bakery activities overnight. It comes as no wonder that the Chinese government, to stave off revolution in its fast-growing cities, treats control of the Internet as a strategic challenge.

The mechanics of social organization in cities (relative to other forms of human settlement) are more efficient, more adaptable, and more difficult to track. People can be physically segregated in specific districts as in Detroit, or excluded from career opportunities as with the dissidents of Gdańsk, Poland, and this can temporarily constrain their urban advantage. But by increasing network efficiencies (i.e., association) through urbanization, the isolation of people with common interests actually increases their effectiveness *as a whole group*. As communist elites steadily excluded opposition-minded people from official spaces and society—removing them from their jobs or sending them to jail—their network efficiencies *as dissidents* actually increased.

At first, they connected as individuals, often under direct police observation and control. Then pairs formed into cells of a handful of people—committees, study groups, or some other configuration. Then cells connected loosely to each other through a particular nodal individual: for instance, a university student with links to Solidarity who also likes punk rock music might seed student-Solidarity-punk-rock activist fusion. Cells become *nodes* in a broad network, which develops common approaches and interests through the efficient sharing of news, underground *samizdat* publications, activist techniques, and plans. Kenney provides an example of how dense networks of resistance could develop in a single city district, as in the strategically important Krakow factory neighborhood of Nowa Huta in 1987. In Nowa Huta "one could find many niches in the opposition," he says: in the Solidarity underground, in social service centers and food banks at the churches, at the meetings of the unofficial Christian Workers' University, in the youth underground, and the employees' councils.[4] It should come as no surprise, therefore, that Nowa Huta became a key geographic center of activism in 1988 to end Poland's communist regime.

Ultimately, networking between such groups within common city spaces enables a new form of association: scaled strategic alliances of otherwise small marginalized groups, giving them access to broader resources and making their actions more effective through coordinated action and shared experience. This cell-based network structure provides urban advantage, yet at the same time protects the alliance against repression because it lacks a single center of control. The aforementioned Network of Free Initiatives and Freedom and Peace were real-world examples of such urban revolutionary networks.

Like everywhere else, the urbanization of Central Europe grew an infrastructure for intercity trade and governance that was used in parallel by activist networks to extend their strategies from city to city. Once extended urban association was established, resistance became ever present, jumping from Nova Huta to demonstrations elsewhere to the international media in a matter of hours. Those who struggled for decades in isolation against the heavy inertia of the system could feel their organizing becoming frictionless; tasks that once required extensive effort, like getting a critical mass out for a demonstration, suddenly happened spontaneously. For the first time, the carnival activists sensed the possibility of real revolution. By the time they felt it, the revolution was already unstoppable. As if overnight, the fringe resisters were transformed into real revolutionaries.

The Philippines' postwar transition from American military control to patronage-based political parties, dominated by the country's rural economic elites, was brutally smooth. But the military dictatorship of Ferdinand Marcos failed to realize that rapid growth of the country's urban population (which more than quadrupled from 1950 to 1985) meant more than a statistical increase in jobs, houses, and roads. It changed the fundamental dynamics of society.

In the 1980s, hundreds of small organizations in Manila, of only a few hundred people each, organized to oppose the Marcos regime. Their "zones of autonomy" were small, informal networks: a typical group was little more than a personal network of like-minded middle-class professionals and lower-income, unemployed people. They operated as cells in shifting coalitions.[5] Learning the techniques of urban revolution in trial-and-error fashion, they suddenly emerged in 1986 as the People Power revolution that brought down Marcos and shocked the world.

In a different way, South Africa's apartheid regime miscalculated the dynamics of urban advantage when it tried to monopolize the nation's cities. The primary strategy of the apartheid regime was based on the relocation of black Africans from cities to rural tribal areas. But the regime also depended on black Africans for mining, industrial, construction, and domestic labor in the cities. It therefore developed dense, large-scale barrack-and-shack townships on the urban periphery, unwittingly creating irrepressible forces of urban association.

In those highly managed workers' colonies, people of different tribal and linguistic backgrounds bonded over common struggles and built common language, viewpoints, goals, and organizations—and ultimately a common national identity. The efficiency of association allowed urban black populations to scale up resistance organizations and activist unions through association in schools, churches, factories, and clandestine political parties in ways that were not fully trackable by the country's extensive police organizations. When resistance leaders were tracked down, many went into exile, creating economies of extension across the cities of Africa, Europe, the Soviet Union, the United States, and Canada. Sending young leaders to foreign urban universities became part of a long-term strategy to extend the global resistance network, which channeled funds and arms to the African National Congress and put pressure on foreign governments to disown the apartheid regime.

Such is the anatomy of power and politics in the Urban Revolution.

Urban revolutions often start in the ghettos of marginalized racial or ethnic groups, but they can also start in communities of middle-class people who have been marginalized from the politics and economic levers of their cities. Hugo Chavez's more contemporary "Bolivarian Revolution," for instance, rose to power with the support of the long-demeaned *barrio* residents of Caracas, Maracaibo, Valencia, and other cities in Venezuela. Yet even as the Chavez regime entrenches control of the military, oil production, and the central government through its support of urban migrants, it remains vulnerable to urban counter-revolution. If Chavez and his successors fail to develop Venezuela's cities into places of opportunity for the middle classes, industrialists, and trade unions, in addition to the growing ranks of migrants, then further revolution will be certain, with or without the intervention of the American CIA.

In the emerging City the struggle for urban advantage has taken many forms, but the underlying logic of power and legitimacy in the urban age is constant. Urban revolutions foment wherever large urban populations are aggressively rebuffed in their attempts to steer the development of their cities to their group's advantage. Urban advantage is a flexible, open-source public good in all urbanizing societies. It can be seized, shaped, and deployed strategically in a myriad ways. Attempts to overly control it reflect a fundamental blindness to the imperatives and ethos of the city.

The regular news of simmering conflict in the informal city districts of China, like the riots in France and Belgium in 2005 or in Kenya in 2008, can be like a drip feed that starts to go unnoticed. But old grievances can easily swell into a new, world-changing tide of urban revolution. In 2005, a special U.S. congressional commission on China released a summary report of sixty-six incidents of unrest in China's cities between 2003 and 2005, most related to forced evictions and demolitions. These incidents typically involved demonstrations of a few dozen to a thousand people, but the nature of confrontation reveals a larger, simmering crisis in that country, reminiscent of the simmering insurrection during America's Great Migration.

October 22, 2004. Changchun City. Four hundred residents of a condemned building attacked approximately one hundred police from the Urban Administration Bureau as they began to tear down the building. According to the source, the residents were dissatisfied with the compensation offered them. Over fifty police and five residents were injured in the confrontation.

November 2, 2004. Wuhan City. Several dozen people staged a peaceful demonstration at the grand opening of a Wanda-Wal-Mart shopping mall to protest the amount of compensation paid to evicted residents of buildings torn down to make way for the shopping mall.

January 4, 2005. Shenzhen City. Over one thousand massage parlor, beauty salon, and restaurant workers protested the proposed demolition of their workplaces, barricading themselves inside the government-owned building.

January 5, 2005. Beijing. More than six hundred police forcibly dispersed 270 vendors gathered at Beijing's Silk Alley outdoor market. The vendors were protesting their eviction and the planned destruction of the market grounds. After several failed petitions, vendors organized a sit-in to stop the demolition of the market area. Following dispersion of the protesters, the market was demolished.

These reports were gleaned from internal news sources in China.[6] Considering the control of information there, they surely represent only a small glimpse of the true state of affairs. In September 2007, Xinhua News quoted the official Communist Party newspaper, *People's Daily*, stating that three million complaints had been filed that month with local government units and national complaint departments over land acquisitions, housing demolitions, and other local government-related matters. In June 2007, the Geneva-based Centre on Housing Rights and Evictions released a report estimating that 1.5 million people would be evicted from their homes in Beijing during preparation for the 2008 Olympics. The director of Beijing's construction committee later tried to calm concerns, stating that only "forty thousand to fifty thousand households had been relocated each year." Given the average size of a Beijing household, this amounts to 130,000 to 165,000 people being relocated each year over the 2000–2008 period, summing to a number remarkably close to 1.5 million. "Most relocated citizens will have to change their living habits," said the official, "resulting in inconvenience in terms of employment, schooling, and access to medical services and transport."[7]

The full picture began to emerge with a report from the RAND Corporation to the same U.S. congressional committee in 2005. "In the past five years officials in China's public security system have confirmed what foreign observers have sensed for some time: social protest has risen dramatically over the past decade, and is now a daily phenomenon," said the author to the committee. The number of sit-ins, strikes, petition campaigns, rallies, marches, traffic blocking, building seizures, and riots increased from eighty-seven hundred in 1993 to fifty-eight thousand in 2003. The report goes on to highlight how extension infrastructure recently developed in China's cities—in particular, mobile phone and Internet service—has provided a major boost to such grassroots protest, alongside undescribed "deliberately hard-to-monitor 'low-tech' methods to organize."[8]

Such a rapid increase in confrontation in China, at such scale, linked directly to the (mis)management of the urbanization process, suggests that we should be braced for a world of further urban revolutions in the decades ahead. China's urban population will increase by nearly three hundred million people over the next twenty years. Adding to concerns, other studies reveal that city dwellers are disinclined to turn to the country's institutions, particularly the police, for help.[9] Disaffection itself is becoming institutionalized. The Chinese government is reproducing a familiar anatomy of revolution in the design and management of its cities. It is marginalizing and then also isolating those marginalized groups together. It is creating common cause among migrants, traditional merchants, and industrial workers as it denies them their strategies for urban advantage. It is burdening its cities and their people's lives with designed inefficiencies that squeeze the poor and force them to create new, disruptive innovations for using the city to their advantage. Everything points to further failure and lost opportunities in our current approach to the Urban Revolution.

CHAPTER 6

What We Can Learn from the Way That Migrants Build Their Cities

Buildings, City Models, and Citysystems

Imagine what might happen if nearly a million poor people came to your city and settled in one place together. They would come from failing agricultural economies where families were just barely scraping by. They would be from the lower castes of society, held down in both subtle and brutal ways by privileged groups who control the opportunities around them. They would have minimal education. Their only economic leverage would be traditional trades that their families had plied for ages—as shepherds, potters, traders, growers, cleaners, moneylenders, metalworkers, tailors, carpenters—and now, their new but vulnerable foothold in your city.

What would happen if they were left to their own devices in this city for thirty to forty years without legal status or investment, but also undisturbed by the kinds of harassment, destruction of their settlements, and forced relocations that have driven similar communities to rebellion in other parts of the world?

Conventional wisdom holds that these people would build a teeming slum and live in squalor. They would be exploited by merchants, employers, and politicians. Their slum would breed crime, addictions, and epidemics. Little good would come of their gamble on city life. Things would have been better for them, and the world, had they stayed, with government help, in their rural homelands.

About a century ago, that experiment began in Mumbai. First, Muslim merchants from Tamil Nadu, followed by Gujarati Muslims who controlled colonial Bombay's trade in animal hides, claimed some peripheral marshlands at the northern edge of the city. Located between the city's isolated slaughterhouses and its central markets, these merchants saw opportunity: the chance to leverage proximity (density) to a ready supply of animal skins, their access to a growing city market for leather goods (scale), and their community's commercial skills (association) into a new tanning industry.

Drawing on their association traditions, the Tamil merchants began recruiting lower-caste Hindu and Muslim laborers from their home district to work in the new tanneries. These workers settled in shacks built on the marshy land near Bombay's waste dumps. They steadily filled the marshes to create solid ground against the annual flooding of their homes. The merchants' venturesome commercial investment and the settlement of workers they recruited sparked the steady transformation of this low-lying land into Dharavi, the world's most notable migrant city and now one of Mumbai's most valuable and contested tracts of land.

Some years ago, during routine visits to Mumbai on business trips, I started interspersing business meetings in the corporate offices and hotels of the city's booming formal economy with an exploration of Dharavi's informal economic life. Dharavi, it seemed, was a Rosetta Stone for understanding the workings of urban advantage free of imported ideas and plans, foreign capital, government regulation, and investment schemes. Here, in Dharavi, the basic logic of city building was laid bare.

A young settlement, Dharavi was born in a legal limbo, without any consistent government investment or planning support. In the early 1960s, during the Urban Revolution's peak migration years, Dharavi grew from distinct villagelike settlements of indigenous Koli fishing families, tannery workers, textile mill laborers, migrant artisans, and slum dwellers pushed from the legal city to the south into a densely packed disease- and crime-ridden slum. Then, from 1985 to 2000, with occasional but minimal government investment, the mega-slum transformed itself again into a massive, globalized industrial economy in its own right. Now, on my visits to Dharavi we met with the executives of export-oriented companies founded by their destitute migrant fathers and grandfathers.

This process of "upliftment," as it is called in Indian English, continues today. Arum's father, the seasonal brick maker in Madurai nearly one thousand miles away, was the first to tell me about the opportunities for migrant laborers in Mumbai. "The boys come back from Bombay and they talk about the nice climate and work opportunities," he said on that hot day in the open brickyard. "So two or three go back with them each time to find work." In Dharavi, one could see the migrant pathway that might soon take Arum to a life across the city.

On one visit, my colleague Prema Gopalan took me to a workers' dormitory, or pongal house, where dozens of Tamil migrant men shared living space, a kitchen, meals, and a wash area between work contracts in Mumbai or abroad and trips back to their distant villages.[1] As one of the founders of a prominent Indian NGO called SPARC, Prema comanaged the first real population census of Dharavi in the 1980s. To me, Dharavi seemed a crammed, horizonless hodgepodge. But with a kind of X-ray perspective and local knowledge, Prema could distinguish Dharavi's intermingled ethnic, caste, and occupational settlements, and literally see the historical development pattern of the place.

We spoke with some established migrants in this heavily Tamil area. Two young men were tying up parcels to take on the days-long train trip south for Eid festivities at their village home. They had purchased pressure cookers and gas lanterns with a down payment from Assadulah Rubena, who also sat across from us. Rubena migrated to Dharavi in 1991, in his early twenties, encouraged by his older brother who migrated before him. He now runs a business selling appliances and cookware on consignment. Each month, he sends half his income back to his family in rural Tamil Nadu—an amount equal to the monthly income of a Madurai brick maker who produces sixty thousand bricks.

Sitting next to Rubena is Inayat Allah. He is from the same district that sent the original Tamil tannery workers to Dharavi. After moving to Mumbai, he found cash opportunities abroad via labor contracts in Saudi Arabia for agricultural and kitchen work. Then he came back and entered the labor-recruiting business himself. Now he goes to the villages of his home district a few times each year and recruits youth for positions in the Gulf region. From the villagers' perspective, the migration of a resident on a foreign labor contract is an investment scheme. The young migrant has to borrow some $1,500 from family members and neighbors—more than a year's household income—to pay visa, travel, and middleman costs.

Then, by working twelve hours a day, seven days a week on a two-year contract, he earns $125 to $200 more per month than he could earn in the village. He lives expense-free abroad. His savings, sent home each month via the expanding global migrant remittance system, are his families' primary route to capital accumulation and investment. Inayat Allah earns $75 from a Mumbai travel agency for each worker he sends overseas. While the visas and contracts for these recruits are being settled, they stay at this Dharavi hostel and explore the other business opportunities available to them in this migrant city upon their return.

Dharavi is no longer a slum. It has a population equivalent to Nashville, Edmonton, Gdańsk, or Leeds. Its gross domestic product (GDP) is far lower, but its economy is every bit as diverse and vibrant as those of Western cities—if not more so. In a matter of decades it has matured into a global manufacturing and trading city built by hundredfold chains of migration from all over India. To use the jargon of Western development, Dharavi has a number of export-oriented industry clusters. It has strong secondary and tertiary economic sectors. Primary industries are supported by networks of secondary suppliers and service businesses, many of which are also located in Dharavi itself. On a walk through the area, one finds a full range of retail shops, warehousing, goods transport, lawyers, accountants, expediters, hotel and entertainment businesses, health clinics, religious institutions, and local political organizations. Altogether, Dharavi has an estimated GDP of $1.5 billion each year. In spite of its remittances to villages across India, its continued economic growth, without significant external finance, suggests a very positive balance of trade.

But in India, few consider Dharavi to be a city. Tradition, entrenched attitudes, and colonial-era ideas about cities consign Dharavi, in the minds of the country's middle classes and elites, to the status of an urban blemish, a slum. For this reason, its success as a poverty-reduction strategy and brilliant contribution to the theory and practice of city building is rarely appreciated.

Imram Khan was born into a family of poor agricultural laborers in a village in Uttar Pradesh, far to the north. Now he sits under an aged tree in a one-lane roadway that also serves as the courtyard of his Dharavi leather-finishing business. Like all things here, the courtyard serves multiple purposes. It is a street, a lunchroom, a playground, a political meeting place, a pathway for religious processions, and part of multiple local supply chains and production lines. As we meet Imram, haulers pass with teetering cart loads of crushed plastic from nearby recycling shops. We step aside as they navigate the steady stream of people who are looking intent on some task. There is no idleness here. It is typical Dharavi.

Imram takes us on a tour of his business. Each stage of the leather-finishing process is divided into a separate building, facing the others across the courtyard. The buildings are made of bare-bones concrete block with corrugated metal roofs, each measuring about fifteen by twenty feet. They are dim buildings, with few windows, but the floors are clean.

In one building you can see folded raw goat and sheep hides. This is where they are cleaned, salted, and treated before tanning. In a nearby building twenty feet away, workmen mix dyes from plastic vats to match the exact color of a customer's sample piece of finished leather, and then they apply the dyes to the skins that they have received back from the tannery. Next door the dyed skins are buffed to a shine. The buffers look like equipment from an earlier industrial era, with big rubberized belts and clanking motors turning the buffing cylinders. A young workman holds up a shiny piece of finished leather, his head cocked back with a half-proud, half-jesting smile. With his fashion-minded dress and cell phone, he is anything but the Westernized poster-image of the exploited young slum worker.

The final finishing and packing takes place in yet another building. The finished skins are then hauled to manufacturers, also located in Dharavi, to be turned into sandals and bags; or they are shipped from Mumbai to manufacturers around the world. One workman inquires about my background. When I tell him that I am from Toronto, he replies that he has taken loads to the Mumbai port addressed to companies there.

Imram Khan's family was part of a chain migration from Uttar Pradesh forty years ago, when Dharavi still had the character of villagelike encampments. As each new family arrived, they joined the leather trade pioneered by those before them. Imram writes the names of his extended family's businesses in my notebook. Wahaz Khan and Sons. Irfun Khan Enterprises. Ilyas Khan Traders. Saba Khan Enterprises. Together they have twenty-eight buildings in Dharavi, not to mention their homes. As a family, he says, they generate about $500,000 in profits each year.

I ask his opinion of a new government plan to tear down Dharavi and rebuild it into a high-rise residential district. "All our workers live nearby," he says. "Dharavi people will not agree to a two-hundred-and-twenty-five-square-foot home like they are proposing. We live now in five-hundred- to one-thousand-square-foot homes. If they give us five-hundred-square-foot houses then we will stay here, but otherwise my business is finished. My workers will move elsewhere."

Imram has touched upon a fundamental tenet of Dharavi's economic system. Profitability and thereby "upliftment"—in the form of hundreds of thousands of jobs and the rising incomes they create—flow from a chain of cost advantages that is unique to Dharavi's unplanned, yet inarguably *designed*, development by its migrant settlers from a slum into a full-fledged city.

The Dharavi story, like that of many cities, begins with land and location. Market demand for Dharavi's marshland was traditionally very low. Pioneer migrants had the mettle not only to build on this land but to invest their sweat and hours into its filling and improvement without gaining any clear legal title to it. What they received in return, just like the tanners before them, was their own claim to unshaped urban advantage.

Even as they improved the land, the cost of a Dharavi location remained low because of the lack of legal titles. With cheap land available, many impoverished migrants could establish residence and begin to save, even on slim incomes. These savings were plowed back into income-generating equipment, like sewing machines, and into their own residential, commercial, and industrial buildings. However, cost pressures forced them to merge these typically separated buildings into unique Dharavi clusters that support a variety of functions in the same space. Dharavi produced a kind of mixed-use building that is not legally permitted in many parts of the world—there are residential-retail buildings, retail-warehouse buildings, even industrial-residential-warehouse buildings. These dense patterns provided the budding unofficial city with four distinct density-related competitive advantages.

To put Dharavi's density in perspective, an estimated 187,000 to 300,000 people live there per square kilometer. This is six to ten times the population density of greater Mumbai, which itself tops the list of the densest cities in the world. This is 16 to 25 times the population density of greater London and an amazing 375 to 600 times the population density of metropolitan Miami. And all of this enterprising human density lives and works, recreates and romances in buildings that rarely exceed three stories' height. Putting aside whether such living conditions are desirable, healthy, or even humane, it is this spatial condition that Dharavi's migrants have consciously used to create their own Industrial Revolution.

The first density-related economic advantage offered by the Dharavi model is low transportation cost. Most of Dharavi's workforce lives there. Workers can work long hours because they don't have to waste time commuting through the city's heaving traffic from distant low-cost settlements. This creates cost savings and income benefits for both workers and employers.

The second density advantage is Dharavi's extremely high utilization rate of property. In more affluent suburbs, where different building uses are segregated, most property is used for little more than half of a twenty-four-hour day. Homes are empty during the day and businesses are empty at night. In Dharavi, the buildings and courtyards are in constant use. Dharavi, one might say, was the first place to invent 24/7.

Dharavi's residents operate some fifteen thousand small workshops. Many of these are also homes. An underutilized workshop building can be transformed into a hostel for someone else's workers. Or a storefront business can be appended onto a small manufacturing workshop. In addition to the manufacturing workshops, there are hundreds of residences that double as retail outlets or service shops. On one stretch of street I passed shops for engine repair, hardware, phones, and food; a barber, cobbler, butcher, tailor, and pharmacy, not to mention a video game room and an aquarium fish store, all of which appeared to be appendages to residences.

A third density advantage is the location of manufacturers next door to their suppliers and retailers. Many of Dharavi's industries have minimal logistics complexity or cost. This is true of local leather- and metalwork and soap making. Whole value chains—from material inputs like scrap metal, skins, or used food oil to goods retailing of belts and soaps—are located within or adjacent to Dharavi.

With cheap land, low transportation costs, efficient utilization of property, and reduced logistics, the resident-worker-entrepreneurs of Dharavi can support their families on low wages and long hours. But Dharavi's low wages and cost of living, which provide continuing waves of migrants with a chance to start accumulating wealth, is just one part of its competitive advantage.

Another advantage combines benefits of density and unique forms of association. Over decades, chain migrations have produced a micro-settlement pattern of eighty-plus distinct ethnic and caste-based residential-industrial areas. Many of Dharavi's neighborhoods have evolved from their original villagelike settlements into units of neighborhood-based specialized production, based on the traditional occupations and business processes of their original settlers. These residential-manufacturing settlements, governed by trust-based relationships, permit the sharing of buildings and the pooling of capital and costs. They further increase the high utilization rate of space and property.

Dharavi's Kumbhar ethnic-caste community, originally migrants from Gujarat state, brought their traditional pottery making with them to Mumbai's huge market. Settling in their own residential-manufacturing encampment, they created unique forms of urban association to advance their joint interests, such as a cooperative that procures their supplies, runs local groceries, and provides day care and a clinic.

Many other chain migrations brought centuries of specialization to the city. Take the example of the leather industry. The Syed family members are cousins of Imram Khan. They own and operate a fashion leather garment company called INMA Enterprises, which makes high-quality garments that are sold around the world for tens of thousands of dollars each.[2] Syed Mushtaq Ali, one of the young executives of the Syed family business, explains how their business evolved from basic knowledge that came with them from rural Uttar Pradesh.

"Dharavi is the head office for raw skins in Maharashtra," he asserts. "Our first business here is to purchase the raw skin. Every Monday Dharavi has an organized raw skin market." He explains how unique expertise in quality skin selection developed from the migrant family's long familiarity with goats and sheep. "There is no technical study on how to buy raw skin," he says. "The grade varies widely between a male and female, the age of the animal, its history of diseases, the kind of food it eats, whether it has been pregnant. You need to know what kind of field it has been grazed in and the kinds of thornbushes that poke it when it goes there. You need a very trained eye to buy raw skin."

Mushtaq Ali's grandfather came to Dharavi in 1947 when it was still largely marshland abutted by tanneries and leather-finishing shops. "He started in raw skin trading," Mushtaq tells us, "but by the third generation here our family got into manufacturing because there was no future in raw skins alone." Stage by stage the Syeds leveraged their expertise in skins into the highest level of value-added leather manufacturing in the world—designer fashion garments.

Dharavi, in short, was designed to gain maximum advantage from density and association. But few Dharavi businesses, whether the traditional Kumbhar potter's craft or the more modern, multinational enterprise like INMA, could have grown without also developing ways to use the combined benefits of the city's scale and extension.

From the start, manufacturers and migrant laborers were dependent upon access to scaled market opportunities in the official city to its immediate south. These opportunities were extended to markets throughout India and the world via Dharavi's location between three main railway lines and its proximity to the port. A basic example of how Dharavi's urban pioneers used the city's scale and extension can be seen along its bordering highways, where dozens of Dharavi-based retailers sell garments and leather wares manufactured only feet away. At the nearby railway station, hawkers sell Dharavi-made snacks and sweets. Thus, in this basic way, Dharavi's entrepreneurs used the city's public extension infrastructure to capture a part of the bigger metropolitan and world market.

Today, Dharavi's more cosmopolitan industrialists use extension to advance the migrant city's legal inclusion in the global City. Dharavi-based garment manufacturers are linking up with major national and multinational companies, and companies like INMA Enterprises are becoming little multinationals in their own right. As they become export oriented they respond to commercial incentives to register their businesses and comply with legal requirements, altering their operations to satisfy the business standards of their buyers. This global legitimation of Dharavi enterprise—ironically in advance of any local legalization of their property ownership and provision of government services—is an important step in the evolution of slums into cities. Extension of business relationships to other cities via the port, airport, and Internet—even as Dharavi is denied the status of a city in its own country—becomes a strategy for further "upliftment," and an important way that multinational corporations exert a progressive developmental impact through their urban extension strategies.

But extension and legalization do not reduce the export company's dependence on Dharavi's unique local advantage. Mushtaq Ali of INMA Enterprises explained the synergy between the Dharavi development model and the global competitiveness of his legally registered companies. Even though regulations and the rising price of land on Dharavi's perimeter forced them to move tanning activities to distant Chennai, they have kept the raw skins, garment design, central management, and cutting and sewing operations in Dharavi. This anchors all the INMA business units in Dharavi's competitive advantages. INMA still purchases most of its skins in Dharavi, where they are cleaned and sent to Chennai. The finished leather is sent back from Chennai to Dharavi, where brothers Irshad Ali and Mushtaq Ali oversee the design and production of coats, jackets, and full outfits. Because Dharavi is so close to the international airport and four-star hotels, Mushtaq explains with a clear sense of pride, "the designers come from Europe to our shop here in Dharavi to teach our tailors how to cut properly or to stitch a collar." Finally, Irshad and his brother Anwar Ali oversee marketing of their products, which are shipped via Mumbai's port to retailers in Austria, Canada, Colombia, Denmark, Germany, Greece, Hungary, Portugal, South Africa, Spain, the UAE, the UK, and the United States. Anwar Ali himself has moved to the United States, where the Syeds have started a retail chain in Florida and Georgia cities.

"We need a place in Dharavi," concludes Mushtaq. "It would be very difficult to do this business anywhere else. The fashion apparel business is seasonal, and time is of the essence on delivery. Leather requires skilled labor at the right time, and they need to have a cheap place to live and to save time by living close by. Here no time is wasted in traveling and labor is available at a cheap price. Other leather-manufacturing companies in Bombay have had a lot of problems with labor because of the time required to move around." The migrant city itself, he knows, is a key part of his competitive strategy.

As garment making, metal smelting, pottery manufacture, and waste recycling developed, the industrial-residential neighborhoods of Dharavi built their savings. These disposable resources, rather than flowing to businesses outside of Dharavi in the form of consumer purchases, supported the development of cost-competitive tertiary services and retail. Dharavi has many jewelry shops, hotels, restaurants, and food vendors. Restaurants are busy throughout the day and night because they are highly affordable. A breakfast staple in Dharavi is the popular steamed rice cake of south India called *idly*. In Matunga, the suburb immediately to Dharavi's south, a plate of *idlis* costs 35 to 45 cents. But in Dharavi a restaurant serves a plate for less than 7 cents. A woman selling idly from a basket on her head will part with them for less than 3 cents. Similarly, a pair of jeans (which is probably manufactured in Dharavi) sells there for $8.75, compared with $12.50 in the nearby middle-class suburb of Bandra. A movie ticket costs 25 cents compared with a $2.50 ticket in a suburban movie house. Dharavi can host such an extensive hospitality and entertainment sector—unlike a typical slum—because the advantage designed into it permits so-called poor people to partake of these urban luxuries.

Building on this foundation of low-cost convenience, businesses diversified to serve Dharavi's growing internal markets. Local bakers are supported by local flour mills. Businesses that use machines are supported by neighboring repair shops. Migrant labor contractors are supported by workers' hostels. "Land owners," smugglers, and money launderers are supported by trusted local lawyers and accountants. Jewelers are supported by local smelters. Statuary makers are supplied by the local plastic recyclers. Garment makers are supported by embroidery shops.

By developing innovative ways to use the four basic economies of the city, Dharavi's settlers have together created a city of distinction. The physical layout, the culture of residential-industrial life, and the diversified markets all work together *as a system* to deliver value to residents and their communities, to local entrepreneurs, foreign companies, and worldwide customers—and to the country as a whole, if only it were to notice.

Dharavi's migrant city, in other words, is a specialized system, designed in a migrant zone of autonomy for overcoming the migrant's marginalization. The strategic priorities of the migrant city are reflected in its every aspect. It may fail to enfranchise residents or gain them legal status or public services, but it provides a powerful commercial platform for their interests. Its basic purpose is to allow very poor people from distant villages to incrementally create financial and business equity within the urban world in the shortest possible time. Dharavi residents suffer and complain of the system's shortcomings: of the migrant city's crowding, the intrusion of new arrivals, the stink of manufacturers next door, the lack of sanitation, and flooding, but they still stay to raise their children because this place is India's premier fast track to "upliftment." Dharavi, the city that migrants built, has achieved the most advanced practice of urbanism: the design, construction, and evolution of what I call a *citysystem*.

Cities are highly complex systems of advantage, which shifting alliances try to shape *to their advantage* by building and using them in often competing ways. To understand the ways that cities grow and how we can shape their overall development toward some common advantage, it is useful to distinguish the four dominant city-building approaches in the world today: (1) ad hoc city building, (2) citysystems, (3) city models, and (4) the master-planned city. Each approach focuses the activity of designing and investing in cities in very different ways and produces dramatically different outcomes.

Ad Hoc City Building

The first and most basic approach is *ad hoc city building*. In ad hoc building each incremental addition to the city is designed for the tactical purposes of individual users; each builder is concerned about how the new building works for him without relation to the others. Ad hoc city building happens everywhere, both within and without government planning guidelines. The builder of a single building (or small clusters of buildings) may have all kinds of purposes, but the most basic purpose is the utility of the building for a relatively small and selective group. A wealthy landowner, government, or philanthropist, working with an architect, may be driven to create a work of beauty, a public attraction, or a legacy. But the key thing about ad hoc city building is that this type of growth does not create any purposeful nature for the city, which is ultimately defined by the way that thoughtfully placed buildings and designed spaces create *a fixed economic advantage* for particular activities and interactions. The material "fixing" of advantageous economics of density, scale, association, and extension for particular pursuits is the raison d'être of the city, which will continue to fuel hyper-urban growth and efforts to control specific local city districts, even in times of the Internet and globalization. In the ad hoc city, however, even when the architect is intent on creating a building that fits well within the context of the buildings around it, and even when the building conforms to planning guidelines on permissible activities, heights, or landscaping, individual buildings may ultimately have little functional relationship to each other. The relationship between buildings and their activities is an ad hoc, experimental one.

Consider an intersection of two main avenues in downtown Toronto. On one corner stands a large, old stone church, a place of worship and historical continuity for the established community around it. Across the street, there is a standard-issue Harvey's fast-food restaurant of the same sort that can be found on just about any highway exit or suburban strip mall between Halifax and Los Angeles. Across from both buildings, an Econolodge budget motel has recently been built. Next to the Econolodge, a lingerie-sex shop abuts a child care center. The two suburban buildings and their businesses—the Harvey's and the Econolodge—create some small symbiosis together. They both serve the transient flow of people through the city. But they create little synergy with the other buildings, which serve different local communities. These communities are advancing their interests in this prime downtown location at potential cross-purposes to each other.

In other words, ad hoc building within the parameters of local planning rules often dilutes the total advantage of an area. Even if some authority initially establishes a greater symbiotic relationship between neighboring building uses, this relationship may dramatically change. The utility of one building can just as easily become disruptive to another, as when a noisy nightclub opens next to private homes, or a small manufacturing workshop next to a hotel or school without any arrangement between the neighboring parties. In the ad hoc city the individual building is the primary unit and not the relationship between them and the activities they host. This is the primary benefit of the ad hoc city. Ad hoc city building offers anyone who seeks a stake in a city and its markets a convenient, expedient locational foothold from which to leverage the city's advantage for individual purposes. But because it often fails to serve any cohesive, common purposes, it often dilutes that advantage along the way.

Sometimes, however, the ad hoc experiment in a district can be astoundingly successful, as in the case of Dharavi. If the builders share interests and a common understanding of a location's unique advantages— if they share a *strategy* to advance their interests through an urban location—then they can master ways to increase those advantages together, and regulate activities and construction that dilute it. They become *a community of city builders* that specializes not only in building but also in the relationships between buildings and activities that create shared economic and social benefits. In other words, they develop *a practice of urbanism.*

Citysystems

More than just a process of building, urbanism is a way that builders, users, and residents codesign, cobuild, cogovern, and combine their activities to support *ways of production and living* that develop their shared advantage. In other words, urbanism uses building to create a particular social and market ecology. The pinnacle achievement of a practice of urbanism is a citysystem, the second major city-building approach. This fundamentally different approach, by which residents, community leaders, investors, developers, and technicians cocreate the city as a community, substantially enhances the city's utility, efficiency, productivity, and emotional benefit or "sense of place" for its owners and users. Refined practices of urbanism, and the citysystems that they can create, are a means for establishing the material space, resource metabolism, and social relations to consistently achieve a community's strategic ambitions in the City, much as a complex industrial facility serves a manufacturing company or an ecological habitat supports a species community.

Now we see that a place like Dharavi is not just a dense collection of buildings or a low-income district. It is the physical home of an urbanist community, which supports distinctive kinds of production and trade, of governance and society, and of resource use and environmental conditions that work as a coherent whole to build that community's advantage. Dharavi may have started in ad hoc fashion, as a slum built shack by shack. But it evolved into a community of practice with implicit knowledge of the spatial relationships that create shared advantage. When you enter a citysystem it is hard not to notice the liveliness and energy relative to adjacent city areas. The bazaar districts of many Middle Eastern cities; the ancient madrassah districts that were adapted by Europeans into the modern university town citysystem; the mixed industrial-residential-commercial neighborhoods that dominated European and North American cities in their first century of industrialization; central business districts and port districts the world over—all are examples of other citysystems produced by unique urbanistic traditions. These traditions define how people conduct business, work together, raise their families, allocate time, socialize, and even court each other.

Consider the *mahalle* citysystem of Turkey, adapted throughout the Middle East and South Asia. From the outside, the mahalle seems like a straightforward residential community. But enter into its life and one discovers a distinct, very localized society. It reveals an urbanism with roots in the Ottoman era, which solved the problem of integrating diverse migrant ethnic groups into a city as relatively self-reliant, disciplined units. The mahalle system adapted ancient village modes of living into a solution for urban life. Mahalles in Turkey still often manage their own water systems and energy facilities. They oversee and organize social life, including marriage, the birthing of children, and festivals. They typically have a local mosque, coffee- or teahouse and grocery. Traditionally each has a leader or "headman" who manages conflicts and acts as liaison with the local government to represent the mahalle's interests and ensure its compliance to law. When I was working with the municipal administration in Bursa, Turkey, in the 1990s, they were reviving this headman role to more effectively engage conservative, lower-income mahalle communities in planning the city's new infrastructure investments and services. The mahalle is far from just a residential development. It is a foundation unit of urban society.

Oddly, we poorly understand the workings of citysystems in any explicit detail, even though we depend on them so fundamentally. In the 1960s–1970s, for instance, governments, planners, and developers throughout North America destroyed central business districts and old industrial-residential neighborhoods, replacing them with marginally viable, master-planned convention districts, government centers, office complexes, and parking lots. Four decades later, many of these same areas remain urban dead zones. The same folly has been repeated nearly everywhere, particularly destroying the citysystems of the poor, like China's *hutongs* and southeast Asia's *kampungs*. Our lack of understanding of the value produced by citysystems hobbles the emerging City.

Citysystems generally grow organically, not by technocratic planning and business investment. Their design is a historical product of trial-and-error by a community of users as they work to optimize the city's density, scale, association, and extension for strategic purposes. Therefore, citysystems are rarely standardized or produced with the suddenness of tract developments and master-planned districts, which dominate the City's explosive growth today. Yet we seem to understand the logic of their replication, like a cultural genetic code. Once discovered, the citysystem "wheel" does not have to be reinvented in ad hoc fashion. City-building communities everywhere are working to evolve slums into migrant cities, master-planned office clusters into mixed-use central business districts, and even monocultural residential suburbs into mixed-use neighborhoods. They succeed if we give them a chance. Architects, engineers, planners, and developers play roles along the way, but they can't design citysystems alone. Consortiums of professionals and companies can build whole new cities if they have the resources, but they cannot install a citysystem for a client. A citysystem has to be designed and brought to life by the community of people who will use it as a hyper-productive system to achieve their own ambitious common purpose. The citysystem is the most potent way to build a city to gain strategic advantage in an urbanizing world because it is the product of a community, rich or poor, that has mastered a very robust practice of urbanism.

Ad hoc building and citysystems, for their considerable differences, are designed and built by their users. But most new urban landscape in the world today is being built in a dramatically different fashion: residential tracts, retail malls, and office parks are typically built *for* anonymous groups of generic users. The bestselling business strategy guru C. K. Prahalad has counseled companies everywhere about the importance of "cocreating" new products and business models with consumers. But the dominant approaches used in today's government and business-led city development lack such a user focus. Their two main city-building approaches offer uniformity, fungibility, basic utility, and rapid, scaled urban growth, but they do not offer *urbanism* to urbanizing societies. They supply offices but cannot build economic communities, construct houses but not homes. They build hot-desks and lodgings for the City's extending networks of migrant workers, whether professional or poor, but not the vital ecology of combined, optimized density, scale, and association that gives stable root to urban life.

City Models

The third approach to city building, what I call *city modeling*, is designed for its own distinct purpose. City models are standardized units of cities, like shopping malls or suburban residential subdivisions, which have been cost-optimized as building-industry *products*. They are the joint practice of urban planners, engineers, architects, financiers, and property developers to create and efficiently replicate a particular kind of zone or neighborhood over and over using a tightly designed, profit-yielding blueprint. They are not built *with* their future tenants and users but are built *for* them.

The precursors to the city model drew upon historic traditions of urbanism, such as the American suburban towns of the early and middle twentieth century, with their villagelike character, or the mahalle-like residential colonies of India. These were often conceived as mixed-use districts and supported the evolution of stable communities to maintain and improve them. Today's industrial-scale city models generally abandoned those urbanist traditions. They were a logical commercial response to the compartmentalization of cities and urban life into single-purpose residential, commercial, and industrial zones, and they served the booming demand for new urban spaces. Along the way, they have replaced downtown retail citysystems with shopping mall "town centers," neighborhood citysystems with housing complexes, and research district citysystems with office "parks."

I call these developments city models, because they combine a city plan for the spatial arrangement of a large group of buildings and a business model for its delivery as a standardized new unit of the city. City modeling is a powerful practice because it combines the know-how of spatial design with that of business—finance, risk management, labor contracting, intellectual property management, logistics, project management, and marketing—to make replication and growth efficient and quickly scalable. City models try to serve two masters: the builders who seek to make a predictable profit from their construction and government agencies that seek rapid, regulated growth of their city (often to increase the local tax base). The designs, infrastructure, and technology embedded in each city model are crafted to profitably provide just enough utility and attraction to target user-consumers. But how the city model works with the rest of the city, and the economics and relationships it creates for its users, is not decided with the end users themselves. The model's total demand for infrastructure and services, and its maintenance and user costs, are vaguely understood and often marginally considered. As a matter of business process, city models rarely foster organized user communities to address these demands. Like fast food, the city model provides individual users with convenience and predictability within a limited range of options but not with any efficient opportunity to shape or evolve their city district to their further advantage.

The Master-Planned City

Fourth among approaches is the master-planned city or city district. Although master-planned city building can include provisions for both ad hoc and city model construction, the typical point of master-planned development is to create a special purpose area—such as a government administrative center or university campus—that reflects the unique vision or philosophy of the builders (and often *not* an existing group of residents or city users).

The master-planned city has generally been the practice of governments with enough concentrated authority and resources to determine a prescribed, detailed spatial organization of activities in a large urban area. In a world of market-driven development, the master-planned city is increasingly rare, replaced by the more expedient and less politically demanding city model. But prominent examples of contemporary master planning remain: in the capital cities of Brasilia, Chandigarh, and Malaysia's new Putrajaya; and in new satellite towns of Shanghai, Singapore, and Stockholm. Even more plentiful are the master-planned street grids and infrastructure systems that can shape the urban form that arises from the piecemeal development of the ad hoc city. Master planning can achieve great social purposes when the dogmas of planners or architects about the "right" or "best" city are outweighed by deep insight about the city's users and their values and strategies, as in Stockholm. At worst, master planning creates a sterile city, which feels and functions more as a huge monument in which people are allowed to work and live than as a living system. Master planning can produce large-scale development that is more tailored to local needs and strategies than the generic city model. But it can also so overdesign the city on behalf of a capital-intensive idea or interest that it leaves little room for users to reshape the city's spatial economics to serve their emerging strategies for advantage.

As we enter the final phase of the Great Migration, which will see two billion more people joining the world's cities by 2035, we need to understand the strategic implications of the city-building approaches used to house and employ them. Will the migrants' own strategies for "upliftment" be factored in the cities to be built for them? Will they play a role themselves, as city builders and coinvestors, in the design and construction of their cities, or will they be forced to choose between flimsy self-built shanties or low-quality government high-rise slums until they can join the ranks of city model consumers? Will the citysystems mastered over centuries be sacrificed and overlooked by technocratic planners, industrial city-builders, and governments fixed on sheer growth and product sales turnover?

One thing is clear. If we aim to build cities—and a City—on robust economic footings, and if we seek urban citizens who are committed their cities and urban leaders who can make cities achieve great purposes, then we need to find a way to accelerate the development of new urbanisms and the citysystems they create. Dharavi, teaches us that. Today we specialize in building cityscapes with little attention to their total productivity and efficiency. They host growing populations of city consumers instead of trained urban citizens and urbanist communities, creating declining common interest in the city. We are at great risk in the Urban Revolution's final phase if we ignore the migrant city's lessons.

PART II

The City Adrift

CHAPTER 7

The Final Phase

Two Billion New City Dwellers in Search of a New Urbanism

There is no better place to witness the struggle between the efficient scalability of the city model and the master-planned district on the one hand, and the empowering productivity of urbanism and its citysystems on the other, than in the free-for-all taking place in Asia's cities. Asia is the Urban Revolution's ultimate frontier. Between 2010 and 2035, more than a billion people will be added to Asia's city populations, accounting for more than 60 percent of world urban population growth during this period. United Nations projections indicate that there will be 3.3 billion Homo urbanis in Asia by 2050—equivalent to the total world urban population today. Importantly, half of Asia's urban growth will be in cities with less than five hundred thousand people—cities whose names and ground-level conditions are still largely unfamiliar to the world and its major institutions.

The unpredictable outcomes of urban development over the next decades, in particular in Asia, place a question mark over every global political, economic, environmental, and security scenario. We already know that the energy demand of these growing cities, if built and managed using current approaches and technologies, will obliterate the rest of the world's efforts to reduce greenhouse-gas emissions. We also know that the continent's lowest-income segments will dominate urban growth. Today about one third of the global City's residents lives in slums; those percentages are much higher in the fast-urbanizing countries of Asia and Africa. More than half of China's growth in urban population—a projected increase of 420 million people by 2050—will come from the migration of poor people from rural areas. A world history of urban revolution now allows us to surmise the turmoil that could arise if new urban majorities are left marginalized, underserved, and disenfranchised like the migrant pioneers before them.

This is a profound challenge for Asian leaders. Do they respond to the quantitative pressures of urban growth by using the most expedient (and profit-yielding) forms of city building: the city model and master-planned city? Or do they seize the qualitative opportunity to empower their new urban majorities as city builders, engaging them in a culturally rooted urbanism and the hyper-productive citysystems it can create? Do they focus now on expedient building or on creating a truly advanced, stable, robust urban society?

Not long ago I had occasion to reflect with a group of international urban experts and the political leaders, planners, and engineers of some thirty Asian cities about the particular problems they faced in managing urban growth. The group included senior leaders from Hanoi, Hue, and Ho Chi Minh City in Vietnam; Cebu, Naga, and Iloilo cities in the Philippines; Bangkok, Phuket, Rayong, and Uttaradit in Thailand; Hyderabad, Indore, and Kolkata in India; Kuala Lumpur in Malaysia; and Shanghai in China. They represented the frontline leadership of the Urban Revolution's final phase.

These local leaders shared many concerns: expanding and financing infrastructure to keep pace with growing populations; securing water and energy supplies, which are often already rationed; enfranchising migrant communities into the formal economy; managing pollution; and securing advantage for their city in the larger global City economy. During our first meeting they received expert input on their plans and made commitments on specific, measurable achievements, agreeing to report back in a year's time.[1] But no one broached the bigger challenge that made everyone feel overwhelmed beneath the bravado of commitments: Could we muster the power and resources to address a legacy of urban problems alongside redoubled urban growth? Could we find some middle way between the profiteering city-building approaches that increasingly dominate local markets and culturally responsive, efficient, and more affordable traditions of urbanism?

One of the most remarkably transformed cities in that group was Kuala Lumpur, among the richest and most developed cities in its region. Anyone who had a chance to visit Kuala Lumpur during the Asian Tiger boom of the mid-1990s would have noticed the fateful city building taking place there. Unlike most Asian cities—and unlike most in the world—Kuala Lumpur had both great resources and concentrated power at its disposal, putting it in a unique position to meet the challenges of the final phase. But the country's strongman prime minister, Mahathir Mohamad, wanted to make Kuala Lumpur "world-class" more than he wanted a real Malay urbanism. The most expedient way to keep up with the Joneses was master-planned and monumental ad hoc city building. Mohamad's local business allies and Kuala Lumpur's technical planners and engineers joined with design and construction firms from Japan, Australia, Europe, and North America to profitably gratify the leader's city-building ambitions: a new international airport, new highways, and a monorail line, and the construction of a master-planned capital city, Putrajaya, and the Petronas Towers, then the world's tallest skyscraper.

The Putrajaya project was Mohamad's most ambitious undertaking. Like earlier feats of modernist master planning—India's Chandigarh or Brazil's Brasilia—Putrajaya's urban genetic code has no organic force within it to evolve any kind of citysystem. It is an architectural theme park of foreign architectural forms and designs with token Islamic, "tropical," and Asian motifs added to them. Its grand boulevards and squares are theoretically made for the public and pedestrian life of an aspiring democracy, like Washington's Mall, but so far they have only provided a functioning habitat for cars. Its residential districts reflect a barracks-like rationality. Somehow, Putrajaya is "home" for more than three hundred thousand people. But it was not designed or constructed with its residents' ambitions or their economic means in mind. It is not the kind of city the average Malaysian knows how to invest in or even to maintain. There is nothing truly Malaysian in it. For all its novelty, it disengages Malaysian citizens from the basic purpose of any city: as a place in which to advance strategies *of their own making*.

Like the Petronas Towers, Putrajaya's primary designed purpose seems to be to upstage and awe—and in many ways it does. But its reference point is the master-planned cities of China, Japan, and Korea, which themselves are more West-imitating (and Western firm–employing) megaprojects than portents of confident, culturally rooted new Asian urbanisms. They are a rejection of the region's best urban traditions. Their subsidized splendor and sterility will sooner or later burden their nations' balance sheets, concentrating the continent's affluent residents, from Shanghai to Dubai, leaving the poor majority to try their own hands at city building on the margins, or to be relocated into new low-quality satellite towns, so shoddily constructed that they collapse in an earthquake's or a monsoon's instant. They suggest no solid foundation for long-term urban advantage.

But even with such concentrated power, Mahathir Mohamad could not dominate his expanding cityscape. The wholesale importation of city models only further transformed Kuala Lumpur into a foreign land. Developments with Anglo-American designs, road patterns, landscaping, and residential functions have claimed the territories of slums, forests, and every city periphery. For all Mohamad's pronouncements about a distinctive "Malay Path" to development, much of the city's emerging land use, infrastructure, energy and water consumption, and pollution and waste production patterns, and even its lifestyles, were being fixed by foreign development consortia to resemble Newport Beach and Sydney. Plot by plot the developers negotiated the replacement of Kuala Lumpur's *kampung* village citysystems, Malaysia's equivalent of the *mahalle*, that once accommodated, served, and governed a substantial part of the city population. For all the central planning, the growth of Kuala Lumpur was creating a total picture that no one really planned or understood. And then the crisis hit.

There are many explanations for the Asian financial crisis of 1997, which halved global economic growth over the subsequent two years. Most analyses found a smoking gun in the speculative, overfinanced urban real estate markets of the Asian tigers. It is not enough to say that the banks that financed the building boom were corrupt or poorly managed. There was a paradigmatic flaw in the approach to development. Governments, sophisticated international firms, local businesspeople, and residents were all making city-building and city-buying decisions without any kind of urbanism to discipline the city's foundation economics, without a way to create or even understand the emerging economies of density, scale, and association in the city. Approaching city building like a string of independent projects, local leaders confused the crass economics of construction with the nuanced socioeconomic development of a city as an economic system. As a result, they had no forecasting models or even data to track the total profit-and-loss and balance sheet of the cities they built. The builder-users of a citysystem are keenly attuned to its full costs, (in)efficiencies, productivity, and revenue potentials, and they constantly debate and problem-solve about them. Master planners and city model builders track their budgets and the metrics of their own financial statements but rarely measure the evolving economics of the city as a whole. They generally do their work and move on. Even in a single city like Kuala Lumpur, investors did not know how much was truly being invested or have a full picture of the sources, uses, and terms of finance. This free-for-all of city building, no matter how much central power or industrial investment, was nothing more than a mildly managed chaos with no real strategy to create some total, stable value.

Rapid city building devoid of any mature urbanism can create a substantial drain on metropolitan and national economies. Economist Edward Leman discovered this through an extensive study of urban form and economic productivity in Chinese metropolitan areas.[2] A great deal of urban growth in China is concentrated in dispersed, high-rise satellite towns that have sprouted out of former villages or rural market towns on a city's historic periphery. These satellite cities do not colocate interdependent economic activities (i.e., providing economies of proximity and concentration). They lack efficient infrastructure, have limited access to metrowide markets, and have sizable marginalized migrant populations. The new, dispersed metropolitan areas of Chengdu and Chongqing, for instance, produced $12 million in gross domestic product (GDP) per square kilometer in 2000. The more integrated metropolitan areas of Guangzhou and Shanghai produced $54 million in GDP per square kilometer. In contrast, on a purchasing-power basis, the practiced urbanisms of Tokyo, Paris, and New York produced around $180 million GDP per square kilometer in 2000. Measures like these do not accurately capture the nuanced economics of each city, but they suggest a productivity gap between cities built on a foundation of local urbanism and the giant construction sites that pass for cities today.[3]

In the final phase, this disconnect between fast-changing local urban ground realities, on the one hand, and the booming import/export of development finance, city models, and global construction supply chains, on the other, creates a unique vulnerability. It prevents the development of local market intelligence and sociopolitical feedback required to make any system efficient and stable. It compromises the emerging forms of urbanism, designed to respond to local social and economic problems—which can be achieved only by designing cities bottom-up from their roots and reflecting local market conditions.

The 2003 severe acute respiratory syndrome (SARS) crisis illustrates the consequences of the disconnect between global systems and evolving urban ground realities. On the one hand, the international community has created an unparalleled infrastructure for global disease monitoring and response through the World Health Organization, affiliated national centers for disease control, and a vast Internet-enabled expert network. It took this global response system only months to prepare a full genetic analysis of the SARS virus genome and the hundreds of mutations it went through to become a communicable human disease. But the very local conditions at the root of the epidemic in China's Guangdong Province caught the world by surprise—and vulnerable.

The SARS coronavirus and recent strains of avian influenza virus (e.g., H5N1) first spread to humans in the Pearl River Delta city-region. The emerging delta city has an utterly unique urban form and social ecology. The main cities of the region—Guangzhou, Shenzhen, Foshan, Zhongshan, Jiangmen, and Hong Kong—are expanding together over an ancient agricultural landscape and society. Satellite images of the region evince an urban-rural fabric with no defined boundary between the expanding "city" and the "rural" parts of the region. Farming and animal husbandry intrude into urban areas and vice versa, through both spatial arrangement and culture, like an interlocking puzzle. One group of Chinese epidemiologists studying the initial SARS outbreaks emphasized the constant movement of people between the agricultural and urban areas as a factor in the spread of the virus. The Chinese residency registration system, which marginalizes rural migrants as "temporary residents," exacerbated this movement between urban and rural life.[4]

Local traditions also played a major part. Even prior to its recent urban boom, the Pearl River Delta was exporting flu viruses around the world, including the virus in the 1918 flu epidemic that killed an estimated fifty to one hundred million people worldwide. There are two major reasons. The first is the tradition of live animal markets in the cities, which facilitate daily interaction between city dwellers and farm families with their living chickens, quail, pigeons, geese, ducks, and exotic wild fowl (and in the case of SARS, civet cats). Different species are caged together for days, allowing a virus from one farm and species to spread and mutate among the animals of many others. Added to this, there are distinct customs of purchasing, such as the practice of determining the quality of a live hen through close examination and smelling, exposing the consumer to the animal's bodily secretions. As one study tactfully puts it, "Eleven early reported [SARS] cases in the communities took animal-related positions. Face-to-face contacts with infected droplets were the main transmission route."[5] In spite of strict measures by the Hong Kong city government to control these practices after that city's bird-influenza outbreak in 1997, they continue as the tradition and business model of agricultural marketing throughout the region.[6]

The second reason is the centrality of Hong Kong not only as a global commercial hub but as the long-standing center of Chinese chain migration. Movements between the upper delta regions and Hong Kong give viruses ready pathways for reaching the world. In hindsight, the exponential increase in rural-urban interaction and interspecies viral exchanges in this one city-region automatically increased viral exchanges across an extended global network of cities, for which Hong Kong serves as a daily hub. This could have been monitored and modeled. To give a sense of the scale of the region's animal diversity at the time of the SARS outbreak, the BBC News reported:

> An official in the southern province of Guangdong said thousands of markets, restaurants and kitchens had been raided to check for protected animal species. The Xinhua news agency

said about 15,000 animal fairs and 70,000 hotels and restaurants had been raided. Officials are reported to have confiscated more than 800,000 endangered animals and arrested 1,428 suspects. Among the animals found were snakes, pangolins, anteaters, cranes, turtles and lizards.[7]

Added to this, the area's crowded, poorly ventilated housing, along with the hot, humid local climate, likely increased aerosol transmission of the virus in the cities. Studies now trace the first human case of SARS to an agricultural area in Foshan in November 2002.[8] Eventually, about fifteen hundred SARS fatalities were recorded in the region.

The source of global transmission was a few infected individuals who visited Hong Kong, from which point networks of association carried the virus to thirty nations in a matter of months: a Chinese emigrant returning to Toronto and her local church congregation; a Beijing medical worker returning to his central China village; traveling businessmen working in the cities of Asia.

Given the epidemiological history of the region, it seems strange that the international community, working with Chinese and local authorities, would not be constantly monitoring and managing it as a special health-risk zone, much as it has been designated a special economic zone for global production and commerce. If we had understood the networked movements of people within the urban region and between other city-regions, we could have better anticipated the routes of the disease's spread. But lacking an urban systems approach to the region and to global affairs, we only took note, once again, of our new reality through the surprise of a crisis that cost thousands of lives, spanned thirty countries, and brought Asian tourism and business travel to a halt at an estimated economic cost of $30 billion to $40 billion.[9]

In the final phase, our global crises will increasingly emerge from such urban blind spots. The subprime mortgage crisis in the United States in 2007–2008 is another case in point—a global financial crisis with distinctly urban roots that could have been arrested had we been paying closer attention to changing conditions in fast-growing cities.

Postmortems of the mortgage crisis generally focus on poor financial industry standards and regulations, but the debacle's basic math involves a multitrillion-dollar gap between paper valuations of bundled loan portfolios and their real estate collateral, on one hand, and the profit and loss statements and balance sheets of borrowers whose economic health was tied to the growing diseconomies of whole regions being transformed by city models. In other words, the underlying problem was a global financial system disconnected from the changing economics of a continent that was rapidly urbanizing with little sense of urbanism.

Cities with strong traditions of urbanism saw this disconnect early and took action. As early as 2000, Chicago passed laws to regulate aggressive "predatory lending" practices that were glutting local markets with capital for high-risk real estate purchases (see chapter 14). But these practices went unheeded in most urban jurisdictions, particularly those in California, Colorado, Florida, and Nevada that were dominated by suburban city model growth. For a while predatory lending remained a specialty of small lenders, focused on credit-starved low-income districts. But once the short-term viability of such subprime lending was demonstrated, larger banks adapted the practices and scaled their offering to middle-class customers for purchases of a new generation of city model products. Portfolios of these high-risk mortgages were built up and traded in the financial system without consideration of the broader economic fundamentals of these models and their consumers, which would determine their ultimate underlying value. In other words, banks not only stopped being prudent about the credit-worthiness of their borrowers, but made sweeping assumptions about the economic health of the urban regions upon which their borrowers depended, even as sprawling city model growth was changing those economics fundamentally.

The cost side of the United States' new urban profit and loss statement was rising rapidly. City model homes were much larger, more energy-intensive, and had more facilities and "plant and equipment," such as central air-conditioning, central vacuuming systems, swimming pools, and outdoor barbecue kitchens. New homes were located ever farther away from employment areas, increasing their owners' mobility costs. As a result, households had to increase the size of their automobile fleets. The per capita capacity of road, water, sewerage, and energy infrastructure had to be increased, and declining economies of density exacerbated the costs. Labor markets had become more flexible, increasing employment churn and related transition costs.

Meanwhile, the revenue side of the urban profit and loss was declining. Federal and state government subsidies for infrastructure construction and maintenance (relative to capacity and serviced land area) were on a steady decline. In many states, local tax revenues were stagnant. Real household incomes and traditional employment benefits were also declining year by year.

The result was a declining net economic equation, which no one was systematically calculating. Builders and home buyers invested in sprawling suburban tracts or high-rise condominium developments without factoring the full costs of operation, maintenance, and lifestyles—and how they would hit borrowers' pocketbooks along with high predatory mortgage rates. Local governments permitted new construction projects without a full-costing of their infrastructure and service requirements.

Other major crisis events are brewing today in the world's coastal areas and earthquake zones, similarly without the disciplines of any urbanism. Authorities, builders, insurers, and development finance agencies are allowing use of generic and inadequate building products in high-risk areas rather than tailoring building materials, designs, infrastructures, and construction to reduce risk. Every year, millions are displaced by disasters along the world's urbanizing coastlines. One in eight city dwellers lives in very low coastal areas, and 75 percent of them (some 300 million people) are concentrated in Asia.[10] International development banks already report that they spend more than half their funds on disaster response and reconstruction, increasingly in urban areas.[11] It is clear that high-risk areas like these require a locally adapted urbanism, not a generic city model approach.

These crises and risks reflect a fundamental disconnect between the development of individual cities and the development of the global City that must be resolved if we are to build a sustainable urban future in the final phase. In the Urban Revolution's preceding phase, strategies for urban investment and migration focused on building advantage in individual cities. Local alliances literally fought each other for development control over specific locations. Civic leaders debated the best way to build their cities to compete effectively against others. But with suc-

cess, the once-local companies, migrant communities, political movements, and criminal groups leveraged their cities' advantage to connect
to markets, business models, and alliances in other cities worldwide.
The modus operandi of urban growth, in other words, steadily shifted
from individual city building to building the City. Along the way, the
foundation economics of local density, scale, and association have been
taken for granted.

The City's development is now dominated by expedient city models, produced by a globalized city-building industry made up of transnational developers and their supply chains. Their products and projects
support the amassing flows of the City: its movements of people, finance, employers, and goods. This industry builds the infrastructure
of extension (e.g., highways and airports). Their office parks and corporate campuses serve organizations whose markets are not local but
are the City. Their high-turnover condominiums and bedroom communities house the worker-commuters of the office parks and corporate campuses. Their big-box and franchise-filled avenues serve the
commuters, who spend much of their lives traversing the developing
cityscape.

Meanwhile, urban advantage and economic fundamentals are still anchored *in places*—in particular, in the efficiencies and productivity of
the citysystem. Their development is disciplined by a local urbanism
that constantly adapts building design, urban form, markets, and community norms to new opportunities and challenges, producing business districts that incubate new industries, arts districts that generate
new culture, neighborhoods that produce social continuity and new
forms of association.

Today, in cities everywhere, the expedient building of the City and
the productive development of citysystems work at cross-purposes and
make our cities incoherent. Crises, not to mention day-to-day gridlock
and inefficiency, emerge from their competing investments, designs,
governance, management, and social norms for city building. In the
years ahead, the economics of the city model, scaled and replicable,
must be reconciled with the economics of the citysystem—creative and
socially responsive. Some of the world's most successful cities have resolved to confront this challenge directly as they rebuild (see chapter
13). Success at this endeavor is a prerequisite for evolving today's form

of globalization, defined by instability, transience, and ungovernable flows, into an efficient, stable, and ultimately sustainable citysystem.

To understand the global consequences of what is emerging within a single city, one has to master the city's subtle, local languages of established or emerging urbanism. This practice of observation and study has recently emerged as a new discipline—*urbanology,* the analysis of social, spatial, and economic relations within a city to explain its workings and evolution.[12]

Gabriel Britto and Prema Gopalan are the kind of ground-level urbanologists needed to understand the unexpected events incubating in our cities. By nature they are perennial sleuths, constantly exploring their seemingly unintelligible home city, Mumbai. Dressed modestly, they enter every crack and corner of the city. They bump into political bosses at tea stalls and gather facts from the city's best-known figures in planning, architecture, and social work. Through relationships developed over decades with local drivers and street traders, they are introduced to informal-sector business clusters, criminal dons, illicit trades, unique labor contracting practices, and disasters past and waiting to happen. Then they disappear into the rural hinterlands, working in regions that have exported families to the city for decades or studying the livelihoods and lifestyles of a particular caste or tribal group. They connect the dots that span the city's multidimensional reach, always tentative in their conclusions, always humble before the city's many-headed complexity, revealing a city that cannot be known from any government desk or corporate headquarters, viewed from satellites, or explained through a computerized geographic information system.

For more than a decade, Britto and his collaborator Molly Charles studied the underworld of Mumbai to understand how to deal with drug addiction in the city. Through the United Nations, they then joined with counterparts in cities around the world to study how transnational criminal organizations rose from the local histories of urban zones of autonomy and extended into a worldwide economic sector.[13] Recent estimates place the annual revenues of transnational criminal organizations in trillions of dollars, creating an entirely new, unpredictable force in the City's final phase.[14]

Mumbai's low-income districts have played an important part in that story. Their smuggling and money-laundering organizations now constitute a multibillion dollar industry establishing one of Mumbai's key roles in the global City economy. So powerful are some Mumbai criminal "companies" and so critical are their role in global markets for gold, diamonds, drugs, and black-market finance that foreign governments—the United Kingdom, the United Arab Emirates, and Pakistan included—appear to turn a blind eye to the offshore operations of Mumbai's dons in their cities.[15]

As with most global industries, there is a very local story. To excel as a center of smuggling, Mumbai needed certain infrastructure. The port city—including its harbor, dockyards, port facilities, and all the businesses and labor contracting systems that support them—developed as Mumbai's first citysystem. When the port itself was modernized in the eighteenth century, Mumbai became western India's premier trading center with the Arabian Gulf, Persia, Africa, and China. Opium was among its major exports.

The British East India Company established an opium trade from the port in the early nineteenth century to solve its balance-of-trade problems with China; Mumbai shipped thousands of tons of opium to China each year. But the British could not entirely control the lucrative trade. More than a hundred Indian (non-British) merchants and firms joined the local opium trade in the early nineteenth century.[16] Opium trading, as Britto and Charles put it, made Mumbai "a paradise for smugglers."

Following independence from Britain, the new Indian government's attempts to control Mumbai's fervid markets further contributed to the hothouse environment for specialized criminal operations. For every new tax and import control the government imposed, a corresponding black market blossomed. Liquor prohibition in the 1950s–1960s created a market for bootleg alcohol. To serve this market, Dharavi criminal entrepreneurs leveraged the same locational economics as the tannery industry before them, making Dharavi a center of bootleg alcohol production and smuggling.

This business developed the capacity and competencies for additional profit centers. Currency exchange controls created large-scale demand for money laundering. Import restrictions and tariffs on gold, gems, electronics, and pharmaceuticals spawned their own massive smuggling operations. Local controls on property development and rents created markets for extralegal harassment, hired killing, and "facilitation." The lack of credit for film production led to the establishment of underground finance for the Indian film industry, and a visible presence of recognized criminal operators in Bollywood.

By seeking control of so many aspects of the city's economic life, the government encouraged black markets large and diverse enough to support the growth of integrated criminal operations. Specialists in smuggling, for instance, made partnerships with specialists in money laundering and property development. Extortion and money laundering, in turn, required nontraceable currency, supporting specialized smuggling operations in gold, India's parallel currency. During the 1990s, annual volumes of gold smuggled into Mumbai reached scores of tons, worth hundreds of millions of dollars.

Added to these core sectors of the criminal economy, operators required specialized business services like insurance policies for smuggled goods, political bribery, and security forces. The growth in the underground economy and its criminal "companies" changed the operating requirements and cost structure for business in the legal economy. For instance, private security agencies in Mumbai were reaping $380 million in annual revenues in 2001 and employing two hundred thousand people, roughly five times the Mumbai police force.

Another contributor to the growth of criminal industry in Mumbai was the persistence of zones of autonomy in strategic city locations. The workers' tenements near the port and maturing slums to the old city's north provided the underworld's equivalent of business incubators, office parks, training grounds, and recruitment centers all in one.

India's first, big-time mafia dons during the 1960s and 1970s—Haji Mastan, Varadharajan, and Karim Lala—all built their syndicates in tight-knit ethnic tenements and slum districts in centrally located Dongri, Dadar, and Dharavi. These areas were close to the dockyards, where their core smuggling business was executed. They were adjacent to the textile mills, which offered a constant supply of new recruits from low-income households. And they were near the marshlands and tidal mangroves of Dharavi and Mahim Creek, where illicit liquor producers and goods runners had established operations.

Varadharajan established Mumbai's first major gang in Dharavi. Building throughout the 1960s with business units in bootlegging, smuggling of gold and other goods, extortion, and gambling, Varadharajan ushered in a period in Dharavi's history where criminality, and not just informality, was a central part of the young migrant city's economy.

This old world of crime still exists in Mumbai but has been eclipsed by a new stage in criminal organization. The next generation of bosses, or *bhais*, such as Dawood Ibrahim and his D Company, rose to power in the late 1970s and 1980s after police crackdowns and slum clearances destabilized the first-generation gangs. Not unlike what happened with MS-13 in Los Angeles, police disruption of territorial control catalyzed extension. The new generation of bhais still built their companies in tenement and slum areas, but intercompany feuds and police crackdowns pushed operations like that of Ibrahim offshore, creating networks across the cities of south and west Asia.

After religious riots and police crackdowns in 1992–1993 rocked Ibrahim's Mumbai territories, a new generation of operators developed yet another strategy for criminal advantage. Arun Gawli, Hitendra Thakur, and Pappu Kilani dominated not only the commerce and real estate development of lower-income districts but also secured election as their districts' representatives to the state legislature, further blurring the line between legitimate and criminal governance.

Criminal companies like these are successful, and can constrain the opportunities of legal multinational companies, because they have truly learned the local language of their cities, constantly tending their local criminal urbanism even as they expand worldwide. They manage not just businesses but urban territories. They develop economic bonds with police, politicians, and residents to create governance processes independent of the official city. As Neeraj Kumar, joint director of India's Central Bureau of Investigation, puts it, "What makes organized crime organized is its ability to serve as a government . . . providing services, allocating resources and territories and settling disputes."[17]

Mumbai may seem like an extreme case, but it is not. The Cali and Medellín drug cartels of Colombia, which expanded into transnational operations, carry their city names for good reason. The triads of Hong Kong have their own histories, business methods, and culture entwined with the urbanism of their city. The city of Fuzhou, China, has fostered a globalized industry in human smuggling.[18] Many other local criminal organizations with unique histories exist in the cities of Russia, Armenia, Azerbaijan, Chechnya, Vietnam, Thailand, Syria, Nigeria, Brazil, Peru, Mexico, the United States, and other countries, and they maintain both local criminal urbanisms and transnational organizations to secure and manage the markets of the City. As they extend, they undermine the progressive possibilities of our cities and the City. Where we fail to link the growth of formal industry with progressive urbanism—to increase everyone's access to transparent markets, to reduce poverty, and to increase environmental sustainability—the urbanisms of criminality are able to flourish.

Since those sessions with Asian city leaders in 2002–2003, I have casually tracked their cities' development via National Aeronautic and Space Administration (NASA) satellite photos. It is a crude way to imagine the complexities and vulnerabilities developing in these places but in some ways not unlike the distance from which governments and their international agencies, corporate executives, and consulting firms make judgments about the emerging urban world.

When I look at photographs of Kuala Lumpur I check first to see what is happening to the slums and *kampungs*. During our meetings in 2002, Kuala Lumpur's chief engineer announced plans to re-house forty-five thousand of the estimated fifty thousand (officially recognized) slum residents by 2005. The official count of slum dwellers in Kuala Lumpur has gone down steadily from 243,000 in 1980 (26 percent of the total population) to 150,000 in 1990 (13 percent) to 50,000 (4 percent) in 2000 to make way for the grander, modernizing developments. But in 2004, Malaysia's new prime minister called the goal of a slum-free Kuala Lumpur an "elusive objective" because of constant immigration required by the city's most recent construction and manufacturing boom. An estimated 2.6 million legal and illegal foreign workers were in Malaysia in 2008—25 percent of the total workforce. Reports cite a growing number of squatter settlements being protected through extortion payments to enforcement officers in spite of the official city plans. But when I look from the telescopic perspective of the satellite I cannot see where all these people are settling. There are no expanding slum districts for the eye to find. Hundreds of thousands of people seem missing from the picture in more than one way, a black hole in our measurement and understanding of the city, waiting to catch us by surprise.

In contrast, large patches of new, affluent city model development stand out in the photos. They are glaring yellow-white patches of exposed earth, so visible from on high, covering many square miles. To the local viewer, I imagine them as described by this promotion from a local real estate company:

> A Gated and Guarded bungalow development nestled cozily on the hillside of Bukit Kemuning Golf & Country Resort. Inspired by Australian contemporary suburban living, these bungalow homes will impress you with their beautifully designed facade, well planned internal floor layout and perfect blend of landscape. Expected to launch early 2007.[19]

On another open patch, the journals of the global city-building industry inform us, a new ninety-acre mini-suburban "city" will appear. It will contain "3,000 residences, hotels with a total 1,600 rooms, 3.8 million sq ft of offices, 3.9 million sq ft of retail space, 500,000 sq ft of conference facilities, a 350,000-sq-ft medical centre and 150,000 sq ft for a cultural centre"—a city model with the ambitions of a citysystem. "Indeed," writes the Malaysian business daily the *Star*, "it is envisioned to be twice the size of Covent Garden in London, three times that of Roponggi Hills in Tokyo and four times that of the Rockefeller Centre in New York."[20] The UK's *Architects' Journal* describes the project's behind-the-scenes details: "Firms on board include Conran and Partners, South Korea's ga.a architects, Heatherwick Studio, U.S. firm the Jerde Partnership, Japan's Kengo Kuma and Associates, and WDA . . . The scheme is being developed as a joint venture between Mycom Bhd and Merrill Lynch Asia."[21]

Thousands of multinational consortia like this one build our cities today, striving to maximize annual product turnover and promoting local real estate market and planning reforms to facilitate acceptance of their city models. As one indication of the scale of effort, the *World*

Trade Atlas estimated that Malaysia's latest urban construction boom generated U.S. $347 million in construction equipment imports in 2004, with 80 percent of the equipment coming from Japan, Germany, and the United States. It would seem that the development of our cities is less and less a locally governable affair.

But look again. The successes or failures of these consortia and their industry, and their positive or negative impacts, are defined as much by very local markets and business practices, cultures and preferences, underworld demands, political relationships and policies as any regulatory reforms they might secure in national capitals. Today, the local and the global dimensions of City building often still evolve as parallel universes. The top-down builders of city models and master-planned districts focus on volumes of production, sales turnover, and the pressing need to rapidly expand the burgeoning cityscape. The bottom-up citysystem builders focus on shaping the city's growth to support their unique strategy for advantage. Both bring critical solutions to the table. We grope for ways to align their competing imperatives and for a vantage point from which to understand the world we are building.

Ultimately, the growth of each city is defined more by its unique history and chaotic complexities than by any general trends. Cities intensify the interaction between social, political, economic, and ecological systems and thereby concentrate their complexities. So there are no fixed types of cities. But to understand the main challenges of the final phase, I find it useful to consider three particular *urban strategy* situations. The first is the City of Crisis. In the City of Crisis, exemplified by Detroit and Mumbai, different socioeconomic groups have mastered distinct city-building approaches or inherited distinct legacies of urbanism, from which they each compete for and secure their advantage (see chapter 8). The more each group evolves a full practice of urbanism to advance its claims on the city against others, the harsher the competition becomes. The result can be a truly embattled condition that leaves the city as a whole in a state of perpetual crisis. The challenge of the City of Crisis is to forge a common urbanism that addresses the different needs and aspirations of each group.

The second condition is the Great Opportunities City. In the Great Opportunities City, as in Kuala Lumpur, Johannesburg, and Toronto, the lack of any consolidated urbanism leaves the city growing incoherently, unable to achieve its often well-financed and officially sanctioned visions and plans (see chapter 9). The vacuum created by the lack of any disciplined urbanism gets filled by ad hoc and city model development and small-scale master-planned projects that do not address the city's challenges or satisfy its aspirations. The challenge of a Great Opportunities City is to develop a stable alliance of interests that fosters a local urbanism tailored to the city's challenges and has the authority to discipline expedient, incoherent city building.

The third condition is the Strategic City. In these cities an alliance has developed and deployed a coherent urbanism across the entire city. These cities, exemplified by Barcelona, Chicago, and Curitiba (Brazil), are *strategic* because their politics, institutions, and practices are so aligned that they can succeed in shaping growth toward broadly supported strategic purposes over the course of decades. The challenge of Strategic Cities (as explored in Part III) is to constantly revitalize their faculties for strategic transformation—their political alliance, their strategic institutions, and their practices of urbanism—in the face of adversity and unanticipated (global) trends.

CHAPTER 8

Cities of Crisis

Sources of Global Vulnerability

One evening in Dharavi my Mumbai colleagues and I visited a notable landlord at his charitable foundation. When we arrived, he was surrounded by accountants, working into the night on their laptops. He seated us around his desk and began a lengthy description of the many good deeds his foundation had financed, showing pictures and newspaper clippings about schools and temples that he'd set up in Dharavi and in his home region in southern India. He complained repeatedly about the people in Dharavi. He would ask them all for donations, but they were stingy, he said. So he had to carry on the good works with his own resources, collected here and there.

This earnest presentation went on for nearly an hour without the slightest grin or sideways glance. Our host, we all knew, was one of Dharavi's old-time underworld *bhais*, specializing in extortion. Throughout our meeting we had been speaking in a sort of Dharavi code. In addition to our host's story line, the code included the trappings of a legally registered charity and a foundation office adjacent to the slum area he controlled. It required framed newspaper stories of good deeds and a hardworking staff who sat around us, busily processing the day's collections and managing funds across who knows how large an extended territory.

Our local guide explained that this man had recently had his wings clipped by the police. This explained the bitter edge in his narrative. But then to demonstrate his kindness, the bhai-cum-philanthropist invited us to his home, so that we could meet his family and celebrate his grandson's birthday. On the way, our interpreter, a longtime Dharavi resident, whispered that our host had recently had his men cook a local baker in his own oven, a demonstration of the consequences of a lack of generosity. Everyone in his family was extremely gracious to us, but the image lingered as he cut his little grandson's cake and served us each a piece.

The next day, visiting a workshop that specializes in collecting, cleaning, and sorting the intestines of goats and sheep to supply Johnson & Johnson Company's Dharavi-based sterile sutures factory, a call came inviting us to meet the successful Long Island mansion-builder Mukesh Mehta. He shared our fascination with Dharavi and had studied it for years.

We met Mehta at a new four-star hotel not far from Dharavi. The hotel was typical of new construction in Mumbai, a lavish high-rise that towered above old residential colonies, maturing slums, and vestiges of other Mumbai city models from earlier times. He pulled up in a sleek black, chauffeured car, dressed in a smart jacket and flawlessly pressed shirt. He had returned to India from a career in New York some seven years earlier to make an impact on his country of origin. Rushing through introductory niceties while he took phone calls and made food orders, Mehta fired up an animated PowerPoint presentation that summarized his proposals for Dharavi.

"Every person is entitled to the dignity of a secure shelter," it intoned, sounding like a declaration from a United Nations summit. He bemoaned the "subhuman conditions" and the stifling of "enterprising slum dwellers." After quoting Mahatma Gandhi, his presentation explained that the project would "retain existing families and businesses" and provide a "sustainable development master plan." It would take a "holistic approach" that is "integrated" into the larger master plan for Mumbai. "The needs of all the stakeholders," he said, would be considered to provide "economic upliftment and empowerment." Crescendoing, Mehta then showed how his plan would help transform Mumbai into "a new Shanghai."[1] Dharavi, the erstwhile slum, would be converted "into a world-class cultural, knowledge, business and health care centre," the presentation claimed. It offered pictures of modern laboratories, museums, and performing arts centers to illustrate his vision of transforming Dharavi into "a premiere destination," making it part of "mainstream Mumbai."

Then he took us through the details. The current migrant city would be razed and cleared. Households with an established residency in Dharavi would be provided with a free 225-square-foot, two-room apartment in a high-rise building near their current location. If people wanted more space, they could buy it at market rates. Sewer lines, drains, and private toilets as well as a safe electricity network would be installed. Recreational areas would be relocated and upgraded. Non-polluting industries would be "rehabilitated," and polluting industries would be relocated to new manufacturing zones, many outside the area. To him, this plan was a humanitarian no-brainer and an urban-development win-win solution. It would bring order, cleanliness, infrastructure, and green spaces to replace the fetid, congested, unsanitary slum.

Wrapping up, Mehta invited us to support his efforts. Whereas he seemed distracted or even defensive at the start of our meeting, now he was friendly. The presentation seemed to reinspire him. And then he dropped the real news, still to be publicly announced: in a closed-door meeting, the chief minister of the state government had decided to implement his plan. He had confronted many naysayers—"vested interests," he called them—and there had been many others along the way who lacked the conviction to help him turn his vision for Dharavi into a "world-class" reality.

As he said this I was staring at his presentation's concluding slide. It was graced with another image of Mahatma Gandhi and read, "It is a challenge to make it slum free . . . it is an opportunity to make it a best suburb."

Dharavi, the bustling, disowned citysystem of Mumbai, was to be dismantled, rearranged, and rebuilt into . . . a suburb. I was numbed by what I'd heard. How could anyone who had observed Dharavi for so long miss the most obvious fact about it: that the residential-industrial citysystem was proving itself every day in the marketplace to be world-class? It stood as probably the most successful, scaled poverty-reduction program in the history of international development. Within the Indian

A street in Dharavi, Mumbai. A view down any Dharavi street reveals dozens of manufacturers, shops, retailers, and homes. The taller building on the left includes the workshop and offices of INMA, the top-quality multinational manufacturer and retailer of fashion leather garments. (Photo: Avik Roy)

context, Dharavi's migrant generations had developed an accessible, replicable citysystem for the advancement of the country's poor majority. It was a stunning example of Indian entrepreneurial ability and ambition. With millions of poor households migrating to India's cities each year, it seemed almost obvious that this migrant city system just needed to be accompanied with the same public investment in urban infrastructure offered to every other Mumbai city model and master-planned suburb, and replicated throughout country.

But like so many brilliant examples of urbanism razed in the name of modernization—like the livable, efficient *hutong* areas of Beijing or the famous West End district of Boston—Dharavi would be replaced rather than transformed by India's modernizers.[2,3] Mehta was speaking the language of transformation and charity, but his proposals for the new Dharavi suggested that he little understood the difference between a citysystem and a master-planned district. The images of the "Slum-Free

Dharavi" were a tailored version of one of the ascendant new city models for Mumbai's growing middle classes—call it the Mumbai new suburb city—intermingled with crowded high-rise residential compounds, not unlike those used to expropriate established African American districts in the 1960s. Mehta's project was the latest skirmish in a protracted low-intensity warfare between competing city-building approaches that makes Mumbai a city of chronic crisis.

The competition started in the decades of state-led development following Indian independence. Government's master-planned projects competed for urban location and advantage with ad hoc private developers and growing slums. The competition created a perverse market for profitability within the government: corrupt bidding for tenure and development rights, building contracts, and ownership from the powerful bureaucracy evolved into a machinery for bribery and kickbacks. Political parties also engaged, developing "vote blocks" on advantageous locations to be bought and sold in the bidding wars for development control. The corruption business thus spawned still dominates the urban development market today. Only now, with market liberalization, development has been steadily turned over to the large private developers and contracting firms.

Mumbai is known for its powerful builders. The nature of their organization remains murky, but stories about corrupt deals between the "builder's lobby" and politicians, or relationships with the criminal underworld, are common.[4] As in any city, local developers typically specialize in a set of city models. These are often adapted from proven models in other markets. Once they adapt the models' business and design elements to local conditions, the developers put together projects—cultivating local political support and acquiring land, permits, finance, and anchor tenants—to construct the models' increasingly predictable products for predictable returns across the city.

Mumbai's new suburb city model is a hybrid of the high-rise, mixed residential, office and retail complexes developed as a kind of plug-and-play solution for aspiring new edge city "downtowns" in North America, for railway station areas in continental Europe, and for mastered-planned districts of Hong Kong, Kuala Lumpur, and Singapore. The model established its first Mumbai beachheads on the city's periphery, far from the old Bombay and Dharavi, at the metro area's northernmost part. A typical project involves a clustered arrangement of apartment towers adjacent to an office plaza alongside a shopping mall. This cluster suggests a potential citysystem. It offers an aspirational, livable, and affordable city unit for the growing ranks of middle-class professionals. If incomes rise to allow these young professionals to rent or buy one of the apartment units adjacent to their office, then they could live, meet, recreate, shop, and collaborate all within a single micro-district. But as a city model, it generates no community of residents who seek these particular locational arrangements. Few large employers have established offices in these new developments; by tradition, most corporations still develop their own campuses or seek a downtown location. Similarly, the new generation of Indian professionals changes jobs frequently. So for now, the new suburb model hosts a residential population that leaves in the morning and a workday population that leaves in the evening, creating little joint advantage together. It works as a shadow of a citysystem.

Now the new suburb city threatens established territories of the old city. Its sorties into the vast slum territories surrounding the international

Mumbai's new suburb city rises next to an established migrant city settlement in the northern Borivali district, adjacent to the Sanjay Gandhi National Park. (Photo: Pradeep Samant)

airport and farther southward to Dharavi has been encouraged by the city fathers of south Mumbai. For them the new suburb city provides workable units of change, which plot by plot respond to the urgings of a commissioned McKinsey & Company report on how to become a "world-class city." Indian cities have centuries-old traditions of urbanism. As in most places, they are poorly understood. So like Kuala Lumpur, the cities' elites "benchmark" themselves to elusive global standards, champion foreign city models, and abandon legacies rather than adapt them to today's challenges.

Other options for Dharavi's renewal are clearly available. The latest urbanist revivals of Europe, North America, and Latin America favor incremental redevelopment of deteriorated low-income areas to increase the equity of established residents and match their building investments with new public infrastructure and facilities. Rio de Janeiro leads the way. Having learned the futile folly of slum clearances and high-rise relocations in the 1960s–1970s, in the mid-1990s Rio started to convert its famed migrant city *favelas* into more stable, lawful, sanitary, mixed-use neighborhoods, with minimal clearing and relocation. In the first phase they organized all of the city's departments—planning, public works, and social services—into a single team that went to each favela to research, design, plan, and build new drainage, toilet and sewerage systems, roads, clinics, and recreational centers in close working partnership with the communities. Then, in 2002, they steadily granted legal titles to the residents, household by household, in exchange for each household's compliance with official building codes.

In Europe, planners learned the folly of ghetto clearance and master-planned urban renewal in the 1960s–1970s, so incremental renewal strategies are now common practice in dilapidated districts, including those dominated by low-income residents, immigrants, and informal enterprise. In Lisbon, 60 percent of recent building permits have been for this kind of incremental revitalization. In North America, gentrification by students and low-paid professionals—a hybrid of the traditional phenomenon of ethnic succession in inner-city neighborhoods—is a common path to regeneration. New renters upgrade apartments and create new social amenities. They eventually become homeowners and establish small businesses. Building their urban association, they secure public investments to match their private ones. Housing subsidy programs can be instituted for low-income home purchases or rents to prevent the wholesale dislocation of established low-income residents.[5]

Even in Asia, there is a history of city building that offers an alternative to the clear-and-rebuild approach. As we were meeting with Mukesh Mehta, urbanologist Matias Echanove was also exploring Dharavi, trying to learn its language. He concluded that Mumbai's migrant city had remarkable similarities with, of all places, the development of modern Tokyo. After Toyko's destruction in World War II, he explains, the city rapidly recovered by melding two traditions of city building into a unique citysystem that Echanove calls the Tokyo Model.[6] It is quite possible to have "locally initiated residential and commercial development" of the nature of Dharavi, writes Echanove, "alongside centralized infrastructure planning." In postwar Japan, the country's central planners focused on rebuilding Tokyo's wrecked water, sewerage and road systems. But the rebuilding of the city's housing and commercial spaces was left to residents. Tokyo did not impose Western-style zoning to regulate and separate land uses and building types. Its citizen city-builders reached back into their traditions of small-town life and created a flexible city of villagelike, residential-commercial settlements, in some ways remarkably like the migrant-entrepreneurs of Dharavi.

The result was a citysystem that families recovering from war could incrementally manage, enabling rapid reconstruction of the world's largest city. Tokyo's densely packed areas of mismatched buildings, notes Echanove, are slumlike in both form and history. The neighborhoods are even somewhat structured like Dharavi, organized along busy commercial lanes crossed by more private, narrow community lanes often hardly wide enough for a single automobile. This structure, he argues, contributes to Tokyo's vibrant small-scale commercial sector and to the safety of its neighborhoods.

Then why so little debate in Mumbai about the possible alternatives for Dharavi's redevelopment? There is a kernel of potential middle ground in Mehta's concept. He would retain the existing apparel, jewelry, and footwear industries within an upgraded manufacturing zone and allocate land nearby to training and research institutes to support these industries. His plan would provide standard infrastructure, health facilities, and amenities. But his lack of commitment to the spatial order of the existing citysystem or to engaging the residents as codesigners of homes and family workshop spaces undermines the basic economics and ethos of the citysystem.

In the end, the plan to "save" Dharavi seems all too crass: if you take close to a million people living in one- to three-story buildings and resettle them into smaller units in seven-story buildings, then you create vast amounts of new, undeveloped land. In Dharavi's case, this land is located in central Mumbai—some of the most valuable real estate in the world. The whole thing reminds one of the charitable "urban renewal" of Black Bottom in Detroit, a grand scheme born of deeply conflicted motivations. Mehta seemed to be telling the same story in Dharavi's vernacular. He would later say that Dharavi also represented "a gold mine that the government was not seeing . . . I've tried to take the opportunity to cash in on that."[7] "Slum-Free Dharavi" would create a massive real estate boon for its proponents and establish a central strategic foothold for Mumbai's emerging new suburb city. It would also create a windfall for the city's political class. Bribery is an industry in Mumbai. Corrupt land deals are as much a part of life as traffic jams and Bollywood films. The total cost of Mehta's plan would exceed $2 billion. The demolition and redevelopment would be divided into five large contracts of $250 to $600 million each. The winning corporate bidders would pay a large "premium" to the government, to use Mehta's words, for their redevelopment rights. Mehta's presentation estimated that as much as a billion dollars would flow in payments to the state government.

But on a bigger historical scale, the momentum behind the Slum-Free Dharavi scheme and the lack of more creative alternatives is a part of a long-standing territorial struggle between Mumbai's two entrenched, competing cities. On one side is the informal city, whose slums develop over time into new migrant cities. On the other side is the official city and its economic strategies. As its builders, financiers, architects, large retailers, and politicians align their interests behind the reliable, world-class profitability of the new suburb city model, their control of the city is reinvigorated. In between these parallel city-building projects is the criminal sector, which extracts money from both sides. When competing alliances—one empowered through sheer numbers, the other through its capital and social status—secure advantage and predictable economic benefits through mastery of fundamentally opposing city-building approaches, their competition inevitably becomes territorial. The battle for Dharavi is part of the larger drama of the City of Crisis.

Back in Dharavi, I ask Imram Khan, the leather businessman, if he had heard about the Slum-Free Dharavi plan of Mukesh Mehta. Did anyone from government come to talk with him about the plan? "No one from government has come," Imram replies. "People like you and journalists come. But for the last twenty-five years no one has come to Dharavi to talk with us. Even the media people come and just meet with the political leaders and go." He says this with an easygoing manner, as if he cannot really be bothered one way or the other. They don't take him seriously, and he doesn't take them seriously either.

It is hard for him to believe that the redevelopment plan will really go through. "The local politicians are not interested in Dharavi's development," he says, "because people will get an apartment, sell it, and then go away. The politicians will lose their vote line."

But then he hedges this comforting view. His back straightens and he speaks faster and more firmly, making me impatient to hear the translation of his words. "My workers will move elsewhere. We will move our business to another part of the city. But I own this place. It is my compound. I will move my business but I will not give up this land." It is clear that he doesn't need someone to come and talk with him about the plan; he fully understands the players and the stakes.

Longtime Dharavi residents have seen it play out before. Mr. Sultanbhai migrated from a coastal area a few hundred miles to Mumbai's south in the late 1950s. He purchased his six-hundred-square-foot property from a notable local *goonda,* or criminal operative. It cost him 300 rupees (about $7.50) then. Now he operates a two-story garment manufacturing and export business on the property, which employs forty-five Dharavi residents. "The place will go for ten million rupees now" on the informal market, he says, the equivalent of $250,000. The informal market price is an incontestable measure of the value that he and his fellow migrants have built on this once soggy ground.

"If my house is coming under the Slum-Free Dharavi project," he tells us, "then I will have to close down my business. I need a lot of space to run my business. If I get a flat of two hundred fifty square feet how can I run it? I am not doing any illegal business. I have a proper license. I am paying income tax. I have insured this place for ten million rupees. I am paying taxes to the municipal corporation and all my accounts are clear. So why can't the government set up an industrial area for us here and give us the place, when we are willing to pay the money that they demand?" He answers his own questions with a perspective gained from watching scores of other slum clearance programs. "All the politicians, the local *goondas*, and social workers are going to earn a good amount of money. Only we will be the sufferers," he says.

"At present Dharavi is one of the famous places in Bombay. Forget about thirty-five years before [when it was built up]. Now all the youngsters are well educated. They all are talking about globalization. This place has improved. If the Slum-Free Dharavi project comes through, many people will lose their jobs and again we will go back thirty-five years and *dadagiri* [thuggery] will start again. *Insaan ko insaan kaiyega.* [Man will eat man.] All the politicians are going to get a good amount of money from the builders, so they are all happy."

Sultanbhai is describing the chronic nature of crisis in a city like Mumbai. As slums mature into a migrant city like Dharavi, the contribution made by criminal activities to local finance and market opportunity becomes less important. Noncriminal local industries mature. The criminally governed slum diversifies into a city with many sources of wealth and power. The migrant city establishes a more stable and even legitimate status through its accumulation of licenses, legal permits, and tax registrations. But when all or part of the migrant city is razed and households are relocated to places without its efficiencies and services, they revert back into destitution, crisis, and even illegality. "Man eats man" again as the migrant community returns to earlier slum conditions, whether in a cluster of crude shacks or in a poorly serviced high-rise building far from employment opportunity—a "vertical slum," as they call it in Mumbai.

Altaf Shah, another Dharavi old-timer, shares Sultanbhai's sentiments. Like the Khans and Syeds, he came to Dharavi from Uttar Pradesh in the 1950s. When Shah arrived, by his recollection there were "hardly forty houses" in his area of Dharavi. He captured some ten thousand square feet of land and established a waste recycling business. The methods used to claim this land are rumored to have been harsh but are not discussed. At present he still owns four shops and twelve rental houses, and he says that he now pays municipal taxes for these properties. "I am not bothered" by the Slum-Free Dharavi plan, he says, because "I know some officers" in the municipal corporation and the regional development agency that will oversee the project. "Whichever builder is coming to this place," he firmly says, "I will tell him, first you solve my problem and then you do what you want."

Altaf Shah speaks in the plainest possible local code. A robust system of influence peddling, bribery, and organized crime is often the primary form of mediation in the trenches of the City of Crisis. Shah understands Slum-Free Dharavi as just another round in an ongoing nasty negotiation. There are few ideals or principles in play.

Dharavi's poorer, less-established residents will be the collateral damage. Sushila Aware and Haseena Shaikh describe their lives after an earlier government-initiated relocation from Dharavi. For thirty-five years, Sushila and her husband lived in a four-hundred-square-foot building in a Dharavi labor camp. Then they were relocated into a 225-square-foot government-sponsored redevelopment unit in another part of the city. Her life there offers a glimpse of what likely awaits the tens of thousands of Dharavi residents who will be relocated under Mehta's scheme. The unit is too small, she says. "It is not even two hundred and twenty-five square feet, unless you include the area outside the door. Only then is it two hundred and twenty-five feet." She says that there are too many robberies in the area away from Dharavi. "It is dangerous to stay over here. And when we came here three years ago, there was a huge problem of water. We had to buy the water for twenty rupees per can . . . There is also a lot of garbage outside the building," she reports, "and because of that we are suffering from various diseases. Now my husband has to travel a lot from here to go to his job in Dharavi. Our expenditures have increased from the traveling."

Haseena's family was also "saved" from Dharavi and resettled into a high-rise building. She too complains of the lack of solid waste collection for her building, far away from the operations of Dharavi's scavengers and recyclers. She blames the unhygienic atmosphere for her husband's death from tuberculosis two years ago. "And in Dharavi, there were lots of job opportunities . . . now over here, there is no chance to work. We are totally depressed."

With the dislocation of migrant city residents and the disruption of their urban ecology, the crises of struggling impoverishment—disease, crime, economic exploitation, flooding, fire hazards—are spread to yet another part of the city. In other words, when the interests of the new suburb city advance their claims against the migrant city—when any two deeply entrenched city models or systems compete head-to-head against each other for the some city land—then the functionality of both is put at risk. Short of a new model that bridges the divergent city-building approaches, Mumbai itself becomes a low-intensity war fought in square-foot units.

Chetan Joshi and S. Tai are ready to fight back. Joshi explains that his family of nine is staying in a four-hundred-square-foot building. Like every Dharavi resident with whom we speak, he unintentionally emphasizes the foot-by-foot measurement of the battleground. "We cannot accept the government plan and live in two hundred and twenty-five square feet," he says. "And since I am also having two shops of four hundred square feet each, the government should also allot equivalent shops to me . . . We, all the brothers of Dharavi, will fight against the injustice done by the government. We are not afraid of anything." S. Tai lives with her husband and five other family members. She came to Mumbai forty years ago and is now running a small grocery. "My shop is three hundred and fifty square feet," she says. "The officer told me that I will get a shop of the same size. If they try to cheat us, then it will create a great problem for us, and we will go for hunger strikes and will not allow them to touch our houses. If the time comes, then we will not be afraid to beat the municipal officers."

Their impassioned attention to what may seem like spatial minutiae further reflects the irrefutable physical, demographic, and economic calculus of the battle over Mumbai, and in cities like it around the world today. In the late 1990s the Mumbai municipality officially counted 2,335 slum settlements spread across the city. There are thousands of other small shack colonies on sidewalks and along railway and water lines. Just as a high-rise hotel (like the one Mukesh Mehta chose to meet us in) serves as an "anchor project" for the development of the new suburb city around it, the slum is the beachhead for the migrant city. It is the poor migrant's first tap root into the city's raw urban advantage.

Mumbai's slums are home to some 6.5 million people, or 55 percent of the city's population.[8] Every day, the migrant city expands from thousands of these beachheads, advancing against every boundary of suburban Mumbai, whether into an undeveloped lot, a tidal marsh, a rail line, or a roadway. And every day, the city model developers and land speculators fight the slum's development into a migrant city by displacing slum dwellers and reclaiming the land for their own projects. They know that demolishing a vulnerable new slum that has not established legal protections, licenses, permits, and registrations is far simpler than the elaborate and expensive maneuvers involved in conquering an entrenched migrant city like Dharavi.

The completed new suburb city. Apartments (left) next to offices and a retail mall (right) are clustered efficiently together, but they serve different users who spend hours each day commuting across the congested city. (Photo: Jeb Brugmann)

But there is another factor that locks the two parallel cities into their grinding struggle. The purveyors of the officially sanctioned city-model developments are dependent on the slum for its cheap labor. The establishment of a slum adjacent to a city model project is even encouraged. It is an important part of their business model. Developers will support its vulnerable limbo for many years and even supply it with a health clinic or school. After construction is completed, the slum provides the cleaning and maintenance staff, drivers, security officers, and household domestics that allow the suburb's residents to work their long hours, to afford their rising standards of living, and to make the new suburb city's tenant companies globally competitive. The de facto strategy of the city model seems to be the encouragement of the slum but the constant interruption of its development into a migrant city, always pushing the migrant's city back to its most vulnerable starting point.

But the migrant city's constant reemergence still secures a fragile dominance in the suburban districts. Sixty-two percent of Mumbai's slum dwellers, or more than four million people, live in Mumbai's suburban wards. As much as 80 percent of the city's employment establishments are located in slums or their roadside borders, indicating the growth potential of the migrant city.[9] *Both* slum-based enterprise and suburban city model development are expanding fastest in the suburban districts; half of the city's office establishments are also now located in suburban wards.[10] This physical proximity of the new suburb city and the evolving migrant city, with their competing interests and strategies, makes every step toward the true stabilization of either full of conflict.[11]

Sometimes this struggle boils over in rioting or sparks street wars between police and gangs or between different caste or religious groups. But generally it takes the form of daily harassments, deprivations, and maneuvering for tactical advantage. Most frequently, these skirmishes are over control of the city's rawest resource, its ever malleable and fungible land. The fight for urban land spurs invasions, expropriations, and legal challenges over each plot. It explains the unpredictable extension or rescission of municipal services, the mystery of unfinished construction, and patterns of harassment by police and municipal inspectors. Each skirmish creates under-the-table revenue opportunities for the bhais and goondas, municipal and court officials, and police officers to expedite someone's desired outcome. In other words, the chronic, predictable competition breeds a massive market in its own right where the dominant business process is corruption and delay and the dominant business solution is organized harassment and security services. This market feeds on failing governance. Corruption, because it becomes more predictable than progress, becomes a form of governance itself. In the City of Crisis, plans, zoning, and permits wither in relevance as they are effectively replaced by thousands of deals, most of which are not transparent. Large parts of the city are undocumented territories of control where rights of ownership, building, housing, trading, and service are constantly challenged. It seems impossible to turn the city's development in any particular direction, least of all away from its spiral of crisis.

In such an environment, no model or citysystem really ever realizes its potential. Even at its pinnacle of achievement, as in Dharavi, the migrant city never consolidates full legal status, legitimacy, or infrastructure. Likewise, the new suburb city's major urban development projects, like the proposed Dharavi plan, materialize as shadow images of their original plans. Too many concessions and expediencies must be managed to move any undertaking forward.

In other cities, the market conditions enjoyed by Mumbai—sustained growth, global demand, abundant talent, flexible labor markets, a growing middle class, plentiful finance—would have supported massive-scale planned developments, like the satellite cities in metropolitan Shanghai and Singapore. But for all its aspiration, Mumbai struggles to achieve any planned, coherent development. Individual buildings rise ad hoc among tracts of run-down, small residential-commercial buildings from another era or along half-finished roadways, and everything abuts a slum colony. The competition between the parallel cities effectively forces the development surge in Mumbai through a funnel of labyrinthine business and policy obstacles that produces a trickle of scattershot progress. Unable to secure advantage over the slum and beholden to the criminal opportunism that feeds on the conflict, suburban city-building practice becomes all the more dominated by short-term cash flow considerations rather than real asset creation.

At the metropolitan scale, there can be no victor in the war between two parallel cities. Even if Mumbai's high-rise suburban revival wins the battle for control of one part of the city, it shifts the crises elsewhere. In 2004–2005, for instance, as part of its campaign to transform Mumbai into "the next Shanghai," the state government violently cleared some eighty-four thousand slum homes, including sixty-three hundred homes in one day. The numbers of homeless from these clearances dwarfed the thirty thousand homes destroyed in India by the 2004 Indian Ocean tsunami. Dislocation and the loss of housing and small businesses spawns new, crisis-ridden zones of autonomy. Old-time slum dwellers like Sultanbhai have seen this many times before.

In an environment of continual conflict and dislocation, everyday urban maintenance also stalls. From 2002 to 2004, courts fined the Mumbai municipality nearly one hundred times for its lack of response to legal petitions against land encroachments and other building irregularities. Acute crises like floods, riots, health epidemics, and collapsing buildings add to the chronic decay, housing shortages, and infrastructure failure.

A major flood in Mumbai in July 2005 illustrates the vulnerability to crisis in such a city. A few days of heavy monsoon rains brought the city to a halt. First the waters overwhelmed the outdated drainage system of the central city and older suburbs, already commonly clogged by construction debris and uncollected waste. The citywide drainage network can carry only half the rainwater volume that falls during a heavy monsoon rain, making flooding an annual occurrence. Drainage problems are further exacerbated by new construction in low-lying estuaries, marshes, and mangroves that would otherwise drain the city. In addition to slums, whole new suburb city complexes and business districts have been built over mangroves in recent years.

With the drainage and natural hydrology overwhelmed, the roads themselves become the drainage system, and the slums become the stormwater retention ponds for vast quantities of sewage and chemical-laced storm water. In the 2005 flood, tens of thousands were forced to wade for hours in waist-deep water to get to their homes or to shelter. The flood shut down Mumbai's major corporate offices, the stock exchange, transit system, airports, ATM networks, and mobile phone services. In thousands of sodden slums, cholera, dengue, and leptospirosis epidemics followed the receding waters.

Another symptom of crisis is loss of life and wealth from faulty high-rise construction. About two hundred multistory buildings simply collapse in Mumbai in an average year, mostly during heavy rains. But the new suburbs and migrant cities both keep building themselves in their expedient, tactical ways.

Even where new rules are imposed, there is dim chance of real enforcement. Take the explanation of the Mumbai municipal commissioner—the city's CEO—for the collapse of a multistory suburban high-rise building that killed twenty-nine people in July 2007. The building was in the northern Borivili suburb where large city model apartment blocks insert themselves into sprawling slum and migrant city areas that daily encroach upon the vast Manori estuary.

"There is no BMC [i.e., municipal] rule to check illegal construction," said Commissioner Jairaj Phatak. "We cannot do anything unless a complaint is filed. The collapsed building is not on the [official] dilapidated list and nobody ever complained about illegal modifications."[12] Ten years earlier a special government commission recommended a wide range of quality-control measures for suburb city construction after thirty-five people died in the collapse of a seven-story high-rise in the Bandra suburb. But none of the measures had been implemented. Granting permits for questionable projects and selling agreements to "look the other way" from nonpermitted construction is too lucrative to give up in exchange for effective regulation. In such an environment, common citizens give up filing complaints to officials that elicit no response. Bribes, favors, and criminal services provide more reliable results. Government often seems reduced to striking committees to perform the latest crisis postmortem.

India has a strong tradition of policy and fiscal measures designed to increase opportunities for its poor majority. Mumbai produces, and exports, world-class talent in architecture and urban design. Yet policy and talent play a marginal role in the City of Crisis. Take a recent initiative by the state government requiring builders to set aside 10 percent of new suburban residential complexes for low-income owners. In return for compliance, the government would let builders increase their building heights and receive tax benefits. Yet a Mumbai real estate lawyer aptly stated the widely expected outcome. "The rich could very well book low-income flats in other people's names and escape detection."[13]

Neither does city planning seem to influence the nature of development. Consider Mumbai's plans to boost the number of recreational spaces and playgrounds. Mumbai has one fiftieth of the open space per person of New York City. The Mumbai Municipal Development Plan has reserved twenty-three hundred plots for recreational grounds and gardens. Since the plan was struck, most have been taken off the list or encroached upon. Less than five hundred of the identified plots were ever developed into public open spaces.[14]

Even a resource as critical as water supply is managed at crisis margins. In the summer of 2005, Mumbai quenched its thirst with only sixteen days of water in reserve. As Mumbai pursues a $50 billion-plus capital works program to repave its roads, upgrade and repair its drainage and water distribution systems, and build more public toilets, it will need to concentrate population growth along these new infrastructure corridors to make them economically efficient. But there seems little hope that Mumbai can control either incessant, ad hoc growth or expedient city model dealing.

In the City of Crisis, every aspect of life is dominated by the implicit battle between its large, competing alliances, their different strategies, and the fallout that this competition creates. The resulting chronic condition again highlights the basic character of what I've called urban advantage. Like other public goods, such as the air and oceans, the economics of a city, and the social life and politics built on their foundation, are vulnerable to the dilemma called the "tragedy of the commons." If competing groups systematically develop and use the city's density, scale, association, and extension economies at cross purposes, as a strategy for their group's advantage at the expense of another's, then the urban advantage of the whole city gets compromised. The more that competing strategies for urban advantage are scaled across the city, the more the city becomes dysfunctional and declines into crisis. By the same logic, the more that urbanizing nations come to depend on their cities (and the global community comes to depend on the City), the more the inclusive governance of urban development becomes critical to the success of nations and global pursuits.

Few can imagine the degree to which a city can spiral out of control as two or more city-building strategies compete over the course of a few decades. But today I am looking at the material record of a City of Crisis end game. Eric Dueweke, a committed, hands-on urbanologist and the director of community partnerships for the University of Michigan's School of Architecture and Urban Planning is taking me on my first real tour of downtown Detroit since the early 1960s.

As we venture along one empty street after another, looking at the run-down houses and abandoned manufacturing buildings, I notice that he intermittently locks the car doors and then unlocks them again when he feels it is safe for me to jump out and take a picture. His grandparents were immigrants to Detroit. He has lived in central Detroit all his life. He works with many of its community development agencies and has committed his family to reside there even as most middle-class professionals, white and black, have left. In other words, he is versed in the subtle routines of safety in Detroit and knows they cannot be taken for granted, even when the streets seem all but abandoned. I didn't make much note of the locking and unlocking while on this tour, amazed as I was by the sheer scale of the city's physical abandonment, but days later it was this sound of the door locks that kept coming back to me, like an imprint of the city's chronic divisions.

Only half a century before, Detroit was still the economic powerhouse that birthed America's metalworking, automobile, and armaments industries. Its inventions in technology, manufacturing process, supply-chain management, logistics, and music shaped the modern world. Today it is remarkable not so much for its industrial productivity or even for the run-down homes, storefronts, and roads of its poor districts as for something rarely seen in the world of cities: a wholesale reversion to open prairie land.

During the same years that Dharavi grew from a marginal marshy slum into a migrant city of nearly a million people, Detroit's population declined by a million. The city left behind—in particular its three main citysystems (the central business district, the industrial city neighborhoods of residences and light industry, and the arterial commerce corridors consisting of wide avenues of commercial and retail establishments), and the main city model (the postwar residential tract)—has steadily collapsed. By 2007, much of Detroit's 139 square miles of land area consisted of empty lots, where ancient prairie grasses from a time before the city re-seeded themselves. Out of 386,000 land parcels in Detroit, approximately 100,000 are empty today. They are roamed by groups of feral dogs and host growing populations of fox, raccoons, opossum, pheasants, hawks, and eagles. Each year the city government tries to sell the foreclosed and abandoned parcels at prices as low as $500, but they do not sell. The upkeep costs exceed anyone's expectations for the city's turnaround. Above all, the city has lost the essential density required to support the economics of any new urban strategy. Local governments therefore maintain a growing inventory of some fifty thousand lots with which they know not what to do.

Detroit is an extreme but concrete example of the City of Crisis end game. The citysystems and models that defined the downtown city steadily declined at the hands of the suburban (white-flight) city, which received all the investment and subsidies necessary for its triumph. Despite intense efforts by some of Detroit's political and corporate leaders, metropolitan Detroit remains shockingly divided. In 2005, 82 percent of the downtown city's population of nine hundred thousand was black, a higher percentage than any U.S. city over two hundred thousand. In the suburban city of 3.5 million people—with its suburban residential tracts, strip malls and shopping plazas, industrial zones, and old town centers—white residents make up more than 95 percent of the population. The city of Livonia, immediately adjacent to Detroit, has the highest concentration of white residents (98 percent) of any city of over one hundred thousand people in the United States.

Divisions along economic lines are also stark. Detroit's downtown city now hosts less than a fifth of the metro region's jobs. One study estimates that 78 percent of the metro region's jobs are now located ten or more miles from the old central business district. A third of the downtown city's population lived in poverty in 2005. One quarter of its neighborhoods did not have a single bank branch. In 2000, Detroit had two thirds of the amount of housing stock that it had in 1960. There is also a record of human collateral damage. The incidence of nearly every health problem—heart disease, poisoning, psychosis, pneumonia, cancer, and infectious and parasitic diseases—is significantly greater in central Detroit than in the largest, adjacent suburban county.[15] Infant mortality in central Detroit is nearly 50 percent higher than the national average. In the downtown city the homicide rate is three times that of the total state of Michigan. Not long ago, when I attended a summit of city mayors from across the United States and Asia, I saw that Detroit's mayor was the only one to travel with a bodyguard. Back in Detroit he had a dedicated bodyguard of twenty-seven officers.

Such divisive growth in a metropolis prevents rational region-wide planning or investment. Take the example of Detroit's regional public transit services. Lacking common interest in the whole metropolitan region, including the movement of people and commerce between the suburbs and downtown, the suburban city suffers from more than seven hundred miles of congested roadways on an average workday. Commute times in suburban Detroit are greater than both the state and national average.[16] As much as it seems that the suburban city prevails over the downtown city, the nearly two hundred small suburban cities and townships cannot extricate themselves from the crisis. They lack the robust advantage of a fully functioning central business district citysystem to lead the region's economic renewal. The process of reconciliation between Detroit's parallel cities has been a constant, sincere process, but the lack of new city-building approaches that can reconcile the divergent needs and strategies of the downtown city and the suburban city prevents the reestablishment of a functional metropolitan region and the rebuilding of the foundation economics of density and association.

A Dharavi leader from the ruling Congress Party has agreed to meet with us to discuss the Slum-Free Dharavi plan. Twenty months have passed since our lunch meeting with Mukesh Mehta.

Varsha Gaikwad is new to her post in the state legislature. She was elected in 2004. But she comes from a tradition of political strength in Dharavi. Her father, Ekwath Gaikwad, is a member of India's Parliament. Their Congress Party has been politically dominant in Dharavi for decades and it now controls the state government that is promoting the redevelopment plan. Congress has been part of many campaigns for slum clearance and redevelopment since the 1980s, most of which have failed and some of which have ended with special commissions to investigate their corruption.[17] Since the 1990s, governments have sought a growing role for the private sector in slum redevelopment. It should come as no surprise, therefore, that the established city models of the local builders' community would increasingly influence plans for development on designated slum lands.

But Gaikwad is enthusiastic about the new plan. She impressively cites figures and statistics. As someone who has spent so much time with people in Dharavi, it strikes me that she speaks of them in an oddly patronizing way. "They are very concerned and loving people," she says. "They are poor but they are good," as if these are inherently contradictory. She means no insult but simply addresses the longtime stigma of Dharavi as a place of crime and squalor, a stigma that can now be used to justify a mega-suburb building project as a form of assistance to the people. She informs us of a number of improvements that her party has made to Mehta's plan. Residents prior to 2000, and not just 1995, will now be "given protection" and provided with a free 225-square-foot unit. Maintenance of their new buildings will be free for fifteen years, and the charge for additional space has been set to construction cost and not to the market rate. The powers behind this project are clearly still negotiating with the power dormant in the migrant city.

I ask her how families with both a residence and a street-level workshop will be able to continue their business activities in a high-rise, but she doesn't have an answer. As for the leather industry, she says, "Maybe we have to consider an industrial zone for them. They will get the same property area, but they may have to change the kind of business." Tenders for the project have already been released, she reaffirms, but many essential details seem undefined. No census has yet been taken of Dharavi's residents, and certainly no analysis has been done of its businesses and complex supply chains and cost sensitivities. Now with global finance at the table in the form of competing international developers, the real plan will be hashed out. I urge her to take time, to engage Mumbai's community of creative architects and urban planners to work with the local residents in designing each building and street. But she takes no heed. The parties to the deal making and terms have been decided: now the details will be negotiated, deal by deal, to the advantage of whoever can muster the most leverage. As in too many other cities, this is a game with little real transparent process or rules. The best talent and the best solutions are never considered.

It is unclear whether Dharavi's fractious ethnic and caste communities, its old-timers and new migrants, its industrialists and its seasonal workers will stand together to demand a better plan, with the details plainly negotiated around a bigger table. More likely, they will be divided into separate negotiations, their loyalties picked away and paid off until, cash in pocket, they split their families between new (but substandard) high-rise apartments and new slums, and relocate production to polluting (and less efficient) industrial estates. What seems to matter most for Mumbai's "Next Shanghai" planners and city model builders is that the crisis is shifted, if only temporarily, to out-of-sight locations where it will fester again. In the meantime, they will have their prized piece of central Mumbai between the airport, Bollywood, and the stock exchange upon which to do something "world-class." Floods, tuberculosis, collapsing buildings, unemployment, pavement-dwelling squalor, and free market criminal enterprise will carry on in the background as the consultants and agencies that rate the world-class nature of our cities prepare their next Mumbai assessment. The point of "world-class," after all, does not seem to be the elimination of crisis or even the improvement in the city's overall economic efficiency. The standards that we have increasingly used to rate the major centers of the evolving City have been narrowing to the concerns of central business districts, neighborhoods for professional classes, and amenities and facilities for tourists and international conventions. In the global City, success is often measured, tacitly, through indexes of the incremental advantage gained by one of the City's major interest groups over numerous others.

Sadly, there is unfulfilled potential in Mukesh Mehta's driving ambition. Greater Mumbai's population is expected to grow by another two million people by 2015. Any model that can elegantly address the need for proximate housing and employment in the sprawling metropolis, that can secure the efficiencies of clustering particular industries and their supply chains and distribution points, and that can advance migrant city industries toward cleaner, value-added production could offer a city-building solution and a business opportunity throughout the cities of India and beyond.

But to overcome the impasse, space must be created for more innovative design. In cities, design is the method that makes alignment of urban strategies possible. The master planners, incremental citysystem creators, local urbanologists, architects, and city model builders would all have to play a cocreating part, long before the deals were cut and terms negotiated. This was the space that Mehta, for all his years at the task, seemed to be imagining, but without the approach to do so; the more expedient opportunity was just too tempting. But in the years to come, the true measure of Mumbai's "world-class" nature and the true test of its ability to tame its chronic crisis will not be its success imitating the models of other cities. It will be whether it musters the will and confidence to create a new urbanism of its own.

CHAPTER 9

Great Opportunities Cities
Stuck in Negotiation

In the City of Crisis, competing alliances stake their economic and political power on city-building approaches that work at cross-purposes. But for many cities the problem is nearly the opposite. They lack a sufficient concentration of power around any stable approach for building common advantage in the city. This lack of any consolidated approach leaves even the most affluent and admired cities unable to steer their development course. The city's development is determined by expedient deal makers and shifting external pressures and is shaped by city models, ad hoc building, and master-planned projects that together create an ad hoc result. The leaders of such a city—such a very typical city—are perpetually focused on negotiations over secondary details without the ability to pursue bigger visions and opportunities. The Great Opportunities City lacks a basic strategic capability to face and shape its final phase of growth. Progress is measured by individual projects and showcase buildings and not by wholesale transformations.

For all the power concentrated in Mohathir Mohamad and his political and business allies, his regime lacked the urbanism experience or confidence to find its Malay Path. No particular Malay urbanism was established by billions in public investments. Foreign city models, foreign urban designs, and mega-skyscrapers as a form of monument building filled the void. Other cities, like Toronto, have a gifted community of urbanists, but their lack of alignment with a stable political-business coalition, able to muster the power to discipline the city's development, has often left them exporting their services to other cities rather than achieving visions for their own.

To the south of my Toronto patch, where a stream once flowed down to the industrial waterfront and harbor, an estimated two thousand acres of largely derelict, open land juts out into Lake Ontario. After Detroit, these Port Lands, as they are called, are perhaps the largest undeveloped downtown terrain in any major North American city. Over the decades, old industries have left the area to seek advantage in cities elsewhere. A constant stream of trucks on the fourteen-lane highway twelve miles to the north has replaced the Great Lakes freighter traffic that once brought economic purpose to the harbor. The land has been steadily cleared, and its substrata of toxic industrial soil has been cleaned, waiting more than twenty years now for some new vision to be imprinted upon it.

But after many visioning exercises, plans, controversies, and soul-searching public debates about the city's purpose, the Port Lands remain a barren place, collecting the random overspill of the city, not becoming part of it. Most activity there is temporary. It is a district of garbage transfer stations, recycling businesses, concrete mixing yards, depots, and machinery repair yards. Anchoring these tenants are an old power station, a huge sewage treatment plant, a roofing factory, and the offices of the city's power utility. "Progress" over the last twenty years has included a golf range, a food store, and the increasing use of the wide, empty roadways by cyclists. If you can find your way through the old industrial lands to where Lake Ontario laps their shores, you will discover an undeveloped northern Riviera. There are sandy beaches, hardly used. Groups have established ad hoc sailing clubs and marinas, unknown but to those who use them. There is a narrow peninsula of land that reaches miles out into the lake. It is the accretion of demolition waste from fifty years of construction booms, but only nature has given it a designed purpose, as habitat for 440 species of plants, 290 species of birds, and even for wild coyotes. This waterfront area is barely two and a half miles from the downtown skyscrapers, but few of the five million people in greater Toronto have visited it. They know it only as a symbol of the impotence of generations of city, provincial, and federal governments, highlighted by the media with each passing election.

For thirty years Toronto's elected leaders, agencies, planners, architects, and developers have casted visions for the Port Lands' redevelopment. The resulting plans range the history and philosophies of urban planning, from large-scale master plans to detailed, community-based designs. Some see the area as "employment lands" for a new generation of inner-city industry. Others envision a compact, smart growth city there, mixing residential, recreational, retail, and "clean" industry into a citysystem served by transit. Others put more emphasis on the restoration of nature at the mouth of the river and the creation of a huge recreation area at the heart of a green corridor that runs the 120-mile length of Lake Ontario's urbanized western shoreline. Others see the Port Lands as a site for competitive positioning in the global City, seeking to build a media and IT cluster to keep pace with other cities. The federal government has placed its bet on renewal of the working harbor. Thrice the city and its private sector champions hitched the Port Lands' fortunes to bids for the Olympic Games and the World Exposition. Many millions were spent on these plans and hundreds of urbanists, politicians, residents, investors, and activists were involved in the belief that great opportunities lie just within the city's reach. Yet the Port Lands remain like a giant warehouse of the city's untapped potential to which no one has yet found the key.

During these decades, Toronto's development firms, architects, and planners have made their marks on cities across the world. One firm led the transformation of London's old industrial harbor into Canary Wharf, one of the most important downtown business centers in the world. Another applied the principles of Toronto's celebrated urbanism—compact, transit friendly, mixed use—to the design of a new Beijing commercial neighborhood, where street-level retail shops, cultural facilities, high-tech offices, and exhibition spaces have been located close to new housing developments. Baltimore, Boston, Chicago, Montreal, San Diego, Seattle, and Vancouver all redeveloped their old industrial harbors. There have been three major real estate booms in Toronto: in the mid-1980s, the late 1990s, and the first decade of this century. These growth spurts have added billions of dollars of new cityscape to North America's fifth largest metropolis. But most of this growth has not taken place according to

Toronto's plans or espoused urbanism. Rather, most of the growth is based on imported American models of residential suburbs, stand-alone condominium towers, strip malls, big-box "town center" malls, and office parks, filling old neighborhoods, industrial areas, and the green fields of the city's agricultural periphery alike.[1]

The population of Toronto's "edge cities" has grown from 37 percent of the urban region's total in 1981 to 53 percent in 2004, increasing by 1.7 million people in those twenty years. Under current growth scenarios, by 2030 the outer suburbs will be home to 61 percent of the region's population, adding another 1.7 million while the central Toronto population increases by only 300,000. If the Port Lands represent the city's strategic incapacity, as an urban community, to build its visions on established urban lands, then the region's Americanized sprawl reflects the community's failure to translate its efficient, vibrant, semi-European urbanism into compelling new solutions for the growing region.

Toronto's dilemma, like that of other great cities such as Los Angeles, Sydney, or Santiago (Chile), epitomizes the urban strategy condition that I call the Great Opportunities City. The Great Opportunities City seems to have everything going for it: a strong economic base and vibrant markets, access to capital and fiscal solvency, civic awareness and engagement, a legacy of infrastructure, talent, and social welfare. It is the kind of place that should be a world leader in urbanism—as Toronto has been in social policy for immigrants, public health, affordable housing, the arts, and even urban planning. But it chronically fails to build the city that it plans, knows is possible, and even sees built elsewhere. Great Opportunities Cities—explored here through the example of Toronto—help us to understand the benefits, as well as the considerable challenges, of establishing and maintaining vibrant, efficient, and productive urbanisms across entire metropolitan regions.

If the dominance of city models and ad hoc building over urbanism teaches us anything, it is this: the renewal of urbanisms in today's market-oriented societies, and with them the establishment of a global urban civilization, requires clear and compelling economic propositions. New urbanisms, even as they respond to unique local conditions, must create commercial opportunities so predictable that they rally a city's private interests to support necessary market disciplines and reforms. We would love to plan and build our cities solely for a great purpose—for equity, environmental sustainability, social empowerment, or something as basic as livability—but these public purposes cannot displace the Urban Revolution's genetic entrepreneurialism. Even in state-controlled societies the commercial imperative was not tamed; public city builders had to come to terms with the often nontransparent forces of wealth accumulation. One of the greatest failings of modern planning has been its misapprehension of this nature of the city. While ideals of urbanism were debated, others mastered the satisfaction of a more basic urban hunger.

The satiating scalability of late-twentieth-century city models has been awesome to witness. These models do not pretend to serve any great purpose; they are an honest, expedient response to a great demand. They are simplified, predictable starter kits for what might later become real cities. In the Urban Revolution's most recent phase they evolved from local products and business models into a global trade in turnkey cityscapes. Models like the residential suburban subdivision introduced a mass market, retail dimension into city development, in principle giving households an empowering consumer choice, but they reduced the city to a commodity. Now we struggle because the economics of city models are so narrowly crafted for short-term paybacks. They seldom seed, and generally undermine, the more robust economics of a truly empowering citysystem. The good news for Great Opportunities Cities like Toronto is that their histories have bestowed technical and design expertise, cultural and political norms from which new practices of urbanism can be forged to outperform the expedient solutions of the city models. Their challenge is to consolidate this legacy into an approach that is so replicable that its practices do not have to be renegotiated every time a new market opportunity arises.

To establish and institutionalize such practices, local political, civic, business, and technical interests have to form a stable alliance to advance them against resistance from both expedient and entrenched interests. Resistance is reliably encountered from competing political jurisdictions whose fiscal footings lie in expanding the territories of city models; from public bureaucracies, industries, professional associations, and labor unions whose business models have been tailored to the old ways of city building; from speculating landowners and development interests; from established residents and tenants; and from criminal organizations. Shared commercial interest, political consensus, legal control, economic muscle, and financial capital must all come together around the new practices if they are to dominate a period of growth.

This alliance must raise hundreds of new standards, and discipline institutions and investors to comply with them. This means the alliance, from its leaders to the community that supports it, must be extremely literate about the details of its practice of urbanism. It is the details that make an urbanism coherent and deliver its citysystem results. The mayor, the chamber of commerce, the newspaper editors, and the community activists all must know, for instance, how a different road or sidewalk width, applied with different retail activities, building densities, or cultural groups, creates different kinds of life and commerce. The substantial impact that a five- or ten- or twelve-foot sidewalk has on the economics, uses, and ambience of a street must be clear to them all. These details cannot be left to the experts. The alliance needs to understand and fight for them not unlike a CEO understands how a product's design and business processes define her company's value proposition, brand, and competitive advantage. The acquisition of sufficient land, the negotiation of the project's design, the financing of the project, the constant monitoring and enforcement of execution, and the relocation of existing activities must all become an efficient, predictable undertaking of *an urbanist community*. To do this, a large part of the alliance's work is to steadily reform laws, government procedures, and standards that prevent the implementation of the new urbanism. The alliance, in other words, needs to create a new institutional regime to support the practice. Time is of the essence. Competing interests share the same windows of opportunity when markets favor and facilitate the city's rapid growth. Having missed many opportunities before, they must now secure the momentum. Their city's final phase is here.

Toronto, like most cities, has gone through phases of different city-building approaches since its initial settlement in the 1790s. As a frontier outpost in the British Empire, it was initially a planned affair. The city began with a carefully surveyed two hundred fifty thousand acres purchased from indigenous people, which was further surveyed into thousand-acre "concessions" and split into two-hundred-acre lots as part of the vast British land survey of Upper Canada. This survey established the rectangular street grid, which today still defines the city's micro-economics of commerce, residential life, and traffic flow. Even as the Crown quickly dispensed large lots to loyalists to create an elite of founding fathers and secure the strategic harbor, the Crown had its own vision for the future city. It declared the land between the lots and the waterfront be "reserved for the use and benefit of the inhabitants [as] a public walk or mall in front of the . . . Town." From its start, Toronto was given to attempts at, and even successful periods of, master planning by supra local authorities. Master planning is the first aspect of Toronto's evolving city-building tradition that has surged and retreated over its centuries.

But plans for public purposes often unfolded contrary to intent. In his aptly titled "The Struggle for Urban Space," historian Peter Goheen describes the opening scene of Toronto's struggle over its waterfront lands. "Private interests soon enjoyed entrenched privileges on these public lands," he writes, and "found no obstacle in appropriating much of it for their own purposes." The history of planning in the city started with "confusion between stated principle and permitted practice."[2] This gap between progressive policy and deference to private interests is another recurring theme during most cycles of Toronto's development.

The initial battle for public use of the waterfront lasted seven decades. It was dominated by scandalous deals between city officials and powerful railway companies, which eventually turned the whole public area into a giant rail corridor and train yard. With the initial waterfront usurped by private interests, in 1840 the Crown asserted that the incorporated city, now all of six years old, must create a new public waterfront "esplanade" by filling in a 350-foot perimeter of the bay. The young city council created this new land, but then gave private interests long-term leases to it, further expanding the railway lands. When scandal forced the council to reconsider those leases, the Grand Trunk Railway plausibly threatened to place its lines down Queen Street, Toronto's main commercial avenue. "The citizens," writes Goheen, "having evinced little interest in the changes surrounding the Esplanade construction, responded with alacrity. When they realized the jeopardy of their private interests" (i.e., to their Queen Street properties) they conceded the new esplanade to the railway. Ever since, Torontonians have fought to reclaim the waterfront for public use. In the 1890s, when the Canadian National Railway pressed to expand waterfront operations, Toronto's first major citizens' organization was established and joined the Board of Trade and labor unions to contest their plans. These struggles ingrained a further aspect of Toronto's city-building tradition: organized civic resistance to master-planned or large-scale private developments. Even during the real estate boom of the 1980s, as the old railway yards were replaced with high-rise condominium towers, there was outcry about the lack of commitment to public interests. But no alliance rallied enough to establish any community standards, not even to stop the towers' hideous architectural designs that encroached on the public esplanade even as they served as the city's new public face.

The de facto master planning of the railway companies provided Toronto with the extension infrastructure it needed for nineteenth-century industrialization. With industrialization, a world of immigrants arrived in the city. Providing housing to the growing immigrant population close to their jobs spawned the kind of industrial city neighborhood citysystems that were characteristic of manufacturing cities from Chicago to Baltimore. Even after industrial jobs disappeared, these robust citysystems still gave Toronto its vibrancy as a city of neighborhoods.

Industrial city neighborhoods are a product of both ad hoc and city model building. Their three main components—clusters of manufacturers, uniform tracts of standardized homes, and commercial avenues mixing retail, service, and light manufacturing—coevolved into citysystems. Density (proximity *and* concentration), combined with limited inner-city mobility, was the enabling force. It created an intensity and regularity of economic and social relationships that allowed the city model residential developments to evolve into a neighborhood where people shared work and social lives, and then into self-standing communities with their own institutions (i.e., association), such as churches, merchants' associations, and social clubs. Most neighborhoods established a distinctive ethnic composition. They became cohesive urban villages; the factories, warehouses, market areas, and offices to which their workers commuted each day were like their outlying fields.

These self-evolving systems of manufacturing, residential, commercial, and social life were further consolidated through Toronto's prescient approach to building schools, parks, and sports and community centers at the unit level of each neighborhood. Acquiring these investments from city hall became a neighborhood rallying point that further organized the citysystems into political communities. Even after the decline of manufacturing, the individual neighborhood defined the social-commercial ecology of Toronto. It provided the groundwork for its successful multiculturalism and tolerance for immigrants, which still allows Toronto to function as a city with a population that is more than 50 percent foreign-born.

Around the larger industrial and commercial areas and university districts, the citysystems became particularly robust. They developed their own leadership and power networks and extended their strategies beyond Toronto, evolving into the central business district, entertainment-arts-tourism district, and university district that make Toronto a world city today. The evolution of Toronto's neighborhoods and districts into robust social-political-economic centers was the ultimate achievement of its as yet unconsolidated urbanism.

Throughout Toronto's history, the above four traditions of city building—supra-local master planning, perversion of plans and visions by private interests, civic mobilization, and strong neighborhood/district systems—always played a part in its growth. But they have rarely, if ever, merged into a coherent, stable practice that would allow the city to realize its increasingly ambitious plans.

Toronto's most successful and stable period of planned development took place between 1950 and 1970 in what Larry Bourne, the senior planning professor at the University of Toronto, calls the golden age of supra-local master planning.[3] In 1953 the provincial government established a metropolitan government for Toronto and its twelve area municipalities. It was the first metropolitan jurisdiction of its kind in North America. Metropolitan Toronto provided a massive tax redistribution machinery—drawing revenues from central Toronto's business and neighborhood citysystems and allocating them to city-building projects in postwar suburbs. Aligned with the construction industry, the new regime built a contiguous infrastructure for those suburbs to develop into part of the city. Somewhat like the railroad-building era of a century before, this was a period of technocratic planning, dominated by engineers. In the new metropolis, historian Richard White told me, "the engineers were in charge and there were no citizens in the way to stop them. They could build to their hearts' content." In little more than a decade there was a regional water and sewer network. The transit system expanded into the second largest in North America. A new provincial housing corporation was created to build large volumes of subsidized public housing throughout the metropolitan area, following a local ethos of creating mixed-income districts that integrated newcomers into established city life. A regional conservation authority was established to control development and prevent flooding along river corridors. A regional planning agency with authority over development in rural areas beyond the new metro municipality was able to substantially contain sprawl during the 1950s. With planning and infrastructure working together, housing and commercial development was concentrated along major transit and arterial road corridors. This maintained a concentration of employment in the central city, "attracting young professionals to settle in older inner city housing,"[4] says Bourne, even as the same demographic fled to the newer, distant suburbs in other North American cities.

The planners in this period also had insight into the efficient economy and social ecology of the industrial city neighborhood. Rather than following the professional planning fashion of the day by separating employment, residential, and commercial activities into sometimes distant zones, they promoted mixed use across the metro area to reduce transportation demand. "This was a carryover of an old-fashioned attitude," says White, "that people move close to their work."[5]

"You have to give them credit," White continues. "Never had cities grown so fast. I have sympathy for the solutions they proposed in the face of the problems. They were indigenous solutions and they worked remarkably well." The infrastructure of the metro project provided Toronto with the structure to surpass American cities in transit ridership, urban energy efficiency, and social peace. But their successes included two miscalculations. Both were based on an underestimation of the impact that the metro government's final infrastructure project—a new highway network—and its economics of extension would have on the social and economic workings of the industrial city neighborhood.

Following the national government's construction of a super-highway across the northern edge of Toronto, the metro government developed a system of expressways feeding southward into the city. This and the widening of arterial roads dramatically increased mobility between metro area districts. The region became commutable, supporting the growth of more distant edge cities with limited fiscal and civic ties to the metro city. With such mobile living, the ad hoc mixed-use areas encouraged by the metro planners failed to evolve like industrial city neighborhoods. Wherever a new highway reached into the city's street grid, the affected area became a corridor of goods and people flows, not a place where a citysystem could grow. Old neighborhood commercial-retail avenues became suburban strip mall corridors. The domination of "flows" over Toronto's traditional place-based living increased in the 1980s–1990s as big-box city model shopping plazas replaced the strip malls. Commercial, retail, and residential buildings now worked against each other, their users anonymous to each other rather than knitting together into a community. For decades to follow, development in the greater Toronto area—the huge geographic catchment of commercial and commuter flows that ties the metro city and its edge cities into an uncomfortable interdependency—reflected the worst kind of ad hocism. The city's form reflected principles of the local urbanism, but the design details of new buildings and streets and the scale of the city models undermined its economics, and the social ecology of the citysystem collapsed. Across the city, residential streets dead-end against warehouses or small factories for commuting workers. High-rise apartments for transient renters are built in settled low-rise neighborhoods. Stores and restaurants designed to serve a neighborhood clientele are crowded out by retail outlets for the flow of commuters. With each opportunistic year of growth, the city became more a hodgepodge of unrelated buildings and uses. For the master planners, this was not a problem, argues White. They planned the city at a macro-level only. "The hodgepodge was the plan," he says. "The market was at work, and letting it run its course is what the planners wanted."

The second miscalculation, in the face of unanticipated change in the city's dynamics, was a powerful backlash from the old industrial city neighborhoods themselves. Toronto's city-building traditions divided against each other rather than dovetailing into a coherent urbanism: neighborhoods and civic activism against master planning and private-interest ad hocism. Industries may have declined or moved on, but the old neighborhoods retained economies of association and commercial-retail vitality with which to fight. In Detroit and Buffalo to the west and south, they saw massive highway projects destroying whole residential districts and creating sterile landscapes of high-rises and parking lots. Toronto's neighborhoods drew battle lines wherever planner-engineers mapped an expressway or private developers a new city model project. In the early 1970s, the civic-neighborhood coalition installed a reform government in Toronto City Hall to fight the metro government's technocratic plans. With this, the central city essentially backed out of the metropolitan project. Toronto and its adjacent municipalities turned inward and away from the problematic development of the region as a whole. Toronto's most advanced urbanism became defensive, focusing on preservation rather than crafting the models and practices for the city that was steadily growing beyond its jurisdiction. Civic protest stopped two major highway projects into the central city; another campaign rallied to tear down the elevated highway along the Toronto waterfront (which replaced the railway lines), renewing hopes for an esplanade. These hopes were dashed by the embattled construction of a wall of brutalist high-rises along the highway corridor. Activists and preservationists fought the neighborhoods' clearance for ad hoc urban renewal. But the steady growth of the Port Lands' miles-long spit of demolition waste measured the progress of their losses.

At the same time, the provincial government started an ill-fated planning exercise. It focused on distributing resources from the six municipalities of the original metro area to develop new town centers in the nineteen edge city and new suburb municipalities of the expanding urban region. Different national government agencies and companies meanwhile promoted their interests through control of the region's old railway corridors, harbor lands, and a former military airport, giving them control over strategic development sites. The municipalities turned competitively against each other. Mayors of the smaller cities surrounding Toronto engaged in tax and subsidy battles to attract businesses and to build up their own imitation downtowns.[6] The new suburbs, writes Bourne, "boomed with little coordination with either development or service provision with Metropolitan Toronto."[7] While their infrastructure and growth was subsidized by Toronto's tax base, they railed against the central city and its special inner-city urbanism and needs.

The result was a grinding halt to any kind of planned growth or coherent urbanism for the emerging city-region. Greater Toronto became a theater of competing visions, city-building approaches, and jurisdictions. Bold ideas about compact growth, pedestrian-friendly development, livability, and the "ecosystem approach" to development continued to be sanctioned in resolutions, strategy papers, and official plans but quickly became impasses in practice. The winners were the experts of expediency: the ad hoc builders (in the inner city) and the suburban city model builders. Private developers and their lawyers mastered ways to override municipal efforts to discipline development. Throughout the 1980s and 1990s, the contrast between the reformers' idealistic plans and the ad hoc reality grew ever wider.[8]

Feuding through protracted impasses—between the city's reformers and its developer allies; between the city, metropolitan, provincial, and federal governments; and between neighborhood groups and private developers—became the city's new master craft. Failing in a renewed urbanism to ally their interests, Toronto's best renewal efforts steadily became a tokenistic stream of publicly subsidized "anchor projects," each re-celebrating the vision but catalyzing little. The distinction between symbols of progress and progressive achievements became lost. Victories were claimed over the passage of new plans and bylaws, but these were rarely truly implemented. New facilities, renovated plazas, sculptures, and ambitious architecture became a substitute for strategic city building. When one mayor made a big event of placing dozens of life-sized moose sculptures around the city (mimicking similar exercises in Chicago and New York) this was understood as token boosterism. But when the city's elite finally succeeded, after more than a decade of effort, in securing a location and financing for a new opera house—a single building—the event was celebrated as a historic breakthrough that would boost Toronto's status and prospects in the world. The opening of the top-class building was feted by a public rally on the city hall square and commemorated in a gush of special media broadcasts and cover stories, suggesting that Toronto had finally arrived. Similarly, the adorning of museums with new facades by David Libeskind and Frank Gehry or the much-heralded construction of a me-too mini Times Square plaza, adorned with flashing advertisement screens, were cited as forms of resurgence in the city. Each successive effort revealed Toronto's shaken confidence in its own urbanism.

Although Toronto's intact citysystems weathered economic downturns and renewed themselves during growth cycles in the 1970s–1980s, in neighborhoods disrupted by imposed urban renewal and in the half-finished cityscape of the spreading suburbia, no act of planning could direct the incursions of condo, office, mall, and big-store city model builders.

As the central city of Toronto wrestled with split jurisdictions, divided power, and querulous civic divisions, the investors, builders, and pioneer settlers of the emerging global City sought advantage in Canada's largest urban region. The migrant pioneers have been arriving by the hundreds of thousands every decade. In the 1990s, more than seven hundred thousand new immigrants settled in the greater Toronto region. Girish is one of them.

Now in his late forties, Girish is a first-generation urbanite. He was born to a land-owning farming caste in a coffee-growing region 150 miles west of Bangalore. When he was a teenager, he lobbied to go to school in the city, where his father had studied before him. He took his first degree in accounting from a small regional college and then went back home to start a small plantation. But his educational ambition was hardly sated. In 1986, he completed his second degree, in law, at a more prestigious Bangalore university. This was during the early years of Bangalore's development into a global IT center. In the spirit of the time, Girish turned away from the more traditional career path of staff accountant at an established firm and joined forces with a local software entrepreneur. This man had secured exclusive license from a British firm to develop one of the first off-the-shelf accounting software packages for the Indian market. When this venture sputtered, Girish stuck to his entrepreneurial path, starting an accounting practice with a colleague. But this proved too small for his ambitions.

"Since a child, I was fascinated by the Western world," he tells me over coffee at the most convenient and convivial meeting place we could find between our respective inner- and edge-city homes—a labyrinthine IKEA store located off an expressway exit. "I knew someone who had gone to Sydney, Australia, who had gotten a job there. He had done very well," he says. This man introduced him to a business that sought an accountant for an Australian start-up, building a credit card payment system for taxicabs. He applied and was hired on a temporary visa.

In Sydney, Girish overcame the loneliness of separation from his wife and two children by spending weekends with a close-knit community of young south Indian bachelors in the city's Liverpool area. Liverpool, a settlement of Serbian, Fijian, Vietnamese, and Italian immigrants, "is the best place," he recalls. The south Indians he met there weren't professionals like him; they were printers, builders, and fitters. "But they were good cooks and they used to do house parties," Girish says. "Four of them would share a one-bedroom apartment and take turns sleeping on shifts, and would share the same car." The men networked endlessly about jobs and plans for further immigration. "It was a lucrative thing," Girish called it, describing the unique association of such an immigrant neighborhood, "to go to that area and talk to everybody and learn what was happening." Through these networking practices, Girish secured a job with Oracle, and then with Compaq.

These advances emboldened Girish, and when his temporary visa expired, he faced a choice: to return home to rejoin the rise of software companies there or to permanently emigrate with his family to Australia or to a city that one of his Sydney contacts had explored before him—Toronto. He tried Australia first, but under the country's strict immigration rules, which prequalify people for certain occupations, he failed to get a visa. He returned to Bangalore in 2001. The economy there was in a slump due to the burst of the dot-com bubble. Salaries were falling, and younger professionals were taking the available jobs. "I applied to Canada on the spur of the moment, and paid my five hundred dollars," he recalls. "Five months later I was called for an interview. It was as casual as you and me talking here. I was approved in a few weeks."

Girish and his family moved to an apartment in Mississauga, a sprawling edge city that proudly tries to rival Toronto and hosts the region's largest Indian community. He soon discovered that his Indian education would not be recognized by the provincial institute that has a near monopoly on chartered accountants, so he applied for more junior positions. "I applied for one hundred fifty jobs. I think I was a great fit for some, but I didn't get a single interview," he explains, the enthusiasm of his Sydney stories waning as he characterized these early Toronto years as "a sinking ship" mentality. "I went to the settlement assistance organizations, but they were not that helpful. They'd say 'here is a course you can join' or 'why don't you upgrade your skills to a Canadian CPA,' but six, seven, eight months had passed and I was depleting my savings.

"It was too frustrating just applying and waiting, so finally I went to a temporary employment agency and got a job on a production line assembling barbecues. It was OK. At least it paid me at the end of the week. Everyone on that line had a profession. There was an engineer from Gujarat. Another was a technician from the Philippines, and another a retired major from the Indian Army. I think," he says, recovering his wit, "that I was the only certified accountant. Then, with one day's notice, thirty or forty of us were laid off."

By the time I met Girish in 2006, he had been a taxi driver for years. "One guy at the factory," he relates, "had a friend who had been a systems analyst in the UK. In Toronto he was a taxi driver. So he told me how to go to city hall in Mississauga and get a taxi driver's license. Then one day I was taking a class to be an income tax preparer. I met a man there who had an airport limousine. He walked me into the airport holding my hand to get me a job there. Otherwise it's very hard to get in. That's a Punjabi-controlled business," he explains, describing the particularly successful chain migration of that ethnic community.

In the course of getting to know Girish, I was helped by a friend, himself an immigrant professional turned taxi driver, to interview a series of airport drivers.[9] They had found their way from India, Pakistan, and African countries via stints at schools and jobs around the world. One had a master's degree in computer engineering, another had been a management consultant, and another a factory manager. Uniformly, their engineering and accounting educations were not recognized by

Toronto's professional institutes. They had worked as security guards, factory workers, or warehousemen. One told me about a prominent Indian astrophysicist who was working on a factory line.

Their stories are reflected in larger statistics. Recent census data show that so-called visible minorities in Canada are 20 percent more likely to have a university degree than white Canadians but that immigrant unemployment rates are two to three times higher.[10] Recent immigrants with degrees made less than half the salary of their Canadian-born counterparts. The average income of an immigrant with a university degree in 2005 was $24,636—in Toronto more than half of this would be needed just to rent an apartment. The gap between the educated immigrant and Canadian-born citizen has been widening for more than a decade.[11]

The problems that immigrants face in their personal development in Toronto have exacerbated the widening spatial gap in the urban region as well. The central city's recovering neighborhood citysystems have been less and less able to serve them. Historically, central Toronto was the landing point for the region's, and indeed for most of Canada's, immigrants. First-generation immigrants still make up half of central Toronto's population and more than a million immigrants have established residence there since 1980. But increasing numbers, unable to find jobs and affordable housing, have settled in the edge suburbs. Now three of greater Toronto's edge cities have a higher concentration of immigrants than Toronto itself.[12]

Toronto's traditional neighborhoods, lacking their local employment base, have lost their potency as vehicles for the immigrant's advancement. Immigrants with lower incomes and skill levels still concentrate in central city neighborhoods, where crowded, extended-family living is accepted or subsidized housing is available. They also crowd into the 1950s–1960s urban renewal projects like Thorncliffe Park. Originally planned for 12,500 residents, today Thorncliffe Park is home to 30,000 people, more than two thirds of whom are immigrants. They often live at the margins and depend on ethnic networks to find work. Informal labor and commerce are an important part of the economic equation in such places. But those who seek homeownership and less crowded conditions have increasingly had to hedge their opportunities in the

Sheppard East Village, a Toronto immigrant neighborhood. The strip malls and auto service shops along this six-lane arterial road, twenty miles from downtown Toronto, are connected by name only into something akin to a town center for this middle-class immigrant district of single-family homes, high-rise apartments, and light industrial zones. Banners on the roadway's light posts exhort drivers to "Stop, Shop, See Sheppard East Village." (Photo: Jeb Brugmann)

suburbs' residential subdivisions, shopping complexes, and industrial-office parks. Here they join the city of flows and a social ecology less of neighborhood building than of extended families and ethnic networks and institutions.

The political impact of this new social geography is concerning for Toronto. The good news is that Toronto's place-based living makes for a more stable society than new suburbs. Census data show that people in the central city change addresses infrequently; they settle in. But central city immigrants don't seem to be the fighting owner-citizens of old. Today, the city's lowest voter participation is in areas with the highest concentrations of immigrants. The strongest predictor of voter participation in central Toronto is the concentration of immigrants in a neighborhood—not education, income, racial background, or form of tenancy. In the 2003 elections, participation in high-immigrant areas was 10 percent to 20 percent less than in the areas with the lowest concentrations of immigrants. In the same elections, immigrant communities in the suburbs were electing their own candidates to office.[13] The citizen-practice of Toronto neighborhood building appears less viable to immigrants than the consumer-practice of suburban home ownership, which offers an appreciating personal asset even if it fails to offer efficient living and community.

In the absence of a renewed urbanism, Toronto has been conceding growth to the suburbs. For forty years, its urbanists failed to offer designs for new city neighborhoods and districts that were commercially robust and politically understood enough to compete against the city models. Between 1960 and 2000, more than a million migrants like Girish transformed large swaths of suburbia into global migrant suburbs. But the political activism of identity-based immigrant communities in the suburbs reflects frustration about hours spent in traffic congestion, about the lack of facilities, about their "ghettoization," "lack of proper planning," and "crazy expansion," as expressed by the participants in our interviews. When I asked Girish and other taxi drivers to tell me their favorite places to visit in the greater Toronto area, they all but unanimously mentioned downtown places. Girish savored a walk in the atrium lobby of a particular skyscraper. Another liked the atmosphere of a particular downtown restaurant; another talked about the liveliness of the downtown waterfront in summertime. They still aspire to be fully *urban* people, even as they feel the city has rejected them.

The more the Toronto region is dominated by the mobile living of the suburbs, with its 24/7 flows of truckers, commuters, and shoppers, the more the city of flows has reached into the old central city of places. As suburb building became the development industry's primary product line and approach, it marginalized Toronto's urbanists and urbanism. The majority of greater Toronto has now been socialized to the designs and patterns of the city of flows; they are the new standard. "Downtown living," as the developers now call it, is but another lifestyle choice. For many, "going downtown" is a visit to a theme park. It's no longer a way of building and living.

On the bright side, the flow of workers between central Toronto and its edge cities remains in Toronto's favor: the number of commuters coming into Toronto to work, relative to those leaving the city each day, has remained well to Toronto's advantage.[14] But the total number of vehicles coming into Toronto during the morning rush hour has steadily increased, from 130,000 in 1985 to 213,000 in 2004. This increase is representative of how the suburb's demands for convenient, private mobility have extended into the city.

Against this tide, in the 1990s Toronto's architects, planners, and builders started renewing the old urbanism of neighborhood citysystems, reworking the old economies of density, scale, and association in new building designs. The traditional two- or three-story storefront with upper-floor housing has been raised to a four- to six-story modern retail-office-residential building that faces wide sidewalks, dedicated bicycle and transit lanes, and narrowed automobile corridors. These new corridors bring investment, street life, and culture back to the worn neighborhoods that they border. They are particularly dominated by the self- and locally employed, who do not depend on long commutes. They are an urbanist's answer to the fortress-like condo buildings that turn local residential life inward, while turning the street into a corridor for commuters and the rising vehicle population.[15] These same urbanists now have the support of a coalition of neighborhood groups, the mayor and city council, the Board of Trade, and a new downtown business and urban development alliance, the City Summit Alliance. With this support they are plotting to extend the old street grid into the Port Lands, into old industrial areas, and into a large 1950s public housing campus. If they succeed, their approach may one day transform parts of the suburbs into a completed city. But for now they compete for the old city's heart and soul. Suburban strip malls and big-box plazas, with their constant traffic between suburb and city, extend steadily toward the downtown. The city's commercial-retail space is allocated increasingly to opportunistic, drive-by customers from locations far away, and less in service to adjacent neighborhoods. The two approaches have met head-to-head in a neighborhood called Leslieville.

Leslieville is not a pretty place. Until recently, it was one of the least inspiring and least coherent places in Toronto. Its modest workers' homes and retail avenues were part of a contiguous district citysystem

Suburban city model building reaches into downtown Toronto. When this suburban-styled shopping mall was approved for construction on a main road within five miles of Toronto's central business district, it was heralded by local architectural critics as a humanizing, inner-city "town center" alternative to the standard mall. It hosts a collection of standard-issue, big-box stores with a vast parking lot and empty sidewalk porticos. It has also created a new nexus of traffic congestion. The controversial proposal for a mall in the Leslieville film district is being promoted by the same developer. (Photo: Jeb Brugmann)

that also included a metal foundry, an ironworks, a large tannery, and other manufacturers and warehouses. By the early 1990s most of these old industries were closed, and many of their sites had been cleared. A mix of depots, maintenance yards, and auto repair shops filled the vacuum but hardly replaced their economic value. Neighborhood incomes had flagged. Housing had deteriorated. Retailers operated at the margins, and there was a booming new trade in crack cocaine.

But then the citysystem started rebuilding itself, a testament to the lasting power of particular development patterns linked to a culture of city living. Small film, recording, and art studios, and printing and woodworking shops rented old brick warehouses. Their ad hoc clustering

Toronto's resurgent urbanism. This renewed streetscape, located a few miles from Leslieville, reflects more than a century of Toronto neighborhood-based urbanism. The fruit store on the right is representative of the twentieth-century streetscape. The renewed urbanism has increased density along the corridor, which is served by a streetcar line on the pictured road. Wide sidewalks support the culture of pedestrianism and outdoor café life. The roadways are being redesigned to provide better bicycle right-of-ways. This development abuts a large, new residential neighborhood that was built according to the traditional Toronto street grid. (Photo: Jeb Brugmann)

spawned restaurants and retail shops to serve them. Investors saw the new potential in the buildings and upgraded them. The young professionals and artisans purchased and renovated neighborhood homes, and their incomes brought new businesses to the avenues. More film companies established studios on the vacant, inexpensive industrial lands. The neighborhood's marginal used-furniture and clothing shops started supplying film and theater productions. More workers and professionals from the film and arts industry moved into the area. New restaurants, cafés, and shops opened to serve them. A 2006 study of the area documented the robust economics reestablished there over just a decade. While the old manufacturers and depots reported that the logic for their continued location in the area was the inertia of history, the film and media companies could articulate unique economic advantages gained from clustering in Leslieville.[16] They had an adjacent pool of skilled industry workers in the neighborhood. Together they created a scaled demand for local specialty suppliers and services. A shallow interpreter of Leslieville's renewal would call it gentrification. But the transformation was in fact an industrial city neighborhood rebirthing itself. Leslieville had evolved again into a citysystem and one of the largest film production centers in North America. A few miles away, near a more affluent neighborhood, the updated approaches of Toronto's professional urbanists were refurbishing the main avenue. With success there, Leslieville was the inevitable next stop for their investments and designs.

But the region's suburban momentum now conspires with Toronto's traditional "confusion between stated principle and permitted practice" (as Goheen called it) to destroy that process. Leslieville lies north of the Port Lands. They are divided by a six-lane arterial road, rebuilt not long ago to channel traffic from downtown and the western suburbs to the Port Lands and Toronto's eastern neighborhoods. Hungry for an "anchor project" on the dormant Port Lands, city hall brokered an exclusive lease for the largest film studio in Leslieville to relocate to a new Port Lands film production campus. Reflecting a deficient grasp of their city's best urbanism, city officials promoted separation of the industry from its neighborhood. Reflecting their worn confidence, they failed to tend to the development's details. When city hall granted the mega-studio developer a ninety-nine-year exclusive right to operate the sole studio on the public Port Lands, the developer finessed a deal to finance its new studio by redeveloping its Leslieville studio site into a $220 million shopping mall. Located along the arterial road, Wal-Mart has signed as anchor tenant. Nearby, down the road, the city has already permitted the first big-box store. Now the formative new urbanist alliance in Toronto stands against a seasoned machinery of mall developers and their lawyers, who traditionally secure their approvals from the provincial government. If the developers succeed, the value of the lands where Leslieville's other studios operate will immediately rise. These studios will be pressured to sell out to retail developers. As studios are economically pressured from their sites, with no chance to relocate to the Port Lands because of the exclusive deal with their competitor, the linkage between Leslieville and film production could be severed. Such are the details that determine the fates of cities and their attempted revivals and make the detailed definition of their urbanisms so imperative. With the precedent set for big-box stores and strip malls in Leslieville, it would be nearly impossible to stop the incursion of the city of flows and its city models into Toronto's waterfront lands of greatest opportunity.

In a City dominated by city models rather than by efficient, productive, resilient citysystems, it is worth considering the possible: against the odds, under conditions similar to Toronto's, metropolitan Vancouver has been fostering new citysystems, even during its most profiteering real estate booms. Its practice remains a work in progress; the region has not yet achieved its own ambitious development targets.[17] But over the decades, metropolitan Vancouver has grown consistent with its plans, even as similar governance problems and commercial expediencies moved Toronto away from its own. A critical difference is the degree to which Vancouver has defined and built community consensus and confidence about the urbanism it promotes.

Greater Vancouver spreads across twenty-one independent municipalities, including the inner city of Vancouver, which makes up a quarter of its 2.2 million population. These municipalities each control planning and development within their jurisdictions. Provincial support for regional planning has wavered over the years, with the province actually withdrawing regional planning powers in the 1980s. Regional planning today depends on voluntary municipal participation in a regional federation. In spite of this, metro Vancouver has developed one of the most stable, coherent urbanisms of any region in the world.

The main tenet of metro Vancouver's urban practice is encompassed in the term *livability*. Livability has particular meanings in the Vancouver context. It reflects a cultural consensus in favor of dense, efficient, mixed-use building that preserves the special green spaces and natural scenery of the region. The region's growth strategies have been consistently linked to in-depth research on the values of the region's residents. The result is four main axioms of Vancouver practice: first, to protect a designated green zone consisting of the agricultural and park lands, watersheds, and environmentally sensitive areas that make up two thirds of the region's total land area; second, to develop compact communities in order to achieve density and scale economies in targeted areas; third, to further build and leverage these economies by designing "complete communities," where people can work, live, and play without having to travel great distances; and fourth, to build a regional infrastructure for transit, cycling, and walking to provide nonautomobile options for living in and moving between these complete communities.

From the start, a group of municipalities refused to fully accept the vision. They continued promoting growth by suburban city model and ad hoc development, reaping their predictable tax revenues. The regional authority, Metro Vancouver, did not have legal means to fight this; it could only compete with a more compelling urbanism, in particular through two other city-building approaches: master planning and cultivation of citysystems.

On the master-planning front, Vancouver had the starting advantage of a stable provincial government commitment to maintain an agricultural land reserve, making up a third of the green zone, which serves as an urban growth boundary. Greater Toronto's first real commitment to a green belt came only in 2005, long after the suburban growth pattern was fully established. Then, not unlike Toronto in the 1950s and 1960s, Metro Vancouver and the provincial government used investment in transit, water, and sewerage infrastructure to reinforce the underlying economic logic of three specific kinds of compact communities: a high-density business and cultural core in downtown Vancouver; eight high-density business district citysystems or regional town centers along transit lines; and nine smaller municipal town centers. The provincial government responded further by locating hospitals, colleges, and universities in the centers. The private sector further responded with medium and high-rise retail and housing investment. Ultimate success—the evolution of the compact centers into complete communities—depended on the pace at which they could engage private builders, architects, and investors to master a market-competitive craft of complete community building, competing against better-tested suburban city models.

Surprisingly, in spite of the race against time, development has tilted in favor of the livable region urbanism. Three main practices supported this success. First was the underlying economics of density and scale established in the targeted areas through infrastructure provision and institutional location. Second was the design of competitively priced office, residential, recreational, and mobility solutions for complete communities, first in the high-demand property market of the metropolitan core. These solutions were developed incrementally, project by project. One result is a notable Vancouver style of slim, high-rise glass towers that are designed to preserve street-level views and prevent the heavy, cavernous effect often found (as in Toronto) with high-rise development. Also contrasting with Toronto and other North American cities, buildings were designed to support street life with sidewalk-facing shops and landscaped public spaces. Designs were developed to maintain pedestrian- and bicycle-friendly spaces between buildings.

A third related practice is the involvement of planners and even communities in detailed review of designs. Although this process falls short of actual cocreation of new city spaces, organizing the trial and error of ad hoc citysystem development into *a business process* has helped builders, regulators, and residents adapt projects to local urbanist principles and culture.

While this approach was being honed in the central city of Vancouver, more-established city model products were rapidly securing their market share, particularly between 1970 and 1985, when the new livable region urbanism was just being developed. The sprawl has not been fully contained. From 1979 to 1996, more than twenty-four square miles of former rural land was suburbanized in metro Vancouver, an area larger than Manhattan.[18] (In greater Toronto between 1976 and 1996, 232 square miles of farmland was suburbanized, an area equal to the entire city of San Francisco or of Kuala Lumpur.[19]) But Vancouver's new compact building approaches came to dominate the residential market. Between 1981 and 1991, 67 percent of the region's new housing units were built within the existing urban area; the percentage rose to 78 percent between 1992 and 2001, a much higher proportion than any major North American city.

Other remarkable achievements of the livable region approach are in mobility, convenience/productivity, and green space preservation. In Metrotown, the livable region's largest regional town center, 30 percent of employees walk or take transit to their jobs. By comparison, 92 percent of the workers in the surburban office parks have to drive to work, and their commute times have been steadily rising. Regionwide, the growth of compact city centers shortened average distances for work-related travel between 1996 and 2006. Regional transit ridership grew faster (39 percent) than automobile ownership (15 percent) and population over this decade.[20] Per capita automobile ownership in metro Vancouver is now half that of greater San Francisco.

Meanwhile, the Agricultural Land Reserve and public land acquisitions helped foster a vibrant regional agricultural economy in the green zone. Between 1986 and 2001 the amount of land in agricultural production in the region actually increased. Gross farm receipts more than doubled. Farm wage payments within the region grew almost five times, to $144 million in 2001.[21]

Consider the choices ahead. The region's population is expected to grow by another seven hundred fifty thousand people by 2030. If this growth is absorbed at the densities of suburban Vancouver municipalities, 216 square miles of new cityscape would be required to house and employ them. This is more than all of the farmed agricultural land in the region today. Even if all these people are housed and employed at the density of the metro and town centers, another eighty-nine square miles of land would need to be urbanized to house and employ them—60 percent of the local agricultural lands. The only real solution is to further increase housing and job densities in the metro core, the town centers, and along the major corridors. Christina DeMarco, the planner leading the latest regional plan, elaborates. The enormous challenge, she says, "is to preserve livability *and* advance sustainability, recognizing the realities of climate change and peak oil while tackling job sprawl, the loss of industrial land, and housing affordability."

To meet this compounded challenge, the livable region must evolve its urbanism to a next stage. In the preceding phase of the Urban Revolution, planners mastered the development of compactness and cultivated many residential solutions for complete communities but failed to transform the commercial and office park city models into a livable urbanism. If they can do this, they might not only complete the envisioned livable region but also create approaches that can be offered across the uncharted horizon of the global City.

CHAPTER 10

A Planet Transformed

Urban Ecosystem or Global Dystopia?

"In something less than thirty years we're going to have to double the amount of urban development in the developing world. Contemplate for a moment what that means," says economist Steven Sheppard. His audience at the World Bank already knows this. He is softening them up for a new, unimaginable killer fact. "That means," he continues, "take all the cities that are currently in the developing world—Mexico City, Calcutta, Mumbai, Bangalore—and build a whole additional copy; that's what doubling that could entail. That's a tremendous burden on the global economy."[1]

Actually, if he and his colleagues at the Center for Land Use Education and Research (CLEAR) are correct, it could be worse: the urbanized area of the developing world, their studies show, might increase threefold. Such is the base reality of the final phase. The scenarios for greater Vancouver are a tamed version of the trends to be managed across the City over the next decades.

To size up global urban growth, Sheppard along with planner Shlomo Angel, natural resources expert Daniel Civco, and the CLEAR team studied a representative sample of the world's nearly four thousand cities that have more than one hundred thousand people. They used satellite photos and surface light intensities in each urban area to track physical growth between 1990 and 2000. Although densities in developing country cities are about three times higher than in developed country cities, the study found that urban densities are steadily decreasing worldwide.

Sheppard continues: "If average densities continue to decline—as they have during the past decade—the built-up area of developing-country cities will increase from 200,000 square kilometers in 2000 to more than 600,000 square kilometers by 2030, while their population doubles."[2] Based on current building patterns, growth at today's urban peripheries—what they call "outspill"—will be seven times greater than growth through urban "infill" in existing built areas. Shanghai, for example, will have to manage fourteen square miles of new growth *each year*, an area the size of Los Angeles' fifteen downtown districts. The growth of all developing country cities (with 100,000 or more people) would cover an area larger than Japan or Germany. To reduce this costly transformation of natural landscape, the world will need to learn from greater Vancouver's livable region.

The CLEAR project's satellite-level analysis concluded that the City's territorial expansion is driven by population and income growth. But the more we zoom in on cities, the more this big picture logic gets tangled in the complexities of very unique local systems. CLEAR's model suggests very predictable trends in the final phase. But we now know that such transformational trends are also chaotic, as in the case of SARS and its chain mutations and dispersion, defined by very local realities. Urban landscapes, like natural ones, constantly evolve as urban*ological* forms, made of diverse citysystems, city models and master-planned developments. The malleability of cityscapes makes them open to our shaping, which is proven by their diversity. Urbanists like Vancouver's Christina DeMarco constantly try to introduce new forms of development to adjust the city's form and growth to serve the purposes and values of their changing populations.

I once worked in the higher elevations of Vermont's Green Mountains, where temperate hardwood forests give way to dense blankets of evergreen fir and spruce. At those heights, cool weather and shallow acid soils produce a southern outpost of a radically different ecosystem located far to Vermont's north, in the boreal zone. Climbing up and down those mountains, I learned to mark my passage between the temperate and boreal zones, and even the impending weather, from the calls of two bird species: the white-throated sparrow and the tufted titmouse.

Sparrows and titmice come in many forms. Like their more famous cousins, the finches, their adaptations to surroundings can inform the observant person not only of entry into a new kind of habitat but even of changes in atmospheric pressure and chemistry. Until 1986, for instance, canaries (a type of finch) were used in mines to inform of dangerous levels of carbon dioxide. Darwin and his successors have studied the exotic Galápagos finches because of their intense speciation in harsh micro-environments.

Contemporary research on the adaptations of the sparrow and titmouse requires no HMS *Beagle*; they can be readily found on city windowsills anywhere in the world. These birds have a remarkable adaptability to the unique—some might say harsh—habitats of dense cities, providing clues about the ecology of the Urban Revolution and the extent to which it is changing our planet.

It is one thing to report that cities are consuming vast amounts of land, changing our politics, society, and economics. It is quite another to argue that they are changing us and other species *biologically*—even changing the ecology of the planet. But this is exactly the case. As cities expand and extend together, geographically and through continuous exchanges of materials, energy, and species, they are reengineering ecology. Until very recently, few ecologists would even venture to understand cities and their role in planetary ecology.[3] But today increasing numbers of scientists are working to explain cities, and the City, as a living system—as a basic *biological event* on Earth. Their work underscores what I see as the primary ecological challenge of the next decades: during the final phase our approaches to city building, in particular our ability to develop ecological urbanisms, will determine whether the City evolves into a truly functional new ecosystem—a citysystem with stable if not synergistic relationships with natural systems—or whether it will continue to function as a parasitic system that disrupts the metabolism of Earth's great green, blue, tan, and white biomes, triggering chaotic ecological collapse.

This challenge might have been apparent sooner had we listened more carefully to the songs of a little bird called the great tit. In the early 2000s, Dutch biologists Hans Slabberkoorn and Ardie den Boer-Visser found that the songs used by the great tit to attract mates and to defend territories in Amsterdam, London, Paris, Prague, and other European cities were fundamentally different from the songs of their brethren in rural or forested areas.[4] Analyzing tonal frequencies, the biologists determined that the birds had adapted them to compete with the low frequencies of city traffic noise, which made their traditional song inaudible. They went on to suggest that this environmental shaping can start the process of speciation, eventually leading to a unique species of urban bird.

Cities abound with unique communities of animals and plants that have adapted, if not started to speciate, in the urban environment. The many-colored pigeons that thrive in large urban flocks throughout the world, for instance, are descendants of domesticated birds. In a nonurbanized environment, these feral pigeons would revert to the natural gray color of their wild relatives. In cities, their differentiated colors reflect new, urban breeding behaviors.

Even the mating practices of Homo urbanis are different from those of their rural brethren. Scientists have found that city dwellers not only look for different qualities in their mates than do nonurban dwellers but have accelerated the tendency to mate with those of similar backgrounds and traits, a biological process called assortative mating. The acceleration of assortative mating in cities is again made possible by their evolving economics of association. People can meet and pair with each other in new ways, including in marriage, because the density and scale of cities makes more specialized selection more efficient and thereby possible.

Traditional human mate selection involves locally distinct criteria of common kinship, cultural and religious group membership, residential proximity, and the size of a wedding dowry. At one level, criteria such as kinship and cultural group membership reflect ways that rural cultures made mate selection economical; the process was facilitated through established networks. But studies of urban mating practices in many parts of the world reveal an entirely different economics of mating. In the United States, biologist Kevin McGraw studied female mate-selection strategies in twenty-three U.S. cities and found that traditional mate selection criteria like shared place of origin, religion, personality, personal interests, and physical attributes were secondary in densely populated cities that had higher costs of living. Women in these cities placed more emphasis on the income-generating potential of prospective mates. Conversely, they placed less emphasis on the emotional qualities or the personal interests of males.[5]

In Russian cities, studies show that educational attainment has become a more critical factor in partnering than the two previously dominant factors: ethnicity and place of origin.[6] In China, couples that married between 1995 and 2001 were ten times more likely to share the same educational level, compared with a sevenfold probability in the 1980s.[7] This increase in mating between people of the same educational level was not found to be associated with China's economic reforms, but it does correlate with urban migration. Another study revealed the logic of this correlation, showing that household income in five Chinese cities increased with each additional year of spousal education.[8] The trend toward urban mate selection on the basis of education levels was even found in Khartoum, Sudan, where female education traditionally has not been an important factor.[9] In order for these practices to work economically, new routines for meeting those with "the right stuff" have to be developed. In recent decades we've witnessed the creation of markets for efficient urban mate identification by new criteria, including personal advertisements, singles clubs, and Web-based dating services.

It appears, but is still too early to conclude, that mate selection may be more different between the City and rural areas than between countries or cultures. By the same measure, studies show that new urban mate selection criteria are contributing to different social structure in American cities. In a study reported in the *Journal of Urban Economics*, Eric Gould and M. Daniele Paserman argued that mate selection by income-generating potential is reducing the marriage rate in American cities.[10] They used marriage data on 300,000 Caucasian women in 321 U.S. metropolitan areas to understand how urban income inequality is influencing female marriage decisions. Their article, called "Waiting for Mr. Right," showed that new urban partnering routines between working professionals have reduced the overall marriage rate because women are taking more time to find an economically attractive mate. Added to this, economists Raquel Fernández and Richard Rogerson warn that increased marital pairing by earning potential "will significantly increase income inequality" in the United States.[11]

But cities are not only changing mating practices; they are also creating new species and subspecies communities. Cities host entirely different densities of species than would be found in rural areas. The office build-ings and hotels of Toronto, for instance, have become habitats for pere-grine falcons, a bird once driven to near extinction by pesticide use in their traditional habitats. Every spring Toronto hosts one of the largest breeding populations of peregrines in all the vastness of wild Canada. Peregrines are extremely picky and territorial about their nesting sites. In Toronto, the downtown Sheraton Hotel seems to be an annual favorite, whereas another breeding pair recently decided to change locations from the Bell Canada office to the spired glass Yellow Pages building. The urban environment, with its high-rise "cliffs" and concentrated, exposed popula-tions of squirrels and other rodents, is ideal for the peregrine's flourishing.

More remarkable in both number and impacts are the city's rac-coons. Until recently, the raccoon has been a predominantly forest ani-mal whose rural/wild population densities varied with weather and predator populations. On average, in rural areas there is about one rac-coon for every twenty-five acres. However, in Toronto their average den-sity is five times greater: there is one raccoon for every five acres. A study of one Toronto neighborhood found that raccoons were clustered in their own "villages" with around one thousand raccoons each.[12] Special-ized raccoon vaccination programs have had to be mounted to manage raccoon-born disease. City raccoons, therefore, like peregrines and tits, represent the emergence of unique urban biological communities.

Ecologists have only recently undertaken long-term studies of the en-tire biological complexity of an urban region. In 1997, fifty scientists from the University of Arizona in the United States started studying the "human-dominated ecosystem" that we otherwise call the city of Phoenix. In ecological terms, Phoenix is itself a recent event. In little more than a century it has grown from a farming town of 3,100 (1890) to a metropolitan area concentrating 3.7 million people (2005). Phoenix now consumes so much that its ecological footprint—the natural area required to supply the city's annual resource requirements—is as large as the country of Greece or the state of Pennsylvania.

"The development of the city has literally been happening as we watch," said one of the principal investigators, zoologist Nancy Grimm. "What Phoenicians have done is to take this river, which was one local-ized area, and capture the water and distribute it over a very, very large area. If you fly in you can see this—you can see that we have a lot more plant biomass, a lot more trees. There are little lakes scattered all over the place. Scottsdale [a suburb] since 1940 has gone from zero to 167 little lakes." "What you have, in fact," adds her collaborator, archaeologist Charles Redman, "is the creation of an urban ecosystem which is quite distinct but not necessarily impoverished."[13]

Many scientists reject the idea that cities represent anything akin to a real ecosystem. Ecologists characterize ecosystems by what they call a trophic structure, the web of relationships—sometimes called food chains—by which each species provides energy and nutrients to others throughout the web. As a natural ecosystem matures it depends less and less on energy (solar radiation) and nutrients from outside its geography because it more and more efficiently recycles its existing nutrients through predatory and symbiotic trophic relationships. This is what makes it sustainable. The University of Arizona study shows how Phoenix developed unique species communities and trophic structures, but these urban communities are young and unstable like our cities themselves. They require vast imports of water, soil, and fertilizers to be kept alive.

But the most basic, irrefutable finding of urban ecology studies offers some hope: urban forms and zones are neither uniform nor fixed. They can be designed to mimic nature's efficiencies and productivity. We are already constantly redesigning them, a trial-and-error method from which we can learn, for instance, how an unsustainable city-model monoculture can be transformed into a more self-sustaining, ecological citysystem.

Take the species communities and trophic relationships in Phoenix. They vary according to the economic status of Homo urbanis in each city neighborhood. "The diversity of plants," says Grimm, "is related strongly to family income—higher family income, higher plant diversity; lower family income, lower plant diversity." In other words, the types of city building and social relations in particular urban areas fundamentally define populations of species, much as the availability of water or seasonal weather defines species' populations and diversity in a natural ecosystem. The way that we build each city creates a local micro- and regional climate (through its building designs and materials), a new hydrology (through its water supply, pavement, storm and waste water infrastructure), new species communities, human culture and markets and their resource consumption patterns. This fact, increasingly probed by scientists of many fields, highlights perhaps the biggest question confronting us in the final phase. If cities are the fastest growing systems on Earth—particularly in the face of declining natural ecosystems—how can we manage the way they are restructuring the ecology of our entire planet?

In 2004, geographer Andrew Coutts and his colleagues at Monash University in Australia attached instruments for measuring carbon dioxide (CO_2), the primary contributor to climate change, on towers above two Melbourne suburbs.[14] They measured CO_2 levels every hour of every day from summer to winter, collecting the data needed to discern the link between a particular city model and this global problem.

They found that each suburb's daily contribution to climate change varied according to minute differences of building density and design, landscaping, vehicle traffic, and home heating requirements. One of the suburbs, Surrey Hills, had a lower density than the other suburb, Preston (i.e., 1,113 versus 1,248 dwellings per square kilometer) and was about 6 percent more forested; but it also had a higher volume of rush-hour traffic. For most of each twenty-four-hour day, the CO_2 levels above lower-density Surrey Hills were lower than those above higher-density Preston. But during morning rush hour, Surrey Hills' higher traffic levels pushed its concentrations up to the level of Preston's. Then, as photosynthesis started during the daytime hours, the larger volume of plants in Surrey Hills sponged up its CO_2 concentrations, again pushing them lower than Preston's. Surrey Hill's peak concentrations were during the morning rush hour. Preston's were in the middle of the night. The study revealed, in other words, how even small variations in the design of a suburb relate to a global environmental problem.

These differences add up. Consider the annual emissions of Preston: eighty-five tons of CO_2 per hectare. If we apply this as an average across the 830 square miles (215,000 hectares) of greater Melbourne, Melbourne's annual emissions are equivalent to nearly *six years* of CO_2 emitted from Hawaii's Kilauea volcano—the most active volcano on the planet.[15] To put it in further perspective, this is also equivalent to the annual CO_2 emissions from Mexico City (Federal District) with its population of nine million people. (Mexico City produces a net average of 128 tons of CO_2 per hectare, but is a much denser city.)

Coutts and his colleagues were measuring the tip of a far greater iceberg. The greater part of Surrey Hill's and Preston's CO_2 metabolism was undiscernible to their instruments. Most of the greenhouse-gas emissions associated with consumption in these places are generated elsewhere in the manufacture, processing, and transportation system that is the global City.

In 1989, Nobel Prize–winning atmospheric chemist Sherwood Rowland and his colleagues counseled Irvine, California, mayor Larry Agran and me on how North American cities could help contain another global atmospheric problem: ozone-depleting CFCs. After gathering leaders from thirty North American cities to pledge to control these gases through local laws, we received a supportive call from Noel Brown, director of the United Nations Environment Programme for North America. A few weeks later he agreed to host the first worldwide summit of local leaders to address the role of cities in global environmental protection. In September 1990, more than four hundred city leaders from forty-five countries gathered there and founded the International Council for Local Environmental Initiatives, the international environmental agency for local governments. It was the first major meeting of urban leaders ever to be held at the United Nations' headquarters.

During the meeting, a small group met in a side room to discuss an even more audacious project. We wanted to determine how a city's infrastructure and physical layout—urban form—gave structure to its urban energy and CO_2 metabolism, not just day to day, but over the life cycle of a city's buildings, vehicles, fuel and electricity demand, industrial production, and household consumption. We wanted to know not only how individual cities emitted CO_2 but how each city contributed to global climate change through its consumption and economic relationships across the entire City. To do this, we had to develop a way to quantify and attribute emissions created elsewhere to each individual city: *to define each city as an extended energy system.* The city councils and mayors of Ankara, Bologna, Copenhagen, Denver, Hannover, Helsinki, Miami-Dade County, Minneapolis–St. Paul, Portland (Orégon, USA), Saarbrüken (Germany), San Jose (USA), and Toronto/Metro Toronto eventually signed on. With financing from the U.S. Environmental Protection Agency, our Urban CO_2 Reduction Project started some of the most detailed analyses of urban energy use and

CO_2 emissions ever made and pioneered a framework through which more than eight hundred cities are coordinating efforts to address a global environmental problem—a new form of global environmental management at the level of the City.[16]

The data from our analysis confirmed the central hypothesis: cities were indeed new, basic units of global ecological change, each having a remarkably different pattern of energy use, which cumulatively created the City's energy metabolism. These patterns were not so much associated with level of economic development and prosperity as with forms of urbanism and other city-building approaches.

The energy metabolisms of northern European cities, for instance, reflected the region's compact urbanism. Decentralized, local energy-generation facilities reduced energy losses from long-distance electricity transmission and supported the introduction of small-scale cogeneration and renewable energy technologies. Helsinki leveraged the density and scale of its urban form—its tradition of large-volume, three- and four-story buildings organized in dense blocks—to support an underground pipe network that channels scalding waste water from its local power station into 90 percent of the city's buildings. This heating system substantially reduces the city's carbon footprint in spite of its heavy reliance on carbon-rich coal. Each urban form created different economies for mass transit and bicycling. In 1990, around 55 percent of the trips taken in both Helsinki and Hannover were made by transit, bicycles, and walking. In Copenhagen the number was 65 percent. (By comparison, in low-density metro Miami only 3 percent of trips were made by transit and walking.) Even after a decade of suburban growth and multiplying traffic volumes, Helsinki was able to keep public transit use at 39 percent of all vehicle trips.[17] Learning from its urbanism, Finland has made urban form management a critical part of its strategy for meeting Kyoto Protocol commitments.[18]

In the lower-density cities of the United States, power generation was more centralized and located at a distance from the urban centers. The Project's North American participants therefore had greater energy losses from transmission. It also took longer for these cities to get their non-local utility companies to truly participate in the CO_2 reduction effort. In addition, their low-density suburban designs made mass transit and decentralized power generation, like solar or cogeneration, less economical. Transportation was generally the largest source of their CO_2 emissions.

In spite of its lower GDP, Ankara benefited substantially from its organization into *mahalle* citysystems. In effect, each dense mahalle ran its own little energy utility for space and water heating and procured its own fuel (typically coal) from the local market. This made it possible for Ankara to rapidly adapt energy sources compared with cities that had centralized, inflexible energy systems. Within a year of joining the Urban CO_2 Reduction Project, Ankara was adopting residential solar and cogeneration systems and retrofitting mahalle heating plants to burn natural gas.

These differences in urban design, form, and infrastructure produced different systemwide results in each city. When Helsinki analyzed all its energy sources, fuel types, and delivery processes, it found that the city's total urban energy metabolism was 68 percent efficient. In other words, 32 percent of the energy brought into the city from ecosystems elsewhere was lost through waste heat or transmission losses. The city's dense, mixed-use form and transit also meant that most of Helsinki's energy use was concentrated in heating and lighting buildings.

In contrast, transportation was the largest consumer of energy in Toronto. In spite of Toronto's high transit ridership, metro Toronto's low-density sprawl in the 1970s–1980s made transport energy use the main inefficiency in its energy metabolism. Another major source of energy loss came from electricity transmission from distant locations. Overall, Toronto achieved only 50 percent efficiency in its energy use. But this was still a step ahead of the American cities, which wasted nearly 70 percent of the total energy they imported into their urban areas.

Although a region's cities share city-building approaches that can give them similar metabolisms, we found that each city was unique, not unlike Melbourne's two suburbs. The cities in our project therefore developed unique ways to reduce emissions; there was no single blueprint. Helsinki was able to increase the efficiency of its energy metabolism from 68 percent in 1988 to 73 percent in 1995 by extending its district heating and transit systems. Hannover, Germany, reduced its total CO_2 emissions by 7.5 percent in a fifteen-year period (1990–2005), in spite of dramatic emissions increases from automobile and air travel. The city reduced oil consumption for power generation by 62 percent and very substantially increased power and heating efficiencies by constructing ninety-one decentralized combined heat and power plants across the city. It reduced total energy consumption for heating, cooling, and lighting of households (-5 percent) and industry (-12 percent)—all in spite of the economic growth and outspill development during this time period.[19]

Though Portland, Oregon, did not have the advantage of Hannover or Helsinki's citywide density, it was able to keep per capita emissions stable between 1988 and 2000, even as America's per capita energy consumption rose 8 percent. Portland counteracted increasing energy demand from sprawl and population growth by advancing its own form of suburbanism: new developments during this period were designed to use half as much land as developments in the average American city. Through an urbanism based on management of form and design collaboration with developers, it found a unique way to manage outspill.

Tellingly, as in Ankara, when it came time for Toronto to take action, the most viable response came from its largest citysystem: the central business district. City hall was able to rapidly forge a partnership with downtown businesses and skyscraper owners to retrofit their buildings—and bring substantial cost savings. Meanwhile, the municipal energy utility leveraged downtown's density and scale to expand district heating and build a new district cooling system in partnership with downtown building owners.

All of these cities did more than apply new technologies or introduce new efficiency standards to achieve their ambitious targets. To change their basic energy metabolisms, they had to further evolve their respective *energy urbanisms*, combining technology, design, form, planning, business models, infrastructure, partnerships, and behavior change to advance how the citywide energy system works.

Variations in urban metabolisms—and opportunities for change—are observable in all other areas of ecology. Water systems draw from different catchments, consume at different intensities, restructure regional hydrology, have different efficiencies, and disperse waste water differently. Each city collects, concentrates, and then redistributes the nutrients from agriculture, horticulture, and human and animal wastes into regional flows in different ways, but always with impacts at larger scales. Each city hosts and redistributes different species and manufactures different materials and pollutants. As much as satellite photos and high-level models indicate gloomy global trends, the diversity and malleability of cities—their basic adaptive capacity—can be used to reengineer their ecological footprints, and those of the City, in the decades ahead.

But can our growing cities become truly ecological through the advancement of their urbanisms? Can the City, which draws unsustainably from the natural productivity of natural systems, be transformed into a *Citysystem* that produces most of what it needs to sustain itself? Or will further decades of low-efficiency, low-productivity urban growth simply scale today's parasitic extraction of nature's production? Ecologist and urban planner Bill Rees likes to talk frankly about this question. Cities, he argues, are anything but ecosystems. To him, a more accurate analogy, for all the refinement of our urbanisms, is that of a messy animal feedlot.

"Anthills, feedlots, and cities share important systemic characteristics," he argues. "All three are characterized by large populations and extraordinary densities of their keystone inhabitants . . . none is ecologically self-contained nor self-sufficient . . . all are sustained by biophysical processes that occur mainly outside." In true ecosystems, he points out, producers like plants take solar energy and local mineral soils and produce food for other local species. The food webs between all these species self-organize in such a way that the waste of each species can be used again by other species within the system. With the ability to draw directly from solar energy, therefore, an ecosystem is self-regulating and self-sustaining. It is also spatially contained. "While there is often minor spatial or structural separation between [the] components in natural ecosystems" (like the layering of forest canopies), in functional terms, says Rees, "ecosystems are operationally inseparable." To put it differently: Ecosystems, like cities, have unique, place-based biological economies that *extend* in fundamentally different ways than cities. As the ecosystem grows and matures it extends its whole system of production, consumption, and nutrient recycling, not just part of it as a form of half-finished outspill. It completely replicates the intricate designs and relationships that sustain its new growth as a complete system. In fact, as it matures, the circular recycling and exchange get more and more efficient.

By contrast, our extended City building draws massively from distant natural areas and scatters wastes across ever more remote hinterlands. The global City is not contained to the cityscape. If we were to encapsulate even the world's most efficient cities, giving them advanced solar and waste-processing technology and a massive budget, they would not survive the transition to a self-sustaining resource system. The design of the city has a *systemic* flaw. The land area of cities, Rees concludes, "comprise only a tiny fraction (typically much less than one percent) of the total area of productive ecosystem required to support [their] urban human populations."

The way forward lies in the word *system*. As illustrated by Ankara's mahalles or Toronto's central business district, cities optimize their productivity, resilience, *and metabolisms* through citysystems: those unique, spatially compact and complete systems. The citysystem's mature urbanism creates a social ecology through which its owner-users can adapt to new challenges, rebuild from crisis, and create new cultural norms for consumption, enterprise, and living. Because they are more self-contained and have honed their efficiencies, they can be most easily retrofitted, redeveloped, and important, maintained by their owner-users. As the world's nodes of extension, citysystems also promote their practices through networks across the City. Can citysystems also be nodes for ecological transformation of the City in the final phase?

Nobel Prize–winner Sherwood Rowland shares Rees's doubts: it is unlikely that individual cities will develop stable, closed-loop metabolisms like ecosystems. But he points to another possibility. "If modern urban systems are undergoing some form of succession," he writes with fellow scientists, "it is now at the earth system level"[20]—in other words, at the level of a Citysystem. Individual urban regions cannot meet all their resource requirements internally and in their immediate hinterlands. But the world's cities have amassed uncounted stocks of materials and nutrients and can supply each other, further reducing collective demands on nature. In other words, much as half-finished ad hoc and city model districts can be evolved into citysystems, the City can be evolved into a Citysystem. But to secure the possibility of the City's ultimate global form, we first need to become masters of a stable, just, and ecological urbanism.

PART III

Strategy for an Urban Planet

CHAPTER 11

The Strategic City

From Global Burden to Global Solution

Precisely because so many of the world's problems now arise from the poor design, weak governance, and mismanagement of cities, it is imperative that we learn how to transform our cities into centers of the world's solutions. This brings the issue of urban strategy into focus. Urban strategy is a practice not only for the political leaders, planners, and builders of cities but also for industries, corporations, civil society organizations, and governments that build their advantage in cities and depend on them. Urban strategy also addresses the larger question of how to develop the City into a more stable system, politically, economically, and ecologically, and how that system can increase equity, inclusiveness, sustainability, and resilience in the world. It shows us how to move beyond Cities of Crisis, Great Opportunities Cities, and other dilemmas that have challenged even the world's finest cities as they try to manage the Urban Revolution.

Urban strategy is a new practice. The need for urban strategy, above and beyond the tactics and technicalities of city building, reflects the scale of our collective challenge in building more common, stable advantage in the final phase.

In the last section we explored basic city-building approaches—ad hoc, master planning, city model—and local practices of urbanism that can evolve different citysystems. Urbanism was distinguished from building. An urbanism is a way of developing, using, and living in the city in compatible ways to make its economics, politics, social life, and ecology coherent with consensus aspirations and values. Urbanism results from effective urban strategy: the alignment of erstwhile individualistic and competing interests behind a common approach to building and sustaining advantage.

In Cities of Crisis, we saw how conflict becomes chronic when the city building of one major alliance fundamentally undermines the city building or urbanism of another. Progress for one alliance requires regress for the other because both alliances depend so completely on their approach to city building to advance their interests. Reconciliation is impossible unless both sides can cocreate a new urbanism that advances their common interests.

In the Great Opportunities City, no particular urbanism is so established, in spite of protracted efforts to do so. There is a lack of confidence or consensus about the practices needed to build a common advantage. No stable, broad alliance of interests has been consolidated to discipline development. City building can revert to ad hocism, and the built city never comes to match the ambitions of its plans. The city's development is negotiated expediently, deal by deal and lot by lot. Such a city lacks a basic strategic capability to achieve the urbanism to which its majority aspires.

Urban strategy therefore has a very clear purpose: to ensure that the many necessary practices of an evolving urbanism can be consistently advanced and ultimately consolidated in the face of external trends and powerful, competing interests. The proposition is simple. Much as military and diplomatic strategy are required to advance the interests of nations, and much as corporate strategy is required to establish and maintain market position in an extending City economy, urban strategy is required to advance the interests of our cities, and our common interest in the global City, during the Urban Revolution's final phase.

Urban strategy begins with the belief that progressive transformation in our cities is possible. We often perceive cities to be tethered to their problematic legacies and fixed development patterns. We tend to define them, as I have so far in these pages, by their entrenched politics, social divisions, sunk capital investments, and gridlock. But cities are engines of self-transformation, more powerful than any established development pattern. They always remain fast-changing, living systems.

We've all seen this transformative potential of cities, for better and worse. Between 1982 and 2003, America's cities consumed more than sixty-two thousand square miles of rural land, an area larger than Florida or Michigan, Greece or Nicaragua. The country's one hundred largest cities alone grew by nearly fifteen thousand square miles between 1970 and 1990, an area equivalent to Belgium or Taiwan. This land was often filled with new kinds of city models. Americans have a whole new vocabulary to describe them: big-box retail strips and "starter mansion" upper-middle-class residential communities; gated communities, "new urbanism" neighborhoods, and master-planned towns; condo complexes and time-shares.

Cities transform so quickly that their political jurisdictions and even our basic notions of urban geography cannot keep up with their change. In fifty years the effective unit of the city has been transformed at least three times. First, towns like Machala (Ecuador), Orlando (USA), Kampala (Uganda), Medina (Saudi Arabia), Khulna (Bangladesh), and Ulsan (South Korea) turned into cities. They developed large populations, built infrastructure, fostered new industries, and gained new legal-political status as city jurisdictions. Most have more than a million residents today. Others grew into urban agglomerations or metropolitan areas, made up of a group of formerly independent cities, towns, and villages. New political and administrative jurisdictions are still being crafted to try to govern even the most established metropolitan cities, like greater Toronto, Vancouver, and Detroit. Meanwhile, metropolitan areas—in their largest form as so-called mega-cities—have been linking together into super-urban regions. A common form of super-city today is the corridor city. Corridor cities evolve when the economies, infrastructure, geography, and politics of two or more metropolitan areas begin to merge.

In Chengdu, for instance, dense new industrial and residential areas grew up in the 1980s from towns and villages on Chengdu's periphery. As road improvements and infrastructure connected these centers to the old city in the 1990s, urban development expanded along these corridors. From 1978 to 2002, the urban land area of Chengdu increased 300 percent. This growth made the legal and administrative definitions of the original city of 3.3 million people obsolete. Today the new

Chengdu Municipality encompasses four contiguous cities, nine urban districts, and seven counties with a total population of more than ten million residents.[1] In the final phase, Chengdu will make Chinese provincial (state-level) territories archaic as it extends beyond the metropolitan city into a Chengdu-Chongqing corridor city. This urban goliath will count more than twenty-six million residents living in the two metropolitan areas and along the urbanizing 221-mile highway between them. Elsewhere, corridor cities cross national borders, like the Los Angeles–San Diego–Tijuana corridor. Extended corridor cities like these are clearly visible from space as long bands of light reaching across landmasses, like Japan's Honshu mainland.

These transformations highlight the extent to which cities have become unbounded. Their growth and most of their basic processes, such as commerce, epidemiology, and hydrology, are not contained within a particular political jurisdiction and are not manageable by traditional means. While local governments still play a critical role, governance requires a strategic capability to align myriad interests seeking advantage in the city, across jurisdictions and sectors, into an urbanist community seeking a common advantage. Lacking this capability, the city becomes an open platform for expedient, instrumental interests and competing extension strategies. Investment and growth occurs in a least-common-denominator fashion, guided by no coherent purpose—and producing no coherent outcome. Without the disciplines of a local urbanism, the City's expedient "flows" overwhelm efforts to build advantage through uniquely productive and efficient places.

By the same measure, these same transformations also evince the malleability of cities. A burned-out Tokyo in the 1940s can become the world's largest urban region by the end of the twentieth century. A place like Dharavi can appear from a marsh as quickly as a place like Detroit can revert back into prairie. A manufacturing center like São Paolo can expand nineteen times in forty-five years (between 1955 and 2000), covering an additional twenty-nine hundred square miles and absorbing fourteen million more people along the way. Dublin can be transformed from a declining old port and manufacturing center with high unemployment in the 1980s into one of Europe's most vibrant centers of finance and high-tech industry, with companies like Microsoft, Google, Amazon, Intel, Hewlett-Packard, and Pfizer staking new claims

on it. As a strategy for both economic development and political reconciliation, major industry associations in Ireland are now promoting a
Belfast-Dublin urban development corridor bridging the 102 miles between them.

Meanwhile, in similar time spans, new skyscraping central business
districts have been erected in the old downtowns of the world, and the
rubble of former city centers has been used to extend the urban land-
mass. In Japan, the debris of urban transformation has reshaped the
coastline of most major cities. Hong Kong's four million tons of annual
demolition waste is now being shipped to mainland China for city building projects. In a ten- to twenty-year period, run-down, centuries-old
city districts throughout southern Europe have been re-parceled and
renovated, given new streetscapes, infrastructure, and social and economic purposes.

These transformations are the sum of myriad alterations to the city.
With this malleability, what a city did wrong twenty years ago can be
re-crafted into something right. Better yet, in the process of remaking
itself, a city can design and scale a breakthrough solution, channeling
its divergent forces of commerce, culture, technology, and demographics into a new force against poverty, inequity, injustice, and environmental degradation. This capacity for *progressive transformation*—the
ability to steer the city's change toward ever more robust *common
advantage*—is the product of effective urban strategy, best demonstrated by the rare but undeniable *strategic city*.

In 1999, I began taking stock of a decade of work by thousands of urbanists worldwide, who were endeavoring to translate the new global
agenda for sustainable development into planning and management
practices for cities. This effort, called Local Agenda 21, was launched at
the United Nations Earth Summit in 1992. It became the largest of
many experiments over the last fifteen years to better understand progressive urban transformation. Ultimately, more than 10,000 cities and
towns in 115 countries got involved, refining a planning approach that
brought together divergent interests to forge a common economic,
social, and environmental program for the next stage of each city's
development. In effect, they were organizing their city's free-for-all

construction into a governed negotiation process. Through efforts like these, urbanists everywhere extended their association in scores of networks for Healthy Cities, Livable Cities, Slum-Free Cities, Competitive Cities, Good Governance Cities, Cities for Climate Protection, and Sustainable Cities. These networks promoted reforms to local laws and municipal organization. They piloted new guidelines, budgeting procedures, management systems, and professional roles to instill a progressive purpose into everyday city building. At times it was like a kind of supra-municipality organizing itself across the City for the final phase. As these networks each built a record of practice, they ran international competitions to identify best practices. The thousands of collected case studies of city-building innovations gave us our first-ever chance to take stock of the City's evolving practices of urbanism.

Reviewing these best practices, it was hard not to notice the often wide gaps between local agendas and actual local development. As I visited urbanists in hundreds of cities, I realized just how divided and unmanageable the urban world had become. Everywhere we discovered the Great Opportunities City: talented and mobilized to create a common good, but chronically pitted against powerful self-interests. Archaic jurisdictions competed with each other, each trying to control a city whose geography and economics surpassed what any of them could manage. Old city management practices posed constant barriers to the experimental practices of a new urbanism. Most everywhere, planners and civic leaders lacked a nuanced, shared understanding of any urbanism by which to shape growth and investment in their cities.

In Japan's cities a shadow governance of urban development overrode efforts like Local Agenda 21. Kanagawa Prefecture was one of the first jurisdictions to take up the Local Agenda 21 challenge. The huge prefecture, containing Yokohama and Kawasaki, has an annual budget of more than $20 billion. Its economy is equal to that of Switzerland. The preparation of the Agenda 21 Kanagawa plan involved thousands of residents, forty-three citizen groups, thirty-seven local municipalities, six trade associations, business representatives, planners, and scientific experts. They hosted neighborhood meetings, conferences, and regional summits to develop their action guidelines. Unified conferences and roundtable discussion groups forged common positions on tough issues. These efforts produced new policies for energy and waste management. They defined new ways to involve residents in planning and designing neighborhood development projects.[2] They established standards for roads (e.g., using permeable materials) and new storm water management systems (e.g., using rainwater collection). New eco-housing projects were launched. Businesses agreed to "green" their office buildings and manufacturing complexes. In the first year of the endeavor, the prefecture launched an impressive fifty-two projects with an annual budget of $149 million, probably the greatest such commitment in the world.

Yet since the launch of its Local Agenda 21, Kanagawa has still developed in ways that don't reflect its efficient, eco-friendly vision. As in a parallel world, planning for major land reclamation projects, roads, port reconstruction, and new districts proceeded as in the past.[3] Massive resources were funneled into mega-scale master-planned "techno parks," "science parks," "new towns," and high-rise commercial districts that have little connection to Agenda 21 Kanagawa. Tellingly, many rooms, offices, laboratories, and industrial plots in these developments remained vacant, demonstrating their lack of connection to any apparent market demand. One of these mega-projects was called Minato Mirai 21, or Port Future 21, an urban renewal project for Yokohama's old port. It sports Japan's tallest skyscraper, financed by the prefecture with national government financing. A decade after its start, the eighty-eight-acre site remained half vacant. The project's logic appears to murkily respond to a city-building machinery that has dominated much of the construction of contemporary Japan.

Construction is one of Japan's largest industrial sectors, historically accounting for about one-fifth of the country's GNP and employing six million workers. Its core is the constant building of Japan's extended corridor city, the highways that connect it, and the dams that provide its water supplies. The industry earns more than a trillion dollars a year, a third coming from public works contracts, a massive slice of Japan's national budget. Because of the close relationship between the industry and the dominant Liberal Democratic Party, construction prices in Japan average 15 percent to 30 percent above international norms.[4] The profits gained from such premiums have generally flowed into political party accounts to fund campaigns or been dispensed as kickbacks to senior officials. Their strategic practice is the so-called *dango* bid-rigging process—ironically, a term that means discussion group—through which construction cartels are formed for each new mega-project. Unlike the public planning of Agenda 21 Kanagawa, dango occurs in the private rooms of restaurants, tea parlors, and golf clubs. According to Stanford economist John MacMillan, these so-called discussion groups account for $5 billion in annual hospitality expenditures alone.

Though dango is illegal, causing jailings of a number of prefectural governors and construction executives, the practice remains widespread. The annual total of dango bribes and kickbacks has at times surpassed $500 million; the sum is more or less officially recorded because construction firms have been allowed to claim a tax deduction for these "business expenses."[5] The dango approach to urban planning lurks behind endless announcements of new roads, ports, airports, and so-called new town projects throughout Japan. The $149 million budget of Agenda 21 Kanagawa pales against such behind-the-scenes power-brokering.

With the establishment of its first democratic government in 1994, Johannesburg was in principle liberated from its City of Crisis dilemma; suddenly the planning and governance was in the hands of a majority urban regime. The new leaders faced four challenges. First, they had to convert barren apartheid townships into real city districts; to do so they had to install basic infrastructure and create functioning property markets. Second, public safety had to be reestablished in downtown Johannesburg so that it could again serve as Africa's main financial and business services citysystem. Third, divided jurisdictions had to be reorganized into a stable form of metropolitan government. Fourth, Johannesburg needed to develop an urbanism that could lead the city's majority along a manageable pathway from shack living to a stable serviced home, to ownership of a small house or apartment, and ultimately to a sustainable middle-class urbanism.

To face these challenges, Johannesburg and other South African cities undertook the most extensive grassroots development exercise perhaps in history, embracing Local Agenda 21, Healthy Cities, Competitive Cities, and other experimental practices along the way. They did so with the full support of their national government, which promised funds for their plans. But before Johannesburg's central business district

(CBD) was stabilized and receiving private investment again, developers and corporations built a new downtown for the financial and IT industries and the stock exchange in Sandton, a former residential district to the city's north. Self-described as "the richest square mile in Africa," it has little connection to the larger city around it. It serves as a kind of extension outpost. Before any post-apartheid urbanism emerged, the white middle classes fled the city for hundreds of square miles of security-protected suburban residential developments. Before the new democratic local government could plan redevelopment of old township areas, new slum townships were appearing on the city's peripheries. Four decades of apartheid prevented the evolution of a functioning urbanism in South Africa; the result has been a sprawling, opportunistic drift into the dilemmas of the Great Opportunities City. Harsher yet, a steady stream of migrants from other African nations in the throes of their own Urban Revolution have joined Johannesburg's impatient slums. The first violent riots in democratic Johannesburg in 2008 suggest risk of a post-apartheid City of Crisis dilemma.

Far away in the northern steel-making city of Hamilton, Canada, regional government was working on another Local Agenda 21, called Vision 2020. Proponents there were seeking to reconcile the demands of businesses and employees attached to a declining steel industry with the new urbanist sensibilities and investment requirements of the service and knowledge industry being incubated from its universities. The lines of debate often seemed stark. Was Hamilton to compete in the world economy as a provider of industrial land, a modernized port, and an expanded network of trucking routes? Or should it rebuild itself as a center of expertise in public health, pollution control, and waste management? Was it to be defined by tolerance for the soot and noise of heavy manufacturing or by the lifestyle of the Niagara wine and theater region? These divergent visions clashed over a planned highway through the Niagara Escarpment, a United Nations' World Heritage Site. The protracted battle over the highway symbolized the city's lack of singular vision.

These experiences, across hundreds of cities, provided a chance to take a more realistic reckoning of the nature of the City. I began reviewing hundreds of "best practice" cases. Which city, I asked, had mastered such a robust urbanism that it could steadily increase its equity, justice, and sustainability in the face of competing external pressures, entrenched local interests, and competing city-building approaches?

Of the hundreds of cities in the best practice databases, most fell off the list with such a demanding filter. They had registered important achievements in regional planning, public-private partnerships, service extensions to the poor, pollution reduction, and energy efficiency. They had prototyped new kinds of low-income or eco-housing or had even renewed a city district or revitalized a waterfront. But in many respects these cities still remained Great Opportunities Cities, developing in ways that undermined their strategies.

There was another group of cities that had undergone amazing transformations through effective, strategic leadership and renewal of their historical urbanisms, as in the case of London or New York. Other cities on this short list were city-states, like Singapore, Hong Kong, and Dubai, or products of highly centralized planning and investment, like Shanghai and other miracle cities of China. These transformations awed with their scale, splendor, economic muscle, and efficiency. Singapore had established world standards in infrastructure and environmental management of industries, and Hong Kong had built a public transit system and urban form to get an unparalleled 80 percent of all city trips on public transit. These cities had cleaned up dilapidated districts and polluting industries. But they had often done so at cost to equity, justice, and sustainability. Their displaced families, low-wage migrant labor, and curtailed rights seemed a necessary, accepted condition for their urban ambitions.

Finally, I came to a list of cities that had mastered transformations with an ambitious social and ecological purpose. Dozens of these cities were clustered in northern Europe, particularly in the Netherlands, Germany, Austria, Switzerland, and Scandinavia. These cities had the benefit of rich economic endowments, slow population growth, and demographic homogeneity and stability. Their deep-rooted historical urbanism allowed them to hit the ground running after the destruction of World War II and they had steadily advanced their efficiency and vitality since. For them urbanism was now a responsibility that included the exercise of responsibility in the global City. They had budgets for international development assistance and led consortia to develop solutions to global environmental challenges. In some ways, they were like a single extended regional City, steered by a common urbanism.

Filtering further, I created a short list of cities that were distinguished by their totally unique local forms of urbanism—Bologna, Italy; Portland and Seattle/King County, United States, and Vancouver, Canada; Porto Alegre, Brazil; and Kitakyushu, Japan. Their practices had evolved more recently, setting new standards in growth management, environmental recovery, economic revitalization, and participatory democracy. But my interest was finally drawn to a smaller group that had managed dramatic transformations against enormous odds. They had been exceedingly fast-growing, destabilized, or destroyed by war, socially divided, economically isolated, and confronted by industrial decline. More than the rest, the strategic practices of Barcelona, Spain; Chicago, United States; and Curitiba, Brazil, illustrated the potency of urbanism over other forms of city building and urban renewal.

Barcelona, Chicago, and Curitiba had each mastered the three main faculties of the Strategic City:

- A stable governing alliance with the power and resources to align interests in pursuit of a common advantage, willing to discipline markets and private development, and negotiate the city's cocreation.
- An explicit and detailed body of urbanist practices, understood and accepted in all parts of the city, for translating the alliance's goals and standards into more productive, efficient, and livable forms of building and design.
- A set of dedicated institutions, with the technical talent and administrative power to develop and implement these new practices of urbanism, establishing the solutions needed to make the urbanism work in every space and aspect of the fast-changing city.

Progressive transformation requires both extreme determination and patience in addition to these strategic faculties. The city is such a complex system that it takes about two decades for transformation to gain momentum. First, competing interests must be aligned behind the strategy. Then the specific practices of the new urbanism—new designs, building standards, services, technologies, kinds of finance, and civic participation—need to be tested and demonstrated. Plans need to be reformulated. Existing institutions have to be transformed. For instance, energy utilities (as in the Urban CO_2 Reduction Project) might be transformed from single-minded suppliers of electricity into providers of services to reduce demand. Schools might be further developed into community health clinics and recreation centers. The culture of the new urbanism—the ways that people govern, use, and live in the city—needs to be defined and widely promoted. In the first decade, a great deal of time is spent cocreating these practices with entrenched and even opposing interests. Oftentimes, new industries need to be seeded to create market constituencies to rally behind the economic and the social purposes of the transformation.

In about a decade a new development momentum can be established. Maintaining this momentum requires consolidation of the strategic alliance into a new urban regime. A key aspect of consolidation is the establishment of institutions—planning agencies, development companies, and utilities as well as new laws—that oversee the practical work of transformation. The process of transformation, in other words, progresses from experimental to entrepreneurial to institutional phases. Now districts, transit and water systems, and even individual buildings are retrofitted or redeveloped to embed the new economics and culture in concrete. The urbanism becomes apparent in the city's large-scale form, in its services and market activities, and even in the micro-level details of streetscape, garbage cans, and park designs, which all convey the new culture and practices to each resident.

By the third decade the city begins to truly transform. With both the macro-foundation of infrastructure and new urban form and micro-practices to support them, the primary city-building approach shifts toward the citysystem. Now with a nuanced understanding of their urbanism, local communities and businesses begin to defend and build the new urbanism in their districts. New business models emerge to support the urbanism on a market basis. New technologies become the new standard products. Even the city's culture and forms of governance transform to support the urbanism as a new status quo.

Urban strategy is the practice of supporting this evolution until the urbanism's progressive ends have been achieved. But in the course of twenty to thirty years, a society also changes radically. The urban strategy, therefore, must constantly forge and adapt new practices of urbanism to steer the thousands of annual investment decisions within the city toward desired outcomes. Curitiba, Barcelona, and Chicago each offer distinct lessons on how to do this. In their own way, each has organized divergent and competing interests *into a broadening city-building community* that achieves shared objectives through constant refinement and renewal of its practices of urbanism.

Curitiba constantly refined its practices through a cocreation approach with local business interests and ethnic communities to create an urban form, infrastructure, and services that transformed the impoverished and flood-prone city into a global center of economic and ecological excellence. Barcelona painstakingly cultivated a local culture for citizens, city builders, and commercial interests to cocreate solutions and discipline the city's redevelopment. And Chicago created the local market dynamics for progressive change, replacing entrenched business models that had stripped the city of its most basic assets and economic viability with a renewed neighborhood-based urbanism. Together each of these cities also illustrates the ultimate strategic practice: the establishment of strong, stable urban regimes with the political, commercial, and cultural clout required to corral the chaotic forces of the world's cities toward progressive, common advantage.

CHAPTER 12

Designing the Ecosystem

A New City Rises on the Serra do Mar Plateau

The flight to Curitiba has cleared the Brazilian coastal mountain range. It arcs to align with the runway. From this angle our landing traverses the distinctive skyline of a city that has amassed over the last thirty years like a parallel mountain ridge on the Serra do Mar plateau. The geologic force beneath its rise was the aligned effort and investment of literally thousands of independent commercial interests, but it was given order by a small group of persistent urbanists, armed with a rare instinct for urban strategy.

This is the game-changing city that all of us have been hearing about: a city that works like a single piece of efficient, living architecture; a product of consistent, incremental design; not the largest but surely the most artful feat of urban transformation in the twentieth century.

Like many on their first pilgrimage to Curitiba, I have arrived eager to experience its unique bus system. If you've read anything about cities in the last two decades, then you've likely heard about this fast-growing and fiscally challenged Brazilian city that figured out how to transform a hundredfold competing private bus companies—often run as quasi-mafias in cities throughout Brazil—into an integrated public transit system that profitably provides 45 percent of the city's passenger trips. In the world of cities, transit systems just don't generate a profit, and this one wins more transit share than most European cities and rivals even transit-packed Tokyo. I soon discover that the transit achievement is representative—but only a small part—of Curitiba's strategic practice.

After checking into a hotel, I go to meet Jaime Lerner, the mayor and master architect of the city's transformation as it grew from a somewhat impoverished small provincial city of 350,000 in 1965 into a metropolis of nearly two million in 2005, now ranking at the top of urban living standards in Brazil. We meet at the Curitiba Research and Urban Planning Institute (IPPUC), the research and development institution established under Lerner's leadership in 1965 to translate a barebones set of strategic guidelines into Curitiba's new urbanism. Over three decades of shifting political fortunes, through military dictatorship and into a new democracy, IPPUC maintained the continuity of the transformation effort. More than just planning, it incubated the hundreds of minute solutions that are required to keep commercial forces aligned and development on a coherent track. IPPUC's challenge was particularly great, as Curitiba was growing faster than any other Brazilian city and, at almost three times the worldwide rate of urbanization, making planning in any traditional sense all but impossible.[1]

After introductions, Lerner proposes that we take a walk. While Detroit's mayor requires a coterie of bodyguards, and most mayors navigate their cities in chauffered cars, he prefers full exposure to the city. I expect him to lead me to the bus system, but he wants to show off the new "24-Hour City," a 24/7 open-air shopping plaza recently established in the successful downtown pedestrian district. Along the way he gives accounts of Curitiba's rise. Lerner's gait and form are like that of a heavyweight wrestler. His eyes squint like a man in constant rumination. And his words come out in a free-form techno-poetry. "Values are an infrastructure," he tells me, giving richer meaning to his subsequent coaching: "If you don't understand the structure of the city, it is difficult to work on it."

The 24-Hour City takes him back to his activist roots in the early 1960s, when modernization plans proposed the demolition of much of the historic city center to build an automobile-oriented city. Upon appointment as mayor in 1972, one of Lerner's first acts was to stop that plan, creating the first six blocks of this car-free district. Still, he makes no reference to the transit system.

Next, he takes me a downtown park. Barigüi Park was also built in 1972 and consists of a large lake surrounded by a nondescript, treeless lawn. I am unimpressed: there is neither landscaping, shade, nor activity. But as we enter on a gravel path, Lerner becomes animated. The pitch of his deep voice rises and a boyish enthusiasm tempers his philosophical manner. He is pointing to the ground, saying something in his broken English that I can't quite understand. At first I think he must have glimpsed a rare insect or small mammal—perhaps he is a hobby entomologist—but he carries on until I realize that the object of the master city builder's enthusiasm is a row of little footlights lining the pathway. They have been placed there for nighttime walkers and joggers. His focus is on the little glass mantles that cover each light. They are made of recycled jars, he explains. And not just by anyone, but by children who live in peripheral *favelas* (slums), the children of migrants, who constituted a majority of Curitiba's annual growth over the last decades. He has enlisted them to help build the city.

Now the whole story unfolds. Like a thread woven deep into the city's fabric, a consistent principle binds the many little parts of Curitiba's transformation, like those little glass mantles: in Curitiba microdetails and macro-form have been incrementally crafted together into integrated systems. With each visit and vignette, Lerner's colleagues disabuse me of the popular understanding that Curitiba was a masterplanned city. Curitiba is the work of negotiators in a melee and the product of intense, customized design by a group of new institutions formed by the so-called Lerner Group. "There is no ideal system," says Lerner, now talking like an ecologist. "The ideal system is integration."

The city lies in a large river basin. Five rivers and nearly two thousand miles of streams flow within its built-up area. Since Curitiba's initial settlement as a cattle town in the early nineteenth century, an annual cycle of flooding, property loss, and disease has been a defining part of its history. As recently as 1995, a major flood caused $40 million in damages. The waters that gather in Curitiba merge into the famous Iguaçú, making their way to the world's second largest waterfall. Barigüi Park is at the head of this great basin. I discover that the porous gravel footpath on which we stand is part of a massive, low-cost flood control system.

The dominant logic for urban drainage and flood control goes as follows: build the city and then make the rivers and local hydrology conform to it. This logic informs the system of levees and canals in greater New Orleans, at great expense, and often human cost. In the early 1960s the World Bank and the national government wanted to straighten the ever-flooding Barigüi River and contain it in a concrete channel. But as a poor city, explains Nicolau Kluppel, the Lerner Group's leading civil engineer, Curitiba had to consider such an investment very cautiously. And he had different ideas.

"The first principle of our approach was to protect the rivers," he says, emphasizing the dominant logic's reversal. "If the rivers could be protected, then the population could be protected from flooding. After mapping the protected areas, then the areas for development could be identified. We treated the rivers as a watershed before the technical term was in parlance."

The Barigüi's protected river corridors range from thirty feet to more than a mile wide, tailored to each stretch and bend of river. Together the corridors form a chain of floodwater collection basins.[2] There was no master plan; such a thing had never been done before. Kluppel explains the process of incremental learning, adjustment, and design used to develop this infrastructure. "By building the banks of the lakes higher," he recalls, "we realized that they would retain more water during the heavy rains. We also realized that a chain of lakes [with a drainage relationship to each other] further slowed the flow of rains into the rivers. This also allowed the storm water to be filtered into the ground; it pretreated the water."

The result was a micro-engineered, ecological flood control system at a fraction of the cost of the usual large-scale concrete solutions. To me, this infrastructure was invisible. That was the point: it doubled as a vast system of public parks. Later, when Lerner had a chance to further explain the story of those glass mantles, he described the addition of a citywide network of sports facilities in this green river belt. They realized that soccer pitches could be designed with a fine gravel base to function as floodwater leach fields during the rainy season. With flood control and park development proceeding as one endeavor, soon Curitiba's level of green space per resident grew from only 2 square feet per inhabitant to 170 square feet in the 1990s—exceeding the level of most Western cities.

But Curitibanos don't live in public parks like Cariocas on their Rio de Janeiro beaches. They are a more somber lot of Eastern European, German, and Japanese immigrants blended with local gaucho culture. "Curitibanos have lots of options for public leisure," explained Lerner, who spent years as a planner in Rio de Janeiro, "but they like to stay home watching videos."

In a fast-growing city, any unused public land is always vulnerable to slum invasion and underhanded private development. Curitiba's pre-emptive response was to use the new parks for yet another objective: to create signature public facilities for each of the city's diverse ethnic communities, where they could celebrate their traditions and cultures. Over time, almost every park has been given a function as an ethnic cultural center, and adopted by a particular community. São Cristóvão park became Italian Wood, joining Pope's Wood, German Wood, Jerusalem Fountain, and Arab Memorial, each outfitted with museums, sculptures, exhibits, and architecture that celebrate its associated cultural group. German Wood has a concert hall; Portugal Wood has a major library; Santa Felicidade park has eighteen chapels celebrating the Italian community.

The thread continues. Soon it was clear that the parks also provided habitat for hundreds of indigenous species; now they also function as environmental education facilities. Pulling on the thread of integration leads to another initiative. There were no roads into the favelas for regular garbage collection, so garbage was piling in their streets and being tossed into ravines and streams. The city began offering a bag of food for each bag of waste brought to a collection point. (The food was purchased directly from regional farmers whose depressed incomes were fueling urban migration into Curitiba.) The children of participating families were invited to join the environmental education program, which ultimately made those glass mantles. The new recreational-social-cultural-ecological-educational-disaster management system was complete. Later, the city offered transit tickets for each bag of garbage collected by the *favelistas*, encouraging new residents to become regular public transit users and giving them access to central city life. But the economics of the transit system also required a concentration of customers living adjacent to bus lines. To encourage high-rise development in these corridors, the city sold development rights. The funds were used to further develop the park system. During our very first walk together, in other words, Lerner was showing me how the thread of transformation exposed in the little glass mantles was ultimately connected to the public transit system and just about every other aspect of the city. Everything was linked together as a designed urban ecology.

"We resisted everything that would separate urban functions," he told me. The first principle of Curitiba's urbanism, in other words, is elegance: responsive solutions that each serve multiple, complementary purposes.

Lerner and his colleagues knew that the fast-growing city was itself flooding out across its periphery, destroying its basic economics and social ecology. Sprawl bore a heavy cost in terms of infrastructure, further marginalization of the poor at the periphery, and lost social cohesion. To renew the city's advantage as it grew, Curitiba had to be given a clear form. Much like the river and stream corridors, people and goods movements had to be structured into their own kind of watershed.

Establishing momentum toward an urban form with robust economies of density, scale and association is a basic task of any urbanism. But the Lerner Group also clearly understood that form alone—the typical preoccupation of a master plan—is not enough to create the social ecology and political economy required to steer a city's incremental, opportunistic daily investments toward a common advantage. To make an urbanism work, people must identify with it. It must be vested with meaning and cohere with local culture and values. As urbanists say, it must offer a "sense of place." Therefore, a distinguishing aspect of the Lerner Group's and IPPUC's practice of urbanism is the extensive resources dedicated to the micro-details of the city's development. It was not enough to have a park. The parks had to be carefully designed as places with particular peoples. The building materials, ornamentation, plantings, names, sculptures, and facilities all needed to be cocreated with that community to generate meaning and a sense of ownership. It was not enough to create a downtown pedestrian mall. The light posts, benches, trash receptacles, and pavement had to be tailored to give them cultural resonance. Unlike the master-planned Putrajaya, which by its conception is designed to bequeath someone else's ideas of the "good city" to an as yet abstract population, the design-centered urbanism of Curitiba made the new pedestrian mall their own. By so doing, it drew the crowds that supported its markets, which in turn created commercial interests to preserve its form and co-invest in its services as a signature citysystem. The symbiosis of form, services and their markets, and micro-amenities made the developing urbanism *coherent*—it made it "stick" and made the city "stick together."

The Lerner Group has been criticized for the lack of popular participation in its approach.[3] During a discussion of the limits of public participation in Curitiba's years under Brazilian dictatorship, Lerner countered that their approach created "transparency" for residents about the city's growth, even when public participation was limited. Continuity and familiarity were guiding principles, in contrast with the sudden, sweeping redevelopment of master planning, as planned today for Dharavi. New urban form and zoning rules were established through incremental, trial-and-error negotiation with landowners. New services and market practices were cocreated with commercial interests. And new micro-amenities were profusely tested with the public. "The city follows the trail of the memory," the poetic Lerner likes to say. "It doesn't function unless it follows the imprint of past social practice and investment. You never rip up the family photograph. The more you are reminded of your family, the more you have identity." At a UN summit meeting in 1996, Lerner would more formally explain, "We must base the development of the city around its history, preserving and appreciating its intrinsic reference points, which have guided generations and provide its basic infrastructure." Constant reference to existing culture and historic uses give a rapidly transforming city a readable structure and cues to help individuals adapt behaviors to the new urbanism. This helps people to align individual strategies and day-to-day life with the planned concept for the city, channeling their activities and investments.

Much has been written about the 1965 "master plan" that started Curitiba's transformation. By the conventions of the day, Curitiba had to develop a *plano diretor*, or indicative plan. But Lerner has always taken pains to distinguish their approach from master-planned city building. He opposed the modernist master planning he studied in France and England and the separation of the city's activities into geographic zones and its infrastructure into separately engineered systems. "The land use regulation in Porto Alegre," the Brazilian city known worldwide for its grassroots participation in city budgeting and governance, "had 900 articles," he notes. "The Curitiba guidelines were four pages." They were a strategic concept of how the city should grow, awaiting the practices of urbanism and the strategic institutions to make them a reality.[4]

Cassio Taniguchi oversaw the development of the famous bus rapid transit system in 1972–1975, and presided over IPPUC for eight years. Then he served as Curitiba's mayor from 1997 to 2005. He explains it this way. "The program was not driven by diagnosis. Rather, we tested a solution and managed the solution. This is the only way to keep pace with such rapid change. By the time a detailed diagnosis is finished, reality has moved on."

For the Lerner Group, a solution was a new system with hundreds of "moving parts": the parks-flood control system or the transit-land-use system that bundled new laws, business models, designs, and technologies into a working whole. Developing and integrating these systems together is the hallmark of the Lerner Group's practice of urbanism. As consensus over each new solution was developed incrementally, institutions and laws were reformed to reinforce them.[5] Locally adapted practice innovations thereby preceded institutional prescription. This process of solutions-development and consensus-building took more than a decade, but it left them with an urbanism whose logic and designs were understood in a detailed way by the major interests of the city. As they aligned key stakeholders around each new solution, their job was to make sure the solutions were connected. Once-separate services and urban management functions—land-use and transit, civil engineering and green spaces, solid waste management and poverty reduction— were rebuilt into an integrated whole, giving the totality of Curitiba, and not just individual districts, the character of a citysystem.

The bus rapid transit system is a case in point. In the early 1960s there were more than a hundred private bus operators competing for customers. These loosely regulated companies had been granted monopoly concessions to operate in particular zones. There were no timetables. Routings were not coordinated, and many areas went unserved. Their routes often met in the central city and clogged the streets. When one military-appointed mayor—who had the added authority of a military general—tried to stop the operators from increasing their fares and extending the permitted age of their buses, the operators organized an end run and got the state government to take control of transit regulation. It was against such coordinated, recalcitrant private interest that the Lerner Group had to build a progressive new transit system.[6] Ultimately, they reorganized them into a new urbanist community.

The work began in 1973 by establishing an altogether new express bus service on a north-south road corridor that was rezoned for high-density residential development. By introducing an entirely new kind of service into a redefined route over which no operator had a legal concession, the Lerner Group created a neutral playing field on which to cocreate the new transit system with the companies. They made a clear offer to operators whose existing concessions covered parts of this territory. The operators would be granted license to run the express service on the city's terms, or the city would organize an entirely new concession on this corridor. At the time, Taniguchi was running another strategic institution, called Curitiba Urbanization (URBS), which would develop and control the new system. He and Lerner knew that pending expiration of existing concessions would force operators to negotiate. The old operators agreed to run the new services, now joining URBS and IPPUC to cocreate the system. Operators rapidly benefited from the dedicated bus lanes along the emerging high-density corridor and became a commercial-political constituency for the eventual development of five such corridors.

Jointly they developed an entirely new business model. Companies owned and operated bus routes according to contractual standards. Curitiba Urbanization set the fares, routes, and timetables and monitored quality. Operators would receive no public subsidies but would be guaranteed a specified amount of revenue per kilometer traveled. Daily fare collections were deposited with URBS. After payments were made to the operators, URBS used remaining funds to further develop the system.

For nearly twenty years this cocreation never stopped; URBS steadily renegotiated concessions with other operators, applying the new model.

In a few years they had reorganized the whole industry, consolidating scores of operators into a dozen companies. Meanwhile, to complete the solution, they had to develop a wide range of practices to make the new road corridors work efficiently for users and profitably for the operators. The first challenge was the physical design of the roadways themselves. The master planners of the 1960s had originally conceived of wide parkways with dedicated bus lanes, but these would require the demolition of existing houses, contrary to the Guidelines. Consulting with homeowners and developers, IPPUC developed the city's distinctive "trinary" road design. The originally planned parkway was split into three distinct, parallel roadways with buildings in between that worked together as a mobility corridor. The main, central roadway consisted of dedicated bus lanes running in both directions. Flanking these lanes on both sides, low-speed, local traffic lanes allowed people in cars and trucks to access the residences and shops. Traditional planning measures were part of the solution: new zoning rules, building requirements, and financial incentives were established to encourage private developers to construct high-rise, mixed-use buildings along each side of this corridor. At the back of these high-rise strips, IPPUC designed dedicated roadways for express, one-way car traffic. With infrastructure and zoning in place for these so-called structural axes for city growth, builders began to incrementally construct Curitiba's distinctive high-density ridgelines. The result was more than a transit system or a new kind of urban form. It was the organic development of a corridor citysystem, based on solid economies of density and scale, in which land use, transportation, commerce, and settlement worked as a carefully designed single system.

Even with this foundation, the cocreation didn't stop. Incrementally the new corridor citysystems expanded from the structural axes. Bus feeder routes and interdistrict lines were created, establishing five distinct types of service. These linked the other districts of the city into the corridors, like streams feeding into rivers. Curitiba Urbanization and the bus companies then developed special bus designs for each of the five services, further developing them with manufacturers. This achieved three main objectives. It matched the bus sizes to routes and passenger volumes, thereby increasing per-passenger fuel efficiency. It kick-started the development of local vehicle manufacturing, eventually making

Curitiba one of the largest automobile manufacturing centers on the continent. It also created transparency for the consumer about the different services, which were connected at integration stations located along the corridors. In further rounds of cocreation, total consumer experience and convenience had to be considered. Trial-and-error experiments over a decade produced a single fare for all services and for travel across the whole city. Tailored ticketing systems and the garbage-for-tickets exchange program in the favelas were all part of the solution. As the system's popularity and ridership grew, subway-like boarding stations and triple articulated buses were all developed to create the operating capacity and efficiencies of a subway system.

The growth of population along the corridor citysystems has been exponential. Their populations doubled in five years alone, between 1980 and 1985. By 1985, little more than a decade from the start of the system's first concession, the density along the structural axes was double that of all the other residential zones. The medium-density residential zone that abutted the structural axes was second in density. Together these two zones represented 7 percent of the city's land area but housed

Curitiba's northern structural axis in 1974, before implementation of the Lerner Group's strategy. (Photo: Curitiba Municipal Archives)

Curitiba's northern structural axis today, with rapid-bus terminals in fore-ground. (Photo: Curitiba Municipal Archives)

nearly 20 percent of the population. Curitibanos had transformed the structure and basic economies of their city. Even after three alternating terms and twelve years in office, Lerner still garnered a 92 percent approval rating. In a 2000 survey, consumers gave the private-operated transit system an 89 percent approval rating. The transit system continues to operate without subsidy. Although Curitiba's rising standard of living has been accompanied with growing automobile ownership—among the highest in Brazil—people still rely on transit. The city uses 30 percent less gasoline per capita than Brazilian cities of similar size.

Other areas of transformation are pursued through this incremental, design-oriented approach, particularly in waste management and social services. The common thread across Curitiba's solutions is economic elegance. In his detailed study of the city's development from 1950 to 2000, economist Hugh Schwartz highlights this dimension of Curitiba's urbanism. "The imaginative construction of public works not ordinarily conceived as economic infrastructure," he writes, "seems to have contributed to the relatively greater rise in income levels as well as to the improvement in the quality of life."[7] Schwartz is referring to what I have called underlying economies of the city, particularly to the robust dynamics created when spatial economies of density and scale, and social economies of association reduce the underlying cost structure of urban life and commerce (in time, effort, and money) and support new markets and models of economic partnership and activity. Things "not normally conceived as economic," like roadway designs, soccer fields, and footpath lights, Schwartz concluded, enabled a meteoric rise in Curitiba's economic development, which he could not explain by conventional macro- and regional economic factors.

Curitiba's ability to shape so many different pressures and parts of city life into new systems reveals another critical aspect of urban strategy: the creation of an *urban regime* with the powers and capabilities required to realize ambitious reforms. Even in cities that have developed new practices of urbanism, such as in Toronto, the leadership's hold on power can be too short, their powers too weak, and jurisdictions too divided to sustain a strategy against competing forces of growth. Alignment of competing interests, and continuity of effort over decades are the two main governance challenges that work against a city's progressive transformation.

Curitiba's challenges in this regard were no less than any other city. Yes, from 1965 to 1988 the mayor was appointed by a dictatorship and therefore in principle had recourse to very centralized power. But Lerner argues that this made mayors more cautious, as they could always be removed from office. Appointment by an unpopular dictatorship—or direct recourse to its authority—could also undermine popular support. Equally important, Lerner and all other Brazilian mayors were limited to serving single consecutive terms, under both dictatorship and the new democracy. These conditions undermined continuity of policy and practice. Dependency on state government and potential challenge by its leaders further exacerbated the challenge.

Governance innovation was therefore also a key aspect of Curitiba's success. The Lerner Group (which included a progression of alternating mayors including Taniguchi) established an innovative institutional apparatus for accomplishing urban strategy. The Lerner Group created a *transformational regime*, because it built institutions like IPPUC and URBS to align and consolidate sufficient power and

The three faculties of the Strategic City.

problem-solving capacity for a long enough time to achieve strategic ends.

As illustrated in the figure above, endowing a city with true strategic capabilities involves the establishment of three strategic faculties. First, the city must have a stable alliance of organizations and interests that together contribute sufficient political and economic power and social legitimacy to reform the legal, policy, and administrative apparatus. Second, the alliance must have stable technical, financial, and entrepreneurial capability at its disposal to energetically advance new practices of urbanism across the city even when the machinery of government is not fully within its control. In other words, the alliance needs strategic institutions to ensure continuity of effort. The third element is an explicit body of practices, which translate the vision—in Curitiba's case, the Guidelines—into the detailed, replicable solutions that shape built form, markets, and culture into a robust urbanism.

Creating a transformational regime can start with any one of these faculties, but to create the apparatus required to shape the city, all three are needed. An alliance without developed practices can inspire and achieve tactical gains, but it cannot dominate the city building of others. Practices of urbanism, without strategic institutions to ensure their consistent application to the city's many different problems, can be piloted but cannot become the city's modus operandi.

The Lerner Group started its work in 1972 with the advantage of city hall control as well as the preceding six years of control of IPPUC, which had a legal mandate to implement the Guidelines. The Group had played a formative role in the conception of the Guidelines and had six years from 1966 to 1972 to conceive practices for their execution. So they entered the stage with a special momentum, which explains the bold establishment of the pedestrian mall, the new park cum flood-control system, and negotiations with the bus operators in their first years in office. But the Group's ultimate strategic coup was the application of all three evolving faculties not to reform the city's existing systems, but to create entirely new systems. Through their incremental cocreation, the Group appeared to be focused on reforms, but their real strategy was disruptive innovation and transformation. Because they were designing the new playing field, they could also redesign the game on their own terms.

CHAPTER 13

Building Local Culture

Reclaiming the Streets of Gràcia District, Barcelona

Toni Pujol is on his job, taking me to city-building projects across Barcelona's constantly renewing landscape. In his thirty years, the city has been completely transformed. In the early 1980s, it was a city that had been isolated for decades by the Franco dictatorship, marked by lost industry and rundown districts, rising poverty, and crime. Today, Barcelona is a global mecca of urbanism. Like Curitiba, thousands of urbanists and city leaders converge here each year to try to understand the genetics of its vitality, creativity, and transformational capacity.

Toni is one of the latest generation of urbanists mentored by this city. The young urban practitioners of most cities—architects, planners, social workers, engineers, or environmental managers—take their university degrees, gain professional certification, and then secure a job with a local government, a developer, or social service organization. Then they ply the textbook methods of their trade and abruptly learn the difference between the ideals of planning theory and the quintessential realism of the city.

In Barcelona, the young practitioner is guided by an additional tutoring: he is *encultured* into a living tradition. He learns this tradition not in the classroom or in an internship. He lives it, as it is constantly changing the city around him. It is part of the debates that he hears when he joins friends for a beer. It supplies the local media with a constant feed of controversy. Barcelona's urbanism never stops testing itself against new challenges, much like the city's most famous building, the Sagrada Familia cathedral of Antonio Gaudí. The cathedral's construction began in 1882 and will be completed sometime between 2030 and 2060. Funded by thousands of patrons, organizations, and common citizens, it is as much a civic as an architectural venture. The 150-year continuity of such a project is itself unique. Like Sagrada Familia, the urbanist project of Barcelona is never finished and never rests.

Without knowing it, Pujol is demonstrating this rich culture of urbanism as we tour the city. On the surface, he's explaining a project that has removed automobile traffic from most of the narrow streets of Gràcia district. The streets have been made level with the sidewalks, turning them into lanes for ambling groups of students, mothers with strollers, and pensioners. Where these lanes intersect with trafficked avenues, barrier posts have been installed; they can be lowered into the pavement with the swipe of a pass card so that local deliveries can be made. But Pujol's narrative is not limited to a technical account. Unlike his manner in other parts of the city, here in his own neighborhood, where he spontaneously meets friends in the public squares, he displays an uncontained exuberance for the place. He explains its history, describes the rhythms of its days, and in the midst of all this he starts talking to me about the little stones in the new pedestrian lanes.

These half-inch stones are used to break the monotony of the black asphalt. They are white. In another lane nearby, they are pink. Frankly, I hadn't noticed, but this was a matter of great controversy in Gràcia's squares and newspapers. Neighbors call them "chewing gum" stones, Toni explains. It is only then that I begin to even imagine the logic for any possible controversy. Here I stand in an atmospheric, architecturally attractive district, free of the automotive ruckus and ad hoc hodgepodge of Toronto. It is the kind of place that most anyone of means hopes to escape to on his vacation. But here there is a controversy: the stones challenge some minute facet of Gràcia's urbanism. They can be imagined as pieces of used chewing gum spit upon the pavement. More difficult to imagine is the intensity of local debate, the consultations between city departments and neighborhood associations, the interventions of local politicians, the letters to the editor. But by local tradition this is how the city is negotiated.

Here the bargaining is a collaborative process working toward a consensus goal. The goal is complex, but is distilled in a local code that the visitor hears time and again: to reclaim *espai public*. The phrase has a very special local meaning, which is not captured in its English translation as "public space." Private spaces, life, and organizations play a big role in Barcelona. City government rebuilds deteriorated districts and constructs and operates its transit systems, water, and energy supplies through partnerships with private companies. Districts like Gràcia are places of conservative, private homeowners and merchants. Espai public, therefore, is not a public zone separate from the private city; it is a third territory of streets and squares where private interests and public uses are vitally interwoven. The practice of urbanism in Barcelona focuses on this private-public territory, which provides the medium in which Barcelona's district citysystems grow.

For example, since the reestablishment of democracy in 1979 after decades of dictatorship, massive public investments have leveraged those of private owners to repair and redecorate square miles of buildings. One priority has been co-investment in the facades of private buildings. But the third territory is not limited to the facades that separate the public street from private interiors. Espai public also penetrates into the buildings. In revitalizing historic districts the city government substantially invested in ground-floor units, cocreating the cafés, lobbies, galleries, and retail shops that revitalized constant interaction between outside public life and inside proprietary life. The pedestrian street effectively flows in and out of the buildings. Similarly, the private has been extended into outdoor public space, with competing proprietors operating their restaurants on the squares and vendors lining both sides of the wide center-city pedestrian Rambla, turning public spaces into a permanent private market. Public facilities nestle among the redeveloped private buildings, old squares are reclaimed from their function as parking lots, and scores of new squares, parks, and *ramblas* have been created in the course of redevelopment projects. It is this expanding zone of interaction between the private and the public that makes Barcelona so dynamic. Looking at a picture of the peeling, gloomy facades and nearly vacant streets of Barcelona's historic center in the 1970s, it is almost impossible to imagine today's vivacious Barcelona as the same city.

Creating espai public and managing the mix of activities in it involves meticulous planning, negotiation, and design. For instance, shifting traffic from some Gràcia streets onto others to create the new espai public of the pedestrian streets reallocates property values, locational benefits, and nuisances between hundreds of families and small businesses. This reallocation involves a fine-grained negotiation, wholly unlike the blunt instrumentality of planning and renewal in most cities. "Barcelona is unique," says Ramon Garcia-Bragado, head of Barcelona's Urbanism Department, "because of the strength of public opinion on all urban questions. Nothing is easy. There's lots of negotiation needed to achieve anything. Just the question of moving a bus stop causes people to get active, to organize demonstrations. They have a sense of public claim to that space, a sense of ownership of the city."[1]

This one project in Gràcia involved sixty meetings among affected households, neighborhood associations, businesses, and schools. There were public demonstrations for and against different plans. It took a year to negotiate. Even then, as thousands of cars and motorcycles discovered new routes through the district, as pedestrians filled the new lanes, new customers filled the shops, and neighbors reclaimed their café-lined squares, there was still a controversy in the new espai public: the all-important detail of the "bubble gum" stones.

At the other end of this counterintuitive citywide transformation through micro-level negotiation was a visionary named Salvador Rueda, the founder and head of Barcelona's Urban Ecology Agency. Rueda's agency conceived and did the technical studies for the Gràcia project. In his office overlooking the seafront, he is projecting an interactive database model of Barcelona for us to view. His agency has documented the traffic patterns and types of activities in most districts of Barcelona, building by building, street by street. The model is a map of the city; he navigates with his mouse to an old neighborhood, part of a traditional Barcelona district citysystem with its dense mix of housing, small industry, and retail shops. He zeroes in on two streets on a short city block. With a few clicks we are looking at an assessment of the activities in this little patch. There are 222 distinct economic activities in the patch, he reports: different stores, tailors, workshops, home-based professions. With a click, his model groups them into 132 different types of activities, an amazing diversity in a small area compared with the zoned commercial or residential districts of a master-planned city. I note that one typically finds this kind of dense economic diversity in a migrant city like Dharavi. But we are looking at an affluent, developed city—at one of the most livable cities in the world. Rueda is pleased by the observation. The notion that his city has retained the organic, vibrant economic character that made cities everywhere historic centers of every kind of revolutionary change is reassuring. But he shares his exasperation with Barcelona's recent drift, like so many cities, toward planned mega-project dead zones, like the controversial seafront convention complex built to host a large international exposition in 2004. "What we are measuring," he explains, coming back to the little urban patch, "is the complexity of organization in this one area."

With his model he computes the resources that are consumed in the patch. Then he calculates what he calls the area's "sustainability." To do this he uses an established scientific formula for measuring entropy—the loss of energy, information, and organizational complexity—in that area. In a stable system, resource consumption is low relative to organizational complexity and activity. In these ecological terms, he explains, the citysystem on this typical Barcelona patch approximates the sustainability of a natural ecosystem. It is this sustainability that Barcelona urbanists are trying to reestablish in Gràcia and in espai public throughout the city.

My Barcelona colleagues don't seem fazed by what we are discussing. They don't realize how much this kind of urban thinking contrasts with the discussions in an average city planning department, where there are no such models, but more important, little time or inclination for such complex analysis. In other cities, Rueda and his model would be exotic, academic, and of marginal use. But here the city has founded and funded his institute and contracts it to plan major transformations of whole swaths of the city. Our discussion about methods for measuring the entropy of an urban patch is only relevant in Barcelona because it is supported by a set of widely held values and urbanist principles about the desirable qualities and benefits of city life. Rueda's model, for this reason, is not abstract or academic; it reveals the underlying logic of Barcelona urbanism and its fixation on espai public. The atmosphere we experience in a Barcelona square or rambla is the designed outcome of a low-entropy place.

The transformative potency of urbanism in any city is derived from its ability to translate the city's core values into a workable, replicable logic of city building. To use the language of business, the Barcelona government and urbanist community has established clear value propositions (e.g., espai public) and a practice for consistently delivering those propositions. Beyond addressing the preferences and needs of citizens in very fine-tuned ways, Barcelona has mastered the process of engaging citizens, landowners, and investors in repeated delivery of these propositions through explicit practices and recognizable types of city development. This is only possible because of the match between the practices of urbanism and local cultural values. Barcelona, in other words, can be said to have a coherent urbanism. Practice is bound to a foundation of shared values; the urbanism is as much a local culture of urban life as a professional practice. The result is a stable, engaged *community of practice*, which gives Barcelona its transformational capacity—its ability to consistently link analysis and policy to action, and to renew the city at a large scale in response to social, economic, and ecological change.

Progressive transformation is values-driven. People and institutions only align their private strategies and instrumental uses of the city to a common strategy because the ends create a more compelling value for them. Achieving strategic alignment in the urban free-for-all is near impossible if local practices of urbanism do not offer a value proposition that relates to the underlying culture of a good part of the city.

This cultural dimension of cities is perhaps the most subtle aspect of urban strategy. Take the example of metropolitan Miami, another Great Opportunities City. For decades Miami's local urban planners, environmentalists, and state-level fiscal planners have tried to insert density into Miami's economic logic. In 1975 they secured passage of one of the first comprehensive urban growth management plans in the United States. It called for concentrated growth along a central, high-density transit corridor. A few years later they received $800 million from the U.S. government to build the first part of that transit system. But even this highly subsidized density initiative did not synchronize with the region's basic values or with the suburban city models developed to serve those values.

During a visit to Miami I have a chance to meet up with my old friend Harvey Ruvin. He's been a fixture on the Miami political scene since 1968 and a tireless instigator of efforts to rein in urban sprawl and protect south Florida's environment. We've agreed to meet at his favorite roadside diner. We each drive half an hour in our separate cars, touching base by mobile phone to report our respective progress through traffic. Now, as we sit together in the air-conditioned diner, the noise of four lanes of traffic is muffled, and Harvey tells the story of their failed efforts to prevent the expansive and expensive sprawl that defines greater Miami today.

"Because the land was cheaper the farther you went west," Ruvin explains, "in the 1980s developers asked the county commission to consider a series of plan amendments to permit development farther and farther away from the designated transit and development corridor and infrastructure systems. I found myself losing votes five to four. The hearings were all perfunctory. Everyone knew what the votes would be. If you were on the 'five' side of that vote you wouldn't have trouble with campaign funding."[2]

Many urbanists have written off Miami as a depressing loss. The head of the Miami-Dade planning department tells me that they even have a hard time getting city planners to apply for jobs there. Ruvin has been constantly, calmly fighting for forty years against the region's strategic impotence. He and his colleagues won the establishment of Biscayne Bay National Park, America's first marine national park, located on the city's shoreline. They got massive funding to restore the Everglades. They passed some of the first local laws in the United States to control development around the region's groundwater resources and to reduce greenhouse-gas emissions. Now, under Ruvin's leadership, they are planning the massive investments necessary to protect greater Miami from rising sea levels and extreme weather events brought on by climate change. But when it comes to development control, according to Ruvin's three decades of stories, it seems to fall apart. In the face of a powerful suburban development alliance, based on low-density city models that depend on cheap agricultural land, the county and state have lacked the will and muscle to see its policies through.

But the triumph of Miami's suburban city models reflects a conundrum more fundamental than political maneuvering and rural land conversion. The underlying issue is a lack of alignment between the dominant values of the local culture and its progressive strategies. The suburban builders have had the clout of culture, not just politics, on their side.

Take the issue of public space and public facilities. In contrast to Barcelona's teeming squares or Toronto's neighborhood parks, the public spaces in greater Miami are generally vacant. It is as if the local government maintains public parks only because they think a city should have them. But residents simply don't use the parks. Miami gives the impression of a region of beach-loving people, but excepting the athletic crowd, most of its beach-going crowds are tourists. Miamians favor their air-conditioned homes and private pools. They also favor their cars over the city's light rail system. When they seek the "public" they most often go to semi-private places like shopping malls, arenas, and attractions. Unlike Barcelona, which specializes in a mixed public-private zone where people of all backgrounds intensely interact, Miami specializes in privatizing public space, bringing public-like activities under private ownership, security, and climate control. Miami and many other American cities are preoccupied with "defensible space"[3]—places where urban design and security services create a privately controlled envelope in which people create their experience of community.

In spite of their origins in public-facing cities like New York, Havana, or Port-au-Prince, Miami's migrant population, as diverse as it is, shares a culture where private ownership and control, personal convenience, and safety rank very high on the hierarchy of local urban values. "There's been a kind of cultural mind-set," says Dario Moreno of Florida International University's Metropolitan Center. "Miami is a city of people who don't want to live in density. It's articulated in a sense that there are too many people or the city is dirty and crime ridden. The feeling about downtown is that there are too many people. Miami is a city where the suburban culture avoids downtown," he says.

Among the competing ideas for greater Miami's development, those that satisfy this value proposition have prevailed. The backyard pool, the restaurant patio, the gated suburban development, and the security-controlled shopping malls are the centers of conviviality. Streets and sidewalks are dominated by the region's vast private automobile fleet. Parking lots are the primary form of espai public.

The drive to assert this culture against the county government's attempts at higher density, mixed-use development and public facilities has taken a political dimension. Even as the county government (and federal prosecutors) began to rein in the suburban builders in the late 1980s and 1990s, clusters of suburban subdivisions seceded from the county and organized into new municipalities. Taking their local zoning and development control out of the county's reach, these new cities represent a further attempt to govern development according to very local core values. As a result of this clash between policy and planning and cultural orientation, greater Miami has never developed a coherent local urbanism.

Few cities pay detailed attention to analyzing their foundation values when they develop plans for their growth. On one hand, leaders try to intuit the likely responses to a new policy or development project, based on past experiences and their own sense of what makes the city tick. More sophisticated cities do opinion polling, but this doesn't give much insight into underlying values. Planners and engineers in most cities take a very technocratic approach, applying standards of the "right way" to design a city that have little reference to unique local values.

Our progressive agendas for sustainability, livability, or equity are often introduced into policy as a further imposition of external values that have little reference to the city's unarticulated values foundation. Except in this case, the values of the progressive agenda are very explicit. They therefore become a lightning rod for all the frustration that a community can feel when the city does not serve their strategies and needs. Policies to contain and control automobile use for environmental reasons, for instance, smack up against the frustrating inconveniences and costliness of living in a city of separate residential, employment, and shopping districts. Attempts to integrate new immigrant groups into an area smack up against the frustrating lack of attention to the existing population's strategies. Because we don't really study local values, we aren't very effective in changing them. We rarely cultivate a consensus value proposition for the city, engage local populations in the design of new city models or citysystems, pilot these models so people can experience and fine-tune them, and ultimately articulate and confront the contradictions of their urban values.

This creates a huge problem for urban strategy. We spend a billion dollars on a transit system, as in Miami or Los Angeles, and people stay in their cars. Or we distribute social service facilities "for the sake of equity" throughout the neighborhoods of a city, and construction is stalled by not-in-my-backyard (NIMBY) battles. We thereby invest our political and financial capital in undisciplined trial-and-error. Take the gentrifying area of my Toronto neighborhood, for example. It is known as one of the most socially progressive in the city. Its residents like to wear their tolerance and appreciation for diversity on their sleeves. But when a socially progressive politician tried to locate a halfway house for teenagers at the edge of the neighborhood, implementing the city's policy of distributing such facilities throughout the city, these otherwise liberal-minded residents revert to an underlying value: ensuring the economic value of their homes. What gets generically labeled as NIMBYism is a distinct values conflict that needs to be understood and solved. People in downtown, middle-class Toronto neighborhoods invest vast sums to renovate and maintain their otherwise modest homes— more than is reflected in their properties' market prices. This kind of pride and upkeep is a core value in Toronto that preserves and improves an otherwise fiscally challenged city. But it conflicts with the social planning ideals that residents would otherwise support. Until a practice is developed to resolve such underlying values conflicts, the city will have problems implementing its progressive policies.

As this Toronto story illustrates, the cultural values in most cities are deeply conflicted. Even Barcelona's urbanism smacks up against values conflicts as it adapts to new challenges. For instance, southern Spain has been experiencing an extended drought. But local values for cleanliness support the daily washing of espai public—for example, sidewalks, lanes, and squares. Developing practices to reduce the use of potable water for this purpose is very controversial.

In Miami, people are deeply concerned with safety in public spaces, but the preferred mode of transportation—the private automobile—is the most dangerous daily activity in the city. People are trading off one strongly held value (i.e., safety) against others (i.e., convenience, privacy, and "freedom") all the time without any clear logic. Adding to the complexity, the values foundations of increasingly multicultural cities are in transition. Even in a citysystem like Dharavi, new ethnic migrant communities from northeastern India are using the migrant city and its markets in a different way from established groups. Few cities have the benefit of a city like Barcelona, whose historic isolation and relative homogeneity over centuries has allowed it to develop stable value propositions.

Traditional planning doesn't offer much help in navigating this landscape. A new practice is required, using anthropology, sociology, market research, and design to incrementally transform the local city-building practice and the values foundation together. The growing gap between official plans and the built city, accompanied by NIMBY and other values-based conflicts, has compelled planners to get increasingly involved in managing detailed design processes. One Sunday morning in Miami, I traveled (by car) to Dadeland, the southern terminus of the light rail transit system that Ruvin and his colleagues on the county commission voted for and lobbied into existence in the 1980s. Ever since, the county has been giving developers incentives to build higher density nodes like Dadeland around the transit stations, all to catalyze the high-density corridor that Ruvin described.

I stop at a number of transit stations but find no passengers there. The development around most of the stations is indistinguishable from any low-density highway strip mall. Along the half-hour drive, I see only two or three people riding on the wide bike path that parallels the train. The only high-density developments along the corridor are a few mega-malls at main highway crossroads. The county built the "right" infrastructure, but the developers didn't come.

But the planning department and developers have approached Dadeland differently. Rather than imposing a fixed paradigm or city model, they engaged each other in a process of more micro-level design. Working from a shared value proposition, they negotiated greater density, mixed use, pedestrian-friendly features into the building facades, orientation, shops, sidewalks, courtyards, landscaping, and streetscape. This design process allowed the builders to test adjustments against their business models. It gave prospective users a chance to react to the new designs. The result is hardly a new urbanism for Miami, but it is a step toward a breakthrough from the high-stakes, rigid, all-or-nothing politics of the suburban builders. Now seven-story buildings abut the transit station; the sidewalks have shaded patios; fountains in the streets slow traffic; street-facing balconies create the sense of public-facing life. Through design collaborations like the one in Dadeland, North American cities are laying a foundation for the reemergence of urbanism.

Constantly renewing its basic practices of urbanism has been a central part of Barcelona's success over thirty years of transformation. Constant debate and self-criticism have kept the practices honest, ensuring their coherence and coevolution with the local culture, as the values proposition for each project is constantly renegotiated. It's no surprise, therefore, to find a person like city councillor Itziar González leading the transformation of another low-income neighborhood, Barceloneta. González is a professional urbanist. She describes her specialty as "conflict resolution and public space."[4] She has been a longtime resident in Barceloneta's adjoining low-income neighborhood, El Raval. She lived in El Raval during its transformation from the city's most run-down area to its prime cultural district. And she is critical of the approach taken and the outcome.

El Raval has been held up as a global best practice in urban regeneration. It is a mandatory stop on the ceaseless pilgrimage of foreign city leaders, planners, architects, and designers to Barcelona. In the nineteenth century, El Raval was an industrial-tenement area not unlike the industrial slums and chawls of south Mumbai. It hosted the city's dirtiest industries—slaughterhouses, tanneries, brick making, and coal-powered textile mills—which attracted migrant workers from the countryside. There was little sanitation. One street was called Chain Street because a chain was installed to pull one's way through the street's deep mud. The southern part of the neighborhood abutted the port, establishing it as a center for brothels, hostels, and taverns.

Thirty years ago El Raval was so degraded that one building collapsed every three weeks. It was one of the most densely settled areas in
the world. The decline of traditional industries made it a center of petty
street crime, prostitution, and drug dealing. The middle class had fled.
Except for its small furniture, printing, and wholesale businesses, it was
a stigmatized residential area without any source of investment. The
idea behind its redevelopment was to clear the most dilapidated and
crime-ridden areas and enhance El Raval's multi-use character with
new cultural industries, public institutions, office and tourist facilities,
and, above all, espai public.

Today El Raval's refurbished streets and squares are buzzing with
activity. In addition to being a residential district it is also a center of
universities, museums, cultural institutions, youthful pan-European
tourism, and nightlife. The city approached this transformation with a
signature method, which has been constantly critiqued and redesigned
as it is applied across the rest of the city. González is currently redesigning the method for Barceloneta.

The basics are as follows. First, the city government designates an
area for intensified redevelopment. When it is designated, all city departments (planning, transportation, parks, police, economic development, etc.), utilities, and social welfare agencies develop a common
plan for new investments, facilities, and services in the area. Then the
city creates a public-private company to ensure coordinated investment
in redevelopment. In other words, redevelopment is approached as an
investment project, led by a group of investor-shareholders. The legal
shareholders of El Raval's transformation included city and regional
government, the telephone company, major savings banks, the city's
parking company, and a joint company of the neighborhood's small
shopowners. To reinforce political alignment, the board of the company includes all the political parties represented on the city council.
Together the initial shareholders in the El Raval project invested 18 million euros, creating a capacity to borrow 200 million euros more.

In parallel with the company's creation, the city amends its general
plan to provide special conditions for investment, land uses, and public
facilities in the area. In the Barcelona approach, Director of Urbanism
Garcia-Bragado says there has been a steady shift away from strict
building requirements "toward more flexible plans," which encourage

creative ways to address the neighborhood's problems and preferences. The revised plan for the district sets the parameters for trading public and private building rights and developing joint investments.

Take, for instance, the new law for low-income Barceloneta. It establishes a legal first option for the city to purchase a property when it is put up for sale. This achieves two objectives. It prevents the aggressive displacement of long-time tenants due to speculative hoarding by private developers who seek to gentrify the area for the pan-European market. It also gives the city landholdings that can be used to attract cultural or social service facilities or to negotiate local building projects—in other words, it makes the city and its public-private corporation a strategic force in the market.

Third, the city establishes what they variously call a "commission" or "consensus-building association." This body facilitates agreement between neighborhood associations and the local, regional, and state governments. It formally establishes the public stakeholders in the redevelopment and defines the policy and business processes for project execution, particularly with regard to housing. In El Raval, the association negotiated a policy on maintaining rental housing, on resident relocation during redevelopment, and on allocating new housing units after completion. "This is part of our institutional culture here," explains Rafael Tormo, the head of a redevelopment project in another Barcelona district. The Barcelona approach is based on a "culture of agreement," he says.[5] "This is the edge of a Damocles sword," he continues. The sword, in the case of Barcelona, is the precarious consensus that makes its urbanism coherent.

With these framework arrangements in place, the work begins. Bragado describes it as a process of "selective, public micro-surgical interventions" implemented across the whole area. The primary task in El Raval was renovating old housing and creating new public housing while repairing streets and facades, opening up new public squares and amenities, and bringing new commerce and employment into the neighborhood. The city co-invested with building owners in the facades and ground-floor shops of old buildings to reestablish pride and asset values. The company negotiated ownership of land parcels and recruited university facilities, museums, and cultural and research institutes to locate in El Raval. It transferred plots of land to the state government for public housing projects. Bragado gives another example of how the city kick-starts investment. When Barcelona was selected in the early 1980s to host the 1992 Olympics it "was not a tourist city or even an interesting city," he recalls. It didn't even have a hotel industry. "The private sector didn't believe that the Olympics would succeed in Barcelona," says Bragado, so hoteliers weren't investing. So the city had to come up with a way to spawn a hotel sector from scratch. The city selected ten locations around the city and zoned them for hotel development. Then it secured properties in these areas and offered fifty-year leases to hoteliers. This dramatically reduced their investment risks. Today, Barcelona has one of the healthiest hotel industries in the world.

Over the El Raval project's fifteen years, the initiative and financing for redevelopment steadily shifted from the public to private sector. Building owners, proprietors, and middle-class residents steadily regained faith in the area. Along the way, private developers were retrained in Barcelona's urbanism. "Now private developers have more interest in historical renewal and in higher-quality mixed-use development," says Bragado. "They found that the market will pay more for this kind of development than their traditional designs."

But González is unhappy with the outcome in El Raval. It has increased the assessed property value in the neighborhood by $11 billion over twenty years, "but the city did the easy part," she argues. "They did planning but not urbanism. They didn't identify the strategic issues that were only known to the neighbors," she says. Lack of attention to the values of the long-isolated tenant and immigrant residents created flaws and incoherence in the urbanism practiced there. As she tells her version of the story, the "strategic issue" becomes explicit: people wanted a stable community life and an affordable, accessible local economy, both of which have been compromised by the more transient, higher-cost cultural district created there.

"The neighborhood perspective," she explains, "is that the development was driven by and for the redevelopment company and local private developers. Now there are no buildings collapsing, but the buildings have been emptied for expensive apartments or hotels. Before, we had subsistence-level criminality, but the local people knew the prostitutes and dealers as neighbors. Now the crime committed here is linked to international networks and mafias. One can argue that there is a degradation of espai public because of the intensity of use by tourists. The old residents are moving out because of the constant busyness and noise." As a result, El Raval has become an area of temporary immigrant settlement and high disease rates side by side with the city's major cultural institutions and tourist district.

González sees this failing as a product of Barcelona's increasing substitution of urbanism with urban planning. Planning, she says, starts from the premise that "we want to reach this goal." Urbanism, in contrast, asks "how do we reach this goal?" She draws a picture of a boat on a large sheet of paper. Then she shows the boat being buffeted by strong winds, just like the pressures a city faces during its redevelopment, which threaten to push its vision off course. "To reduce the pressure of the winds on the boat," she argues, the planner makes the boat bigger and bigger. In other words, the project becomes less responsive to local values and priorities. It increasingly focuses on the needs of the boat. In contrast, she explains, as she continues her paper illustration, "urbanism is adding and developing solutions for all the different interests." She draws each "interest" as a little boat. "Urbanism is getting lots of little boats moving in a similar direction."

The starting point of strategic urban practice, in other words, is the constant articulation and evolution of the local values foundation that drives the citizens' choices, behaviors, and uses of the city. Strategic capability arises when urbanist practice is aligned with that foundation and develops numerous tailored solutions to create shared advantage on it. This approach to Barcelona's transformation is echoed by administrators and technical staff I meet throughout the city. None of this is taught in university courses for planners, architects, or civil engineers. It is learned as a local culture of practice. Jordi Campillo is the new managing director of the city's environment department. We're having a casual conversation about his new job and he expresses the same view. "The construction of the city," he says, "is not something that the city imposes but is built through consensus."

Campillo's words remind me of the transformational accomplishments of Kitakyushu, one of Japan's most historically burdened cities. A major postwar center of steel, chemical, and automotive production,

Kitakyushu was ranked by the United Nations as one of the top pollution hot spots in the world. Then, between the late 1960s and 1990, it underwent one of the largest industrial cleanups in history. It did so largely without national regulation or forced measures. The transformation started with a grassroots campaign by housewives. Before it was over, major manufacturers like Nippon Steel, Hitachi, Mitsubishi, and Toshiba and the city government had entered into 183 voluntary pollution control agreements and 883 written promises of action, altogether exceeding national law requirements. By the early 1990s, Kitakyushu had some of the best air and water quality in Japan. More than one hundred species of fish and marine birds were reestablished in what had been the largely dead Dokai Bay. Building on this success, Mayor Koichi Sueyoshi and his administration decided to make Kitakyushu a leading world center for sustainable urban development. One of his many initiatives was to re-create the natural watershed that flows into the bay.

During my first visit to Kitakyushu, Sueyoshi had me visit one of the many canalized streams that flow more like an engineering diagram than a natural watershed through the city. This particular stream canal ran along a road through a working-class neighborhood. At first I was unimpressed at the thought of this canal as some kind of environmental restoration. But the process of transformation in this city of engineers and heavy industry was unexpectedly subtle. The managers had us climb down the banks to look closely at the edges of the stream where the water lapped against the canal walls. Here and elsewhere, Sueyoshi's team had mobilized the neighbors to install rocky nooks and crannies in the stream beds. They had also established a nursery in each neighborhood for growing insect larvae. When ready, the citizens planted the larvae in the nooks. These were not just any larvae; they were larvae of the firefly.

The engineering of the watershed, they understood, had destroyed not only the fireflies' breeding grounds but also a cherished piece of local culture: the famous annual children's firefly festival. The firefly, Sueyoshi knew, was an indicator species that predicted not only the health of the whole riverine ecology but also of the human culture that had evolved around it. The river project was one of many ways his administration was engaging and educating citizens about their connection to global environmental issues.

Sueyoshi's ultimate ambition was to complete Kitakyushu's transformation from a top-ten pollution hot spot to a top-ten center for urban environmental sustainability. But to succeed he realized he needed more than political support; he needed a cultural momentum. To prepare one of the most ambitious environmental programs in the world of cities, Sueyoshi started not with a host of international experts but with a local citizens' commission. Its purpose was to renew the voluntary agreements approach used to clean up Dokai Bay and the city's air quality in the era before environmental regulation. The first task of the commission's industry, professional, NGO, and government representatives was to reach consensus on an explicit values foundation, consisting of ten consensus principles. The voluntary agreements were then negotiated on the basis of these principles.

Kitakyushu has excelled in the environmental arena and mobilized hundreds of millions of dollars behind its program because its strategies rest so explicitly upon such deep-seated, implicit cultural understandings. Many of the resulting principles are truly meaningful only to local people.[6] Consensus value statements, not technical prescriptions, served as their strategic planks.

Now Barcelona is testing its practice of urbanism against a different global challenge: building an urban value proposition in which the competing values of established local communities and of global industries begin to work together. Barcelona's powerful urbanism and its strategic capability evolved from its cultural homogeneity, regional commerce, and political isolation. But it also aspires to be a fully cosmopolitan city, supporting progressive transformation across the City. Managing the two-way process of extension in the final phase—the ways that global migrant companies and professionals seek to strengthen their global advantage in Barcelona, and the ways that Barcelona seeks to build its advantage across the City—is Tormo's new Damoclean sword. It is the fundamental challenge to the global City's coherence: the reconciliation of the local citysystem with the foreign city model, of the local *city of places* with the extended *city of flows*.

In an old, deteriorated textile and apparel manufacturing district called Poblenou, once known as the Spanish Manchester, Barcelona urbanists are facing this challenge. Now designated in the city's official plan as a special redevelopment area called district 22, the District 22@ Project is working to reconcile the high-tech campus city model of the global ICT, design, media, and data industries with a very local citysystem that is hungry for renewal.

Poblenou is a conservative, lower-income community of some sixty thousand residents. Most of the families there have lived in the industrial neighborhood citysystem for generations. Its economic design is not unlike early industrial districts throughout the world. Residences are located among local manufacturers, shops, and warehouses. But Poblenou has a special local design, based on a grid of hundred-by-hundred-meter blocks or "islands" that mix these uses in a cellular, micro-citysystem structure.[7] The only problem is that Poblenou's industry began rapidly disappearing in the 1960s. The 22@ Project proposes to insert new industry into this existing citysystem structure and culture. The design challenge for the new, so-called innovation district, in other words, is to integrate more than three million square meters of new productive activities into 115 island blocks while stabilizing the local population and adding four thousand new affordable housing units, along with new infrastructure and more public amenities, all without undermining the values of the established community.

Barcelona is hungry for the new industry. "We're not a primary city," explains Xavier Romero, the philosophical marketing manager for the company that was established to lead the project. "We need to find creative ways to make ourselves attractive to these big companies. At the same time we have to resist the pressure from them" to accept their standard models. "We don't want a downtown here; we want a life here after seven P.M.," he says. Under a more typical redevelopment approach, he adds, local developers "would put in all middle-class residential buildings," given the region's booming housing market. Their aim is to renew the community of the existing population, not replace it.

To get started, the project had to "establish its DNA," as Romero puts it, and define "the rules of the game." The rules are as follows. First, to preserve the islands and their mixed-used vitality as the basic unit of Poblenou urbanism, the island and not individual land parcels were defined as the basic unit of regeneration. No redevelopment can take place in an island until 60 percent of the landowners agree to its

transformation. This condition forces integrated planning for each island.[8] Second, landowners are given an economic incentive to agree together on their island's redevelopment: they can rebuild the island at a
substantially greater building height (density), automatically increasing
their land value if they participate in the 22@ Project.[9] In this way the
project facilitates the organization of *a community* to plan, build, and
foster the renewed island citysystem. Third, as a quid pro quo for the
increased density allowance, each landowner must transfer 30 percent
of his lot to the municipality. Under the new density allowance, this still
leaves the landowner with a bigger opportunity than before, but the
municipality secures land for progressive investment in each island:
one third is used for affordable housing, one third for espai public,
and one third for educational, studio, and research facilities that support the targeted new industries. The fourth and final rule provides infrastructure for the renewed district, adding to its progressive character:
each developer must pay a fee to cofinance a district heating and cooling system, a pneumatic underground waste disposal and transfer system, and a fiber-optic cable system.[10]

Within these rules, landowners and the city negotiate the transformation of each island. Meanwhile, a special citizens' commission oversees
protection of 140 designated historical buildings and other structures,
like old factory chimneys and walls, thus retaining the district's ties to its
past.

By traditional measures, the project has already been a success. After
decades of stagnancy, it has mobilized an enormous private investment: more than 60 percent of the 115 blocks are in the process of transformation. A remarkable 80 percent of the developers and more than
half of the mobilized private investment are local. But 22@ still rebuilds
on the sharp edge of the sword. We visited one particular block whose
construction had been completed. It was a classic example of mixed-
use development: a university facility abutting an office building for IT
companies, which was next to a classy new hotel, which in turn abutted
new affordable housing. In the middle of the island, shared by all, was a
small, smartly designed open square—a newly minted piece of espai
public. But the sterile quiet of the new island and this square constrasted
starkly with the run-down island across the street, yet to be transformed.
There you could see children playing in the street. There you saw people

transacting business in their street-front espai public. In the transformed island the only functioning espai public was the few tables of a
street-front café, awaiting their lunchtime customers. In short, the old
island was a place where people were at home. They lived, worked, argued, made their noise and money, and chased their children there. The
transformed island was not yet either a neighborhood or a downtown.

It remains to be seen whether Project 22@ will evolve a common
ground between the placed-based urbanism of the island citysystem
and the globally extended building of the city model. But there can be
no question about Poblenou's renewed historic significance. Project
22@ is breaking a path for the final phase, much as the *illes* of Poblenou
gave shape to modern industrial life in the nineteenth century. This latest phase of Barcelona's twenty-year transformation is nothing less
than an ambitious work in progress to discover an urbanism for the
City.[11]

CHAPTER 14

Governing the Entrepreneurial City

Local Markets and the Resurgence of Chicago

There's an old theater called the Uptown at the center of a gritty commercial area at the intersection of Broadway and Lawrence Avenue in Chicago. It is thought to be the largest movie house in the United States, bigger even than New York City's famous Radio City Music Hall. But since 1981 it has been boarded up and closed.

On the plywood that covers the huge entranceway someone has pasted a reproduction of the theater's gala opening program. This event in August 1925 included orchestras, three choruses, jazz music, and elaborate dancing and stage performances. Twelve thousand people stood in line to get tickets. A parade of two hundred floats converged on the theater that summer day, and the Uptown opened its forty-four hundred seats, turned on its ten thousand stage lights, bellowed a greeting from its huge sixty-five-foot pipe organ, and demonstrated its first-of-a-kind air-conditioning system for the first of many full-house crowds. Thereafter, the Uptown would sell more than twenty thousand movie tickets on a single weekend day, the pinnacle act of commerce of the local citysystem that birthed America's film industry.

Only a century earlier, Chicago itself had been a marshy outpost for a dozen or so traders and farmers. By the start of the twentieth century it was one of the ten largest cities in the world. In the first decade of the twentieth century, the district called Uptown emerged as Chicago's second downtown and changed the face of American culture.

In 1880, after the city's reconstruction following its great fire, Chicago had five hundred thousand people, but it still ended far south of the forest that covered Uptown. This land was cleared in the mid-1880s for celery farms. As streetcar and rail entrepreneurs extended their lines northward in the late 1880s and 1890s, speculating developers built new housing tracts on these farmlands. The communities that started there, still half-built and half a dream, attracted a mix of Scandanavian, German, and Irish immigrants who were leaving congested, slumlike neighborhoods in the central city. The annexation of the new housing tracts to Chicago in 1893, driven by these same development interests, suddenly enabled the district's rise into a city center of its own right. It began with the northward extension of the city's water and sewer lines and police and fire services. In 1901 a new end terminus of the famous elevated transit line was built there. No one anticipated what would happen next.

Now linked to the markets of Chicago, Uptown rapidly created an entire industry value chain, which served a nationwide market, from production to distribution to consumption. Within two decades of its annexation, it became the center of America's new film and recording industry, the Hollywood before Hollywood. By 1920, Uptown could have stood as a city in its own right. It would have been one of the largest in the United States.

The first seed of the Uptown citysystem lay in the late-nineteenth-century establishment of summer resorts along the area's lakeshore. Their clientele created demand for restaurants, bars, and entertainment, and a labor market of entertainers to serve them. Leveraging the concentration of entertainment talent, one of America's first film companies, the Essanay Studios, established its studio there in 1907. Essanay attracted even more talent and entertainment technicians. Some, like actress Gloria Swanson, were "discovered" among local residents, but many, like Charlie Chaplin, were transient employee-residents in Uptown's project-to-project cultural industry. Essanay, produced four of five American silent films in the early twentieth century. It also established America's first nationwide film distribution model. A while later, the first "talkie" movies were produced in Uptown too. Then one of the country's first record companies started there. More than 480 movies and television shows would be filmed in Uptown.

In 1913, the Plymouth Hotel opened. Uptown's growing mix of vacationers, technicians, and transient entertainers had created demand for a new kind of housing. The Plymouth was the first of more than ninety apartment hotels to come, providing the dominant form of housing in Uptown. The apartment hotel offered units on a daily, weekly, and monthly basis. Along with their modern amenities like elevators, telephones, and even swimming pools, their flexible terms supported the transient lifestyle of entertainment employees and tourists alike. They also attracted growing numbers of young working singles, including a contingent of America's first generation of single, working women, who gathered in lively Uptown from across the country. Uptown created the social ecology of the North American yuppie district.

In the 1920s "most of the 400,000 Uptown area residents," writes historian Perry Duis, "were singles or childless couples who worked during the day, frequented the theatres, clubs and dance halls at night, and took the majority of their meals outside of their living quarters."[1] In response, an entrepreneur named Mary Dutton added a further component to the emerging citysystem, opening the 1,226-seat Ontra Cafeteria to serve youthful residents and entertainment-seekers. The next market of opportunity for Miss Dutton's cafeteria business was a certain emerging film center in Los Angeles. The Uptown citysystem was extending itself, and with it a new national industry and urban culture.

This cluster of young professionals, studios, apartment hotels, and eating places reinforced the retail entertainment sector. As elsewhere, new union contracts and shorter work hours spawned a culture of leisure and consumption.[2] On weekends, Uptown's theaters (the Uptown, Deluxe, Lakeside, Riviera, and Pantheon) and dance halls and cabarets (the Aragon, Arcadia, the Green Mill, and Rainbo Gardens) were filled to the brim. But in 1981, not long after Bob Marley and Bruce Springsteen performed big-ticket concerts at the Uptown Theater, its doors were permanently closed. It had been the last holdout of a citysystem whose residents and businesses had been boarding up windows and fleeing for more than a decade.

During the 1960s–1970s, Uptown's middle class fled. When remaining residents reported drug dealing, muggings, gang violence, and prostitution, the police officers would ask them, "What's someone like you doing living here?" Chicago's police and firemen were moving out of the city themselves; city hall had to pass a law making Chicago residency an employment requirement. The entertainment district citysystem gave way to new markets and business models. The apartment hotels were filled with a new demographic of transients: low-income elderly pensioners, thousands of deinstitutionalized mental patients, prisoners on early release, and refugees from Cuba, Vietnam, Laos, and Ethiopia. Chicago's main newspaper called the area "a psychiatric ghetto." Banks refused to give mortgages for property there. Slumlords took over buildings and rented their units to gang members and drug dealers, who took control of the parks and streets. When the slumlords drained the last cash from their dilapidating buildings, the buildings became opportunities for a new kind of entrepreneurship spreading around Chicago: locals called it "arson for profit." One twenty-four-block corridor of Uptown apartment buildings earned the moniker Arson Alley.

The crisis in Uptown was replicated across Chicago as old industries and associated neighborhood citysystems collapsed one by one. Chicago became the sum of dozens of deteriorating neighborhoods.

But over the last twenty-five years, Uptown and Chicago's other neighborhoods have been on a remarkable rise. Chicago has reemerged as America's busiest commercial, conference, tourism, and entertainment center. This is a stark contrast to Detroit, which shares a common history of manufacturing, shipping, immigration, racial division, and industrial decline. Detroit has not been able to develop a new urbanism to reunify and rebuild. In stunning contrast, Chicago has transformed itself district by district to resume its position as one of the most productive, creative, and vibrant cities in the world.

But the Uptown Theater still stands idle, a monument to the fragility of urban economies, even when organized into robust, efficient citysystems. It demonstrates the third major challenge to a city's progressive transformation: the governance of the city's entrepreneurial impulses through the design and management of its many markets. This process, as shown by the story of Uptown, often begins at the level of each individual building.

It's best to be clear about what we mean when we talk about a market. A market can be simply understood as a regular, patterned set of transactions between a group of buyers and sellers, which results in the predictable exchange of some mutually recognized value. That's how we normally think about markets. This makes markets seem like generic exchange mechanisms but markets are anything but.

The different markets within a city—whether for fish, houses, parking spaces, or engineering contracts—are defined by local and regional customs, laws, conventions, infrastructure, and spatial relationships. Many different forces in the city, not just its buyers and sellers, shape how each market works. In turn, each market determines which business models can thrive in a city. By constraining the types of business models that succeed in a city, a market also shapes the way the city itself develops, as the continuing story of the Uptown district will illustrate. At their most mature stage of development, different local markets cluster activities together to create unique efficiencies and synergies in the physical form of a citysystem.

To explore the local character of markets, take the example of housing in a residential neighborhood. Theoretically, the housing market involves a generic product unit, a square foot of living space. The price for that unit is determined by supply, demand, and the cost of its production. There may be a real estate agent who mediates the transaction between buyers and sellers and takes a fee, and a local bank that finances the purchase and charges a fee and interest. But in reality, the nature of the product, its value on the market, and how the transaction is managed are all determined by dozens of local cultural, political, legal, and institutional factors. The cultural or social background of neighbors determines whether a home in this neighborhood secures a premium price. It also determines the allowable activities and income that can be derived from the building, such as whether an owner can operate a home business or rent units. Political and legal factors determine whether and how the building can be expanded on its lot and how much it will cost to do so (e.g., in the form of legal fees or illegal bribes). Institutional factors determine the availability and cost of finance, or whether owners have to look after their own water and sanitation services. These factors are part and parcel of the residential housing market. They greatly determine its prices and the nature of the building, its ownership structure, liquidity, and sales transactions. These local factors are not separable from the market. They define and *govern* it as much as the market governs the moments and ways that a city can pursue transformational change. To the extent that a city can shape its markets, it can also shape its own development. ·

Local markets are *socially* regulated, even in free market economies. There are vast differences between the forms that a particular market takes in different cities. It is hard to compare North American clothing stores, with their fixed prices, ready-to-wear garments, and relatively anonymous shopping, to a traditional clothing district in Istanbul or Delhi, where prices are negotiated and there is an expectation of hospitality and customization. Each distinct market uses different buildings, supports different activities, and produces different externalities, such as waste streams and noise. These conditions arise from historical compromises between different ethnic and economic groups and from political accommodations to religious, mercantile, labor, and government institutions. Conceiving a market that is void of culture, historical conventions, and institutions is a truly academic or ideological exercise.

To the extent that we manage national economies and multinational companies without reference to the diverse, evolving urban markets on which they stand, we welcome a world of economic surprise.[3]

From the first orderly plots imposed on marshy prairie lands in the early 1800s, Chicago was conceived as an economic powerhouse of intercontinental consequence. Early Chicago was the material product of an explicit urban strategy, promoted by a loose alliance of speculators, businessmen, and investors to build a shipping, warehousing, and trading nexus between the world's largest emerging agricultural region and the world markets reached via the Mississippi and Great Lakes shipping basins. The transformation of the area's waterlogged landscape into a city and the transformation of its lousy harbor into an industrial shipping canal to connect the two great basins was driven by self-selected entre-preneurs who instilled a permanent commercial disposition in the city.

The city's early markets were the product of shifting alliances and set-tlements between four main actors: speculative investors, pioneer busi-ness ventures, immigrant communities required for staggering building projects and workloads, and the public institutions called upon to un-derwrite so much infrastructure. Consistent renewal of these settle-ments, although often brutally negotiated, enabled market growth and the multiplication and scaling of tested Chicago business models into new industries. Then the industries clustered to service each other. They synchronized with government, private developers, and slum-building immigrant communities to create the urban form, construction innova-tions, and infrastructure that would congeal into Chicago's industrial neighborhood citysystems. The citysystems evolved the social ecology of the *neighborhood* and the political economy of the *ward*, and Chicago developed one of the most palpable urbanisms in the world.

By the early twentieth century, Chicago's massive economy was dom-inated by large-scale, specialized industrial zones (like the stockyards), mixed-use industrial city neighborhoods, and middle-class residential-retail city model towns on the city's expanding periphery. Some of the latter, like Uptown, evolved into industrial neighborhood citysystems in their own right. All of these districts and activities were connected by scores of private railway and streetcar lines. Chicago may have been sec-ond to Detroit in manufacturing or to New York in finance, but it earned a legendary primacy as the continent's center of commerce.

The momentum of Chicago urbanism and reinvestment in the city's manufacturing and infrastructure was interrupted by the 1930s' Great Depression. Reinvestment was further delayed by subsequent, all-out production for the Second World War. These crises left Chicago in the 1950s with a base of early-twentieth-century infrastructure, plants, and equipment. Exactly at this time, when the city was challenged to re-new, the governance of the most basic metropolitan markets—for land and infrastructure—was removed from the hands of local institutions and commercial interests and commandeered by the social engineer-ing and untested master planning of the national government. The U.S. government started a massive city-building experiment on the subur-ban fringes of most of the country's major metropolitan areas. It redistributed tax revenues generated in cities and their citysystems for the construction of highway, water, and sewerage infrastructure for semi-urban city models that had no basis in any established local market logic. It subsidized finance for suburban home purchases, thereby also subsidizing the business models of the new suburban city model industry. The result was a division of metropolitan Chicago, much as in Detroit, into two competing market systems.

In earlier phases of Chicago's development, decisions to build or modernize were made locally and were often strategically aligned through evolved urbanism. The city's organic growth was based on trial-and-error consolidation of local business models in locally disciplined markets. The national suburban program traded urbanism for city building and eschewed the established logic of local investment decisions. Its reengineering of the cost equations in urban regions destabilized existing markets. Federal highway construction suddenly reduced the importance of locating manufacturing facilities adjacent to rail lines, a central feature of Chicago's industrial districts and neighborhoods. Highway networks underwrote a new business model: the commercial trucking company. Soon the trucking industry consolidated a new market for freight transportation. Almost overnight, a location on the city's rail network shifted from being a competitive advantage to a cost burden.

The combination of trucking, low suburban land costs, and subsidized suburban infrastructure made suburban industrial development feasible and attractive for the first time. But to stabilize this new form of urban development, suburban municipalities had to overcome their underlying lack of organic economic footing. A permanent revenue stream had to be created for long-term upkeep of the new infrastructure. Without a public finance solution, the suburbs could not stabilize the industrial land development market.[4] Property taxes from old residential suburbs would not be enough. In a zero-sum game, the suburbs sought to capture a major part of Chicago's historical tax base. In a brilliant strategic move against the city, suburban municipalities developed new forms of market governance. Municipal land grants, tax holidays, and site development incentives traded off today's revenues and land values against a long-term future stream of industrial and commercial taxes.

Faced with the choice between a subsidized new industrial landscape and full-cost capital investment in established city locations, Chicago's manufacturers moved to the suburbs. The property development markets of Chicago and its surrounding suburban jurisdictions were suddenly joined in a wholesale competition.

By 1965, more than half of the manufacturing jobs in metropolitan Chicago had shifted to suburban highway corridors. Between 1965 and 2000, Chicago lost 70 percent of its manufacturing jobs. The relocation destroyed the economics of Chicago's industrial city neighborhoods and special industrial districts. The city lost not only tax revenues to renew aging infrastructure, schools, and parks but also gained a substantial new liability: square miles of idle, contaminated old industrial sites. Chicago residents followed industry's move to the suburbs, spreading the crisis to the city's commercial and residential real estate markets. Between 1960 and 1990, Chicago's population dropped by almost eight hundred thousand people. This was the first time in Chicago's history that its population had ever declined.

Few expected to ever see Chicago, of all cities, struggling for basic market viability. But there was a fatal flaw in the genetic code of the city's advantage. The economics of association in Chicago worked within ethnically or racially homogenous industrial city neighborhoods, but association broke down when those neighborhoods were confronted with a common external challenge. From the beginning, Chicago industries and districts had been built on the principle of community. Immigrants pursued their strategies through chain migration communities. They gained prominence in specific trades and industries. They invested together in residential districts and ethnic- and race-based churches, newspapers, clubs, and charities. They focused within their often segregated districts or neighborhoods on internal development. Political power was gained and parceled out to ethnic political bosses whose wards were gerrymandered to ensure that they maintained a coherent ethnic base. Political "machines" developed to apportion patronage jobs and services between wards, developing a political culture of divide and conquer. This divided association, which had worked at the scale of the neighborhood citysystem, left Chicago without mechanisms or mentality to forge true alliance in the face of the region's reshuffled economic deck. In the fight for what remained, the city's communities cannabalized each other.

An ungoverned market arose to exploit these conditions, supporting four interrelated business models, which used coercion, collusion, and misinformation to stealthily strip the remaining wealth from emptying neighborhoods. The first model was predatory finance: the charging of exorbitant interest rates and fees for basic home and small business finance by usurious moneylenders and predatory quasi-banks. The market for predatory lending was made possible by citywide redlining: institutionalized collusion between private banks and insurers to withhold mortgage finance and insurance policies to households in selected neighborhoods, particularly those with large African American populations.[5] Predatory finance operations emerged as an opportunistic strategy to legally and quickly secure the remaining income streams and assets of the redlined populations and their neighborhoods. It accelerated the city's depletion by driving people into bankruptcy, and it increased the barriers to Chicago's bootstrap renewal by inhibiting the most basic investment in a city of immigrants: the purchase and improvement of a home and its leveraging into an enterprise.

The second business model to emerge was blockbusting. Blockbusting was a logical extension of redlining and predatory lending that preyed on the city's racial division. The model required two market conditions: the lack of affordable finance for African American families in their redlined neighborhoods, and the fears of white residents that their homes would immediately lose value if black families moved to their neighborhood. Agents started their blockbusting street by street by spreading rumors that black families were moving in. To make their point, they would hire black women to walk the streets of targeted neighborhoods with their children. The agents would then spread information that this was driving down property values. White residents would sell their homes to these agents at a discount and join the flight to the suburbs. Then the homes would be quickly resold at premium prices to incoming black families.

The third business model of Chicago's decline was slumlordism. Predatory lending and job losses created high loan default and tax delinquency rates. The slumlord would purchase homes, commercial buildings, and even major cultural facilities like the Uptown Theater in foreclosure sales or city tax auctions. The slumlord's basic business model was to take an asset built through the prior investments of others and squeeze as much short-term cash rent from it as possible, without any capital investment in maintenance. The slumlord strips the city of assets just as a junkyard strips the salvageable parts from a wrecked car.

Finally, the fourth business model finished the job of urban destruction: arson. Once a slumlord had drained the possible cash streams from a declining property, building owners would hire an arsonist to burn them down to collect on their fire insurance policies. With the destruction of each property, or even a whole city street, Chicago's new business cycle of decline was completed. The city government would take possession, clear the lot, and add it to a growing inventory of raw, de-urbanized land.

Together these four models corrupted the market system at the foundation of Chicago's economy: neighborhood property value and the tax base for renewal of infrastructure and services. Tax increases on the remaining residents and businesses were not enough to stem declines in city services. Flight from the city became self-perpetuating. The only solution was to rebuild the property markets of Chicago's neighborhoods, building by building, lot by lot, and block by block.

In Chicago, die-hards prevail. It has been that way since the city's start. In its moment of greatest crisis, the city's most powerful urbanism legacy was revealed: a self-help culture of urban pioneering in its neighborhood communities. It was in local districts like Uptown and Edgewater that Chicago launched an eventual citywide recovery.

Some residents refused or simply could not afford to flee. These were stubborn people. I'd met a number of them, like Gail Cincotta, in earlier decades. At the start of Chicago's collapse in the 1960s, Cincotta was the female head of a working-class family with no experience in taking on the large-scale market failures, redlining, and blockbusting that were destroying America's inner cities and her westside neighborhood of Austin. "I learned to organize by running a household of three generations," she told me. The gravelly-voiced, heavy-smoking Cincotta became one of the most influential figures in the history of American banking. She led the successful nationwide campaign for passage of the U.S. Home Mortgage Disclosure Act in 1975, which forced banks to reveal redlining practices, and the Community Reinvestment Act in 1977, which forced them to stop.

Die-hard neighborhood citizens like Cincotta joined together by the tens of thousands as an implicit urbanist community and led the reclamation of their city. Their achievement was to reestablish effective governance of markets, starting from the micro-level. To do this they had to fight the perverse entrepreneurialism that was destroying neighborhood assets and regeneration potential.

Their model was endemic to the Chicago neighborhood: the citizens' group, led by the community organizer. During the decline, each limping Chicago neighborhood organized dozens of groups: block clubs, neighborhood associations, community councils, community development corporations, tenants' organizations, cooperatives, and mutual aid associations. Many such groups still play a central role in Chicago's development and planning today. They are the new foundation upon which the powerful mayoral regime of Mayor Richard M. Daley now rests. Under Daley, the community group has been transformed into a strategic institution. Uptown and Edgewater, for instance, have fifteen active residents' councils and neighborhood associations, six active block clubs, and three community development corporations whose roots were set in the 1970s and early 1980s. Along with local business, ethnic, and condominium associations, these groups now constitute the district's official zoning and planning committee, which reviews and recommends all development proposals for the neighborhood.

Back in the 1970s, these groups were informal neighborhood shareholder associations, fighting slumlords and gangs on one front and the self-serving machine of Chicago's Democratic Party on another. Their modus operandi, to use the language of their activists, was to protect or "take back control" of their community. In commercial terms, their job was to undermine the business viability of gangs, slumlords, blockbusters, corrupt officials, criminals, arsonists, and redlining banks, and thereby break the market for urban dismantlement and recover the city's remaining assets, building by building. They were the de facto asset managers for their neighborhoods, eventually retaking the city into a kind of voluntary receivership. They made inventories of every building, school, park, and lot. They debated and agreed on the sources of value in each neighborhood that should be redeveloped under their strategic control.

In Edgewater, just north of Uptown, community groups gave priority to the district's architectural heritage, to the retail hubs adjacent to transit stations, and to its public lakefront. Many of the activists had themselves prevailed against the redlining system to purchase their own homes. They therefore brought the mind-set of investors to their activities. They secured planning grants, which they used to define the mix of housing products and markets they wanted to reestablish, which buildings to preserve, and which to let the city demolish for parks or new commercial purposes. Edgewater and Uptown activists opted for a neighborhood economy based on diversified, mixed-income housing models. They literally recruited new owners to buy and manage the buildings designated for each of these models—single-occupancy rentals, family rentals, owner-occupied homes, cooperatives, and condominiums—and trained and monitored them to do so within their community-defined market parameters. They recruited investments for their schools, parks, and historic buildings to supply the amenities of a fully functioning residential-commercial system. It was in this way that today's Chicago was first rebuilt.

All this required leverage over apathetic police precincts, nonresponsive city departments, and the unaccountable city hall machine. Over decades, employment in city government had been converted into a market in its own right for exchanging political power and government resources. Chicago's Democratic Party rose to power in the 1930s by organizing rival ethnic political fiefdoms into a centralized regime for governing the city under control of the mayor as the machine boss. This party machine allocated politically controlled resources—access to city jobs, property development opportunities, infrastructure contracts, and city services—to local party leaders at the ward level. The ward leaders ran extensive vote-mobilization organizations, staffed by recruits whose loyalties and services were maintained through the provision of patronage jobs. With near control over local election outcomes, these ward leaders promoted candidates for city council who would be fully loyal to the mayor and his positions. The steady accumulation of jobs under the control of the ward bosses over the decades created a massive pool of patronage workers in nearly every city department. It was a black market in its own right. Single ward leaders and aldermen controlled large parts of the workforce in particular city departments. The inefficiencies of this political pyramid scheme were borne by neighborhood residents. The job of a patronage worker was not to do the job—or even to attend work; it was to get the machine reelected. This disconnect between employment and work performance made city government all but impotent at the level where Chicago's markets had to be reclaimed.

When resident-activist Marge Britton and her husband purchased their home in Edgewater in 1968, she recalls, "People were asking why we would live there. Uptown looked like it was bombed-out." In the early 1970s, the residents decided that they had to "take over the political machine so there wasn't a machine here any longer." In addition to the slumlords and the gangs, they had to eliminate the patronage market. Lacking a political party to turn to for support, the residents created their own political organization, mobilizing block clubs and residents' councils to elect what locals called their first "community candidate" to the city council in the 1980s. In their lifetimes, this was the first alderman elected from their ward who had not been part of the machine. The old ward boss in Edgewater-Uptown would eventually be convicted for taking payoffs from local real estate operators. "Every alderman since," Britton says, "has come from the community."

Today's alderman for Edgewater, Mary Ann Smith, is one of those community people. She moved to Uptown in 1971 and started working on a campaign to stop appointment of judges by the machine. Then she joined a group that fought to clean up and ensure public access to the city's lakeshore. In 1987 Smith moved eight blocks north into Edgewater. In 1989, she became the area's alderman and entered a new alliance formed by today's Mayor Daley during his election campaign.

"You can't imagine a problem that wasn't happening here," Smith recalls. "My first two years in office were all about crime. I had two years to show that we could tackle it. All the blocks had block clubs by this time. We tracked crime by address to identify the problem corners and buildings. In order to get the police to patrol these areas, I had to sit in a lawn chair at the most crime-ridden street corners. I'd call them in advance to tell them where I would be and this would force them to do a sweep of the area before I got there so I wouldn't get harmed."

Across the districts of Chicago, a similar logic of community inventory, intervention, stabilization, political mobilization, and bootstrap redevelopment was unfolding. In 1973, a group of bankers in the redlined African American neighborhood of South Shore established ShoreBank, the country's first community development bank. It almost immediately generated profits. ShoreBank became the largest inner-city bank for low-income households in the country, with branches throughout the United States. Grassroots entrepreneurial efforts like these incubated the new business models to address local challenges. Because Chicago's urbanism was so neighborhood-based, these neighborhood associations, block clubs, and community development corporations became the ground-level strategic institutions of the emerging transformational regime. They provided the training ground for many of the professionals who would later assume executive positions in the administration of Richard M. Daley.

One such professional is Jack Markowski. His first experience was in the poor South Side of Chicago in the late 1960s. He was immediately drawn to what he calls "self-help" as opposed to "welfare" models for regeneration. "Call it the 'private sector bootstrap model,'" he tells me. In 1981 he became executive director of the Edgewater Community Council. For Markowski and his council, rental housing was a strategic market that they had to reshape and govern. In the 1980s, the rental market served 65 percent of Chicagoans; today that figure is still over 50 percent.

The Edgewater Council focused efforts on the most rapidly disinvesting area, the legacy of Uptown's heyday. "Ninety-five percent of the housing there was rental housing, and most was single-resident occupancy," Markowski recalls. Edgewater's rental housing had been designed for the transient young professionals. After the Second World War and Uptown's decline, the small units seemed tailor-made for halfway houses, poor senior citizens, new immigrants, and other vulnerable people, often under the management of slumlords. "First we did an inventory of owners and residents in all three hundred buildings. We realized that we had to organize the owners, many of whom did not even live here," he recalls. "Our work focused on training them in good property management; even in simple things like keeping the buildings clean and selecting good tenants." Markowski and his colleagues, in other words, were reestablishing the most basic practices of Chicago's neighborhood-based urbanism. The regeneration practices that they pioneered would then be scaled into strategic institutions with citywide mandates.

Take the Community Investment Corporation (CIC), which Markowski now serves as CEO. The corporation was established by a consortium of banks in 1977 to fulfill their legal obligations under Cincotta's hard-won Community Reinvestment Act. It has since provided more than $800 million in loans to rehabilitate thirty-nine thousand multifamily units, securing affordable homes for one hundred ten thousand residents. Mission-driven corporations like CIC represent a second level of strategic institution in the city's new regime, reinforcing community-level initiatives. For example, CIC's Troubled Buildings Initiative helps community organizations secure ownership of their neighborhood's most divested apartment buildings. The corporation rehabilitates them, secures quality tenants, stabilizes their operations, and then recruits, trains, and finances new private owners to operate them on the reconstructed marketplace. Outfits like CIC have reengineered the way that land and housing markets work for a significant segment of the Chicago population, squeezing out slumlord and predatory lending practices.

By the end of the 1980s, these two levels of new market governance provided a foundation of partners and tested practices for a third tier of new entrepreneurial governance, operated directly by city government under the governing coalition of Mayor Daley. Under Daley, community organizations have steadily replaced ward bosses as a base of political power. Now the mayor's loyalist aldermen serve as solution and resource brokers between community groups and city hall. The new city hall regime, thus articulated from the level of the block to the neighborhood to city council to the mayor's office, can exert direct entrepreneurial leadership of markets over vast areas of the city. While the old model of machine patronage has withered, much of its culture of discipline and loyalty has survived, giving tremendous stability to the regeneration effort.

An early example of the new approach under the Daley regime is NeighborSpace. NeighborSpace is a not-for-profit corporation created by city hall to convert the city's large inventory of abandoned residential lots from near-worthless symbols of abandonment into new community parks, playgrounds, and gardens. NeighborSpace acquires these properties from the city at a substantial discount and works with community organizations to plan, develop, and maintain them under a contracted management agreement. To facilitate the transformation of these spaces it provides insurance coverage for the properties, secures funds for necessary environmental cleanups, and gets facilities like city water hydrants installed. NeighborSpace exemplifies the entrepreneurial working partnership between Daley's city hall and the neighborhood organizations to re-create assets and market values in the disinvested city.

Under Daley, Chicago's most significant mechanism for guiding rede-velopment has been the use of tax increment financing (TIF). The TIF mechanism is Chicago's market-based answer to the suburban subsidies and incentives that originally drained the city of its industry. Disinvested areas are designated as TIF districts. Any incremental growth in tax rev-enues from development or market appreciation in a TIF district are held in a separate fund, to be invested in land rehabilitation, infrastructure development, and private sector partnerships in the district. As these sub-sidies attract further private investment, local property values increase. Each increase in property values creates further revenues for the TIF fund, which are fed back into further investment in the district. The TIF mechanism thereby reestablishes competition between the city and the suburbs on the basis of real locational advantages rather than one-sided government subsidies. There are 136 TIF districts in Chicago today, which cover more than 30 percent of the city's land area. They have generated more than $400 million in investment. As a reflection of these areas' re-covery, the combined assessed value of property in TIF districts increased by $11.4 billion, or nearly 16,000 percent, between 1986 and 2005.[6]

Funds from TIF serve a market governance function, establishing the commercial terms of engagement in an area in a more robust way than traditional city planning, by backing policy with investment funds. But Daley's widespread use of TIF funds is not without risks and criticism. The TIF mechanism removes the tax revenues of a large part of Chicago from the general fund under control of the elected city coun-cil. This raises legitimate red flags, especially for those who witnessed the closed-door shenanigans of the old machine. But reform politicians like Alderman Smith have created community governance mecha-nisms to keep the TIF strategy accountable. More than sixty neighbor-hood, tenant, condominium, and local business associations have been organized into her ward's zoning and planning committee, which she uses to review and vote on all but the most routine developments in her area, including TIF projects. The committee is Smith's grassroots re-placement for the ward committee of the old machine.

Market-oriented policy has been another aspect of city hall's assertive new approach. One example is the use of city hall's purchasing power to establish new banking standards and prevent the emergence of new predatory lending. In the late 1990s the mayor and city staff noticed a growing number of empty homes in low-income neighborhoods. "We found mortgage companies that we'd never even heard of before," recalls Markowski. "They were offering high-interest loans with minimal down payments based on simple drive-by property value assessments, not on the basis of the borrower's ability to pay." The empty homes were foreclosed properties secured by predatory lenders—the pioneers of the subprime mortgage lending to come, whose collapse bludgeoned world markets in 2007–2008.[7] Years before the crisis, Chicago was the first U.S. jurisdiction to prohibit government departments from doing business with any company engaged in or connected to these practices. The law was passed against the strong lobbying resistance of some of the world's largest banks, which would later buckle under their own subprime loan portfolios.[8]

Chicago's preemptive action against the subprime crisis included the 2003 launch of an initiative with the Federal Reserve Bank of Chicago called the Home Ownership Preservation Initiative (HOPI). Officers of HOPI preemptively identified and counseled more than fifty-four hundred homeowners, most of them victims of predatory lending, in restructuring their home financing. Between 2003 and 2007, the program prevented fifteen hundred foreclosures and reclaimed three hundred foreclosed buildings.[9] To promote the program, the city established a mortgage crisis hotline and engaged religious leaders and community organizations to urge vulnerable families to seek help. While Chicago foreclosures increased between 2000 and 2003, by 2004 the city's foreclosure rate had returned to 1999 levels.[10] While Chicago's home foreclosures decreased, foreclosures increased by 20 percent in suburban Chicago municipalities during the same period.[11]

"Few governments have changed as deeply and as rapidly as Chicago's," writes University of Chicago sociologist Terry Nichols Clark, "without a visible or violent revolution." Clark is not your normal academic. He's been deeply involved in the planning and politics of his city for decades. He argues that Chicago politics between the 1970s and 1990s have "been revolutionized in many similar respects to the revolutions in Eastern Europe, Latin America and Asia" during the same years.[12] When Richard M. Daley revealed his ambition for the mayor's office not long after the death of his legendary father, Richard J. Daley, many who had fought to reclaim Chicago from the old machine feared a dynastic return. But the new Mayor Daley did something unexpected. He systematically broke down the old party patronage machinery and replaced it with a broad-based, inclusive, reform-oriented regime that is no less powerful. An ingenious, instinctive politician, he understood that the locus of power and solutions in Chicago had shifted from the ward bosses to the community organizers.

"Revolution" and "regime" may seem like overstatements, given their association with antidemocratic leaders and state-controlled societies. But both express a critical feature of the urban strategy challenge. The transformation of a city, particularly when in crisis, requires constant engagement and alignment of competing interests behind common purposes. This is particularly difficult in pluralistic, capitalist societies with traditions of individualistic commercialism and ethnic-based allegiance. If ever there was such a society, it is Chicago. Alignment behind a common strategy under such strained and divisive circumstances is revolutionary in its sheer improbability. In Chicago's crisis, this alignment was achieved at the neighborhood level by the "die-hards" through grassroots organization, coalition-building, legislative battles, and entrepreneurial ventures to reestablish local market viability. The new progressive Daley regime was only possible with a foundation of such community-based organization and innovation, which gave Daley a political base and legitimacy independent of the old machine. It was his genius that forged a new electoral coalition from the numerous community networks that had emerged to redevelop suffering districts. He further developed the coalition into a chain of authority and accountability between organized communities, their elected officials, and the mayor's office. This allowed predictable mobilization of support for his policies, executive interventions, and entrepreneurial initiatives. Today this community-based system parallels and constrains the remnant machinery of party bosses, precinct election organizations, and patronage networks. Daley manages their interaction and balances their power. Like a master of corporate merger and acquisition, Daley did what seemed impossible: he developed and integrated the two competing systems into a single progressive governing machinery.[13]

Daley also proved a master of the politics of inclusion. He was elected in 1989 with overwhelming electoral support in every area of the city except the African American wards.[14] He entered office with the support of community candidates like Mary Ann Smith and rapidly appointed young, reform-minded staff "from outside" to senior positions in his administration. With no fanfare, he gave them sweeping mandates to clean up the patronage legacies of whole departments and reorganize them into community-focused service providers and incubators of further innovation.

Take the Chicago's Parks District, the largest urban parks organization in the United States. It manages a $2.5 billion real estate portfolio of 550 parks, 540 recreational buildings, thousands of sports fields and playgrounds, a major zoo and sports stadium, and 31 miles of prime Lake Michigan shoreline. Today, Chicago parks have more users than any other park system in the country. But as recently as the 1980s many parks were controlled by gangs and "were more like ghost towns," says Forrest Claypool, the political reformer who was selected as Daley's cleanup man for the District.

In the early 1980s, the Parks District was being run by Ed Kelly, a prominent old machine ward boss. Kelly oversaw selection of Democratic Party candidates in countywide elections and had accumulated some four thousand patronage jobs to dispense to his loyalists. Under Kelly's control, the Parks District ran a chronic deficit, even though it had a dedicated municipal tax. It had been prosecuted by the federal government for racial discrimination. Everything worked for the convenience of the District's patronage employees. On major holidays, for instance, when people most wished to use the parks, they would be closed for the convenience of park employees. Claypool recalls a comment made to him by a District employee: "Don't you understand," the employee said, "this is a no-work job?" One study revealed that it took eighty-four administrative measures and more than a year's time to fire a single Parks District employee.[15]

The appointment of Claypool as superintendent of parks and Alderman Smith as chair of the city council Parks Committee was a classic Daley move. Both were machine outsiders. Claypool learned the complexities of transforming city government and earned the confidence of the mayor as his chief of staff. Daley gave him a full mandate: to rebuild the parks as what Claypool called "anchor assets" to stabilize neighborhoods. Smith could be counted on to provide political cover on the city council. Both had a deep connection to the city's resurgent neighborhood urbanism. Like the Lerner Group in Curitiba, Claypool created space for innovation by dramatically changing the playing field. He privatized major facilities to increase efficiency and break the machine's control. He brought in private consultants to streamline the organization, eliminating two thousand patronage jobs and reorganizing the budget and programs.[16]

In similar fashion, in one city operation after another, Daley leveraged his coalition to launch corporate-style turnarounds, placing outside reformers, progressive businesspeople, and a new generation of managers in sensitive executive positions. The head of community lending at a major bank was brought in to clean up and restructure the housing department. When Daley took over the dysfunctional Chicago school system in 1995, he appointed his budget chief and his chief of staff to head the turnaround. Under their leadership, $3 billion was invested in the renovation of five hundred schools and in the construction of seventy-one new ones. Student scores increased for six years and summer school programs were expanded. Finances were stabilized and extended labor strife was brought to an end.[17] City departments, heretofore managed as independent political fiefdoms, forged partnerships for the first time. The Parks District, for example, created a partnership with the school board to build hundreds of new parks in school yards. Again emphasizing the urbanism practice of the new regime, Claypool describes the partnership "as a way to make the schools into community assets."[18]

As the 2007–2008 U.S. mortgage crisis unfolded across the United States, the mayor selected Myer Blank, another outsider and the senior analyst of Chicago's main government watchdog organization to lead the effort to stabilize property markets.[19] They did what few governments have ever considered: make property tax rates function as an elastic, transparent market that adjusts rapidly to rises and falls in property values. By making taxes elastic to immediate market conditions they reduced the risk of delinquency and foreclosures in depressed areas. The program seemed to reveal Daley's basic strategic logic. In Daley's view, the fundamental unit of economic vitality is a complete, viable community. If the city has to take a cash-flow risk to prevent deterioration to that fundamental asset, then Daley will take it. One official cited a federal home heating assistance program for low-income households, which typically runs out of money before the winter is over. Most city governments leave the household to fill the gap. But the result in wintry Chicago's low-income districts has often been tax delinquency and the loss of a home, restarting the downward spiral. Daley's choice was to finance the household's remaining fuel purchases until springtime.

"I've never seen a more intuitive politician," says Claypool from his posting in the Barack Obama presidential campaign headquarters. "He looks at the whole citizen experience," recounts Gery Chico, Daley's former chief of staff. "He looks to make sure that there is a seamless experience for the citizen, without having to get caught up in our internal nonsense."

Late one afternoon Mayor Daley receives me in his office. He has just returned from inaugurating the city's famous St. Patrick's Day parade. Earlier in the day, he decided to go ahead with a reorganization of the police department, a major event in any city. He seems tired and preoccupied. He has fought so many battles in his city's turnaround. Soon, in his plainspoken way, he is ranging over every issue that touches a city, from the subprime crisis to the Olympics, from urbanization in Asia to the role of education in a global economy. When he speaks of Chicago he repeatedly uses the words "infrastructure" and "asset." It takes me a while to realize that he is referring to libraries and individual building lots. "What you have to do," he says with rising animation, "is take what is a liability in a community and turn it into an asset. Once you take an abandoned building down, the land becomes an asset. Then you start building schools, parks, libraries, senior centers, and every time you build a new infrastructure it's like a puzzle; you build one here and here and here and then all of a sudden you start connecting. You put in a row of trees and you put in a median and flowers over here." Like the urbanists of Barcelona and Curitiba, America's most powerful mayor is describing a kind of micro-surgery of the citysystem. "Then you put in some new housing over here and everything starts connecting. Once you start rebuilding a community, nothing can separate it."

Of course, Daley knows the arcane details of the Uptown Theater. His top staff have told me about his constant drives around the city and the daily stream of notes he passes to them with micro-observations from these explorations. One reported his appearance in the middle of the night to inspect a project to replace the light fixtures beneath city bridges. Daley himself just told me how he was sitting in a symphony concert distractedly jotting notes to his staff: "Why is this?" "Why is there an abandoned building here?" "What's happened to this vacant land?" The vacant Uptown stands as a challenge to everything for which he stands. Since a slumlord sold the property in the 1980s, it has been caught in a labyrinth of ownership disputes, liens, and court battles resembling a Mumbai standoff. One would think he'd just stop there with a flag on his way to work one morning and lay claim to it.

But urban strategy advances through a tangle of uncounted histories, details, and changing variables. Daley and his city council ally Alderman Smith have steadily advanced the city's claim on the building, stepping in to make repairs as its ownership languishes in court. Across Lawrence Avenue from the theater's boarded entrance, large signs beckon passersby to the newly established big-box Borders bookstore and Starbucks café. These outfits are shadows of the Ontra Cafeteria and they will never replace the district's lost industrial vitality. But the Green Mill, Aragon, and Riviera and dozens of scattered new cafés, bakeries, pubs, book-shops, and galleries are making Uptown a residential and entertain-ment destination once again. "The city follows the trail of the memory," said Lerner. Too much of Uptown's old citysystem has been replaced by pieces of suburban city model—strip malls and their parking lots and drive-through pharmacies and banks—but the area has been designated a TIF district. The community registered the theater as a national histor-ical landmark. A proposal by a major entertainment company to refur-bish and re-open the theater has been cleared by the community's zoning and planning committee, part of a plan for a whole, renewed en-tertainment district. "We do community-directed development," says Alderman Smith to highlight the meaning of the neighborhood com-mittee's decision. "This is a binding vote on me"—and ultimately on Daley and his regime.

CHAPTER 15

Cocreating the Citysystem

Toward a World of Urban Regimes

In 2008 world markets collapsed under the weight of an American city model building boom, the financing of which was remarkably disconnected from the evolving economic ground realities in those cities. As the crisis rippled across the global City, it provided another harsh reminder of our flawed grasp of the Urban Revolution. Business strategist Michael Porter once put it very simply. "The more there are no barriers," he told *BusinessWeek*, "the more things are mobile, the more decisive location becomes. This point has tripped up a lot of really smart people."[1] In 2008, it tripped up the world.

While postmortems of the subprime mortgage crisis focused on bad business practices and the ideological naïveté of financial deregulation, we've overlooked the larger failing: a lack of urbanism to shape and maintain the quality of "location" in a rapidly urbanizing world. The Americans were not alone. We have been building cities everywhere like industrial commodities, measuring them in undifferentiated square footage, while marketing them with names that stimulate our memories of citysystems and their community life. A suburban residential city model might be called Deer Path Village, a shopping mall is now a "town center," a multi-theater movie complex is an "entertainment district," or an office park an "innovation district," but this landscape is not the carefully crafted product of a community that has a shared strategy and method for building and maintaining urban advantage in the world.

Throughout these pages I have argued that avoiding crisis on an urban planet requires that we design cities and their districts as efficient, productive systems governed and managed by communities with strategic purposes. And to address the major global problems of our time—poverty, marginalization, conflict, and environmental decline—we need to align the strategies of these communities to shape the City as it completes its evolution in the final phase. None of this will be achieved in cities made of corporate city models—even with the best technology and infrastructure designs. It will require something more than scaled construction to achieve ambitious ends at the City's scale. I have argued that this "something" is the development of local urbanisms, which allow cities to align their myriad endeavors; optimize efficiency and productivity; adapt to external challenges; and forge new solutions through urban form, markets, and culture. Urbanisms, and not just plans and building, are the method of an advanced urban society. They empower even divided and downtrodden communities, as in the recent histories of Barcelona, Curitiba, and Chicago, to transform their cities into livable, efficient, creative agents of global change. Urbanisms are the foundation of healthy urban civilizations with the capacity to realize their aspirations.

It is often written that the era of the nation has passed. Tremendous power and capacities remain within the apparatus of the nation-state, which can be further applied toward these common purposes, to be sure. But nation-states and their strategic institutions—the United Nations, international development banks, international laws and conventions, and intelligence agencies, to name a few—are steadily losing their centrality in the economic, ecological, and political end games that will play out in this century. The momentum of development has steadily shifted to the city, a territory still poorly understood by most nations. Nations have often tried to regain position in this shifting strategic landscape or to advance progressive policies by intervening in their cities. But throughout the world they have generally lacked a sufficient sense of urbanism to solve urban problems rather than creating new ones.

Many note that the strategic challenges of our time are transnational, but the antiquation of national boundaries and controls has been wrongly understood as an end of geographic significance. The world is *not* flat. As Porter counseled, cities and even specific locations within them are the new source of advantage. Porter championed what could be called an economic theory of the citysystem by documenting how the shared economies of density, scale, and association of colocated firms or industrial clusters produce such advantage. He discouraged the view that competitive advantage is gained through operational efficiencies, obsessively counted and reported not only in the corporate world but also in a plethora of city benchmarking reports and best-city-for-this-or-that indexes. Competitive advantages in regions are not really comparable. They come from differentiation, he argued, not from the race to generic "world-class" standards. The urbanisms of Curitiba, Barcelona, and Chicago prove his argument that "operational effectiveness means you're running the same race faster, but strategy is choosing to run a different race because it's the one you've set yourself up to win."[2]

Richard Florida, in his *Rise of the Creative Class*,[3] elaborated an important aspect of the creation and maintenance of urban advantage. The competitive advantage of an industry cluster is not produced in a master-planned factory compound, corporate campus, or city model office park in a locational vacuum from the larger city. These competitive advantages of density, scale, association, and extension are produced, maintained, or lost within the wider city. When a firm chooses a particular urban location for its chain migration, it must work with the unique (in)efficiencies, costs, conflicts, values, culture, and competitive advantage of the entire city region. But since these advantages are accessible to and used by all, the corporation is challenged to a new role: to work to sustain them as a public good. To truly secure advantage, corporations must also practice *urban strategy*.

Corporations, in many cases more than nations, must play a central part in the evolution of this practice. The nation-state has focused its craft more on trying to control the city—its growth and urban migration; its economic and social activities; its politics, fiscal affairs, and police forces; and its infrastructure for international trade. Meanwhile the corporation was finding new ways to serve the city's demands and build wealth within it. This alignment with the underlying entrepreneurial modus operandi of the city, in a time of rapid urban growth, has been a significant contributor to the rise of the corporation's global strategic position vis-à-vis the nation-state.

But few modern corporations have any real developed sense of urbanism. One of their major influences on the city has been the city model and its emergence as a primary mode of city building, which has converted much of the expanded cityscape into something less efficient and synergistic in its potentials. The city model has brought speed, scale, and predictability to the city-building process—important achievements in a time of such rapid urban growth. But its business processes and products need to be reconstructed to allow for substantially greater participation in design and customization, so that the suburb, commercial corridor, or office district can provide a managed platform for the evolution of citysystems and new forms of urbanism. Embuing corporate city model building with a process of cocreation with communities, users, and local urbanists is one of the most important challenges and opportunities of urban practice in the final phase. To maintain urban advantage, in other words, the corporation must join the effort to build a local urbanist community.

Corporations have been learning from their pursuit of urban advantage over the last decades. Their positioning vis-à-vis cities and their investments in them have slowly evolved from opportunistic locational cost-comparisons and biddings for public subsidies, to firm-specific forms of corporate citizenship through which they have expanded their notion of location into one of community and longer-term civic engagement. From these engagements with the problems of the broader city beyond their immediate, expedient concerns, they have joined experiments in city building and even instigated new practices of urbanism and urban strategy. Chief among these practices is the development of *urban regimes*.

The concept of the urban regime was pioneered in the 1980s by the American urban planners Norman and Susan Fainstein and by the political scientists Stephen Elkin and Clarence Stone.[4] The question that most concerned them was how cities were made governable, given their multiplicity of private, market-oriented interests, public interests, and community interests. In particular, they wanted to understand how cities could facilitate accumulation of wealth by businesses *in a way that also advanced* the economic and social interests of the city's citizens. In 1989 Stone published the first complete analysis of the evolution of an urban regime, revealing how elements of Atlanta's white establishment forged alliance in the 1950s with African American leaders and institutions to create a governing regime that differentiated Atlanta's development from the rest of the racially divided American Southeast, increasing the city's leadership position in the U.S. civil rights movement and its eventual centrality in the global economic system.

"How, in a world of limited and dispersed authority," Stone asked, "do actors work together across institutional lines to produce a capacity to govern and to bring about publicly significant results?" Cities, he goes on to say, are organizations that lack a structure of command "that guides and synchronizes everyone's behavior." "Because local governmental authority is by law and tradition [limited] . . . informal arrangements assume special importance in urban politics." An urban regime therefore arises as "an informal yet relatively stable group *with access to institutional resources* that enable it to have a sustained role in making governing decisions . . . the regime is purposive, created and maintained as a way of facilitating action. In a very important sense, *a regime is empowering.*"[5]

For about a decade, the study of urban regimes advanced within the United States, but its relevance was generally considered to be limited to the private, market-oriented character of cities there, in contrast to the more state-centered control of land, development, infrastructure, and services elsewhere. But as nations transformed into more market-based societies in the 1990s, by both policy decision and the extension of their cities, the urban regime concept gained increasing international relevance. Today the concept and the rich literature that supports it helps us understand important aspects of urban strategy—what I have earlier called the strategic alliance and its strategic institutions.

My argument is that the success of cities and the viability of the City in the final phase require the rapid development of progressive urban regimes, capable of transforming their cities, as they grow, into more equitable, ecological, stable, and creative places. Without such regimes, the problems of governability in cities and the City will increase in proportion to their irreversible growth beyond the territories, powers, and resources of the nation-state's municipal and even provincial jurisdictions. But for an urban regime to succeed in managing this kind of transformation, it must also develop the kind of robust, nuanced urbanism displayed in cities like Curitiba, Barcelona, and Chicago. In other words, a strategic alliance is not enough. It must create strategic institutions whose purpose is to hone a local practice of urbanism that is designed to achieve progressive ends within the unique local context. This is the basic challenge of strategy in the world's new geography. Only through a world of urban regimes will we effectively govern our affairs, protect public goods, create common advantage, and have a chance to address the kind of hard ecological logic of thinkers like William Rees, transforming the City into a more complete and self-contained ecology, the Citysystem.

In the world of "locations" and industrial clusters, Silicon Valley, California, the city-region that encompasses the small cities of San Jose, Santa Clara, Palo Alto, and more than a dozen other municipalities, is the indisputable archetype. So firm is Silicon Valley's status as the sin qua non of urban agglomeration economies (i.e., density and scale) and cluster dynamics (industrial economies of association)—or simply as the ideal business address—that cities aspiring to similar urban advantage can't stop declaring their goal to become "the next Silicon Valley." Aside from their false assumption that such an urbanism can be imported and copied, Silicon Valley itself has been facing a lot of problems.

The Silicon Valley phenomenon has roots in the university town citysystem of Palo Alto, which consists of Stanford University, colocated residential and commercial districts, and importantly, the Stanford Research Park, the serviced technology commercialization facility established by Stanford's dean of engineering, Frederick Terman, in 1951. Today, the Stanford Research Park is home to more than 140 electronics, software, biotechnology, and other technology companies, employing more than twenty thousand people. But the governance arrangements were not in place to protect the advantage of such a compact social and commercial geography, particularly as businesses and institutions leveraging this advantage grew. The genius of the region's early urbanism was poorly understood. So the city's growth spilled out across the old fruit orchards of the Santa Clara Valley in a sea of uncritically accepted suburban city models and master-planned corporate campuses whose flaws of density and scale have started to undermine the region's vibrant economies of association and burden it with inefficiencies, costs, and drags on its productivity. Traffic congestion, a growing geography of economic segregation, rising housing and business costs, energy supply and environmental problems, and the unmanaged risks of such intensive development in a major earthquake zone have left the region groping for new urban solutions.

The response has been a slow yet explicit formation of a regional urban regime, engaging hundreds of companies and corporate leaders, civic organizations, and the municipalities in new networks, formal and informal, for regional governance. This process started with the Silicon Valley Manufacturing Group, founded by David Packard of Hewlett-Packard in 1977. Over the years, as regional development challenges impinged upon its advantage, the group (now the Silicon Valley Leadership Group) has greatly broadened its agenda, focusing on the maintenance of "a high quality of life in Silicon Valley for our entire community by advocating for adequate affordable housing, comprehensive regional transportation, reliable energy, a quality K–12 and higher education system and prepared workforce, a sustainable environment, and business and tax policies that keep California and Silicon Valley competitive."[6]

Then, in 1993 many of the same companies joined with local government, labor, university, and civic leaders to endow the informal collaboration with a new strategic institution. Going by the name of "Joint Venture: Silicon Valley Network," the organization somewhat misrepresents itself. It is far more than a network. It is a Silicon Valley–styled version of the Curitiba Institute for Research and Urban Planning, trying to align the region's many companies and municipalities, and to develop new practices with and for them. It is a cocreation facility for their new urbanism. Joint Venture coordinated a regionwide review of disaster preparedness and put a process in place to establish the first regional prevention, response, and recovery plan. It established the first coordinated economic development apparatus for the whole of Silicon Valley. It engages in urban design activities, such as an initiative to transform the main avenue passing through the region, El Camino Real, into what it calls the Grand Boulevard. "The Grand Boulevard," it explains, "is a collaboration of nineteen cities, counties, [and] local and regional agencies united to improve the performance, safety and aesthetics of El Camino Real . . . the initiative brings together—for the first time—all of the agencies having responsibility for the condition, use, and performance of the street." And it now leads an effort to engage municipalities and companies in developing plans to reduce their greenhouse-gas emissions. Joint

Venture gives the emerging urban regime an apparatus for developing the region's urbanism. As it says in its own words: "Our quality of life is founded on the region's unique 'habitat of innovation.' Joint Venture is committed to . . . maintain this habitat and create the Next Silicon Valley."[7]

The flagship of this revival is a district in North San Jose that transforms the established, isolated, one- and two-story corporate campuses (which are mostly allocated to parking lots) into what San Jose planners call "intensified campuses" of four to eight stories with colocated amenities, and into "mixed-use innovation districts" with downtown-like, pedestrian-friendly residential and commercial life fully integrated with high-tech offices. The economics of these districts are reinforced with public services, such as public transit and bikeways.[8]

Silicon Valley is not alone. It is part of a larger, hopeful trend to empower cities with progressive urban regimes. Much as the Chicago story illustrates, these new regimes stand out from an earlier era of machine organizations and elite networks. They still secure their power and resources from the city's elites, but their purposes are generally different. Their agendas almost uniformly embrace the larger progressive concerns that are the unfinished business of the Urban Revolution. In the United States, for instance, some one hundred regional alliances have been formed to create ways to govern the growth of city regions that now extend beyond any municipal jurisdiction. About fifty of these alliances are affiliated with the Alliance for Regional Stewardship, which describes its mission as fostering "collaborative multi-sector regional stewardship as a means for advancing economic, social and environmental progress, while maintaining a sense of place, in America's metropolitan regions."[9] These alliances see a continuum of regime formation, starting with relationship networks as described by Stone, evolving into formal partnerships and leading to structural change.

These kinds of intentional efforts to start the process of urban regime formation are increasing in other parts of the world. In Bangalore, for instance, the state government invited the corporate sector to get directly involved in planning, infrastructure development, and public administration through a Bangalore Agenda Task Force (BATF) of corporate and civic leaders. Established in 1999, the BATF began working as a kind of management consultancy to the city administration. It cocreated new accounting, traffic management, tax assessment, and solid waste management systems. More than eighty-five hundred public works projects were documented and placed under new management controls. In a nation built on the premise of state-led planning and investment, such wholesale engagement of the private sector in the affairs of government was viewed by many as a private sector commandeering of the city for its own interests.[10] But the progressive agendas of BATF and other public-private alliances and their engagement of a broad range of interests make them not unlike the Local Agenda 21 planning efforts of the 1990s—except that this time the corporate city builders are also at the table.

In Bangalore, the BATF was just one part of a new civic drive for urban regime formation. Two other organizations, the Public Affairs Centre and the citizen-activist Janaagraha movement, have re-engaged the middle class in planning and governance after years of civic alienation from local government corruption and incompetence. They have organized a regular "citizens' report card" on municipal services, championed major legislative reforms to strengthen municipal government, and developed detailed proposals for a new public transit system. Before Bangalore's inconceivable growth, during its high-tech boom, the city benefited from strong civic engagement in urban affairs. These efforts are both rekindling and expanding that engagement, involving not only architects, planners, and social workers but also artists, designers, engineers, ecologists, and medical, computer, and media professionals, this time in collaboration with *both* government and the new titans of industry. These alliances are building a new sense of ownership for the city, a sense that the city is actually a common home.

The stakes are enormous. According to the United Nations Environment Programme, cities are responsible for 70 percent to 80 percent of the world's energy consumption; we cannot address climate change without their transformation. There is not enough fresh water in the world to quench the demands of the future City at current rates of consumption. The supply chains that feed our cities' growth and appetites are destroying habitats everywhere. The only imaginable stable future is one in which we transform the burgeoning City into a Citysystem, a truly self-sustaining biome for our gathering and multiplying species. This cannot be achieved without the proliferation of Strategic Cities, which in turn requires a proliferation of urbanist communities organized into new urban regimes.

The success of these nascent regimes will be determined by their resolve and skill at cocreating new urbanisms in their regions: the managed creation of efficient urban form; the development of new services and infrastructure; the progressive governance of their markets; and the binding development of a culture and cultural language for understanding, using, and living in the city toward shared strategic ends. Lacking a creative and open process for engaging migrants, neighborhoods, local urbanists, corporate investors, and government officials in the design of their practices of urbanism, these emergent regimes will lose their fragile legitimacy as the continuance of today's expedient urban growth depletes their cities' advantage.

"You have to keep sucking water up from your own roots," says David Crombie, talking to me about urban strategy. He was Toronto's mayor for nearly a decade—the mayor supported by Toronto's immigrant urbanist par excellence, the late Jane Jacobs—and has served as the city's uncontested Leader Emeritus for more than thirty years. Over these decades he has constantly remobilized his large informal network to align the city's separate pursuits and to consolidate a regime and urbanism that might ultimately transform his city-region. He has seen Toronto through many battles—to stop the downtown freeways, to preserve so many neighborhoods and build a few new ones as well, to mobilize the city to recover its public waterfront, to align the overspilling city as a growing regional system and not as an assortment of half-empowered, bickering municipal jurisdictions.

Crombie is one of that breed of true urbanist-mayors who never cease negotiating and fine-tuning their city's tacking course into the strong winds of the final phase. During his years at the helm in the 1960s through the 1990s, the Urban Revolution's significance and challenge were not yet fully clear. But now they are. A city must know its purpose in a world that demands so much from it. To fulfill that purpose, the city must "suck from its own roots." This is the counsel he gives me. "You can't copy," he says, eschewing the idea that there are any truly useful "best practices" from elsewhere. Neither can a city gain advantage from securing a "world-class city" title. When Toronto started receiving accolades from the United Nations and other city indexes, he says, "people got complacent. We'd thought we'd made it. Toronto ended up in a golden funk."

Now he constantly reminds Toronto to seek the reempowerment of its root urbanism. His fractious progressive reform movement arose in the 1960s as they watched so-called urban renewal in the United States destroy the legacies of urbanism in Detroit, Buffalo, and Boston. "Back then our thinking was: we could follow others. Then we saw Detroit in flames, the destruction of Buffalo's wonderful park system for a highway, and we realized we had to find our own model."

The functioning unit of Toronto urban society, he explains, is a neighborhood. It is the urban patch that remarkably welcomes and holds so much of the world, renews it, builds its leadership, and pioneers its new solutions and economic sectors even as it harbors its problems. "Toronto's great legacy," he says, like the chairman of a powerful agency with a world purpose, "is how people live together. It's hard to get people excited here about good buildings. Beauty ain't us. But people come here for opportunity." It is therefore concerning to him, and to those working with him, that Toronto may be slipping in its abilities to serve as a premier strategic site for the global migrant. "It cuts close to who we think we are. We have always understood the immigrant experience better than most."

In the past, he explains, people thought what Toronto did well, its advantage, was "in the air here. So people put down their weapons." They stopped insisting on their urbanism. Crombie's name now tops a list of opponents to the shopping mall in Leslieville. For him this very local matter is a strategic battle; he and his associates worked so long to clear those Port Lands for something greater than a highway strip mall: the next great opportunity for Toronto to be fully itself, and by doing so, to make something great happen for the world.

He reflects on strategy. The toughest battles, like the one in Leslieville, he says, "taught me something about mediation. Mediation is not about compromise. You have to find out what the new space is. You have to spend time finding out where you're going. When you see the new space emerge, then you help others to see it," he says. "Then you all go to that new space."

He is sounding both like a corporate strategist talking about a new market "opportunity space" and an activist talking about a new "social space" for change. Surely, he means both and also something more. When Crombie the urbanist uses the words "new space," he means more than the discovery of a new way to align supply and demand or competing social interests. He is also talking about a physical space and the potential to give it a particular three-dimensional form of buildings, roads, courtyards, shops, landscapes, and facilities and to host all the activities that people themselves invent to locate there. The space that Crombie speaks of is a material one, the new geography of global opportunity—or of crises, depending on our ability to imagine and build the city differently—a three-dimensional human habitat that liberates our energies and aligns our creativity and the solutions latent in them.

Like thousands of other committed urbanists, Crombie is always imagining the City's better potential and trying to help us to see it. Together they do this day and night, because they cannot help it: The city is their passion. Imagining and corralling the better potential of their cities is their embrace of the twenty-first-century's true human nature. They accept their cities as their true homes and the City as our common fate. If hope, potential, and opportunity are what we seek in the face of the global challenges we know too well, then we also need to learn how to see the new spaces that these urbanists imagine and to rally with them behind our cities—and the City they are fast becoming.

Acknowledgments

Writing this book required both in-depth and broad exposure to the world of cities over an extended period of time. This exposure was granted to me by the International Council for Local Environmental Initiatives (ICLEI) during my tenure there between 1990 and 2000. The leaders and professionals of ICLEI member municipalities, the ICLEI staff, and the executive committee members were unwittingly instrumental informants and assistants in this project. They are too many to acknowledge here. I remain deeply grateful to that community of urban strategists for their collaboration in getting cities on the international agenda, and for their ongoing commitment to building a sustainable Citysystem.

Five individuals have played particularly important roles as mentors and supporters of the work that underlies this book. Frank Duehay and Larry Agran provided unwavering encouragement for the municipal foreign policy experiments of the 1980s, when the City first became politically self-conscious. Larry prodded me to organize ICLEI. Noel Brown and Maurice Strong opened the doors of the United Nations system for full engagement on urban issues. Maurice has been a persistent mentor and generous advocate of all my endeavors with cities. C. K. Prahalad has been my mentor *par excellence* in the field of strategy, providing a hands-on crash course through our collaboration in The Next Practice. More than anyone, C. K. has helped me to see possibilities for alignment between seemingly competing public, private, and community interests through the cocreation of solutions at the microeconomic level. In a world preoccupied with tactics and short-term thinking, he has renewed my belief that strategic change is possible.

The initial conception of this book arose from an engagement with the Planning Department of Metro Vancouver (then the Greater Vancouver Regional District) in 2002. In particular, Johnny Carline, Ken Cameron, Hugh Kellas, Christina DeMarco, and Ralph Perkins stimulated my thinking about urban strategy as a distinct field of practice, by including me in debates over their Livable Region Strategy. Metro Vancouver hosts one of the most sophisticated communities of urbanists in the world. In every discussion with practitioners there, I was forced to clarify my ideas. Thanks in particular to Christina DeMarco for keeping the facts straight. Cheeying Ho, Sebastian Moffatt, William Rees, and Mark Roseland have also been very helpful and encouraging.

The accounts of particular cities in these pages draw on extensive literature on each. But the project was only possible with the support of many who helped me learn directly about their cities. Any misinterpretations or misstatements about their cities are entirely my responsibility.

Madurai: Muthu Velayudham and V. C. Nadarajan helped conceptualize the exploration of urban migrant strategies in Madurai and gave it their organization's full support. A. Juli provided tireless linguistic and contextual interpretation. N. Rajeswari, P. Saravanan, C. Parthasarathy, R. Padmini, and Ms. Akhila made it all possible by organizing and facilitating interviews and assisting with interpretation. I am very grateful to the people who opened their homes and life stories during these interviews. I hope the text serves them in some way.

Toronto: Rod Cohen, David Crombie, Jeff Evenson, Saddeiqa Holder, Michael Miloff, and Richard White generously shared knowledge and insight about different aspects of the city. Special thanks to Sachin Sharma and Devyani Srinivasan for their research assistance on Toronto immigrant life.

Detroit: Thank you to Eric Dueweke for providing the kind of insightful tour of Detroit that is only possible from one who has made his city his lifelong commitment and work.

Mumbai: Gabriel Britto, Prema Gopalan, Avik Roy, and Abdul Wahab Suharvarthy were generous guides, hosts, interpreters, and fellow explorers of the city, which otherwise would have been largely impenetrable to me. V. K. Das, Sheela Patel, Shirish Patel, and Rahul Mehrotra provided invaluable insight and lessons about the city's development history. Special appreciation is due to the many residents of Dharavi who took time to share their stories and opinions. Thank you to Mukesh Mehta and Varsha Gaikwad for sharing their plans for that district. Although my written assessment of those plans is not a positive one, I hope that for the sake of the builder-residents of Dharavi they prove me and other doubters wrong.

Bangalore: This book did not provide an opportunity for full exploration of the strategic lessons that can be derived from Bangalore's history and transformation. A whole chapter had been included in earlier drafts under the heading "How a City Remakes the World," but the story was too big to contain in these pages. Nonetheless, the following Bangaloreans were extremely generous in helping me understand some of the city's lessons: Samuel Paul, S. Sadananda, Ramesh Ramanathan, Swati Ramanathan, V. Ravichandar, and A. Ravindra. Thank you also to Shankar, our family's local aide de camp, who opened other parts of the city and south India to me.

Curitiba: I am thankful to Mayor/Governor Jaime Lerner for a ten-year tutorial on Curitiba's transformation during my visits there. Mayor Cassio Taniguchi, Jonas Rabinovitch, Nickolau Kluppel, Maria do Rocio Quandt, Eliel Rosa, Fric Kerin, and Irene da Paz Vieira also gave very generously of their time and insight. Eliel Rosa provided enthusiastic interpretation and organizational support. Special appreciation is due to Hugh Schwartz, who has authored the most complete and insightful English-language book on Curitiba, and who generously shared his manuscript prior to its publication.

Barcelona: Deputy Mayor Jose Cuervo, Helena Barraco Nogues, and Toni Pujol opened the world of Barcelona to me. Deputy Mayor Imma Mayol Beltran, Deputy Mayor Ramón García-Bragado Acín, Councillor Itziar González i Virós, Judit Albors, Jordi Frigola Almar, Jordi Campillo, Txema Castiella, Francesc Roma, Salvador Rueda Palenzuela, Rafael González Tormo, and Xavier Gracia Romero explained *and exuded* the city's fascinating urbanism. Their untiring intellectual curiosity and love for their city, individually and as a community of practitioners, has been captivating.

Miami-Dade: Over the years, clerk of the courts and former county commissioner Harvey Ruvin has generously shared four decades of colorful south Florida political and development history. Dario Moreno and Mark Woerner both guided me with their own rich understandings of the region.

Kitakyushu: Mayor Koichi Sueyoshi and Reiji Hitsumoto have been constant supporters since we first met in 1992, and I thank them for keeping me abreast of the details of their many initiatives.

Chicago: In the 1980s, Gail Cincotta and former alderman and current Cook County clerk David Orr gave me my first tutorials on Chicago. They revealed Chicago's distinctiveness as a place where people fight for the "right to the city" as a matter of local culture. In researching the book Mayor Richard M. Daley, Alderman Walter Burnett Jr., Alderman Mary Ann Smith, Rita Athis, Myer Blank, Lee Botts, Marge Britton, Gery Chico, Forrest Claypool, Paul Green, Rep. Greg Harris, Jack Markowski, John McCarron, Tom Samuels, and Tim Samuelson gave generously of their time. Special thanks to Mary Ann Smith for her constant support and for providing such a full introduction to Edgewater, and to Sue and Bob Henning for being gracious hosts.

Specific appreciation is also due to Alfredo Sirkis and Tania Castro of Rio de Janeiro, Christina DeMarco and Mark Roseland of Vancouver, Hans Mönninghoff and Karin Rumming of Hannover, Kim Walesh of San Jose, and Wayne Wescott of Melbourne for keeping me updated (and for correcting me) about developments in their cities. Former Honolulu mayor Jeremy Harris, Lynette Char, Karl Hausker, and Dinky van Einsiedel gave me a chance to further understand the Urban Revolution in Asia. Gabriel Britto, Chris Taylor, and Devyani Srinivasan provided invaluable research support. Professor Karen Seto and Rebecca Kim helped with particular technical questions. Gabriel Britto, Paul Brugmann, Craig Cohon, Deborah Doane, Hamideh Heydari, Saddeiqa Holder, Ethan Kay, Michael Miloff, Konrad Otto-Zmmermann, James Waite, Harvey Ruvin, Lou Siminovitch, Mary Ann Smith, and Sue Zelinski provided encouragement, critical reactions, and other support in various aspects of the project.

I would have never written this book without the encouragement, frank counsel, and faith of my agent, Jackie Kaiser at Westwood Creative Artists. She was an unflagging advocate, working with me to focus the book concept and to secure its publication. Natasha Daneman, also at Westwood, was equally determined to make the book available for a larger audience beyond North America. Dan Smetanka provided extremely useful editorial coaching and support at a critical early stage.

Thanks to Peter Ginna at Bloomsbury Press and Diane Turbide at Penguin for their early faith in this project, and for their counsel during writing. Pete Beatty at Bloomsbury has had a tremendous impact on the final product. He edited the manuscript with an informed passion for the topic, providing a critical reading and skillful taming of text. Bloomsbury production editor Jenny Miyasaki, with Patterson Lamb and Maureen Klier, ushered the manuscript through the final editorial stages with meticulous care for every last word. Thanks also to Sean McDonald at Riverhead and to Tim Bartlett and Paul Taunton at Random House for early feedback on the book proposal, which changed its execution.

Anyone who tries to wrestle the complexities of the world into a single argument is indebted to others who have domesticated unruly reality beforehand with their intellectual legacies. I am particularly indebted to the works of Hernando DeSoto, Jane Jacobs, Bob Jessop, Henri Lefebvre, Karl Polanyi, Saskia Sassen, Clarence Stone, and Michael Storper.

Finally, a book project can take creeping possession of a household, beginning with the writer's preoccupied state and research travels and ending in a torrent of round-the-clock production. Saddeiqa, my spouse and intellectual sparring partner, has been tremendously supportive of my professional pursuits and intellectual passions. She filled many roles and gaps during this project, and I thank her more than anyone for being able to pursue it. Rashad and Kareem abided my absences and cloistering in the home office. They developed a supportive excitement about the book even as it reduced walks, lunches, and games of catch together. Above all, the three, together with the neighborhood friends of our Toronto urban patch, provided an anchoring city home from which to explore the City.

Notes

Preface to the U.S. Paperback Edition

i William H. Lucy and Jeff Herlitz, "Foreclosures in States and Metropolitan Areas: Patterns, Forecasts, and Pricing Toxic Assets," unpublished manuscript (February 2009), p. 5–6. http://www.virginia.edu/uvatoday/pdf/foreclosures_2009.doc (accessed November 2009).

ii Ibid, p. 1. Lucy and Herlitz highlight the folly of the financial institutions that created yet a further gap between real property values and their real estate investment dealings. They write: "Damage to the balance sheets of large banks and AIG occurred not mainly from losses on foreclosed residential mortgages, but because of borrowing short-range to buy long-range derivatives and from selling credit default swaps insuring derivatives backed by mortgage payments. These financial manipulations had high speed forward gears, but when the housing bubble burst, the banks and AIG discovered they had neglected to create a reverse gear with which they could separate foreclosed properties from some forms of mortgage backed securities. Obstacles to disentangling toxic components of mortgage backed securities magnified many times the actual housing value declines."

iii William C. Wheaton and Gleb Nechayev, "Past Housing 'Cycles' and the Current Housing 'Boom': What's Different This Time?" unpublished manuscript (May 2006). http://econ-www.mit.edu/files/1760 (accessed May 2009).

iv Thomas J. Holmes, "The Diffusion of Wal-Mart and Economies of Density," *NBER Working Paper no. W13783* (2008): 1. http://sticerd.lse.ac.uk/seminarpapers/ei07112005.pdf (accessed July 2009). A video map of Wal-Mart's cluster growth pattern can be found at http://www.metacafe.com/watch/yt-EGzHBtoVvpc/the_diffusion_of_wal_mart_and_economies_of_density/.

1. Look Again

1 In this book the word *city* is used to denote a contiguous urbanized area and the word *City* is used to denote the extended geography that cities together form through their import of people and resources from rural areas and their trade, shipments, travel, and financial and information flows between each other. Unless otherwise noted, the word *city* is not used to denote a political or legal jurisdiction such as the City of London but rather the contiguous urbanized area that typically includes numerous political jurisdictions and that takes many forms, including metropolitan areas, corridor cities along major transportation routes, and regional city systems such as the eastern seaboard of Japan.

2 The most detailed analysis of the development and Gounder origins of the Tiruppur knitwear industry has been made by Sharad Chari at the University of California, Berkeley. Sharad Chari, *Fraternal Capital: Peasant-Workers, Self-Made Men, and Globalization in Provincial India* (Palo Alto, Calif.: Stanford University Press, 2004).

3 These terms were agreed to in 1989 by a negotiating group involving representatives of the White House, Senator John Chafee (chairman of the Senate Committee on Environment and Public Works), the major manufacturers of CFCs, and the Natural Resources Defense Council. The ban on local and state regulation of CFCs and other greenhouse gases was included in the resulting Senate version of the 1990 Clean Air Act. Responding to protest from state and local governments, then-senator Al Gore submitted a floor amendment to the act, striking the local legislative ban. The Gore amendment won with a strong majority.

4 This movement is called the Cities for Climate Protection (CCP) Campaign. After staffing the earlier CFC effort, the author first conceived the CCP at a major international meeting of city leaders that he organized at the United Nations in New York in 1990. Starting in 1991 with fourteen cities on three continents to develop the methodology for quantifying urban-generated greenhouse-gas emissions, the CCP was then scaled by Toronto environmentalist Philip Jessup, American urban activist Nancy Skinner, energy expert Ralph Torrie, and the author under auspices of the International Council for Local Environmental Initiatives (ICLEI). It was launched with the sponsorship of the United Nations Environment Programme at the United Nations in New York in 1993. For more information about the Cities for Climate Protection Campaign, see http://www.iclei.org/ccp.

5 Ana Arana, "How the Street Gangs Took Central America," *Foreign Affairs* (May–June 2005). http://www.foreignaffairs.org/20050501faessay84310/ana-arana/how-the-street-gangs-took-central-america.html.

6 The software technology for the Internet (i.e., packet switching) was developed somewhat independently of any particular urban market or city network, though it was developed in particular high-tech urban centers like Cambridge, Massachusetts. E-mail was a related parallel development, based on the development of off-line readers, which involved the same technical community in Cambridge. Off-line readers were effectively a productivity enhancement of telephone networks that allowed users to rapidly send and download material via dial-up connections and work with it off-line. The first computer-to-computer network was created for the U.S. Department of Defense (ARPANet) by the early 1970s, but once the technology was developed other government agencies and universities created their parallel networks. Similar networks then developed in Europe. The Internet came about in the early 1980s when protocols were established to connect those specialist user networks. Throughout the 1980s, the Internet was effectively a system for connecting largely urban-based universities, technology companies, and government agencies. In parallel, similarly inclined technical professionals in universities and computer-related companies started using e-mail. The first commercial e-mail service started in 1983, but these services were limited to urban markets because of the existing telephone infrastructure in these markets and the concentrations of users there. With the advent of the Internet, largely university-based concentrations of specialist users started using the World Wide Web. Internet service providers were concentrated in cities in the United States until the mid- to late 1990s. In other words, though the technology could support participation from any place with a phone connection, in reality the Internet infrastructure was initially as fixed in its urban orientation as the first interurban infrastructure, the shipping port. Truly worldwide Internet service was only made possible on the foundation of established urban-scale economies and could not likely be sustained without them.

7 A telling example of the Internet's tethered relationship to urban markets is Craigslist, the seventh-most-used Web site in the United States. As the *New York Times* (May 12, 2008, pp. C1–3) reports: "Once, an announcement that Craigslist was expanding meant adding cities like Miami, Minneapolis and Philadelphia. These days, it means smaller places like Janesville, Wis., (population: about 60,000) and Farmington, N.M., (roughly 38,000) as well as Cebu in the Philippines and . . . Ramallah on the West Bank." The population of Cebu City and the Ramallah area was eight hundred thousand and two hundred thousand, respectively, in 2007. In describing the Web site's competition with eBay's classified advertising site, called Kijiji, the article goes on to report: "The competition between the companies is also heating up . . . Craigslist in the last few weeks has added 120 cities, half of them overseas, where Kijiji has been dominant." This story suggests that Internet-based consumer businesses are still following urban markets and not necessarily creating their own market spaces.

8 Rural access to the Internet in the United States only started catching up with urban access in the late 1990s, by which time the Internet had been a going concern for nearly two decades. In the United States, urban Internet use, both as a percentage of urban population and as a percentage of total national Internet use, continues to exceed rural use measures in spite of the high percentage of low-income households in U.S. inner cities. See U.S. Department of Commerce, *A Nation Online: Entering the Broadband Age* (Washington, D.C.: U.S. Department of Commerce, 2004). Also NTIA, *Falling Through the Net: Toward Digital Inclusion, a Report on Americans' Access to Technology Tools* (Washington, D.C.: National Telecommunications and Information Administration, 2000). http://www.ntia.doc.gov/ntiahome/fttn00/Falling.htm#t31 (accessed March 14, 2007). See also an earlier version of the same report: NTIA, *Falling Through the Net: A Survey of the "Have Nots" in Rural and Urban America* (Washington, D.C.: NTIA, 1995). http://www.ntia.doc.gov/ntiahome/tables.htm#Table%2015 (accessed March 14, 2007). In Canada, a 2000 government survey of household Internet use tellingly focused only on metropolitan areas. See Statistics Canada, "Household Internet Use, 1999," *Daily*, May 19, 2000. http://www.statcan.ca/Daily/English/000519/d000519b.htm (accessed March 14, 2007). Reference to the initial establishment of Internet services in urban areas in China and Afghanistan is drawn from media reports.

These U.S. data reflect a worldwide trend of growing rural penetration of mobile phone technology, driven in part by the efforts of low-income households to access information related to (generally urban) market opportunities. For instance, U.S. rural households with very low incomes (less than $10,000) and low income inner-city households (with incomes between $15,000 and $20,000) were percentage-wise the highest users of the Internet to search classified (employment) advertisements. Rural black households were percentage-wise the highest users of the Internet to take online courses. In developing countries with large émigré communities, information and communication technology (ICT) is being used to help rural and small town populations access income, via remittances of family members who are working in cities abroad. In the Philippines, the telecom company Smart Communications Inc. provides a service with mobile operators in Asia, Europe, and North America to transfer funds via mobile phone, which local family members can collect at (urban) retail outlets like 7-Eleven stores, McDonald's, and gasoline stations.

9 See Clare Ribando, *CRS Report for Congress: Gangs in Central America* (Washington, D.C.: Congressional Research Service, 2005).

10 Throughout this book my citations of national, regional, and international urban population data are drawn from the United Nations report *World Urbanization Prospects: The 2003 Revisions* (New York: UN Economic and Social Council, 2004). Like most population data on cities, the figures in this report are a best estimate, based on the different definitions of *urban* and approaches to data collection of national census studies. National census data tend to undercount urban populations in three ways. First, they count the population only within an officially defined geographic *urban area*, even if the typical growth pattern at the periphery of metropolitan areas today is to integrate what would otherwise officially be considered villages or rural settlements into the economic and social life of the city. Second, census data undercount people who do not have legal residency in a city, such as slum dwellers. Even where census takers do surveys in slum or other informal areas, the vulnerability of these people to harassment and relocation by government bodies makes them reticent to cooperate in these surveys. Third, in many parts of the world, particularly in China, cities are inhabited by large numbers of seasonal migrants who alternate between agricultural work and residency in rural village and labor and residency in the city. These people are generally not counted as urban residents in census reports.

11 A huge academic undertaking was started in the 1980s to collect the data and to build the databases for tracking and analyzing global flows of finance, commodities, and people between cities on a continental and global scale. This multidisciplinary project, known as World Cities studies, has given us the first detailed grasp and disciplined insights into the formation, structure, and dynamics of the City system. See J. Kentor, D. Smith, and M. Timberlake, *The World-System's City System: A Research Agenda*. http://www.irows.ucr.edu/conferences/globgis/papers/Smith.htm (accessed March 16, 2008). Also P. J. Taylor, "Hierarchical Tendencies Amongst World Cities: A Global Research Proposal," *Cities* 14, no. 6 (1997): 323–332. Also J. Beaverstock, R. Smith, and P. Taylor, "World-City Network: A New Metageography?" *Annals of the Association of American Geographers* 90, no. 1 (2000): 123–134.

However, the field's theoretical bias toward understanding global development through the single lens of corporate investment and expansion provides us with a very partial view of the City, its drivers, and its impacts. In contrast to the field's view of corporate and generally top-down economic restructuring of the world City, I argue that much more fundamental drivers inherent in the nature of urban settlement have instigated numerous parallel efforts by many different and competing social and economic interests, such as migrant ethnic communities and criminal organizations, to shape and gain advantage in the City. The corporate economy and its strategists are but one, albeit central, part of that rush to shape and control the City. The City also needs to be understood in more than just its economic aspects—in particular, in the way that it is restructuring ecological flows, dynamics, and relationships in the world.

12 Our bias toward measuring countries and industries leaves us with no exact estimates of the annual urban consumption of materials used to build and

rebuild the offices, homes, bridges, roads, tunnels, sewers, sidewalks, and ports of the world's cities. This estimate is based on the conservative assumption that since half the world's people live in cities, then 50 percent of the world's construction is located in cities as well. Figures on annual consumption of concrete are taken from industry association sources.

13 R. Kumar Mehta, "Greening of the Concrete Industry for Sustainable Development," *Concrete International* 24, no. 7 (July 2002): 23–28.

14 Estimates of migrant remittances are taken from International Fund for Agricultural Development, *Sending Money Home: Worldwide Remittance Flows to Developing Countries* (Rome: IFAD, 2007). http://idbdocs.iadb.org/wsdocs/getdocument.aspx?docnum=1172190 (accessed April 5, 2008). The IFAD report attempts to estimate both official remittances through regulated financial channels and informal remittances through the global *hawala* system. There are no established worldwide data sets that distinguish urban and rural remittances or migration flows. However, country data on population settlement patterns in the main foreign migrant recipient countries and on the main outgoing sources of remittances (e.g., in Europe, North America, the Gulf States, the Russian Federation, Japan, Singapore, Hong Kong, South Africa, Argentina, Brazil) clearly indicate a very substantial urban settlement pattern, both in gross and marginal terms. Data on official foreign direct investment (FDI) flows are taken from World Bank, *Global Development Finance Report* (Washington, D.C.: World Bank, 2007). Total FDI flows to developing countries were $800 billion in 2006. For an overview of the informal hawala remittances system, see World Bank/IMF, *Informal Funds Transfer Systems: An Analysis of the Informal Hawala System* (Washington, D.C.: World Bank, 2003).

15 Lewis Mumford, "The Natural History of Urbanization," in William L. Thomas Jr., ed., *Man's Role in Changing the Face of the Earth* (Chicago: University of Chicago Press, 1956). http://habitat.aq.upm.es/boletin/n21/almum.en.html (accessed February 18, 2008). Mumford's writings about cities and urbanization, at the start of the last phase of global urbanization, demonstrate both his prescience and the degree to which we have so far failed to develop an effective practice of urban strategy.

2. The Improbable Life of an Urban Patch

1 An excellent NASA image of Earth at night can be found at http://apod.nasa.gov/apod/ap001127.html.

2 The use of satellite imagery and remote sensing has opened a new dimension of scholarship in the study of cities. No single remote-sensing methodology has yet been established as a standard for measuring the cityscape, but a general consensus exists that the described light patterns are one of the primary indictors of urbanized terrain. Measurement of the density of light, in particular, is an established proxy used to measure the geography of urbanized territories. See Mark R. Montgomery, "The Urban Transformation of the Developing World," *Science* 319 (February 8, 2008): 761–764. Among a number of research endeavors recently established to document and model the land areas and growth patterns of cities worldwide, the tri-university research project managed by the University of Connecticut's Center for Land Use Education and Research (CLEAR) offers the fullest data set. This study, as well as the research of Karen Seto of the Center for Environmental Studies and Policy at Stanford University, uses land cover data and not visible surface light to determine urbanized area. Seto's work uses infrared photography to distinguish different land covers. The CLEAR Project clusters micro (pixel-level) data from daytime imagery into fifty different land-type clusters and then sorts these into urban and nonurban land uses. In an interview for this report, Seto noted that visible light intensity is also used as an accepted technical measure of urbanized area, particularly for industrialized countries, although it is a more accurate measure of energy intensity. In higher income, industrialized countries, she explains, the intensity of light creates a "bloom effect," or glow, that extends beyond the actual land area from which the light is emanating. This has to be corrected for in measuring urbanized area in these countries. Conversely, in lower-income developing countries there may be urbanized areas with low energy intensity and little light marker.

3 Human Rights Watch, *Funding the "Final War": LTTE Intimidation and Extortion in the Tamil Diaspora*, March 14, 2006.

4 See C. A. Schubert, I. K. Barker, R. C. Rosatte, and C. D. MacInnes, "Density, Dispersion, Movements and Habitat Preference of Skunks (*Mephitis mephitis*) and Raccoons (*Procyon lotor*) in Metropolitan Toronto," in D. R. McCollough and R. Barrett, eds., *Wildlife 2001: Populations* (London: Elsevier Science, 1992), pp. 932–944.

5 A. D. Tomlin, "The Earthworm Bait Market in North America," in J. E. Satchell, ed., *Earthworm Ecology* (London: Chapman and Hall, 1983), pp. 331–338. http://sci.agr.ca/london/faq/tomlin01_e.htm (accessed September 2007).

3. The Great Migration

1 For an excellent study of the role of distinct cultural communities in the development of urban commerce and capitalism in India, see David W. Rudner, *Caste and Capitalism in Colonial India: The Nattukottai Chettiars* (Berkeley: University of California Press, 1994).

2 Richard N. Juliani, *Building Little Italy: Philadelphia's Italians Before Mass Migration* (University Park: Pennsylvania State University Press, 1998).

3 Adam Mckeown, "Global Migration, 1846–1940," *Journal of World History* (2004). http://www.historycooperative.org/journals/jwh/15.2/mckeown.html (accessed September 5, 2007).

4 Jan Lucassen, *Migrant Labor in Europe, 1600–1900: The Drift to the North Sea* (Wolfboro, N.H.: Croom Helm, 1987).

5 Saskia Sassen, *Guests and Aliens* (New York: New Press, 1999), pp. 7–11.

6 Ibid., p. 8.

7 David Eltis, "The Volume and Structure of the Transatlantic Slave Trade: A Reassessment," *William and Mary Quarterly*, 3rd Ser., 58, no. 1 (2001): 17–46.

8 Over a seventy-year period, an estimated six million people emigrated from Hong Kong alone, setting the stage for Hong Kong's early prominence as one of the world's first and most truly globalized cities. As is the case with many major historical migrations from other countries, the great majority of Chinese migrants came from a few primary contributing regions and cities, particularly from Hong Kong and Guangzhou. In essence, this was not really a Chinese migration but more of a regional one that finds its origins in the political and trade history of the Hong Kong–Guangzhou region, as well as in the distinct culture of people from this region. For an overview of Chinese migration, see Ronald Skeldon, *China: From Exceptional Case to Global Participant.* Migration Information Source. http://www.migrationinformation.org (accessed September 5, 2007). For a glimpse into the cultural particularities of the pioneer migrants themselves, see George C. S. Lin, "Hong Kong and the Globalization of the Chinese Diaspora: A Geographical Perspective," *Asia Pacific Viewpoint* 43, no. 1 (2002): 63–91.

9 At the peak of German immigration to the United States between 1881 and 1885, for instance, the United States received one million German migrants, many of whom left declining wages in Germany to ply their trades in the booming cities of the American Midwest. (See David Khodour-Casteras, *The Impact of Bismarck's Social Legislation on Emigration Before World War I* [eScholarship Repository, University of California, 2004].) Irish immigration during the entire period of 1820–1930—again largely to the cities of the East Coast and Midwest—counted about five million people, and it took from 1820 to 1980 for an equal number of Italians to emigrate, once again predominantly to East Coast cities. Even at the peak of the more recent migration of Latin Americans to the United States in the 1980s–1990s, the United States received an average of three hundred ninety thousand per year, concentrating in the cities of Florida, Texas, the Southwest, and Southern California.

10 The figures are similar for Canada: historically, immigrants have focused their ambitions on Canada's cities. Immigration played a major part in driving up Canada's urban population from 25 percent of total population in 1880 to 54 percent by 1940, and again to 76 percent by 1990.

11 UN Population Division, Department of Economic and Social Affairs, United Nations, *World Urbanization Prospects: The 2003 Revision*, Table A.17 (New York: United Nations, 2004).

12 My hosts, guides, and supporters in Madurai have been the staff and associates of the Covenant Centre for Development (CCD), which has specialized in micro-finance and the development of community-owned enterprises that help low-income rural families, confronted by their declining agricultural economy, to develop new livelihoods through production for and trade with urban markets. For more information on CCD, see http://www.ccd.org.in.

13 It was not hard to find willing, real-world "experts" on urban migration to share their stories. Some of the young people who worked for CCD had family members who were first-generation migrants. These CCD staff also approached members of their rural micro-credit groups, asking them if they had family members who had migrated to the city. Using this snowballing technique to secure contacts and introductions, we together interviewed forty migrant households and discovered some of the hundreds of migration chains that had been creating the new face, culture, and economic dynamics of a growing Madurai.

14 Carmen Elisa Florez, "Migration and the Urban Informal Sector in Colombia," paper presented at the Conference on African Migration and Urbanization in Comparative Perspective, Johannesburg, South Africa, June 4–7, 2007. http://pum.princeton.edu/pumconference/papers/4-Florez.pdf (accessed September 2007).

15 Cindy C. Fan, "Migration and Labor-Market Returns in Urban China: Results from a Recent Survey in Guangzhou," *Environment and Planning* 33 (2001): 479–508.

16 Katy Cornwall and Brett Inger, "Migration and Unemployment in South Africa: When Motivation Surpasses the Theory," paper presented at a conference of the Centre for the Study of African Economies, Oxford University, 2004. http://www.csae.ox.ac.uk/conferences/2004-GPRaHDiA/papers/5f-Cornwell-CSAE-2004.pdf (accessed September 2007).

4. Anatomy of Urban Revolution

1 Eliyah Zulu, Adama Konseiga, Eugene Darteh, and Blessing Mbera, "Migration and Urbanization of Poverty in Sub-Saharan Africa: The Case of Nairobi City, Kenya," paper presented at the 2006 annual meeting of the Population Association of America, Los Angeles, California, March 30–April 1, 2006. This

study provides a full profile of slum demographics and migrant strategies. http://paa2006.princeton.edu/download.aspx?submissionId=61368 (accessed January 2008).

2 Richard U. Agesa and Sunwoong Kim, "Rural to Urban Migration as a Household Decision: Evidence from Kenya," *Review of Development Economics* 5, no. 1 (2001): 60–75.

3 Fernando Cruz, Kerstin Sommer, and Ombretta Tempra, *Nairobi Urban Sector Profile* (Nairobi: UN Habitat, 2006).

4 Nancy Luke, "Individual Pursuits and Community Ties: New Theory and Evidence on Remittances in Western Kenya," paper presented at the Wits/Brown/Colorado/APHRC Colloquium on Emerging Population Issues, Nairobi, Kenya, May 2006. This was a study of Luo migrants to Kisumu, Kenya's third-largest city. The survey found that "88% of male migrants remitted to their rural families in the last year, and 66% sent financial transfers to their rural communities. Family remittances made up 25% of migrants' yearly incomes of those who remitted."

5 See Nicholas Lemann, *The Promised Land: The Great Black Migration and How It Changed America* (New York: Vintage Books, 1992).

6 For a characterization of the stages of migration, see, for instance, Peter Gottlieb, "The Origins of Black Migration," in Gottlieb, *Making Their Own Way: Southern Blacks' Migration to Pittsburgh, 1916–1930* (Urbana: University of Illinois Press, 1987).

7 Kevin Boyle, *Arc of Justice: A Saga of Race, Civil Rights, and Murder in the Jazz Age* (New York: Henry Holt, 2005).

8 Information about black housing conditions in 1920s Detroit is drawn from the report of Elizabeth Anne Martin, *Detroit and the Great Migration, 1916–1929*, bulletin no. 40 (Ann Arbor: Bentley Historical Library, University of Michigan, 1993). Much of this report is based on primary documents of black associations, like the Detroit Urban League, which monitored migrant living conditions at the time of the migration. The full account is available at http://bentley.umich.edu/research/publications/migration (accessed November 2007).

9 Facts about the demographics of Detroit are drawn from the U.S. government's Decennial Census reports for 1920, 1930, 1940, 1950, 1960, and 1970. The figures cited in this paragraph are drawn from the 1940 Census of Population, state report for Michigan, Table #34. http://www.census.gov/prod/www/abs/decennial/1940.htm.

10 Julia Isaacs, *Economic Mobility of Black and White Families* (Washington, D.C.: Economic Mobility Project, Pew Charitable Trust, 2007). www

.economicmobility.org (accessed November 2007). Another recent study of the lending practices of a major American bank shows that blacks still lack equal access to the home mortgage refinancing that is required to leverage their home equity into family educational and business investments. See Michael Hodge et al., "A Case Study of Mortgage Refinancing Discrimination: African-American Intergenerational Wealth," *Sociological Inquiry* 77, no. 1 (2007): 23–43.

11 Jack M. Bloom, *Class, Race and the Civil Rights Movement: The Changing Political Economy of Southern Racism* (Bloomington: Indiana University Press, 1987), p. 11.

12 Dale Wittner with Bud Lee, "Newark, the Predictable Insurrection: Shooting War in the Streets," *Life* 63, no. 4 (1967).

13 Max Herman, *Ethnic Succession and Urban Unrest in Newark and Detroit During the Summer of 1967* (Newark, N.J: Rutgers University, Cornwall Center for Metropolitan Studies, 2002), p. 29. Herman used the location of riot deaths as an indicator of the geographic location of riot events in Detroit and Newark in 1967; his statistical analysis reveals that the riots in Detroit and Newark in 1967 took place, not in well-established black districts, but in areas where blacks were newcomers and had not yet gained economic control of housing, commercial life, or representation in the police and other government services managing the area. "The black population proportion was increasing in most Detroit neighborhoods, but the neighborhoods where riot deaths took place had a significantly greater rate of black population increases.... As change in percent black [residential population in a census tract] increases, the likelihood of multiple riot fatalities in a tract also increases . . . For Detroit, economic indicators fail to predict the likelihood of multiple riot fatalities in a tract. Neither percent males unemployed nor . . . medium household income has a significant independent effect on the dependent variable [i.e., riot fatalities] when controlling for racial/ethnic composition . . . Areas with a higher degree of homeownership were less likely to be touched by riot violence than tracts inhabited primarily by renters" (pp. 25–27). He concludes that the riots were part of a process of "ethnic succession."

Herman's paper is accessible at http://www.cornwall.rutgers.edu/pdf/Herman-July%202002-Report.pdf (accessed in 2008). The full study by Herman was published as a book: Max Arthur Herman, *Fighting in the Streets: Ethnic Succession and Urban Unrest in Twentieth-Century America* (New York: Peter Lang, 2005). Herman also provides oral history video clips of residents of the riot-affected areas at http://www.67riots.rutgers.edu/d_questions.htm.

14 Robert D. Kaplan, "A Bazaari's World," *Atlantic Monthly*, March 1996. Kaplan's article provides an excellent exploration of the post-Revolution rise of the bazaari class as economic managers of the businesses that the new theocracy captured from the shah's economic allies.

15 Guilain Denoeux, *Urban Unrest in the Middle East: A Comparative Study of Informal Networks in Egypt, Iran, and Lebanon* (Albany: SUNY Press, 1993).

16 Ibid., p. 136.

17 Arang Keshavarzian et al., *Bazaar and State in Iran: The Politics of the Tehran Marketplace* (Cambridge, Mass.: Cambridge University Press, 2007), pp. 228–229.

18 Iranian landowners were traditionally served by two groups of peasantry. The first was the sharecroppers. These people organized into teams of six to twelve men and negotiated agreements with landowners to cultivate their property for the season. They paid an agreed percentage of the harvest back to the landowners and divided the rest among themselves. The second group was agricultural laborers. They lacked any traditional rights like the sharecroppers to directly cultivate the land. These people depended on seasonal wage labor for mere subsistence. As land reforms made the sharecroppers the new landowners with government subsidies, they employed their own families in farming tasks. They evolved their traditional sharecropper cooperation into farming enterprises, allowing mechanized production. Work opportunities for the landless laborers therefore steadily disappeared, and they began migrating in droves to the cities.

19 Farhad Kazemi, "Urban Migrants and the Revolution," *Iranian Studies* 13, nos. 1–4 (1980): 257–277.

20 Ibid., p. 269.

21 Asef Bayat provides the most nuanced, detailed analysis of migrant and slum-based association and politics in the Iranian Revolution and in cities throughout the Middle East, providing an antidote to tendencies to simplify the nature of the poor and the dynamics of the slum. See Asef Bayat, *Street Politics: Poor People's Movements in Iran* (New York: Columbia University Press, 2007), pp. 38–58. Bayat provides a brilliant analysis of the nuanced character of revolutionary urban coalitions in his article "Workless Revolutionaries: The Unemployed Movement in Revolutionary Iran," *International Review of Social History* 42 (1997): 159–185. The mobilization and organization of squatters and slum tenants in the years preceding the Revolution continued in the years that followed. Unemployed migrants and industrial workers, emboldened by their revolutionary experience, organized together into an unemployed workers movement seeking a forty-hour workweek, unions, unemployment benefits, and other government support. This brought them into alliance with leftist (and soon to be job-seeking) students who clashed with the core coalition of clerics and bazaaris who formed the new conservative regime. Their new organizations managed an intense period of demonstrations and negotiations with the new regime in cities large and small, including Teheran, Isfahan, Tabriz, Ghazvin, Gachsaran, Khorram Abad, Kord, Sari, Mahabad, and Kermanshah.

22 Jahangir Amuzegar, *The Dynamics of the Iranian Revolution: The Pahlavis' Triumph and Tragedy* (Albany: SUNY Press, 1991), pp. 34–35. Describing the partial influence of religious fervor in the revolution, Amuzegar quotes an eyewitness reporter at the 1979 mass demonstrations against the shah: "The recent waves of widespread rioting across Iran are the work of little people lashing out against inflation, unemployment, unequal distribution of wealth and corruption in high places." The comment fails to note that almost all of these riots took place in the fast-growing cities.

23 Denoeux, *Urban Unrest in the Middle East*, p. 93.

24 Ibid., p. 42. Denoeux describes these highly organized, neighborhood-based networks as the foundation unit of urban society throughout the Middle East region. Social, economic, political, and religious life in Middle Eastern cities has traditionally been tightly bound together within city districts. These districts, called *hara* (e.g., in Cairo and Damascus), *mahalla* (e.g., in Mosul and Baghdad), and *hawma* (e.g., in Algiers and Tunis), organized residential, social, and commercial life into a small city system. The people in them shared common trades and merchant roles, kinship and religious affiliations, and neighborhood identities. Their interests were generally represented to outside powers by the strongest merchant interests within their quarters. Governments often turned to these local strongmen to serve as their agents, further entrenching the strongman's authority. For instance, as far back as the ninth through fifteenth centuries, these strongmen had organized policing and paramilitary organizations. Because urban society was structured—both spatially and socially—into these informal, decentralized districts with their own entrenched power, they continued to be the norm and the basis for political organization in the twentieth century.

In the early years of modern Lebanon's development as a nation, specifically through the 1943 National Pact, power was distributed according to religious sectarian affiliation. As urban sectarian society was structured into these established neighborhood districts, power accrued to the strongmen in the modern state as well. "Formal political institutions never acquired a reality and logic of their own," writes Denoeux, ". . . the urban Sunni population, which had at its disposal a variety of sectarian, kinship, neighborhood-based, and patron-client networks, withdrew around these networks to participate in politics" (p. 82). In the twentieth century the traditional Beirut strongmen managed extensive networks of street leaders who both policed the neighborhood and operated smuggling and racketeering operations in parallel with their political roles. As a result of the codified sectarianism of national politics and the organization of urban society through such robust, neighborhood-based economic-social-political units, Lebanon never established a modern governing elite, drawn from its different social-religious sects.

But as Christian and Shiite populations migrated into the cities in large numbers in the 1960s and 1970s, the old strongman organizations were not able to expand to serve and integrate them into the established political system. These new populations, particularly the Shiite migrants, were ultimately organized into leftist political movements and militias, ultimately leading to the 1975–1990 civil war. Although their primary function was that of military organizations, they also took on the traditional role of providing a full range of basic urban services, social services, schools, radio stations, telephone networks, and so on to their low-income populations.

The development of the Iranian-supported Hezbollah movement is distinct from these slum-based political-militia movements. Hezbollah could be said to have roots in the Urban Revolution, in that it is a direct outcome of the Iranian Revolution and the vast economic resources this granted to Shia clerics from Najaf, Iraq. Although Hezbollah did early establish its religious schools, social welfare services, and cells in low-income Shia districts of Beirut and Tyre, its primary focus has been territorial control of the more rural and small town southern Lebanon. Hezbollah also has a different organizational character from that of the old neighborhood-based strongman organizations and the left-oriented militias. Its model is derived from the Islamic clerical model of organization into schools and learning cells, linked to individual clerics. Hezbollah was initially a network of these small units that formed shifting and splintering alliances, but in more recent times the movement has appeared to be more stable and consolidated under Hassan Nasrallah (since 1992). Hezbollah also established a more prominent presence in Beirut in 1988 and has since become entrenched in the territorial fabric of the city.

25 Ibid., pp. 92–97.

26 Nizar Hamzeh, "Lebanon's Islamists and Local Politics: A New Reality," *Third World Quarterly* 21 (2000): 739–759.

27 Asef Bayat, "Radical Religion and the Habitus of the Dispossessed: Does Islamic Militancy Have an Urban Ecology?" *International Journal of Urban and Regional Research* 31, no. 3 (2007): 579–590. Bayat's analysis of the relationship between Islamic movements and low-income settlers in Cairo focuses on the instrumental rather than the ideological nature of their political activities.

28 As a measure of the Muslim Brotherhood's potential as a new urban political force in Egypt, in the 2005 parliamentary elections, "independent" candidates associated with the Brotherhood secured 80 of 444 total seats, in spite of alleged, widespread government manipulation, making them the country's largest parliamentary minority.

29 http://www.igmg.de/verband/islamic-community-milli-goerues/organisational-structure.html (accessed April 2008).

30 For scholarly articles on both Milli Görüş and the IGP, see Lorenzo Vidino, "The Muslim Brotherhood's Conquest of Europe," *Middle East Quarterly* (Win-

ter 2005). http://www.meforum.org/article/687 (accessed April 2008). Also Gökçe Yurdakul, "Muslim Political Associations of Turks in Germany," Council for European Studies, Columbia University, 2005. http://www.councilfor europeanstudies/pub/Yurdaku_sep05.html (accessed April 2008).

5. The Tyrants' Demise

1 Padraic Kenney, *A Carnival of Revolution: Central Europe, 1989* (Princeton, N.J.: Princeton University Press, 2002).

2 Ibid., pp. 4–5 and pp. 12–13.

3 Ibid., p. 11 and p. 14.

4 Ibid., pp. 41–47.

5 For a description of the organizational structure of the People Power movement, see Masataka Kimura, "The Emergence of the Middle Classes and Political Change in the Philippines," *Developing Economies* 41, no. 2 (June 2003): 264–284.

6 For the full list of sixty-six reported incidents, see http://cecc.gov/pages/ virtualAcad/rol/forcedevictionchart.pdf?PHPSESSID=59d757e59c64d8b21d 530b45cd9a1c97 (accessed December 2007). The Congressional-Executive Commission on China was created by Congress in October 2000 to monitor human rights and the development of the rule of law in China, and to submit an annual report to the president and Congress. It consists of nine senators, nine members of the House of Representatives, and five senior administration officials appointed by the president.

7 Nick Mulvenney, "Olympics-Beijing Residents Support Relocation— Official," Reuters, August 15, 2007.

8 Murray Scot Tanner, *Chinese Government Responses to Rising Social Unrest: Testimony to the U.S.–China Economic and Security Commission, April 2005* (Santa Monica, Calif.: RAND Corporation, 2005).

9 See Rance P. L. Lee, Danching Ruan, and Gina Lai, "Social Structure and Support Networks in Beijing and Hong Kong," *Social Networks* 27, no. 3 (July 2005): 249–274.

6. What We Can Learn from the Way That Migrants Build Their Cities

1 *Pongal* is a typical south Indian breakfast food. The pongal house is a typical migrant city business model that maximizes the efficient use of space and

buildings. A lodger buys an eight-hour right to sleep, bathe, eat, and do personal work, so that the house serves three shifts of people around the clock.

2 If you go into Dharavi, you will not find INMA without a guide because the operation is indistinguishable from a home or any other workshop. But you can read about INMA on its Web site: www.inmaenterprises.com (accessed November 2007).

7. The Final Phase

1 The occasion for these meetings was the Asia Pacific Urban Institute (2002–2003), established under the leadership of Honolulu mayor Jeremy Harris and technically and financially supported by the Asia Development Bank, US–Asia Environment Program of US AID, Canadian International Development Agency, and a substantial group of domain experts.

2 Edward Leman, "Metropolitan Regions: New Challenges for an Urbanizing China," paper presented at the World Bank/IPEA Urban Research Symposium, April 4, 2005 (Ottawa: Chreod, 2005). http://www.worldbank.org/urban/symposium2005/papers/leman.pdf (accessed February 2008).

3 A more useful measure of the internal productivity of a city area would be the amortized total cost of building and maintaining an "urban patch" relative to the area's economic productivity.

4 See J. F. He, R. H. Xu, D. W. Yu, G. W. Peng, Y. Y. Liu, W. J. Liang, L. H. Li, R. N. Guo, Y. Fang, X. C. Zhang, H. Z. Zheng, H. M. Luo, and J. Y. Lin, "Severe Acute Respiratory Syndrome in Guangdong Province of China: Epidemiology and Control Measures" [article in Chinese], published by the Center for Disease Control and Prevention of Guangdong Province, July 2003: 227–232.

5 Ibid.

6 For an epidemiological assessment of the contribution of local live market practices in the emergence and spread of new virus strains, see Robert G. Webster, "Wet Markets—a Continuing Source of Severe Acute Respiratory Syndrome and Influenza?" *Lancet* 363, no. 9404 (January 17, 2004): 234–236.

7 BBC News. "Animals Suffer in the War on SARS," April 30, 2003. http://news.bbc.co.uk/1/hi/world/asia-pacific/2989479.stm (accessed May 2008).

8 See Ih-Jen Su, "Predicting an H5N1 Influenza Pandemic: A Great Challenge to the Scientific World," *Epidemiology Bulletin* (January 25, 2006): 12–17.

9 "International Air Arrivals to Asia Dropped 13 Percent in 2003, the Year of the SARS Crisis," *Global Tourism Report* 3 (2003).

10 Catherine Brahic, "Coastal Living—a Growing Global Threat," *New Scientist* 14, no. 54 (March 28, 2007). http://environment.newscientist.com/channel/earth/dn11483-coastal-living–a-growing-global-threat-.html (accessed September 2008).

11 For an overview of the role that urban development plays in the design of disaster risks, see Janet Abramovitz, *Unnatural Disasters*, Worldwatch Paper 158 (Washington, D.C.: Worldwatch Institute, 2001).

12 The concept of urbanology as a new field of study is sometimes attributed to Serbian architect and former Belgrade mayor (1982–1986) Bogdan Bogdanovic. For him, urbanology was a way to understand the dynamics and possibilities of cities independent of what he called "practical urbanism," which he described as "a treaty zone between politicians, large companies and capital." By his European experience, he says, practical urbanism "has become the inviolable domain of the mafia." See Miroslav Marcelli, "The Architecture of the European City: An Interview with Bogdan Bogdanovic," *Eurozine* (2003). http://eurozine.com/pdf/2003-10-20-bogdanovic-en.pdf (accessed January 31, 2008). The urbanology concept has since taken off in Europe and beyond. Niels Albertsen of the School of Architecture in Aarhus, Denmark, has aptly explained in his course called "The City Between Disciplines" that the city is not the subject of any particular discipline but is by nature interdisciplinary. Urbanology is an effort to bring some systematic approach to that interdisciplinary study. Two of the field's most interesting grassroots practitioners are Rahul Srivastava and Matias Echanove. Their reflections and analyses are accessible via http://www.urbanology.org.

13 I am indebted to Gabriel Britto and his partner Prema Gopalan for their accompaniment on many explorations of Mumbai; also, this exploration of the emergence of global criminal organizations draws heavily on the work of Gabriel Britto, Molly Charles, K. S. Nair, A. A. Das, and numerous researchers in UNESCO, G. Fabre, and Michel Shiray, *Globalisation, Drugs and Criminalisation: Final Research Report on Brazil, China, India and Mexico* (2002). http://www.unesco.org/most/globalisation/drugs_1.htm (accessed December 2007).

14 Misha Glenny, *McMafia: A Journey Through the Global Criminal Underworld* (New York: Random House, 2008).

15 Mumbai's Dawood Ibrahim has controlled a large part of the underground *hundi* banking system in Pakistan as well as Indian gold smuggling through operation centers in Dubai, Karachi, Islamabad, Mumbai, and Delhi. His company manages a massive real estate portfolio in these and other cities and is said to have made an emergency U.S. dollar loan to the Pakistan Central Bank. Many intelligence service professionals link his organization to Al Qaeda's smuggling and money-laundering activities. Another operator of modest Mumbai origins, Iqbal Mirchi, began as a Mumbai taxi driver and roadside spice vendor and now

oversees a drug and smuggling operation that extends across India, Afghanistan, Pakistan, Dubai, Hong Kong, Kenya, Nigeria, Mozambique, South Africa, Canada, and Australia. He is estimated to own a $50 million real estate portfolio in Mumbai, Dubai, and London.

16 Amar Farooqui, *Smuggling as Subversion: Colonialism, Indian Merchants and the Politics of Opium, 1790–1843* (New Delhi: New Age International, 1998).

17 Neeraj Kumar, "Organized Crime," *Police Speak* 483 (November 1999). http://www.india-seminar.com/1999/483.htm (accessed October 2007).

18 David Kyle and Rey Koslowski, eds., *Global Human Smuggling: Comparative Perspectives* (Baltimore: Johns Hopkins University Press, 2001), pp. 187–253.

19 http://www.amrealty.com.my/comingsoon.asp (accessed April 2008).

20 L. K. Yap, "Mycom Teams Up with Merrill Lynch: They Will Jointly Develop Land in Kenny Heights," *Star*, September 5, 2007.

21 Clive Walker, "Adjaye, Benoy and Foster Team Up on Huge Kuala Lumpur 'Suburban City,'" *Architects' Journal* (2008). http://info.architectsjournal. co.uk/article.php?jchk=1&nolog=1&p_id=381&jlnk=cslo220 (accessed April 2008).

8. Cities of Crisis

1 Much as Kuala Lumpur has measured itself against Singapore, Mumbai's political leadership has oddly selected Shanghai as their city's paragon. In announcing the "next Shanghai" goal, the chief minister of Maharastra state remarkably set forward a time frame of five years, until 2010, to mimic the growth achievements of this utterly different city. The irony of the chaotic and anachronistically democratic metropolis of Mumbai modeling itself after the development practices and objectives in such a different political-economic system has not been lost on the general population. See "Mumbai Government Vows to Be Next Shanghai," *Times of India*, April 30, 2005, p. 1. Quoting from the article:

"MUMBAI: Maharashtra Chief Minister Vilasrao Deshmukh, who has vowed to transform Mumbai into another Shanghai, is setting up a team of ministers with special powers to oversee the city's modernisation . . . Deshmukh is plugging for large-scale investments in infrastructure in the next few years, officials said . . . The team, comprising ministers from the ruling Congress and Nationalist Congress Party, will coordinate with various agencies and arrange for funds for different aspects of the project . . . This includes relocation of slum dwellers displaced under urban infrastructure and transportation projects."

2 The *hutong* is a distinctive Chinese citysystem that has proven adaptable over centuries to provide a convenient, safe, socially vibrant, walkable form of inner-city urban living. Its primary units of development are the single-story Shi-He-Yuan house with its courtyard and its narrow hutong lanes where a mix of residences, shops, and markets offers a lifestyle where everything is in reach within the neighborhood. With the privatization of property development in China, developers of high-rise buildings managed the centralized planning system to secure approvals to destroy square miles of hutong districts. During the 1990s, an average of six hundred hutong lanes were being destroyed per annum. Ironically, like the Dharavi plan, displaced hutong residents were offered housing in these new buildings, but the actual livable area they received was less than their Shi-He-Yuan residences and was not at ground level. As well, many people displaced by hutong demolition—an estimated two hundred thousand in the 1990s—were granted housing in only isolated areas on the city outskirts.

3 The West End of Boston was a historic residential-commercial district of multistory brick buildings along narrow winding lanes, much like Boston's historic North End today. In the mid-twentieth century, the district deteriorated after waves of immigration. As in Dharavi today, it and other Boston immigrant areas were classified as slums, even though local residents valued them as neighborhoods. Forty-six acres of the West End were cleared in the 1950s to make way for Boston's elevated expressway, nondescript high-rise apartment buildings, and brutalist government facilities. By the 1980s, the West End was one of Boston's most sterile areas, while the nearby old North End, spared the wrecking ball, became one of the most attractive residential and tourist areas in the city. As a final demonstration of the folly of the West End's urban renewal project, the city and federal government spent $15 billion over a seventeen-year period to put the Boston expressway underground.

4 See, for instance, Rahul Mehrotra, *Mapping Mumbai* (Mumbai: Urban Design Research Institute, 2006), p. 42.

5 It has often been argued that this kind of gentrification displaces low-income households and destroys established ethnic neighborhoods, yet the incremental nature of the process generally supports an extended coexistence of old and new residential groups. It surely provides a far less disruptive way to renew the built city than master-planned urban renewal or developer-driven city model projects. Incremental gentrification is part of a long tradition in American inner-city neighborhood citysystems called *succession*, whereby one district citysystem is used and renewed repeatedly by different waves of immigrants as their first city foothold, from which each immigrant community moves on to more middle-class areas once their metropolitan advantage has been established. Since the birth of American

cities, succession and, more recently, gentrification in such industrial neighborhood citysystems have been accompanied by social conflict between ethnic and income groups. These conflicts can be manipulated by business and political elites to secure territories for their designs, or they can be managed through facilitation and co-investment to create mixed ethnic neighborhoods. See L. Freeman, "Displacement or Succession? Residential Mobility in Gentrifying Neighborhoods," *Urban Affairs Review* 40 (March 2005): 463–491. Also, for a constructive effort to distinguish types and stages of gentrification, see A. Duany, "Three Cheers for Gentrification," *American Enterprise* 12 (April–May 2001): 36–39.

6 This term was coined and defined by Matias Echanove, *The Tokyo Model of Urban Development* (2007). www.urbanology.org/dharavi/The_Tokyo_Model_of_Urban_Development_Echanove_1.7.07.pdf (accessed January 23, 2008). The summary of Tokyo's postwar redevelopment and its comparison with Dharavi is drawn from Echanove's analysis.

7 Philip Reeves, "Bid to Develop Indian Slum Draws Opposition," National Public Radio broadcast, *Morning Edition,* May 9, 2007. http://www.npr.org/templates/player/mediaPlayer.html?action=1&t=1&islist=false&id=10089935&m=10089936 (accessed November 2007).

8 D. P. Singh, "Slum Population in Mumbai: Part 1," *Population* 3, no. 1 (March 2006): http://www.iipsenvis.nic.in/vol3no1/slum.pdf.

9 I have used the number of employment establishments that do not officially have a source of electricity or other power as a proxy for the number of establishments associated with the slum-city economic system. Further data on employment establishments can be found in the Mumbai Metropolitan Region report titled *Population and Employment Profile of Mumbai Metropolitan Region* (MMRDA, 2003).

10 Ibid., p. 18. Fifty-one percent of Mumbai office establishments were located in the central business district in 1980. By 1998, 46 percent of the total office establishments were located in the city's suburban wards.

11 The migrant city and the new suburb city are not monolithic. They too are pulled in many different directions by internally competing interests. Frictions between different waves of migrants sometimes break into violent conflicts over land claims, lifestyles, and conflicting activities. Each side may have its own lawyers, NGOs, and politicians advocating its position. Dharavi's residents may prove too divided by ownership and tenancy, length of residency, ethnic and caste group, political party, and criminal networks to ally against the Slum-Free Dharavi plan. Similarly, in the new suburb city different alliances advance their interests by steering public resources and policy in favor of development in the lands and industries where they have greatest leverage or control.

12 Sanjay Sawant, "BMC Has Nobody to Supervise Buildings," *DNA Mumbai* (newspaper), July 21, 2007, p. 4.

13 Rukmini Shrinivasan, "Soon, Cheaper Homes in Every Project," *Times of India*, July 27, 2007, p. 1.

14 G. Singh and S. Kuber, "Megamorphosis," *Economic Times of Mumbai*, March 4, 2005, p. 3.

15 Michigan Department of Community Health, *Vital Statistics: Michigan County Profiles for Oakland and Wayne Counties* (2006). http://www.michigan .gov/mdch/0,1607,7-132-2944_4669—,00.html (accessed December 2007).

16 Southeast Michigan Council of Governments, *Commuting in Southeast Michigan, 2000* (Detroit: SEMCOG, June 2003).

17 One scheme, established in the late 1990s under the Shiv Sena/BJP governing alliance, provided slum land rights to private developers for residential-commercial developments in exchange for building minimum-sized apartment units for the displaced slum dwellers. The government established and financed a private development company, which in turn contracted the construction of projects to private sector builders. Although the scheme originally announced the construction of 800,000 new units of 225 square feet for slum dwellers, the target was soon scaled back to 200,000 units. A government investigative committee set up in 2001 under a highly respected former official found that only seventy-five hundred units had been completed with another forty thousand under construction. The committee's report cited millions of dollars taken by developers, lack of enforcement of building standards, and special deals between government/development agency officials and builders.

9. Great Opportunities Cities

1 By *city*, I refer to the current boundaries of the City of Toronto, which between 1953 and 1998 was the thirteen municipalities of the Metropolitan Municipality of Toronto (later merged into six). By "metropolitan area," I refer to the Greater Toronto Area, which refers to the City of Toronto and the four suburban regional municipalities of Durham, Halton, Peel, and York, which I refer to as the outer suburbs. The divergence of growth between the city and the outer suburbs is therefore the difference between the City population and the combined populations of the four regional municipalities. Data are drawn from the following source: Larry Bourne, "Designing a Metropolitan Region: The Lessons and Lost Opportunities of the Toronto Experience," in Mila Friere and Richard Stren, eds., *The Challenge of Urban Government: Policies and Practices* (Washington, D.C.: World Bank Institute, 2001), pp. 27–46. Also

from the Web site of the Greater Toronto Marketing Alliance: http://www
.greatertoronto.org/investing_demo_03.htm (accessed March 2008).

2 Peter Goheen, "The Struggle for Urban Public Space: Disposing of the
Toronto Waterfront in the Nineteenth Century," in A. G. Murphy and D. L.
Johnson, eds., *Cultural Encounters with the Environment* (Lanham, Md.: Row-
man and Littlefield, 2000), p. 61.

3 The writings and interpretations of Toronto's planning and development history by planner and geographer Larry Bourne and by historian Richard White
of the Neptis Foundation were particularly helpful to me in preparing this description of planning practice in Toronto. See Bourne, "Designing a Metropolitan Region," and also Richard White, *Urban Infrastructure and Urban Growth in
the Toronto Region, 1950s to the 1990s* (Toronto: Neptis Institute, 2003).

4 Bourne, "Designing a Metropolitan Region," p. 33.

5 This and the following quoted from an interview with Richard White, January 8, 2008.

6 One city, North York, had some success in creating a downtown, but its location along the country's busiest expressway corridor made it function more
like a city model for the daytime use of a large catchment of commuters than a
citysystem. Other municipalities fared even worse: Mississauga, the region's
second-largest city, created a "downtown" with tokenistic plazas that works
more like an office park. Scarborough, also along the busy expressway corridor, created a "town center," which is in fact a sprawling shopping plaza with a
few high-rise office and condominium towers.

7 Bourne, "Designing a Metropolitan Region," p. 35.

8 In 1997 I was hired to develop a new environmental management system
for the new City of Toronto that was being formed through the merger of the
six remaining, separate municipalities of the 1953 Metropolitan Toronto
government. This involved the review of all the official plans and environmental policies of the six municipalities. The distance between their stated
goals and planning obligations and the kinds of development that had been
taking place in these jurisdictions over the preceding decade was shockingly
wide.

9 These interviews were conducted by a university-educated fellow driver using a standard questionnaire.

10 In 2006, Canadian-born holders of university degrees had an unemployment rate of 2.8 percent compared to a 6.3 percent unemployment rate for
university-educated immigrants with five to ten years of residency. Those
residing in Canada less than five years had an 11 to 12 percent unemployment rate. The unemployment rate among all immigrants who had lived in
Toronto for five to ten years, with or without a degree, was 7 percent. See:

Danielle Zietsma, *The Canadian Immigrant Labor Market in 2006: First Results from Canada's Labour Force Survey* (Ottawa: Statistics Canada/Ministry of Industry, 2007). Also: "Visible Minorities More Likely to Hold University Degree than White Canadians," *National Post*, May 26, 2008, p. A4.

11 See Elizabeth Thompson/Canwest News Service, "Immigrants with Degrees Losing Ground on Salaries, Study Argues," *National Post*, May 4, 2008. The researcher behind this analysis, Jack Jedwab of the Association of Canadian Studies, is reported to conclude that Canada places too much premium on educational attainment when vetting immigration applications. The implication is that an immigration policy focused more on less-educated immigrants might lessen the record of unsuccessful integration into Canadian society represented by people like Girish. But it raises other problematic questions regarding the development of a low-income immigrant segment in major cities with little chance at social mobility.

I argue that the chronic gap between immigrant qualifications and economic achievement in greater Toronto arises from three key barriers immigrants face in trying to access Toronto's markets. These barriers can and should be addressed to create a more clear and effective pathway for immigrant advancement in Canadian society.

First, like Girish, they often cannot access opportunities in their professional trades, even in good economic times, because of restrictive and effectively exclusive certification standards for foreign university degrees and professional licensing procedures for regulated professionals such as accountants, nurses, and engineers. These standards and procedures are jointly regulated by the provincial government and independent professional institutes and colleges. The arrangements with these institutes function like de facto cartels. Little relief has been offered for immigrants other than establishing an appeals process for their degree or licensing application rejections. Remedies are thereby formally available but practically onerous, often requiring immigrants to make "all or nothing" decisions as to whether to take a new university degree or abandon their established, practiced career.

Second, metro home prices are prohibitive and housing finance is restrictive for new immigrants, particularly at their salary levels. This barrier is directly related to local urbanism practice. The immigrant's housing path often starts in the inner city in a subsidized or low-quality rental unit, as the new resident often shares housing with extended families or roommates. Immigrants then typically find their way to an ethnic residential-retail beachhead established by the ethnic migrants before them. Upwardly mobile groups, for whom home purchases are within reach, generally establish their beachheads in the edge city suburbs, where housing prices are lower and where ethnic ties and financing schemes are used to overcome problems in accessing traditional bank mortgages.

Third, there is a cultural barrier. For all the city's internationalism, greater Toronto employers generally undervalue foreign work experience and give an extreme premium to prior Canadian work experience when selecting candidates for interviews. The question "Do you have any Canadian experience?" functions as a catch-22 conversation stopper in most application processes. As an executive of a Toronto-based international organization that placed a premium on foreign experience, I interviewed many university-educated, experienced immigrant professionals who had spent more than a decade as clerical-level workers in Toronto because they could not find an employer willing to take the smallest risk of granting them their first "Canadian experience" opportunity.

12 According to 2006 census data, the cities of Markham, Mississauga, and Richmond Hill had 56 percent, 51 percent, and 51 percent foreign-born residents, respectively, compared with 49 percent for the city of (central) Toronto. Even where chain migrations have established major communities in the edge cities, many new immigrants, including those I interview, had entered Toronto life through a period of residence in the central city, whose dense old neighborhoods still offer shared rental units and boardinghouses. Those who did not secure or seek a life in subsidized housing then migrated to their ethnic community areas in a suburb. Others moved farther away to try to purchase an affordable home, for which they described innovative financing schemes involving extended families and ethnic real estate agents.

13 Myer Siemiatycki, "Immigrant and Minority Political Engagement in Toronto: Problems and Possibilities," paper presented at the Canadian Urban Insitute Seminar "The Changing Face of the GTA: Practical Solutions Needed to Welcome New Canadians," April 14, 2005. For an outstanding study of the geography of foreign-born urban migrants in greater Toronto and their participation in the city's politics and social affairs, see Myer Siemiatycki and Engin Isin, "Immigration, Diversity and Urban Citizenship in Toronto," *Canadian Journal of Regional Science* 20, nos. 1 and 2 (1998): pp. 73–102.

14 The data to support this conclusion are drawn from peak-hour traffic counts performed on a biannual basis by the City of Toronto Planning Division and the Joint Program in Transportation (JPT) of the University of Toronto. The ratio of inbound vehicles during the morning rush hour rose from 1.4 in 1987 to 1.6 between 1991 and 1998. It has, however, dropped again to 1.4 in 2004. The specific reports are Data Management Group, JPT, *Greater Toronto Area Cordon Count Study: Analysis of Traffic Trends, 1985–2004* (Toronto: University of Toronto, 2007); and City of Toronto, Planning Division, *City of Toronto Cordon Count Program—Overview Report* (Toronto: City of Toronto, 2007).

15 Toronto's new inner-city urbanism is best represented by the work of architect-planners A. J. Diamond and Ken Greenberg, both of whom have

been taking every chance since the 1970s to steadily update the residential-commercial-retail model of the old downtown and industrial city neighborhood. Their starting premise is the maintenance and extension of Toronto's original rectangular street grid. Working from this structure for arranging commercial-retail and residential uses and for organizing traffic, transit, and pedestrian flows, they have created a design that brings many of the successful features of European city building into the main streets and avenues while retaining the original character of the residential neighborhoods that these avenues surround. The model at once increases densities (from a typical two to four stories to four to six stories on the street fronts) and public spaces and amenities. For an introduction to the emerging inner-city new urbanism of Toronto, see City of Toronto, *Toronto Waterfront Design Initiative: Urban Design Report* 1. http://www.toronto.ca/waterfront/pdf/twf_booklet.pdf (accessed April 2008). Yet, for reasons cited, this model of development has made scant headway beyond the inner city and some of central Toronto's main commercial-retail arteries.

16 The "South of Eastern Planning Study" was undertaken by the city's planning department and submitted in a report to the Toronto City Council on July 25, 2006. The report can be accessed via http://www.toronto.ca/legdocs/2006/agendas/council/cc060725/te6rpt/cl012.pdf (accessed May 2008).

17 For a thorough assessment of metro Vancouver's development outcomes relative to its planned targets, see Ray Tomalty, *Growth Management in the Vancouver Region* (Waterloo, Ontario: University of Waterloo, Department of Environment and Resource Studies, 2000). www.fes.uwaterloo.ca/research/asmtplan/pdfs/BC_4.pdf (accessed May 2008). Tomalty makes a solid case that metro Vancouver has failed to achieve most of its long-term development targets. It is not the purpose of his assessment to evaluate whether the original targets were realistic given the constraints on development planning and control in the greater Vancouver region. Considering the weak form of regional government, the persistent resistance of critical municipal jurisdictions to even accepting the regional targets, the market-oriented nature of urban development in Canada, and the high rate of growth in the region relative to the limited public resources for infrastructure development, it comes as no surprise that the targets were not fully met. What is surprising, relative to the development trends in most North American cities during the period of his assessment (1990s–2002) is that the region made steady progress in the direction of the targets and not, as in greater Toronto, in the opposite direction.

18 Ibid., p. 5.

19 Pamela Blais et al., *Inching Towards Sustainability* (Toronto: Neptis Institute, 2000), p. 9.

20 The statistics in this paragraph are drawn from Greater Vancouver Regional District, *Advancing the Sustainable Region: Issues for the Livable Region Strategic Plan Review Draft* (Vancouver: GVRD, 2005). As an indication of the role of the metro/regional town centers in the development of compactness in the region, between 1991 and 2001, the population of the metro core and regional town centers grew by 41 percent, compared with a region-wide population growth of 29 percent. In 2001 there were 32.5 persons per hectare in the growth concentration area (green spaces included) and 13.4 per hectare in the other areas of the region (p. 16).

21 Ibid., p 38.

10. A Planet Transformed

1 Steven Sheppard, presentation at the Poverty Reduction and Economic Management Conference, World Bank, April 25, 2006.

2 Schlomo Angel, Stephen Sheppard, Daniel L. Civco, et al., Center for Land Use Education and Research Web site, University of Connecticut. http://clear.uconn.edu/Data/Urban_Growth/index.htm#3 (accessed May 2008). Full details of their remote imagery and economic analysis are provided on this site.

3 James P. Collins, Ann Kinzig, Nancy B. Grimm, William F. Fagan, Diane Hope, Jianguo Wu, and Elizabeth T. Borer, "The New Urban Ecology: Modeling Human Communities as Integral Parts of Ecosystems Poses Special Problems for the Development and Testing of Ecological Theory," *American Scientist* 88 (2000): 416–425. Their article notes that between 1995 and 2000, only twenty-five of nearly sixty-two hundred articles in the top (nine) English-language ecological sciences journals dealt with cities or urban species.

4 Hans Slabberkoorn, and Ardie den Boer-Visser, "Cities Change the Songs of Birds," *Current Biology* 16 (2000): 2326–2331.

5 Kevin J. McGraw, "Environmental Predictors of Geographic Variation in Human Mating Preferences," *Ethology* 108, no. 4 (2002): 303–317.

6 L. A. Atramentova and O. V. Filiptsova, "Genetic Demographic Structure of the Bologrod Population: Age, Ethnicity, Education, and Occupation," *Genetika* 41, no. 6 (2005): 823–829.

7 Hongyun Han, "Trends in Educational Assortative Marriage in China from 1970 to 2001," Department of Sociology, University of Wisconsin-Madison, 2006.

8 Junsen Zhang, Chong Huang, Hongbin Li, and Pak Wai Liu, "Why Does Spousal Education Matter for Earnings?: Assortative Mating or Cross-productivity," Department of Economics, Chinese University of Hong Kong, 2006.

9 Abdelrahman I. Abdelrahman, "Education and Assortative Marriage in Northern and Urban Sudan, 1945–79," *Journal of Biosocial Science* 26, no. 3 (July 1994): 341–348.

10 Eric D. Gould and M. Daniele Paserman, "Waiting for Mr. Right: Rising Inequality and Declining Marriage Rates," *Journal of Urban Economics* 53 (2003): 257–281.

11 Raquel Fernández and Richard Rogerson, "Sorting and Long-Run Inequality," *Quarterly Journal of Economics* 116, no. 4 (2001): 1305–1341. Also see David S. Loughran, "The Effect of Male Wage Inequality on Female Age at First Marriage," *Review of Economics and Statistics* 84, no. 2 (May 2002): 237–250.

12 C. A. Schubert, I. K. Barker, R. C. Rosatte, and C. D. MacInnes, "Density, Dispersion, Movements and Habitat Preference of Skunks (*Mephitis mephitis*) and Raccoons (*Procyon lotor*) in Metropolitan Toronto," D. R. McCollough and R. Barrett, eds., *Wildlife 2001: Populations* (London: Elsevier Science, 1992), pp. 932–944.

13 Quotes by Grimm and Redman taken from *Urban Ecology Study Witnessing the Birth of a "Designer" Ecosystem* 12, no. 28 (January 4, 2005). http://www .physorg.com/news2552.html (accessed April 2007). For a more detailed description of the approach taken by the University of Arizon team, see Nancy B. Grimm, Lawrence Baker, and Diane Hope, 2001 "An Ecosystem Approach to Understanding Cities: Familiar Foundations and Uncharted Frontiers," in A. R. Berkowitz, C. H. Nilon, and K. S. Hollweg, eds., *Understanding Urban Ecosystems: A New Frontier for Science and Education* (New York: Springer-Verlag, 2002), pp. 94–114.

14 Andrew M. Coutts, Jason Beringer, and Nigel J. Tapper, "Characteristics Influencing the Variability of Urban CO_2 Fluxes in Melbourne, Australia," *Atmospheric Environment* 41 (2006): 51–62.

15 The cited measurement of daily CO_2 emissions from Kilauea (8,500 t/d) reported in T. M. Gerlach, K. A. McGee, T. Elias, A. J. Sutton, and M. P. Doukas, "CO_2 Degassing at Kilauea Volcano: Implications for Primary Magma, Summit Reservoir Dynamics, and Magma Supply Monitoring," paper presented at the American Geophysical Union, fall meeting 2001; abstract #V22E-10.

16 For more information about the Cities for Climate Protection Campaign, see www.iclei.org/ccp. Initial modeling support for this effort was provided by Germany's Oko-Institut, using its TEMIS model. This model was succeeded by the development of a custom-made modeling tool for urban baseline emissions inventory and scenario-building, developed by Ralph Torrie and Torrie-Smith Associates of Ottawa, Canada. Torrie did the detailed analytics, along with each city's technical leaders, on the CO_2 inventories of each city and their implications, as cited in this chapter. The executive director of the Urban CO_2 Reduction

Project was Philip Jessup. In 1993, the fourteen founding municipalities of the project, with their elected leaders and technical teams, launched the Cities for Climate Protection Campaign at ICLEI's second summit meeting at the United Nations in New York. The unique campaign model, which linked individual cities together into a standardized approach for analytics, scenario forecasting, and action planning and thereby to the early international diplomacy on a climate convention, was developed by Jessup and organized along with Nancy Skinner, Tanya Imola, and myself. Additional financial support was provided by the W. Alton Jones Foundation, Pew Charitable Trusts, the German Marshall Fund of the United States, the City of Toronto and Municipality of Metropolitan Toronto, the Province of Ontario, and the Joyce Foundation.

17 Axel Borsdorf and Pierre Zembri, eds., *European Cities Structures: Insights on Outskirts* (Paris: Blanchard, 2004), p. 41. http://urbamet.documentation .equipement.gouv.fr/documents/Urbamet/0259/Urbamet-0259438/EQUTEX 00010091_1.pdf=UTEX00010091_2.pdf (accessed May 2008). Both Helsinki and, particularly, Hannover have been challenged to increase or even maintain their transit/bicycle/walking shares of total trips during the period of urban sprawl in their regions since the early 1990s in spite of very substantial investments to expand their transit infrastructure and services.

18 See Irmeli Harmaajarvi, Sirka Heinonen, and Pekka Lahti, *Urban Form, Transportation and Greenhouse Gas Emissions: Experiences in the Nordic Countries* (Copenhagen: Nordic Council of Ministers, 2004), pp. 24–25. http:// www.norden.org/pub/miljo/transport/sk/TN2004540.pdf (accessed May 2008).

19 Hans Mönninghoff, *CO2-Bilanz, 1990–2005: Energie- und verkehrsbindigte Emissionen*, Heft-Nr. 44 der Schriftenreihe Kommunaler Umweltschutz (Hannover: Stadt Hannover, 2007). For a full English-text explication of Hannover's CO_2 metabolism, see http://www.hannover.de/de/umwelt_bauen/ energie/leitstelle_energie_klimaschutz/klima.html (accessed March 2008).

20 Ethan H. Decker, Scott Elliott, Felisa A. Smith, Donald R. Blake, and F. Sherwood Rowland, "Energy and Material Flow Through the Urban Ecosystem," *Annual Reviews of Energy and Environment* 25 (2000): 685–740. Quotation taken from page 721.

11. The Strategic City

1 For an outstanding report that uses remote sensing to document an individual city's (e.g., Chengdu's) rapid spatial growth, see A. Jackson, K. Seto, D. Webster, J. Cai, and B. Luo, *Spatial and Temporal Patterns of Urban Dynamics in Chengdu, 1975–2002* (Stanford, Calif.: Asia-Pacific Research Center, Stanford Institute for International Studies, 2003).

2 An excellent example of Yokohama's attempts to create more transparency and a more robust citizen role in development decision making is the "public involvement" system tested for a major road project, which gave citizens the option, for the first time, to formally recommend "no development." Writes journalist Ichie Tsunoda: "This 'road construction project based on public participation' proceeded through trial and error, but the Onmoto Road plan made a decided stir in the debate on the decision-making process for public works. For example, the Japanese Ministry of Land, Infrastructure and Transport is including public involvement (PI) in its implementation of a road construction project for the Tokyo Gaikaku Expressway, an outer beltway around central Tokyo. In this project, the ministry has undertaken PI from the conceptual phase—the first time for this to happen with an expressway project in Japan. The ministry is disclosing information to residents and users along the road and discussing the plan through opinion exchange." See Ichie Tsunoda, "Yokohama City: Pioneer in Public Involvement" (Web publication, 2004). http://www.japanfs.org/en/public/gov_14.html (accessed October 2007).

3 See the tactfully investigative article by David McNeill, "Building Projects Defy Huge Cash Woe: Forests of Cranes Don't Suit Japan's Recession," *Japan Times*, March 11, 2003.

4 John MacMillan, *Reinventing the Bazaar: A Natural History of Markets* (New York: W. W. Norton & Company, 2003), pp. 136–147. Also see Ben Hills, "Silencing the 'Voice from Heaven,'" http://www.benhills.com/articles/articles/JPN06a .html (accessed October 2007).

5 Hills, "Silencing the 'Voice from Heaven.'"

12. Designing the Ecosystem

1 The average annual population growth rate of Curitiba was around 6 percent during the period 1965–1995. During this same period the urban population growth rate of Brazil was 3.6 percent, and average worldwide urban growth was 2.6 percent per annum.

2 The Lerner Group reserved the future option of channelizing stretches of river if its floodwaters could not be otherwise contained. They did build channels in already developed riverside areas. Meanwhile, the World Bank became a supporter of the Curitiba approach, financing its extension to downriver municipalities in the metropolitan area. Carlos E. M. Tucci makes the case against the traditional canalization approach as follows. "According to past practice the usual approach would have been to carry out construction works to increase the river capacity (i.e., via canalization) so as to cope with the 50 or 100-year flood. Under these conditions, because of the fact that flood

frequency decreases as a result of these works, the population would feel protected and start to occupy the floodplain. Parallel to this, after a few years the development of the upstream basin would increase the flood frequency and peak of the floods (i.e., due to pavement and storm water run-off). Under such a future scenario, there would not be more space available to allow increasing the section width of the channel, since the flood plain would be occupied. Thus, flood control would only be possible by means of dykes (with pumping station and internal drainage), or deepening the river along a reach of at least 50 km, all of which would represent a very high cost." Carlos E. M. Tucci, *Brazil: Flood Management in Curitiba Metropolitan Area* (Washington, D.C.: WMO/GWP, n.d.), p. 2. http://www.apfm.info/pdf/case_studies/brazil.pdf (accessed May 2008).

3 Recent critical analyses of the Lerner Group and its transformation process emphasize the lack of any broad citizen participation in consultations, planning, and solutions design, highlighting this as a critical flaw in their urbanism. Clara Irazabal (2005) suggests that the technocratic and business orientation of the Lerner Group's urbanism, coupled with this lack of mass engagement, threatens the continuation of public support for established practices as metropolitan growth and congestion develop. (See Clara Irazabal, *City Making and Urban Governance in the Americas: Curitiba and Portland* [Aldershot, UK: Ashgate, 2005].) This debate has powerful historical and political roots. Lerner and his political colleagues gained their offices via appointment under military dictatorship and are thereby associated with it, even if they were repeatedly elected following the establishment of democracy in 1988. One of the major opposition movements to the dictatorship gave birth to the socialist Workers' Party (PT), which pioneered very profound participatory governance practices in the many cities where they gained office. The "participation" of the Lerner Group—which focused more on aligning commercial, industrial, and property interests behind transformation initiatives—contrasts significantly with the popular, mass participation urbanism of the PT. The Curitiba approach was a necessity and not a choice during the military era, during which time public participation was not a possibility. Given the historical context, and even in a general theoretical context, it would be dogmatic to use one form of participation as the legitimate normative measure of the other, or even to use broad public participation as a sine qua non for progressive transformation. The Lerner Group and PT approaches to governance were used to develop different kinds of urban political-economic regimes and local urbanisms. Similarly, to single out the Lerner Group for its "technocratic" orientation would require ignoring the much greater dominance of engineer- and planner-driven development in many other Brazilian cities, and in cities generally during the 1960s and 1970s. If anything, the Lerner Group softened the technocratic orientation of the times with its more incremental, design-oriented approach.

In this context, Lerner's decision to impose the initial portion of the pedestrian district against the opposition of businesses has been used as evidence of a technocratic and even authoritarian aspect to their approach. Over the course of one weekend, while shops were not open, he ordered the street closed to traffic, the removal of the street, and the full construction of the pedestrian plaza with its lighting, benches, and landscaping. This was not the only singular event during his tenure but must be understood as the establishment of a negotiation process and his effort as a newly appointed mayor to build some popular legitimacy. Lerner's administration did consult with shopowners prior to this action, but resistance was strong enough that they determined a demonstration was needed. If it did not work in a matter of months, they planned to return the street to its old form. The forceful yet still incremental move attracted people into the plaza to see the results, and the sustained increase in customer volumes resulted in requests from shopowners on adjoining blocks to expand the pedestrian district by nine more blocks, this time with their cooperative participation in the design.

4 The Curitiba Guidelines were adopted as the legal plan for the city, and as IPPUC's first president, Lerner was legally charged with their implementation. The Guidelines included the preservation of the old historic city center and the creation of a pedestrian-friendly zone. They called for the integration of land development, population growth, and transportation into the four high-density corridors or structural axes—a fifth axis was later added—that aimed to contain the outspill growth of the city. They included the integration of the favela populations into mainstream city life and the provision of their settlements with essential urban and social services. And they included the creation of a large area for low-pollution industries—the future "Curitiba Industrial City." All the elements of Curitiba's ultimate transformation were there in those four pages. But their authors had no master blueprint for their realization or any political-commercial alliance to see them through. Building this strategic capacity was the basic work of the Lerner Group.

5 That being said, even traditional land-use zoning in Curitiba—the primary tool for disciplining development in conventional urban planning and management—was used very flexibly. Hugh Schwartz writes in his seminal account of the Curitiba transformation: "The spatial specifications that were laid down reflected a rough logic, but also a certain measure of arbitrariness. A tendency was observed to take account of *de facto* situations in drawing up *de jure* regulations . . . No explanations were offered for the precise boundaries of land use that were specified, nor were there discussions of the tradeoffs involved or the alternatives that were considered and rejected." Hugh Schwartz, *Urban Renewal, Municipal Revitalization: The Case of Curitiba, Brazil,* chapter 3 (self-published, 2004, ISBN:0914927434), p. 6.

6 Dr. Arturo Ardila-Gomez provides a unique and detailed political-economic analysis of the development of the bus rapid transit system, thereby also theorizing the role of Lerner Group planners in the city's complex power dynamics. See Arturo Ardila-Gomez, *Transit Planning in Curitiba and Bogotá: Roles in Interaction, Risk and Change* (Cambridge, Mass.: Massachusetts Institute of Technology, 2004).

7 Schwartz, *Urban Renewal*, "Introduction," p. 3.

13. Building Local Culture

1 Statements in this chapter by Mr. Ramon Garcia-Bragado Acín, Barcelona mayor for urbanism, are from an interview in Barcelona on June 17, 2003.

2 Interview with Harvey Ruvin, Miami-Dade County Clerk of Courts, September 16, 2007. Miami's pioneering Cuban immigrant developers knew that orderly single-family homes with private yards, built in large tracts on agricultural land, offered an affordable way to satisfy the economic and psychological aspirations of hundreds of thousands of immigrants who were abandoning turmoil in their Caribbean and Latin American countries or who were escaping the inner-city strife, decline, and congestion of U.S. cities to the north. The resulting spatial development of greater Miami into a sea of what Florida International University's Dario Moreno calls a landscape of residential "theme parks" with no urban center was inextricably linked to the business and product model of these influence-wielding Cuban developers. Within a decade, single-family tract developments were expanding across hundreds of square miles, into the farmlands to Miami's north and south, toward the marshy Everglades to the west, and into the mangrove coastal areas to the east. The built area of the metropolis more than doubled over the next twenty years, consuming an average of fourteen hundred acres of undeveloped land each year.

This "Cuban Model" was a lucrative mix of sociology, politics, finance (household, bank, and public), and raw business ambition. Profitability for the Cuban builder was most easily found on the urban periphery, where the builder purchased large tracts of agricultural land. Here there was no complicated legacy of divided land holdings and community interests to contend with and no costly demolition. The opportunity was at once affordable and big in scale. To advance their model against the density-oriented planning of progressives like Ruvin and the organized environmental community, the builders created an alliance of financiers, lawyers, and municipal politicians to incrementally rezone peripheral agricultural land for residential uses. This alliance to circumvent the Comprehensive Plan took public shape as the Latin Builders Association (LBA). As described on its Web site, "since its establishment in 1971, Latin Builders Association has embodied the interests of builders, developers, contractors, architects, engineers, plumbers, electricians and tradesmen associated with the business of construction, striving to provide a vital forum for . . . representation at the local and state level."

The Cuban builders thereby offered an affordable, convenient product for what came to be a mobile, churning population. Home buyers certainly secured economies of scale and extension. But greater Miami's sprawling suburbs required massive public investments in uneconomical (low-density) water, sewer, highway, and road networks. These infrastructures and their operating and maintenance costs remain a constant subsidy for the Cuban Model. By value-engineering the city model for its builders, the Cuban Model leaves greater Miami's resident-taxpayers to their own devices to manage the costs and inefficiencies of low-density urban life.

3 The concept of "defensible space" arose from studies by Oscar Newman and others of crime in low-income, high-rise housing projects in American inner cities during the period of racial conflict in U.S. cities in the 1960s and 1970s. The basic focus was how urban design and security monitoring could be used to secure more private control or even ownership over traditionally public spaces, like building lobbies, thereby reducing the attractiveness and vulnerability of public spaces to criminal control. The objective of defensible space design, argues H. Cisneros and others, is to create opportunity for community to take place by giving people a greater sense of safety in public interaction and activity. In the end, the largest manifestation of defensible space concepts in the United States has been in public venues of the middle class, like shopping malls. See Richard H. Harold and Ted Kitchen, *Planning for Crime Prevention: A Transatlantic Perspective* (London: Routledge, 2002). Also H. Cisneros, *Defensible Space: Deterring Crime and Building Community* (Darby, Penn.: Diane Publishing, 1995) and Oscar Newman, *Creating Defensible Space* (Washington, D.C.: U.S. Department of Housing and Urban Development, 1996).

4 Statements in this chapter by Itziar González, Cuitat Vella District councillor, are from an interview in Barcelona on April 4, 2008.

5 Statements in this chapter by Rafael González Tormo, CEO of the public-private company responsible for Barcelona's Poblenou, or "22@" district, redevelopment, are from an interview in Barcelona on June 17, 2003.

6 One principle states that Kitakyushu will intensify the "environmental power of the city through the laughter and strength of the people." Another establishes that it will value "the significance of visible local ties." Another commits the city to protect "valuable urban assets in the quest for beauty." Working from these principles, the action program prescribed fifty-six "directions," each of which includes a set of specific "actions."

7 Barcelona's modernist landscape of *illes*, first designed by Ildefons Cerdà,

covers almost 3-square miles, or 7.5 square kilometers, of the Eixample district, but the same grid and island pattern also dominates the 4-square-mile (nearly 11-square-kilometer) Sant Martí district in which Poblenou is located. While the islands imposed a master structure to the city with fixed ratios and patterns typical of modern master planning, this structure was used to support the private development of each ille into a mixed-use economic microcosm. In other words, the master planners started the work and the citysystem builders finished it. The result is efficient, coherent, villagelike city units that allow the city to work and renew itself at scale. The central courtyard of each ille provides it with espai public. The wide rambla market boulevards connect the illes socially and give them access to a mix of services and amenities.

8 Other features include mandatory compensation to dislocated residents and businesses and special provisions for transforming only half of a block if landowners cannot agree to a full transformation. Once a group of landowners agrees to a plan for redevelopment of their island, they must secure approval on the general plan and individual building plans from the municipal planning department. In cases of controversy, the municipality can force a redesign of the plan.

9 Standard zoning permits construction of floor space that is double the lot area. When the lot is converted by agreement of the island's landowners into a 22@ lot, they can build 2.7 times the lot area.

10 The infrastructure charge to developers is 50 euros per square meter built. This has covered 60 percent of the new infrastructure cost. Another 30 percent of the infrastructure cost is the investment of the district's telecommunications services providers.

11 Barcelona's Salvador Rueda argues that the only viable scale for a citysystem that embraces traditional neighborhood urbanism and global economic forces is what he calls the *super island*, a cluster of illes that can contain the life of old Poblenou, of new knowledge industries, and their shared espai public. The present attempt to cluster traditional Poblenou neighborhood life and new industrial life into a single island is artificial and produces only a symbolic, circumstantial proximity, not a real symbiosis.

14. Governing the Entrepreneurial City

1 Perry Duis, *Challenging Chicago: Coping with Everyday Life* (Chicago: University of Illinois Press, 1998), p. 162.

2 Average work hours had dropped from around sixty hours per week in the late nineteenth century to around fifty hours per week in the 1920s. The five-day workweek was becoming the norm.

3 The concept of a free market (i.e., a market in which prices of goods and services are determined by sellers and buyers who have equal access to information and who do not coerce or mislead each other or get coerced by any outside party—by government regulation, for example) is highly theoretical in the context of a city. The city is not *free* in this sense; it is a constant negotiation over competing efforts to use it and develop it. Coercion and misleading behavior are typical of the entrepreneurial ventures launched upon a city, particularly when the forms of entrepreneurship are *governed* for private, opportunistic interests rather than for common, strategic interests to build a particular form of advantage.

Stalwart advocates of the free market idea contradict themselves when it comes to their prescriptions for cities. Few bemoan, for instance, the historical involvement of public institutions in creating the infrastructure (e.g., harbors, canals, ports, and road systems) and providing the basic services (e.g., water supply) for cities that make their markets viable. Similarly, even as they promote free choice of housing location and building types in defense of all forms of land development, they uncritically accept the vast subsidies that governments provide to supply the infrastructure and services to uneconomical urban forms, such as low-density suburbs.

I have argued that cities are fundamentally a market phenomenon with strong entrepreneurial origins. But the reconciliation of competing entrepreneurial impulses in the city toward some more robust strategic advantage naturally requires that urban markets be designed, governed, and managed. As noted, this is achieved in more ways than just government regulation. The Strategic City uses local legal, financial, infrastructural, social, and cultural means to align the city's changing entrepreneurial interests and talents behind the achievement of shared developmental objectives—to create some shared, stable forms of advantage. With the expansion, extension, and global integration of markets within the City, local government has increasingly developed forms of what is called entrepreneurial governance, evolving numerous market-oriented practices to create and shape the development of markets directly. Short of such entrepreneurial governance, markets (and their externalities) develop in favor of specific entrepreneurial interests at costs to others in coercive and nontransparent ways, and the typical outcome in the city is not freedom, but conflict, inefficiencies, reduced productivity, and simmering crisis.

4 Historically, property development on Chicago's periphery consisted of new residential tract developments. Over a few decades, the early suburban developers refined Garden City residential city models, reflecting the City Beautiful urban planning movement of the day. These city models rarely established any primary economic activities but focused on the creation of local retail and transportation hubs within or adjacent to the tract developments. They therefore maintained a specialized, peripheral function within the overall

metropolitan market system and did not substantially compete with the citysystems that established Chicago's centrality as the metropolises' center for industry, employment, and services.

5 Redlining itself was also started by the U.S. government in the 1930s, when it published "residential security maps" for 239 cities. These maps rated black and low-income immigrant neighborhoods as high-risk lending areas and indicated them on the maps with red lines. Banks never questioned or updated these market assessments but used them instead to limit the development of functioning local financial and real estate markets in the marked areas of the city. In spite of the national outlawing of redlining in the 1970s, based on grassroots organizing in Chicago, Chicago continues to fight predatory lending practices to this day.

6 Civic Federation, *Tax Increment Financing: A Civic Federation Issue Brief* (Chicago: Civic Federation, 2007).

7 The creation of poor-quality loan portfolios through predatory lending practices was the first step in the development of the subprime mortgage crisis. In most American urban markets, these portfolios were built up without reference to or monitoring of local supply and demand, employment conditions, and demographics. Without the disciplined governance of real estate finance, they provided a new form of subsidy to real estate developers, with effects not unlike the subsidized housing finance of the postwar years, further exacerbating America's urban sprawl. Builders and home buyers alike made investment decisions unrelated to the full costs of the inefficient urban form that new suburban developments were creating or the rising evidence of housing oversupply. From these permissive origins, the bad loans were then traded in a financial system whose valuations were fully disconnected from the fundamentals of the city markets—in Cleveland, San Bernadino, Sacramento, Detroit, Las Vegas, Miami–Ft. Lauderdale—to which they were tied. Their transactions broke an essential standard for effective governance of mortgage lending: that the loan valuations in secondary markets reflect the actual value and risk of the properties held as collateral.

8 Another example cited by Markowski of Chicago's resistance to practices of the subprime lending crisis is its refusal to accept terms proposed by corporate financial consultants for hundreds of millions of dollars in home mortgage revenue bond issues. These bonds are widely used by Chicago and other cities to generate a pool of mortgage funds to finance home purchases by low-income families. During the subprime years, financial consultants urged the city to offer these mortgages with only a 3 percent down payment and forty-year amortization term. "The mayor held out against such terms," Markowski reports. (Interview, March 11, 2008).

9 D. Swint, "A Helping Hand for Subprime Mortgage Holders, *Medill Reports*, July 11, 2007. http://news.medill.northwestern.edu/chicago/news.aspx?id=40771 (accessed April 2008). Although the figures on prevented foreclosures may seem small, the impact on local property markets is profound. A 2005 study of the impact of a foreclosure on nearby houses in Chicago found that the cumulative values of properties surrounding a foreclosed home dropped by $159,000 to $371,000 per foreclosure. Dan Immergluck and Geoff Smith, *There Goes the Neighborhood: The Effect of Single-Family Mortgage Foreclosures on Property Values* (Chicago: Woodstock Institute, 2005).

10 Geoff Smith, *Key Trends in Chicago Area Mortgage Lending: Analysis of Data from the 2004 Chicago Area Community Lending Fact Book* (Chicago: Woodstock Institute, 2006).

11 Chicago foreclosures rose again in 2007 but remained well below the rates in the city suburbs and in many other U.S. cities. The city's initial measures stopped the predatory lending practices by regulated banking institutions, but the vacuum was filled by a second wave of unregulated "exotic" lending targeted at low-income neighborhoods. See "Exotic Loans Push Families over the Edge," *National Training and Information Center Online Reports* 99 (Summer 2006). http://www.ntic-us.org/publications/reports/nticreports.htm (accessed April 2008).

12 Terry Nichols Clark, ed., *Trees and Real Violins: Building Post-Industrial Chicago,* chapter 1 (book draft manuscript), p. 2.

13 Historically, Chicago seems to have swung between periods of free-for-all commercialism with unruly divide-and-conquer politics and efforts to align commercial interests and political factions behind some common purpose. One of Chicago's most famous periods of strategic practice took place in the early twentieth century, during the same period that saw Uptown's initial rise. During this time Chicago's industrial, mercantile, and real estate interests spearheaded major public works, cultural institutions, parks, the reorganization of railway lines, and the construction of major new avenues under the strategic coordination of the Commercial Club and Merchants Club. Their vision was expressed in America's most famous urban plan, the 1909 Plan of Chicago, or Burnham Plan, which promoted a transformation of the laissez-faire city into the orderly design of a Paris, Washington, D.C., or Barcelona. Although the Plan offered much to serve the interests of its commercial sponsors, it also promoted a pluralistic city of schools, parks, and recreational and cultural amenities to create a common culture and shared interests between and with its diverse communities and even its poorest residents. But by the 1920s, Chicago had entered an era dominated by criminal organizations and interethnic rivalries. "This was a brutal place," explains Chicago political scientist and media commentator, Paul Greene.

"Chicago had never really been a city. It was a collection of ethnic enclaves" and separate suburban towns. These communities, Greene explains for emphasis, "were defensive perimeters. People stayed in their enclaves." (Interview, March 12, 2008.)

After Mayor "Big Bill" Thompson ruled the city in service to its dominant middle-class Irish community and the rising criminal commercial interests of the Prohibition era, the Czech immigrant community's alderman, Anton Cermak, knitted together the fractured, feuding ethnic neighborhoods of poor Irish, Scandinavians, Germans, eastern and southern European, and recent African American migrants into the first Chicago political machine. "Because of its absolute Balkanization," Greene argues, "the only way to govern Chicago as a city was with an incredibly strong mayor. But the system was set up with a weak mayor and a strong city council." Cermak's model was later institutionalized under Mayor Richard J. Daley in the 1950s–1970s. During this period, Chicago went through a period of mega-project investment typical of the time. It extended and reinforced the lakeshore waterfront, built inner-city highways, and built a sizable stock of public housing, but the machine left little entrepreneurial legacy other than its exclusive trade in patronage.

After the first Mayor Daley (Richard J.) died in 1976, the most powerful ward bosses under the machine tried to parlay their well-endowed political organizations into the mayor's office. Their internal power struggle opened a window of opportunity for the many communities that had been ill-served or excluded by the machine to coalesce around the reform candidate, Congressman Harold Washington, in the early 1980s. Washington, also Chicago's first black mayor, defeated today's Richard M. Daley in his first run for the office in 1983. Local political observers highlight two impacts of Daley's 1983 defeat. The first was the realization that the old machine could not be trusted as a stable ally. The second was the chance to learn from Washington about the new political space emerging in Chicago.

Washington himself had risen politically within the structure of the old machine, which also dominated politics in the black community. He understood that Chicagoans had developed new de facto political units for governing the city, loosely called communities and neighborhood organizations and represented politically by reform candidates and independents. He was the first to leverage their grassroots efforts into a new political coalition even as he managed an opportunistic cooperation with the machine's old ward organizations. In many respects, it was Washington who forged the activists in communities like Edgewater into a coherent sector. "Harold taught Richie Daley the importance of inclusion," as Lee Botts, a longtime Chicago activists, put it. (Interview, March 11, 2008.)

With his election in 1989, Richard M. Daley more fully developed and institutionalized the Washington type of politics and entrepreneurial reforms. For instance, the Washington administration had started housing market reforms by getting housing courts to increase the liability of owners (read "slumlords") for building code violations. Tax delinquency periods were shortened and the city was given greater license to take delinquent or code-violating properties into receivership.

14 Paul M. Green and Melvin G. Holli, eds., *Restoration 1989: Chicago Elects a New Daley* (Chicago: Lyceum Books, 1991). Also Paul M. Green, *1999 Chicago Mayoral Election: A Ward and Precinct Analysis* (Chicago: School of Policy Studies, Roosevelt University, 2000).

15 James G. Clawson, *Chicago Park District (A), Darden Case Study UVA-OB-0618* (Charlottesville: University of Virginia Darden School of Business Administration, 1996), p. 5.

16 Ibid., p. 1.

17 Jody Wilgoren, "Chief Executive of Chicago Schools Resigns," *New York Times*, June 7, 2001.

18 Statements attributed to Forrest Claypool were made by him in an interview on March 11, 2008.

19 The Civic Federation was established in 1894 by the city's most progressive reformers, including Nobel Prize–winner Jane Addams, and regularly releases public analyses of city budgets, tax policies, and TIF practices. www.civicfed.org.

15. Cocreating the Citysystem

1 "Q&A with Michael Porter," *BusinessWeek*, August 21, 2006.

2 Michael Porter, "What Is Strategy?" *Harvard Business Review* 74, no. 6 (1996): 61–78.

3 Richard Florida, *The Rise of the Creative Class: And How It's Transforming Work, Leisure, Community and Everyday Life* (Cambridge, Mass.: Basic Books, 2002).

4 The Fainsteins' originating works on the topic are Norman I. Fainstein and Susan S. Fainstein, *Urban Policy Under Capitalism* (New York: Sage, 1982); Norman I. Fainstein and Susan S. Fainstein, "Regime Strategies, Communal Resistance, and Economic Forces," Susan S. Fainstein and Norman I. Fainstein, eds., *Restructuring the City* (New York: Longman, 1983), pp. 245–282; and Susan S. Fainstein, *The City Builders: Property, Politics and Planning in London and New York* (Cambridge, Mass.: Blackwell, 1994).

Elkin's seminal works on the topic are Stephen L. Elkin, "Twentieth Century Urban Regimes," *Journal of Urban Affairs* 5 (1985): 11–27; and Stephen L. Elkin, *City and Regime in the American Republic* (Chicago: University of Chicago Press, 1987).

Stone's seminal works on the topic are Clarence N. Stone, "The Study of the Politics of Urban Development," in Clarence N. Stone and H. T. Sanders, eds., *The Politics of Urban Development* (Lawrence: University Press of Kansas, 1987), pp. 3–22. And most important, Clarence N. Stone, *Regime Politics: Governing Atlanta, 1946–1988* (Lawrence: University of Kansas Press, 1989).

5 Quotes taken from Stone, *Regime Politics*, Chapter 1, "Urban Regimes: A Research Perspective," pp. 3–10.

6 See http://svlg.net/ (accessed June 2008).

7 See http://www.jointventure.org/programs-initiatives/programs.html (accessed June 2008).

8 My thanks to Kim Walesh, assistant director, Office of Economic Development, City of San Jose, for informing me about these developments, although the interpretation is my own. She highlights a second aspect of the "Next Silicon Valley" urbanism, organized through a program called the "Strong Neighborhood Initiative." This initiative engages neighborhood residents in municipal capital budgeting and services planning, and explicitly seeks to develop neighborhood leadership to support the broadening of the new regime. Between 2001 and 2006, the initiative developed nineteen active neighborhood coalitions, completed 113 priority capital projects, addressed 9,300 identified problem conditions, and allocated $85 million according to neighborhood priorities. Kim Walesh, "The Power of Civic Collaboration: A View from San Jose/Silicon Valley," presentation to the CIC/Janaagraha conclave on Bangalore's future development, January 2007 in Bangalore.

9 See http://www.regionalstewardship.org (accessed May 2008).

10 In addition to providing one of the most exhaustive analyses of Bangalore's twentieth-century development, Janaki Nair makes a strong cautionary argument regarding the risks of an imbalanced corporate influence in the affairs of the local state. One of the challenges—which leaves these nascent regimes open to critical interpretation, much as was the case in Curitiba—is the lack of mechanisms for engagement of the lower-income majority in reform of governance and cocreation of solutions. But one can also make the case that the early stage of urban regime formation first requires the engagement of government, corporate and commercial, and middle-class civic interests, which not only hold different forms of authority but have direct access to institutional resources. See Janaki Nair, *The Promise of the Metropolis: Bangalore's Twentieth Century* (New Delhi: Oxford University Press, 2005), specifically pp. 333–345.

Index

Note: page numbers in *italics* refer to illustrations; those followed by n or nn indicate an endnote or endnotes.

INDEX

A Note on the Author

For more than two decades, **Jeb Brugmann** has developed strategies for governments, corporations, international agencies, and NGOs to tackle global issues on local levels. His initiatives have involved thousands of cities in more than fifty countries. Visit his Web site at www.jebbrugmann.com.